JAPANESE-RUSSIAN RELATIONS UNDER BREZHNEV AND ANDROPOV

Distant Neighbors

Hiroshi Kimura

Volume 1
**Japanese-Russian Relations
Under Brezhnev and Andropov**

Volume 2
**Japanese-Russian Relations
Under Gorbachev and Yeltsin**

DISTANT NEIGHBORS
VOLUME ONE

JAPANESE-RUSSIAN RELATIONS

UNDER

BREZHNEV

AND

ANDROPOV

Hiroshi Kimura

M.E. Sharpe

Armonk, New York
London, England

Copyright © 2000 by M. E. Sharpe, Inc.

An earlier version of this work was published in
Kyoto, Japan, under the title *Islands or Security?: Japanese-Soviet Relations
Under Brezhnev and Andropov*. Nichibunken Monograph Series No. 2.
Copyright © 1998 by the International Research Center for Japanese Studies.
The text has been extensively revised for this edition.

Library of Congress Cataloging-in-Publication Data

Kimura, Hiroshi, 1936–
    Japanese-Russian relations under Brezhnev and Andropov / by Hiroshi Kimura.—
New, rev. ed.
        p.cm—(Distant neighbors; v. 1)
    Rev. ed. of: Islands or security? : Japanese-Soviet relations under Brezhnev and
Andropov. 1998.
    Includes bibliographical references and index.
    ISBN 0-7656-0585-6 (cloth : alk. paper)
        1. Soviet Union—Foreign relations—Japan. 2. Japan—Foreign relations—Soviet
Union. 3. Soviet Union—Foreign relations—1945–1991. 4. Japan—Foreign
relations—1945–1989. 5. National security—Soviet Union. 6. National security—
Japan. I. Kimura, Hiroshi, 1936– Islands or security? II. Title. III. Series.

DK68.7.J3 K56 2000
327.52047′09′047—dc21   99-086081

Printed in the United States of America

The paper used in this publication meets the minimum requirements of
American National Standard for Information Sciences
Permanence of Paper for Printed Library Materials,
ANSI Z 39.48-1984.

BM (c)   10   9   8   7   6   5   4   3   2   1

To Professor Masamichi Inoki

Contents

Preface

Japanese-Soviet relations are a neglected subject in contemporary scholarship, despite their significance—which hardly can be overemphasized now and which probably will increase in the future. One reason for this academic neglect is the difficulty of studying the subject. To begin with, those who want to specialize in this topic must be fluent in at least three languages: Russian, Japanese, and of course, English, a standard means of communication in today's scholarly community. Furthermore, since Japanese-Soviet relations are strongly influenced by events occurring in the world in general and in Asia in particular, analysis of these bilateral relations would not be complete unless the broader framework of international relations is taken into consideration. In other words, those who want to study Japanese-Soviet relations need to be familiar with at least the quadrilateral power configuration in Northeast Asia, consisting of the United States, the USSR, the People's Republic of China (PRC), and Japan.

These and other difficulties notwithstanding, several books have been published on Japanese-Soviet relations. These publications include Donald C. Hellmann's *Japanese Foreign Policy: Domestic Politics and The Peace Agreement with the Soviet Union* (1969); Savitri Vishwanathan's *Normalization of Japanese-Soviet Relations, 1945–1970: An Indian View* (1973); John J. Stephan's *The Kuril Islands: Russo-Japanese Frontiers in the Pacific* (1974); Young C. Kim's *Japanese-Soviet Relations: Interaction of Politics, Economics and National Security* (1974); Bhabani Sen Gupta's *Soviet-Asian Relations in the 1970s and Beyond: An Interperceptional Study* (1976); Rodger Swearingen's *The Soviet Union and Postwar Japan: Escalating Challenge and Response* (1978); and Rajenara Kumar Jain's *The USSR and Japan: 1945–1980* (1981). These books help to fill the scholarly gap but are not sufficient, as a number of them are limited in terms of the time period or the field of relations they cover, and others are superficially comprehensive.

What may distinguish the present work from books published in the past under similar titles are the following salient features: (1) specific emphasis on national security rather than the "Northern Territories" issue; (2) examination of the dynamic relationships among geography, politics, security, and economy; (3) discussion of determinants, capabilities, strategies, and the limits of Soviet policy toward Japan; (4) analysis of the dynamic process of action-reaction in the relations between Japan and the Soviet Union; and (5) detailed examination of Japanese-Soviet relations in the late Brezhnev era and the Andropov era (1976–1983).

Acknowledgments

I express my deep appreciation to John W. Lewis, director of the Center for International Security and Arms Control, Stanford University, and his staff, for their kindness to me during my stay there as a visiting research fellow. Without their most generous assistance, advice, and arrangements, I would never have thought to begin writing this book. Particularly, the late Henry Hayase, Anne Blenman-Hare, and Barbara Johnson were most helpful. I appreciatively acknowledge the advice and comments made by Coit Blacker, Condi Rice, Daniel I. Okimoto, Paul Langer, Tsuyoshi Hasegawa, and Peter A. Berton, who kindly read the whole manuscript and recommended its publication. Special thanks are due to Nancy Okimoto for her warm support, encouragement, and arrangement for the writing and publication of this volume. Without her help, the miracle of my completing a book in a nonnative tongue in so short a time would not have been possible.

I also wish to thank my former colleagues at the Slavic Research Center of Hokkaido University, who tolerated my frequent and long absences from the center during this book's writing, and generously undertook my share of teaching, administrative, and other responsibilities.

Academically, I have benefited from numerous works by Russian, West European, American, Asian, and Japanese scholars and specialists in international affairs and in Soviet politics in particular. Here, however, I must limit myself to mentioning only those who specialize in Soviet-Japanese relations and with whom I had the opportunity to meet in person and discuss common interests. These people include James Morley, Donald Hellmann, Joseph M. Ha, Robert A. Scalapino, Peter A. Berton, Rodger Swearingen, Paul Langer, Michael Blaker, the late George Lensen, Robert Legvold, Peggy L. Falkenheim, Joachim Glaubitz, Bhabani Sen

Gupta, Masamichi Inoki, the late Hayao Shimizu, Keisuke Suzuki, Kazuo Ogawa, the late Dmitrii V. Petrov, Igor′ A. Latyshev, Vsevolod V. Ovchinnikov, Boris N. Slavinskii, Georgii F. Kunadze, and Konstantin O. Sarkisov. I am particularly indebted to Young C. Kim, who encouraged me to enter this new academic field in 1977, when we first met in Washington, D.C. Special gratitude goes to John J. Stephan, who has not only been the outstanding giant in this field but has also constantly enlightened me personally through his valuable advice, comments, and observations, for which I shall never be able to reciprocate.

For the collection of research materials, I owe a great deal to the excellent services provided by the following bibliographers and librarians: the late Paul Horecky (Library of Congress); Patricia Polansky (University of Hawaii); Toshiyuki and Takako Akizuki, and Jun Matsuda (Hokkaido University); Joseph D. Dwyer, Hilja Kukk and Emiko Moffitt (Hoover Institution); Wojciech Zalewski (Stanford University); and Kayoko Ōkubo (American Center, Sapporo).

I am grateful to those personal friends of mine who kindly took the time to read, comment on, and edit parts of my manuscript: Basil Dmytryshyn, Vladimir Kusin, Paul Horecky, Roger E. Kanet, Joyce Ōkawa, Tilly C. Friedman, Dan Caldwell, Leslie Moonshine, David Holt, Carmen Wyatt, Meg Young, Tim Bartz, Laurie Freeman, and Stewart Chisholm. Without their assistance, I would not have been able to write this book. I am also thankful to those who kindly typed my manuscripts: Nana Luz, Anne Blenman-Hare, Jeannette Thomas, Marilyn Weber, Akiko Mōri, Atsuko Kamiseki, and Maki Sueno.

I cannot fail to affectionately note the cooperation of my wife, Noriko, and my two children, Michiko and Akatsuki. They patiently tolerated my devotion to a self-imposed deadline that deprived them almost completely of opportunities to enjoy the marvelous California weather together with their father, who ended up not even fulfilling a promise to drive them to San Francisco.

On a fine Saturday morning in August 1983, when I was close to completing the manuscript, I received a telephone call at Stanford from my sister in Kyoto, who informed me that our mother had suffered a heart attack and was in critical condition. I was told that if I did not return to Japan immediately, I might never see my mother alive again. I drove immediately to the San Francisco airport and flew to Kyoto, leaving my work unfinished. Fortunately, my mother was able to continue living for several more years. However, in the meantime, I had entirely lost my momentum. I finally resumed work on this book after returning to the Slavic Research Center, Hokkaido University, Sapporo, while commuting regularly from Sapporo to Kyoto in order to take care of my mother.

To make matters worse, during this difficult period of trying to work on my book and take care of my bedridden mother, radical changes were taking place in the Soviet Union. Andropov died and Chernenko came to power. Shortly thereafter, Chernenko died and Gorbachev assumed the leadership. I expected that Gorbachev would make drastic policy changes toward Japan—changes that I thought would force me to radically revise my manuscript. However, the innovations in policy toward Japan made by Gorbachev proved far less significant than expected. Naturally, this dénouement greatly disappointed me and others who were hoping to see a great diplomatic breakthrough in Soviet-Japanese relations; but it also carried an advantage. Precisely because a dramatic breakthrough did not occur in bilateral relations between Japan and the Soviet Union, the manuscript that I had almost completed at Stanford was still of value, and only minor amendments were needed for publication.

June 19, 1999
Hiroshi Kimura

Abbreviations

AFP	Agence France-Presse
ASEAN	Association of South-East Asian Nations
BBC-USSR	*British Broadcasting Corporation Monitoring Summary of World Broadcasting:USSR*
CBM	Confidence-building measures
CC	Central Committee
CCID	Central Committee's International Department
CDPSP	*Current Digest of the Post-Soviet Press*
CDSP	*Current Digest of the Soviet Press*
CIS	Commonwealth of Independent States
COCOM	Coordinating Committee for Multilateral Export Control
CPSU	Communist Party of the Soviet Union
CSCE	Conference on Security and Cooperation in Europe
FBIS-SOV	*Foreign Broadcast Information Service:Soviet Union*
GKChP	State Committee for the State of Emergency in the USSR
IDV	Institute of Far Eastern Studies
IMEMO	Institute of World Economy and International Relations
IMF	International Monetary Fund
INF	Intermediate-range nuclear forces
ISKAN	Institute of the USA and Canadian Studies
IVAN	Institute of Oriental Studies
KGB	Committee for State Security
LDP	Liberal Democratic Party
MEiMO	*Mirovaia ekonomika i mezhdunarodnye otnosheniia*
MID	(Soviet/Russian) Ministry of Foreign Affairs
MITI	(Japanese) Ministry of International Trade and Industry

MOFA	(Japanese) Ministry of Foreign Affairs
MZ	*Mezhdunarodnaia zhizn'*
ODA	Official development assistance
OSCE	Organization for Security and Cooperation in Europe
PDV	*Problemy dal' nego vostoka*
PECC	Pacific Economic Cooperation Conference
RSFSR	Russian Soviet Federated Socialist Republic
RIMPAC	Rim of the Pacific Exercises
SDF	(Japanese) Self-Defense Forces
SLBM	Submarine-launched ballistic missile
SSBN	Nuclear submarine equipped with strategic ballistic missiles
UPI	United Press International
USSR	Union of Soviet Socialist Republics

Introduction

Relations between Japan and the Soviet Union, now the Russian Federation, have remained cool throughout most of the postwar period. They were particularly unstable and strained in the period covered in this book—the late Brezhnev era and the Andropov era (1976–1983).

Evidence of strain in the bilateral relationship is plentiful. To begin with, politico-diplomatic relations between the Soviet Union and Japan have lacked a stable legal basis. Although diplomatic relations between the Soviet Union and Japan were normalized in 1956, a peace treaty has yet to be concluded. Without a peace treaty, some schools of thought on international law[1] maintain that these two countries have not put a complete end to the state of war between them. For example, the late Professor Lawrence Oppenheim of Cambridge University stated in one of the authoritative standard textbooks on international law: "The most frequent end of war is a treaty of peace. Many writers correctly call a treaty of peace the normal mode of terminating war."[2] A Soviet textbook on the same subject, edited by the Institute of Law of the USSR Academy of Sciences, states the same view: "A peace treaty legally ends a state of war between the signatory states, thereby establishing political and other relations between them."[3] One way to illustrate the abnormal degree to which Soviet-Japanese relations are stalemated is to compare them with the bilateral relations between Japan and the People's Republic of China (PRC). Japan and China normalized relations in 1972 and concluded a peace treaty only six years later, in 1978.

The poor record of visits exchanged by top political leaders of Japan and the Soviet Union also demonstrates that diplomatic relations between the two countries have been neither warm nor smooth. The underlying assumption here is that communication and contacts between top political leaders are indicative of the state of relations between countries. In the twenty-seven years between the normalization of relations between Moscow and Tokyo (1956) and the end of the period covered in this book (1983), only one Japanese prime minister (Kakuei Tanaka) visited the Soviet Union (in 1973); and the highest Soviet political leader ever to visit Japan was USSR Deputy Prime Minister Anastas I. Mikoyan (in 1961 and 1964). During the same period, six Japanese foreign ministers visited Moscow, whereas their Soviet counterpart, Andrei A. Gromyko, traveled to Tokyo only three times (in 1966, 1972, and 1976). Compared with the diplomatic intercourse between the USSR and other Western capitalist countries (such as the Federal Republic of Germany, France, and the United States), visited by both Nikita S. Khrushchev and Leonid I. Brezhnev, the number of high-level exchanges between the Soviet Union and Japan was extremely small. Of particular significance is the fact that both Soviet and Japanese leaders refused to visit one another's capitals; instead, they held brief meetings in New York while attending the United Nations General Assembly. This is a clear indication of the abnormal state of affairs in Soviet-Japanese bilateral relations.

Soviet-Japanese relations have been unstable and strained also in terms of security. Publicly, Tokyo has been advocating the so-called omnidimensional or all-directional (*zenhōi*) foreign policy—diplomacy aimed at developing friendly relations with all countries. It is an open secret, however, that Tokyo regarded the USSR as almost the sole "potential threat"[4] to the security of Japan, particularly since the conclusion in 1978 of the Sino-Japanese Peace and Friendship Treaty, by which the PRC ceased being a potential Japanese enemy. In much-disputed remarks made during a January 1983 trip to Washington, Prime Minister Yasuhiro Nakasone made no secret of the fact that his country was demanding increased Japanese security efforts. The outspoken prime minister declared that "the whole Japanese archipelago should be like an unsinkable aircraft carrier against infiltration by the [*Soviet*] *Backfire* bomber" (emphasis added by Hiroshi Kimura).[5] He also stated that "Japan should have complete control of the four straits that go through the Japanese islands so that there should be no passage of *Soviet* submarines nor other naval activities" (emphasis added by H.K.).[6]

Although Moscow did not regard Japan as a threat to Soviet security, Japan's increasingly independent diplomatic and defense postures did evoke concern. The Soviets began to worry about Tokyo's possible participation in such anti-Soviet security alliances as a "Washington–

Tokyo–Seoul" or "Washington–Tokyo–Beijing" axis, or JANZUS (Japan–Australia–New Zealand–United States) alliance. Moscow showed particular concern over the expanding United States–Japan military cooperation. In an attempt to check Tokyo's decision to accept U.S. advanced F-16 fighters at the Misawa airbase in northern Japan and to counter Nakasone's remarks cited above, Soviet leader Iurii V. Andropov threatened the Japanese with nuclear retaliation. This escalation of action and reaction on security matters further strained relations between these two neighboring countries.

Soviet-Japanese relations were similarly strained in nonpolitical and nonmilitary areas, such as economic, scientific, cultural, and sports activities. It may be true that exchanges between countries with different political and economic systems were not as frequent as those between countries with the same or similar systems, and it may also be true that such exchanges inherently had serious limitations. It is undeniable, however, that with the global tendency toward increasing interdependence, we were gradually overcoming ideological barriers and systemic disparities, especially those in trade and finance and in cultural and athletic activities. Trade relations between West Germany, France, and the Soviet Union and those between Japan and the PRC provided good illustrations of this. Yet, even in nonpolitical and nonmilitary fields, Japan and the Soviet Union were unsuccessful in developing a good, stable relationship. Unlike West Germany, France, Italy, Finland, and other West European countries, Japan failed to conclude a long-term intergovernmental agreement on economic cooperation with the USSR;[7] Japan's trade with the Soviet Union in the period covered in this book constituted less than 2 percent of Japan's entire foreign trade. Nor was a long-term fishing agreement signed between Japan and the Soviet Union. Exchanges of high government officials and government-sponsored cultural and athletic delegations between Japan and the Soviet Union were irregular at best, and at times were even frozen.

JAPANESE-RUSSIAN
RELATIONS
UNDER
BREZHNEV
AND
ANDROPOV

Part One

WHAT MADE JAPAN AND THE SOVIET UNION "DISTANT NEIGHBORS"?

Chapter 1
Basic Determinants of Japanese-Soviet Relations

Japan and the USSR have been appropriately described as "distant neighbors."[1] Although they are geographically close, a severe gap has existed between the two nations, and a distinct feeling of remoteness.[2] The following questions arise: Why does such a paradox exist?[3] And what caused them to be "distant neighbors"? Part One of this book examines the fundamental differences at the root of this estrangement.

In bilateral relations between any countries, there are usually two sets of factors influencing the relations: those factors that prevent cooperation between the two countries and those that encourage good relations between them. In the case of Japanese-Soviet relations, the former elements consistently overwhelmed the latter elements. It is my assessment that some of the factors customarily classified as those fostering good relations—e.g., geographical proximity and economic complementarity—tend to be overrated.

The number of factors influencing bilateral relations between Japan and the USSR is boundless. Any factor that exerts influence in one way or another on their relationship can be regarded as one of its determinants. The factors examined here are limited to those that seem to the author to be the most relevant. For the sake of convenience, they are classified into four groups: (1) *background factors*, such as geographic proximity, economic complementarity, and culture and historical heritage; (2) *basic framework*, such as politico-social systematic structures and military-strategic associations having mutually antagonizing alliances and diplomatic orientations; (3) *perceptions, policies,* and *foreign behaviors*; and (4) *issues and disputes,* the most important of which is the Northern Territories question.

3

1. Background Factors

Geographic Proximity

Geographically, Japan and the USSR are neighbors. In my view, the customary proposition that geographic proximity leads to, or ought to lead to, good-neighborly relations (a conclusion drawn by many Soviet and Japanese commentators) warrants criticism. Japanese politicians and journalists frequently made the point that Japan had no choice but to be friendly toward and live peacefully with the Soviet Union, regardless of ideological differences and subjective preferences. For example, Munenori Akagi, former Japanese Minister of Agriculture and Forestry and the President of the Japan–USSR Society, stated, "The main factor in our [Japanese-Soviet] relations is that Japan and the Soviet Union are neighbors, and we must live like good neighbors."[4] Soviet spokesmen frequently quoted a statement allegedly made in 1973 by former Japanese Prime Minister Kakuei Tanaka: "Though the distance between the capitals of Tokyo and Moscow may be great, the USSR and Japan nevertheless are close neighbors (*blizkie sosedy*)."[5] "Therefore, it is not surprising," another Soviet spokesman continued, "that both Moscow and Tokyo attach much importance to the expansion of Soviet-Japanese relations."[6] Elaborating further, Soviet writers drew the bold conclusion that geographic proximity (*geograficheskaia blizost'*) "necessitates" or provides "objective conditions" (N. N. Nikolaev and A. Pavlov) or "objective necessity" (G. Krasin, V. Dal'nev, O.V. Vasil'ev) for developing good-neighborliness and mutual cooperation between the Soviet Union and Japan.[7]

Unfortunately, however, our complex experiences in international relations have revealed that geographical propinquity does not necessarily lead to good-neighborly or friendly relations. Occasionally, such good relations do occur among neighbors (e.g., Canada and the United States),[8] but this is not always the case. At times, even the exact opposite occurs. Just as close relatives sometimes have a strong dislike for each other, neighboring countries sometimes conflict with one another more harshly than they conflict with more remote states. This occurs, in part, because they compete for the same objectives.

Geographic contiguity tends to facilitate conflict.[9] As demonstrated by history, disputes over territorial boundaries between geographically adjacent nations have constituted one of the most significant sources of international conflicts. Some specialists on international affairs have gone so far as to regard conflicts over boundaries as "the most important single cause of war between states in the modern world."[10] Research by Lewis F. Richardson revealed that the number of frontiers shared with other countries was positively related to participation in war.[11] This should not, of course, be taken to mean that states sharing common territorial borders always tend to fight each other. As Bruce M. Russett put it, they have "an *opportunity* to fight because they are close. Proximity becomes the catalyst." (emphasis in original).[12]

The late Dmitrii V. Petrov, one of the top Soviet Japanologists in the Japan Section at the Institute of Far Eastern Studies (IDV) of the USSR Academy of Sciences, astutely recognized the dual function played by geographic proximity. While admitting that the close geographic location of Japan and the Soviet Union, together with their cultural affinity, encouraged the two countries to agree on many complicated issues,[13] he did not fail to emphasize that this very closeness simultaneously created a potential source of conflict. He wrote, "Geographic proximity between the USSR and Japan not only makes exchange of information between the two countries prompt and convenient, *but also gives rise to a number of difficult problems* that must be solved by their joint efforts," (emphasis added by H.K.).[14]

Although Petrov himself said nothing further on the subject, we can easily enumerate the following as concrete examples of "difficult problems" requiring special consideration: demarcation of frontiers, territorial waters, economic and fishing zones; distribution of underwater resources; emigration; and military security—just to name the most pressing. The worsening of relations between Japan and the Soviet Union was largely ascribable to these unresolved problems, which stem from geographic proximity, as best illustrated by, for example, such incidents and events as the MiG-25 incident, the 200-nautical-mile fishing zone negotiations, the awakening of a sense of a "Soviet threat" among the Japanese, and of course, the Northern Territories dispute.

Economic Complementarity

Soviet specialists and some Japanese—especially business community members—never tired of emphasizing the existence of a "mutual economic complementarity" (*ekonomicheskaia vzaimodopolniaemost'*) between Japan and the USSR as a basis for expanding Japanese-Soviet relations. According to D. Petrov, this complementarity stemmed from "differences in the natural conditions and national economies of these two countries."[15] Japan lacks most raw materials, but due to advanced technology and capital, she enjoys the status of an industrial superpower, second only to the United States. In marked contrast, the former Soviet Union may be the world's richest nation in terms of potential natural energy resources; yet, except in space programs and military fields, the Soviet economy remained sluggish, operating at the level of a "developing" country. Viktor B. Spandar'ian, chief Soviet representative of trade and commerce in Japan, noted the existence of an economic complementarity between the two countries:

> Soviet exports to Japan consist largely of such commodities as timber, petroleum products, cotton, coal, non-ferrous metals, platina, potassium salts, whale meat and fish products, all of which are essential for the Japanese economy. . . . For its part, the Soviet Union imports from Japan goods that are necessary for its own economy. . . ferrous metal goods, including steel pipes, rolled ferrous metals, tinplate, engineering equipment and chemical and textile goods.[16]

In view of such economically complementary relations, the prospects for joint Soviet-Japanese development efforts—in Siberia and the Soviet Far East, for example—seemed promising, with a potential for enormous benefits to both countries. In their strenuous efforts to woo individuals in Japanese business and government and to convince them of the benefits to be drawn from closer commercial interactions, Soviet commentators on Soviet-Japanese relations made exceedingly optimistic and even exaggerated statements. For example: "The mutual economic complementarity between Japan and the Soviet Union is of a kind *very rare in the world*" (V.N. Berezin);[17] "Such mutually supplementary relations provide an *objective condition* for the successful development of Soviet-Japanese ties over the long term and on an extensive scale" (Spandar'ian).[18] Because of this complementarity, "the Soviet Union and Japan have transformed themselves into important trade partners and can no longer regard one another as secondary or reserve partners" (Pavel D. Dolgorukov);[19] and "the mutual complementarity between these two economies creates *extraordinarily favorable prospects* [for the future]" (D. Petrov) (all emphases added by H.K.).[20]

As proponents (mostly Soviet) of active trade and economic relations between Japan and the USSR emphasized, there indeed was an economic complementarity between the two countries. However, for Japan, a country poor in natural resources yet highly industrialized, *any* resource-rich country is economically complementary and in a position to develop an economic partnership. From the Japanese vantage point, then, the USSR was merely *one* candidate with the potential to become a good trade partner. In other words, economic complementarity constitutes only *one* of the necessary conditions for economic partnership. Those who conclude that the Soviet Union and Japan were logical or reliable trade partners[21] simply because of their geographic proximity and economic complementarity, wittingly or unwittingly, overlook or underestimate other equally important factors that affect economic relations between states.

Culture and Historical Heritage

Among what I call "the background factors" exerting a great influence upon Soviet-Japanese relations are the ethnic, cultural factor and the historical heritages of the two neighboring nations. A U.S.–Asia specialist at George Washington University, Harold C. Hinton, once made the following bold statement concerning the Japanese and Russians:

> The Japanese and the Russians are highly *culture*-bound peoples cordially disliked by most of their neighbors, including one another. It would be hard to name any [other] pair of peoples less well suited by *temperament* and *culture* to get along with each other. [emphasis added by H.K.][22]

If Hinton's observation were close to reality, we would be forced to accept the situation regardless of how hopeless it might seem. After careful examination of this highly controversial statement, however, we are hesitant to accept it without major reservations. Among other things, Professor Hinton presents a rather simplified, one-sided answer to a complex question: Can a pair of nations that are close to each other in race, culture, temperament, attitude, and behavior get along better politically and diplomatically than nations that are culturally and racially remote? This is indeed a broad and complex question, to which no single, authoritative answer has been or is likely to be found. We have already observed two ways in which geographic proximity influences politico-diplomatic relations—either by distancing a pair of neighboring countries (e.g., China and Russia) or by promoting closer ties (e.g., Canada and the United States). The same rule probably can be applied to racial, cultural, and other (e.g., ideological) types of affinities.

To further complicate the issue, there are *both* similarities and differences between the Russians and the Japanese with regard to race, culture, attitude and behavior. These similarities and differences between the Soviets and the Japanese work in two directions: both to alienate the two countries and to attract them. Due to this *dual* nature, neither similarities nor differences in these domains are to be viewed as *direct* determining factors of Soviet-Japanese relations. Rather, they are to be regarded as *indirect* or *potential* determinants, in the sense that they accelerated, reinforced, and amplified the direction determined by other variables.

Probably a more direct, and hence a more important, determining factor of Soviet-Japanese relations is history and its legacy. The distinct historical experience of each of these neighboring countries exerted a profound impact upon their bilateral relations. History is an integral part of the present because it forms and predetermines the present possibilities and limitations. (Recall, for example, that the "Northern Territories" issue, a major stumbling block between the two countries, according to many observers, is nothing other than a "result" of World War II.)

Anyone reviewing the historical record is struck by the fact that relations between Japan and Russia tsarist or "socialist" were dominated by conflict rather than cooperation. A partial list of these conflicts includes the Russo-Japanese War (1904–05); the Russian Civil War, during which Japan sent troops into the Soviet Far East (1918–22); Japanese participation in the anti-Comintern Pact (1936); recurrent military clashes along the Soviet border (late 1930s and early 1940s), including the Changkufeng Incident (1938) and the Nomonhan Incident (1939); the Red Army *Blitzkrieg*, which violated the Japan-USSR Neutrality Pact (1941); the illegal Soviet occupation of the "Northern Territories" (1945); and the Soviet internment of half a million Japanese in Siberian camps (1945–52).[23] The periods of cooperation and alliance between Japan and Russia were contrastingly brief (1909–16 and 1941–45).

To what extent past experiences determine present relations is difficult to ascertain. Concerning this question, however, two things can be said. In general, images once formulated tend to last for quite some time. A strong psychological factor mechanism works to preserve cognitive consistency with pre-existing beliefs, even in the face of information refuting these beliefs (see Ole Holsti and Robert Jervis).[24] Only when very powerful evidence to the contrary is presented, does one begin to doubt or modify one's perceptions. Needless to say, less frequent exchanges of personnel and information between Japan and the Soviet Union did not encourage any profound change in the historically conditioned images each held of the other.

However, it is important, as Alexander Dallin correctly warns, not to overestimate the validity of historical legacy. To be sure, we are all captives of our past, real or imaginary.[25] Yet, the past does not always predetermine the future. The present and future can never be assumed to be a simple repetition or extension of the past. To his observation that "history does not repeat itself; historians do," Dallin added a remark by Sidney Hook that "those who always remember the past often don't know when it's over."[26] In short, here again one must be aware of *both* the uses and the limitations of historical legacy and analogy.

2. Basic Framework: Politico-Diplomatic Factors

Systemic Differences

The ideological and systemic (political, economic, and social) differences between Japan and the USSR should not be either overestimated or underestimated. On the one hand, the USSR was the self-proclaimed founder and prototype of "socialism"— a country allegedly putting into practice the teachings of Marxist-Leninist ideology. In contrast, Japan has exemplified a skillful and successful model of the capitalist system and Western-style democracy—a model which, despite its brief experience, has become one of the most powerful "locomotives" of the Western camp.

Ideology remains an ambiguous and elusive term.[27] If, however, Soviet ideology is narrowly interpreted to mean Marxism-Leninism, then there is considerable consensus that over the years, ideology played a progressively less important role in Soviet foreign policymaking.[28] Marxist-Leninist ideology functioned less and less as a guide to action, and it increasingly fulfilled the function of legitimizing the regime and rationalizing or justifying actions taken or changes made in existing policy.[29] One of the major goals of Marxism-Leninism is the transformation of the world along "socialist" lines.[30] Though this ultimate goal might have remained entrenched in the long-range Soviet scheme, it long since ceased to play a major role in the daily conduct of Soviet foreign policy. Instead of the philosophical commitment of Marxist-Leninist doctrine, it was Soviet national interests, as perceived by Soviet decision-makers on particular issues at given moments, that played a more significant role in Soviet foreign policy formation. However, there is no such thing as "pure" or "objective" national interest, as Seweryn Bialer has correctly observed.[31] In Soviet society, the national interest was inevitably imprinted and defined by the will, predispositions, and aspirations of policymakers, whose "socialization" process was in turn conducted by Marxist-Leninist ideology. In short, ideology and national interests are not two completely separable things, but rather, are inextricably interwined with each other.

Soviet foreign policy toward Japan was no exception to this general rule. It is true that the Soviet leadership regarded Japan as a capitalist nation with which "socialism" not only had little in common but that also bore many antagonistic and irreconcilable features. However, it is quite conceivable at the same time that "pragmatic" Soviet leaders even preferred, to a certain extent, a "capitalist" Japan to a "socialist" Japan. Politically, a "socialist" Japan might have even become a source of trouble to Moscow, in light of the Soviet experiences with China, Yugoslavia, Albania, and "Euro-communism." Under a "socialized" economy, Japan would have been far less efficient and less productive. This would have made it notably less useful to the Soviets and even more burdensome than a "capitalist" Japan, evidenced to a certain extent by the Soviet experiences with Vietnam, Afghanistan, Bulgaria, and other socialist "brethren" countries. Indeed, it might have been more desirable and beneficial for the Soviet Union to continue peaceful coexistence, or détente, and economic cooperation with "capitalist" Japan. In an article commemorating fifty years of diplomatic relations between the Soviet Union and Japan, N.N. Nikolaev, a Soviet commentator on Soviet-Japanese relations, stated unequivocally: "True to the Leninist principles of developing and strengthening relations with all countries *regardless of their social system*, the Soviet government is doing its utmost to insure that relations with Japan become sound and friendly" (emphasis added by H.K.).[32]

For its part, Japan in the postwar period had made clear its intention to pursue the so-called omnidimensional, or all-directional (*zenhōi*), diplomacy. Explaining this, successive Japanese prime ministers and foreign ministers have repeatedly stated that the basic foreign policy principle of Japan is to maintain and develop friendly relations with all countries, regardless of their political systems, although giving priority to Japanese-U.S. relations, which remain at the center of foreign policy.

Thus, Marxist-Leninist ideology *per se* appeared unlikely to constitute an insurmountable obstacle to any deals between the Kremlin leaders and Tokyo. If an obstacle to agreement existed, it would not be Marxist-Leninist ideology in itself but rather the *embodiment* of the ideology—that is, *the Soviet system* and *the mind-set* of the Soviet leadership and elites. The Soviet political and socioeconomic system had adverse effects upon the

USSR's relations with Japan. For instance, the so-called totalitarian political regime that the USSR maintained continued to pose a serious threat that prevented most Japanese from establishing closer ties with the USSR. The completely state-monopolized trade system, coupled with bureaucratic inefficiency and data secrecy, also constituted serious obstacles. All of these factors discouraged Japanese businesspeople and government officials from seeking closer trade and economic relations with the Soviet Union except as a last resort for procuring raw materials and energy resources or for coping with a severe Japanese economic recession.

U.S.–Soviet Relations

Bilateral relations between Japan and the Soviet Union were influenced and determined by the *international* environment and by *global* circumstances. The most important international environment influencing bilateral relations between Japan and the Soviet Union was the relationship between the two nuclear superpowers, the United States and the USSR. The Soviet Union often made foreign policy decisions with regard to a given country in the context of a global confrontation with the West led by the United States and not on the basis of bilateral considerations. Once, in 1959, at the height of the Cold War, Nikita S. Khrushchev remarked: "The case of international tension is like a cabbage. If you tear off the leaves one by one, you come to the heart. And the heart of this matter is relations between the Soviet Union and the United States."[33] Andrei A. Gromyko, Soviet foreign minister for 28 years, expressed a similar bipolar perception of the world in his statement: "International situations depend largely upon Soviet-United States relations."[34] The Gromyko-type, bipolar interpretation of international relations was widely used among Soviet spokesmen. Iurii N. Bandura, former Tokyo correspondent and later deputy director of the International Department of *Izvestiia*, for example, wrote the following in an article contributed to the Japanese periodical *Jiyū* (Freedom): "The title prepared for my article by the Japanese editor, 'What Does the Soviet Union Want from Japan?' is misleading and somewhat perplexes me, because there is nothing that can be specifically called a Soviet policy aimed solely at Japan among Soviet foreign policy goals. . . . Even when concrete questions regarding Japan are being considered, they are based on the general line of foreign policy adopted for the party and government."[35]

Changes in U.S.-Soviet relations—changes in Washington's policy toward Moscow, and changes in Moscow's policy toward Washington— influenced Soviet-Japanese relations. According to this bipolar concept, Soviet-Japanese relations were ultimately a function of U.S.-Soviet relations, and Soviet Japan policy was merely a spinoff of Soviet global strategy toward the United States.[36] The deterioration in Soviet-Japanese relations, most notable in the late 1970s and early 1980s, and the sign of a "thaw" were closely linked with, and even a faithful reflection of, the global shift from détente to a "new cold war," and again to a "new thaw" between the two military superpowers.

At the beginning of the 1960s, the Soviet government started to argue that it refused to hand over to Japan even the Habomais and Shikotan, which they had agreed to return previously in the joint Soviet-Japanese Declaration of 1956. Explaining the reason for this shift in Soviet policy toward Japan, the Soviet government pointed out that the Japanese government in 1960 had renewed the Japan–United States Mutual Treaty of Security and Cooperation (hereafter, referred to as the Japan–U.S. Security Treaty). The Soviet Union apparently took the U.S.– Japanese political-military alliance quite seriously—probably more seriously than we might imagine. The Soviet Union's reluctance to return the Northern Territories to Japan, even at the expense of the bilateral relationship, is ascribable to the global confrontation between the USSR and the United States.

The question we must therefore address is whether or not any possibility existed for improvement in Soviet-Japanese relations as long as Japan remained a close ally of the United States. In general, as mentioned above, the Soviet Union pursued peaceful coexistence and close economic cooperation with advanced capitalist countries, most of which had more or less close diplomatic and even military-strategic relations with the United States, including the NATO member countries in Western Europe. Japan was no exception to this general rule. Advocating improved relations with the Soviet Union as Japan's alternative road to increased "authority and influence in international affairs," D.V. Petrov stated in 1972: "*This road will not harm such United States–Japan ties* as long as both sides regard it to be necessary and mutually advantageous at this stage" (emphasis added by H.K.).[37] This statement by a relatively "dovish" Soviet specialist on Japan might be taken to indicate that, taking the close U.S.– Japanese ties as a *fait accompli*, the Soviets were ready to improve their relations as much as possible within the framework of Japan's close relations with the United States.

The next question to be addressed here is to what extent Soviet-Japanese relations could have improved within the framework of Japan's close ties with the United States. As long as we continue to interpret Soviet official writings literally, we cannot easily find the right answer to this. A Soviet diplomat stationed in Tokyo, however, said during a private conversation: "We are realistic enough to believe that even with the existence and continuation of the U.S.-Japanese security treaty there still exists considerable room for improvement in our relations with your country." According to some astute Western observers of Soviet foreign policy, it was not utterly inconceivable to speculate that the Soviet government did not necessarily oppose, and in fact might even be ready to tolerate, the Japan–U.S. Security Treaty. The Soviets may even prefer—so they speculated—a Japan controlled within the U.S. military-strategic system to a completely free, independent, and militarily strong Japan, which might have been more harmful to Soviet interests. Lilita Dzirkals, a senior researcher at the RAND Corporation, noticed that "some Soviet spokesmen" did not necessarily advocate abolishing the Japan–U.S. Security Treaty or taking Japan out of the U.S. military-strategic system.[38] Their basic assumption seemed to her to be that "U.S. control over Japan would be guided by the primacy assigned by the United States to its relationship with the Soviet Union and hence could constitute a restraining influence on Japan."[39] Instead, "they [some Soviet spokesmen] suggested possibilities for enhancing Japan's autonomy within the framework of her alliance with the United States."[40]

Sino-U.S. and Sino-Japanese Relations

Bilateral relations between Japan and the Soviet Union were also shaped by the *regional* environment in East Asia, particularly, by the quadrilateral power configuration among the USSR, the United States, the People's Republic of China (PRC) and Japan.[41] With the aim of proving this, let us examine the impact events in Sino-U.S. relations or Sino-Japanese relations exerted upon Soviet-Japanese relations.

One example is the Sino-U.S. rapprochement of the early 1970s. President Nixon's announcement that he would visit Beijing in March 1972, ending two decades of conflict with the PRC, shocked Moscow as much as it did Tokyo. Faced with a change in the regional and the overall international environments, Moscow appeared to regard a new approach toward Tokyo as a necessary countermove. In January 1972, Foreign Minister

Gromyko canceled a scheduled visit to the Warsaw Pact summit talks in Prague in order to visit Tokyo—his first visit there since 1966. During his stay in Japan, Gromyko took, or at least appeared to take, a very concilia- tory posture, which was at the time referred to in Tokyo as "Mr. Nyet's smile diplomacy." Japan always held that it could not sign a peace treaty with the Soviet Union without the return of the Northern Territories, the islands off the coast of Hokkaido—Etorofu, Kunashiri, Shikotan, and the Habomai group of islets—that were seized by Soviet military troops in 1945. Before leaving Tokyo for Moscow, Foreign Minister Gromyko told Japanese reporters that the Soviet Union had agreed to "negotiate a peace treaty and discuss related problems." At the time, Western and some Japa- nese Kremlin watchers predicted that the Kremlin would agree to return some or all of the islands to Japan.[42] The joint communiqué issued at the end of the Japanese Prime Minister's visit to Moscow in October 1973 also mentioned the importance of settling the "outstanding questions left over from World War II." The Soviet Union, however, failed to return even one of the disputed islands. In his speech to the 25th Party Congress in 1976, Leonid I. Brezhnev stated unequivocally that Japan's demand for the return of the Northern Territories was "unfounded and unlawful," making it crystal clear that the USSR did not intend to return any of the islands.[43] What accounts for this shift in the Soviet position, from slightly conciliatory to uncompromising? First, the Soviet Union was greatly dis- appointed that Japan, under the leadership of Prime Minister Kakuei Tanaka, had promptly moved closer to the PRC. It was also disappointed by political developments in Japan when the powerful Tanaka was sud- denly replaced by the weaker Takeo Miki. Moreover, by that time, the Soviet Union had already obtained half of what it wanted from Japan: Japanese government participation in economic development projects in Siberia. The Soviet leadership under Brezhnev may have thus concluded that it was unnecessary, particularly after the oil crisis in 1973–74, to make any political concessions to Tokyo.

Another example is the conclusion of a peace treaty between Japan and the PRC in the late 1970s. It is quite clear that the USSR wanted to block, or at least delay as long as possible, the conclusion of a treaty that included the so-called "antihegemony" clause, which was perceived by both the PRC and the USSR as being directed at the Soviet Union. (For more details, see chapter 8.) Soviet actions both before and after the con- clusion of the treaty were extremely counterproductive. For example, in January 1978, Gromyko insisted that his Japanese counterpart, Sunao

Sonoda, agree to receive a Soviet draft proposal for a Treaty of Good-Neighborliness and Cooperation between the USSR and Japan, which included, among other things, the shelving of the Northern Territories issue. This Soviet action strengthened the Japanese view that no matter how long and patiently Japan might wait, the Soviet leadership had no intention whatsoever of negotiating a peace treaty with Japan. The USSR also threatened Japan, saying that it would take "countermeasures" if Tokyo concluded a treaty with Beijing. The Soviet military buildup at bases in the Northern Territories, which first became public knowledge in Japan in 1979, appears to have been such a countermeasure.

3. Perceptions, Policies, and International Behavior

In section 2, we examined the significant influence that international circumstances, particularly the *global* confrontation between the United States and the USSR, exerted upon the relationship between Japan and the Soviet Union. I have also stressed that *bilateral* relations, such as those between the PRC and the United States and between the PRC and Japan, also greatly influenced Soviet-Japanese relations. Finally, in this section, I would like to point out that the policies of *individual* countries (the United States, the PRC, Japan, and the USSR) also played a large role in shaping the bilateral relations between Japan and the Soviet Union. Since the policies of the United States and the PRC are discussed partially in the previous sections, let us deal here with Japan and the USSR.

Japan's domestic and foreign policies were an important determining factor in Japanese-Soviet relations. Domestically, for example, Japan's successful shift in its economic structure from predominantly smokestack industries to an economic structure that consumes less energy greatly decreased its need to cooperate with the Soviet Union in Siberian and other economic development projects. This contributed to an improvement in Tokyo's political bargaining position vis-à-vis Moscow. Due to the "high yen–cheap dollar" phenomenon, Japan surpassed not only the USSR in terms of GNP but also the United States in terms of per capita income. Though very few Japanese feel they are richer than Americans, the majority of Japanese started to look down upon the materially poor living standard of the Soviet Union, increasingly self-confident of the Japanese economy's superiority over the inefficient Soviet economy. More and more Japanese began to feel that Japan can get along well without the Soviet Union, whereas the Soviet Union needed Japan even more.

In Japan's foreign policy, what I call Japan's "globalization" trend, with Japan beginning to assume a more positive role in the Western community, was one of the single most important determinants of Soviet-Japanese relations. Many factors contributed to this trend and to subsequent policies in Japan, including Japan's perception of a relative decline in American supremacy in political, military, and economic spheres; increasing recognition that Japan's security was inseparable from that of the rest of the Western world, and hence the need to share the defense burden with Western nations, as best illustrated by Japanese Prime Minister Yasuhiro Nakasone's endorsement of the joint communiqué issued at the Williamsburg summit in 1983, which stated that "security is indivisible"; and growing self-confidence and even some elements of nationalism brought about and buttressed by economic achievements and other successes. But the most important single factor leading to, or at least accelerating, Japan's "globalization" was the Soviet worldwide military buildup, particularly in the vicinity of Japan.[44] It is difficult and perhaps impossible to say precisely how much the enhancement of Soviet military forces contributed to this transition in Japan, but there is no question that without the rapid, massive Soviet armament efforts, the policy shifts in Japan would not have occurred. Soviet allegations of "a resurgence of militarist tendencies" in Japan summarily characterized a complex situation for which the USSR was at least partly responsible.[45]

Thus, the Soviet Union's domestic and foreign policies were a principal determinant of Japan's foreign policy and Soviet-Japanese relations. The determining factors of Soviet domestic and foreign policies are limitless. They include ideology, geographic conditions, history, culture, religion, military-strategic elements, economics, politics, the decision-making structure, national characteristics, and the Soviet *Weltanschauung* (world view). Therefore, we must limit discussion here to only a few of these variables. (For more detail, see chapter 5, section 3.)

A most important variable is Soviet perception of and behavior toward Japan. To put it simply, the Soviet perception of Japan consisted of a combination of two somewhat opposing images—the Soviets perceived Japan as a dwarf in military terms and a giant in economic and technological fields. Although the Soviets became vigorous in their criticism of "the revival of Japanese militarist tendencies," the Soviets' actual assessment of Japan in the military field remained low. In an article titled

"The Militarization of Japan: Threat to Peace in Asia," D. Petrov remarked in 1981: "Today and in the near future, Japan will be unable to independently resolve strategic problems and offensive large-scale operations. Japan's military doctrine envisages the use of the American 'nuclear umbrella' and complete cooperation with the military forces of the United States and its Asian allies."[46] As long as Soviet foreign policy makers continued to regard military strength as the most important component in their concept of a "correlation of forces," Japan did not rank high in the Soviet Union's list of foreign policy priorities.

In contrast, however, the greater the weight that Soviet leaders attached to economic and technological elements, the higher was the position that Japan occupied in their list of priorities. The remark made by Vitalii Kobysh, chief of the U.S. section in the International Department of the CPSU's Central Committee, provides a good example. In a report on his visit to Japan in 1982, Kobysh wrote: "Toward the end of this century, Japan's GNP will constitute 12 percent of that of the whole world. It is unrealistic not to take this into consideration when analyzing the correlation of forces in the whole arena."[47] Of course, it would be premature to emphasize this remark as indicating any significant change in the Soviet assessment of the relative weight of variables. Yet, it is worth keeping in mind that a change in the relative weight of variables was slowly taking place. In place of the traditional assessment of Japan, derived from a heavy dependency upon military factors, a new mix, with more emphasis upon nonmilitary components—above all, economic and technological factors—was gradually emerging.[48]

Furthermore, the realization of the dawning of a new era in the Asia-Pacific region contributed to the change in Soviet perceptions of Japan. The Soviet Union has been described as a Eurasian country but an essentially European power. Its Europe-oriented attitude began to change as the weight of world economic activities shifted from Europe to the Asia-Pacific region. How much significance the Soviet Union came to attach to this region may be illustrated by the fact that the Soviet Pacific Fleet quickly grew into the largest of the Soviet Union's four fleets (Northern, Baltic, Black Sea, and Pacific Fleets). Despite its strong desires and claims to be a major Asia-Pacific power, however, the Soviet Union did not acquire either the prestige or the influence to be a full-fledged member in the Asia-Pacific regional community.

There may be multiple reasons for this failure, but no one can deny that one of the obvious ones is the poor record of Soviet foreign policy toward Japan, one of the most important countries in the region.[49] Geopolitically, the bow-shaped Japanese archipelago lies in the way of Soviet access to the Pacific Ocean. From a diplomatic perspective, not to mention from an economic point of view, Japan also occupied a significant position, and its voice was becoming more and more audible and influential in the region. It may be no exaggeration to consider that without improving relations with Japan, the USSR would not be able to become a full-fledged member of the Asia-Pacific community. In spite of the vital role that Japan played in Soviet strategy in the region, what Moscow was in fact doing diplomatically toward Japan amounted to almost a total disaster. There was a marked discrepancy between the apparent significance of Japan for Moscow's objectives in the Asia-Pacific region and Moscow's foreign policy conduct toward Tokyo.

In sum, the Kremlin's foreign policy toward Japan was based on a mix of the two perceptions described above: the traditional underestimation, bordering on outright contempt for Japan, on the one hand; and the reassessment of Japan as an increasingly important independent actor, particularly in the Asia-Pacific region, on the other. The former perception was contented with a Soviet policy toward Japan that was more or less an extension of Soviet strategy toward the United States. The latter encouraged the formation of a distinct foreign policy toward Japan that was sufficiently independent to be distinguishable from Soviet policy toward the United States, taking full account of the specific conditions of Soviet-Japanese relations.

4. Issues and Disputes

Between Japan and the Soviet Union were a number of issues that either helped these neighboring countries become closer to each other or prevented them from becoming friendly with each other. Recognizing this, D. Petrov writes the following, as cited previously: "Geographic proximity between the USSR and Japan gives rise to *a number of difficult problems* that must be solved by their joint effort" (emphasis added by H.K.). Solutions to or methods for solving most of the problems that arose between Japan and the Soviet Union in the postwar period were already found. Although fishing negotiations still needed to be conducted every year, these negotiations became business-like and come to almost completely exclude, for better or worse, political and other considerations.

Only one important issue remained unresolved: the conclusion of a peace treaty solving the territorial dispute.

No one denies that the issue of the Northern Territories—known to the Russians as the Southern Kuriles—hampered the improvement of Soviet-Japanese relations. It may be an exaggeration, however, to state that the Northern Territories issue constituted the greatest stumbling block to harmonious Soviet-Japanese relations. To begin with, to test this assertion, let us assume that the Kremlin were to return the Northern Territories to Japan. In that event, Japanese national feeling toward the Soviet Union surely would have improved, and hence Soviet-Japanese relations certainly would have greatly improved. Yet nobody can predict for sure to what extent Japanese feeling toward the Soviet Union would have improved. The reversion of Okinawa from U.S. to Japanese rule was greatly appreciated by the Japanese but not to the extent that some Americans expected. The Japanese appeared to take the United States's action somewhat for granted. The great "China euphoria" following the signing of the Sino-Japanese Peace Treaty in 1978 turned out to be very short-lived. It would also be overly optimistic to presume the following: that with the return of the disputed islands, all friction would cease between the two countries; Tokyo–Moscow relations would suddenly become rosy; and conflicts or other problems would not reoccur. It is understandable in light of past Japanese behavior that Kremlin leaders were reluctant to take risks for such an intangible, volatile, and unreliable thing as Japanese national sentiment. Indeed, they could not ascertain what benefits they might obtain from Tokyo in exchange for a return of the islands.

Another reason for Soviet intransigence on the territorial issue was of a military-strategic nature. Located just northeast of Hokkaido, the islands could affect the access of Soviet ships to the Pacific Ocean. Their strategic importance was publicly affirmed by Joseph Stalin[50] and Nikita Khrushchev.[51] Furthermore, the military-strategic significance of the Sea of Okhotsk increased, largely because of the new Soviet "bastion strategy."[52] Owing to the development of military technology, Soviet submarine-launched ballistic missiles (SLBMs) were capable of reaching almost all ports in the United States. However, U.S. anti-submarine warfare technology is capable of detecting Soviet nuclear-powered ballistic missile submarines (SSBNs). In order to prevent the U.S. tracking of their submarines, it became vital to the Soviets that the Sea of Okhotsk remain a sanctuary defending the SSBN bastion area. This bastion strategy certainly invested the Northern Territories with increased military importance in Soviet eyes. If we accept the above interpretation, it leads us to the position mentioned formerly: the importance of the role that the global confrontation between the United States and the USSR played in Soviet-Japanese relations. According to that school of thought, what really obstructed harmonious Soviet-Japanese relations was Japan's postwar diplomatic-military ties with the Soviets' principal archenemy, the United States. The Northern Territories issue was merely the tip of the iceberg.

Chapter 2
Approaches to National Security

There were both similarities and differences between the Soviets and the Japanese with regard to the *a posteriori* factors that determined Soviet-Japanese relations. The most fundamental disparity between Japan and the Soviet Union arose from the different doctrines and principles upon which the two states determined their own national priorities since the end of World War II. From this basic disparity flowed other major disparities, including divergent views on and attitudes toward matters such as resolving international disputes, attaining national security, and using military force. The Northern Territories issue, usually viewed as the most important stumbling block to relations between the two countries, is merely a spin-off from these more fundamental differences.

1. Solving International Conflicts: The Legacy of World War II

At the end of World War II, Japan and the Soviet Union stood apart as the defeated and the victor, respectively; yet, both had suffered such widespread physical and economic destruction that efforts to redevelop and reconstruct their individual economies began from virtually nothing. As we review this history, we realize with astonishment what contrasting lessons each drew from their separate experiences in World War II.

The psychological shocks the Japanese suffered as a result of their defeat in World War II—the first such experience in their entire history—are beyond imagination. In 1945, the Japanese were compelled to recognize how much the war had cost them: a toll of two million lives; eight million injured; two atomic bombardments which took (an additional) 300,000 lives; destruction of one-third of the national wealth; and loss of nearly half of their national territory,[1] as well as many less significant losses. The Japanese national psyche was shattered further by the sudden realization that their emperor was not infallible and that their military not invincible.

One of the most significant results of the war experience was a dramatic change in Japanese philosophy, from militarism to pacifism and mercantilism.[2] The Japanese no longer trusted the effectiveness of military might as a tool for achieving national goals, neither for themselves nor for any other country. After the end of the war, the Japanese, instead, became firm believers in nonmilitary strength, particularly in economic power. The man who provided the foundation for this new philosophy of national strength was Shigeru Yoshida, who, in his capacity as prime minister, dominated Japan's foreign policy for almost ten years (1946–47 and 1947–55) immediately after World War II. His primary principle was that since "Japan lost in war, it must win in diplomacy."[3] This principle or approach—which has been conveniently termed "the Yoshida Doctrine"—has been pithily described by Masataka Kōsaka, professor at Kyoto University, as a "merchant's view of international politics"[4] and has been faithfully followed by every Japanese head of government since Yoshida. Partially as a result of policies that grew out of this doctrine, the Japanese made a startling postwar economic recovery and achieved a level of prosperity that has put Japan in a position of economic power second only to that of the United States.

Successive Japanese prime ministers have firmly pledged that "although Japan has become a powerful economic giant, it need not and must not become a commensurate military power."[5] In a speech on May 9, 1983, in Kuala Lumpur, Prime Minister Yasuhiro Nakasone also reiterated that "our country [Japan] is determined not to become a military superpower," further stating, "This is not simply a policy but stems from unchangeable, deep-rooted Japanese national sentiment based on the profound repentance of the past."[6] Some Japanese believe that Japan should be proud of this "novel historical experiment," i.e., becoming the first *nonmilitary* superpower.[7] Whatever one calls it, this unique approach to world affairs is best described in the constitution of postwar Japan, which stipulates: "The Japanese people forever renounce . . . the threat or use of force as a means of settling international disputes." (Article IX)

The lesson which the Soviet Union learned from World War II was, unfortunately, quite the opposite. As a victor, it emerged onto the postwar world scene both exhausted and exhilarated. True, the war had demanded tremendous sacrifices, including the lives of 27 million Soviet citizens. It was also true, however, that the war brought tangible and intangible benefits and profitable by-products to the nation. Despite the principle of "territorial non-expansion" agreed upon by the Allied powers in the Atlantic Charter (1941) and the Cairo Declaration (1943), the USSR took full advantage of the war to expand its territory. In fact, it succeeded in obtaining 670,000 square kilometers, an amount equivalent to the combined land area of Great Britain, Italy, and Greece. Additionally, the Soviets expanded their sphere of influence over Europe; the USSR succeeded in establishing several "socialist" regimes in Eastern Europe, thereby finally fulfilling its long-term dream of having "socialist" countries outside its own boundaries. The victory tremendously increased the Soviets' self-confidence and international prestige, providing the USSR with a good foundation from which to grow into a superpower at a later stage.[8] From an impoverished, inexperienced, and underdeveloped pariah in the family of nations, the USSR grew into a formidable superpower. According to the perception of Soviet leaders, nearly all the USSR's profits and achievements were brought about through the victorious Red Army. This, then, was the most important legacy of World War II: Soviet leaders became convinced that the stronger military power gets the greater "spoils"— a proposition that does not always prove true.

By no means did the Kremlin's devotion to military power begin at the end of World War II. A perusal of the works of Lenin and Stalin shows a pervasive stress on military power. Their writings are permeated by military terms and concepts, such as "struggle," "conflict," "war," and "front."[9] Bolshevist leaders drew on the tradition of terrorism left as a legacy from tsarist Russia, both tying it to the Marxist belief that violence is the midwife of revolution and strengthening it through the sophisticated development of modern military science. The use of military force to achieve political goals became one of the core principles of the Soviet belief system. This trend, which existed even before World War II, was merely amplified by the experience of the war and by a combination of factors after it ended.

The postwar developments contributing to the Soviet attraction to military force include: the Soviet Union's successful development of nuclear weapons, which made it a superpower equal in military strength to America; the tendency of U.S. leaders to overestimate the significance of Soviet military power; Soviet recognition that the Soviet Union had nothing in the nonmilitary realm with which to demonstrate its superiority in the world, since Soviet-style "socialist" ideology had decreased in appeal, the "socialist" economy had stagnated, and Soviet culture had withered with the exile of the new generation of writers and other artists; the escalation of political displays of power growing out of the nuclear stalemate; and the formation of a military-industrial complex within the Soviet Union. Due to these conditions, the Kremlin clung tightly to its devotion to military power, buoying itself up by the constant expansion of its forces.

Official Soviet pronouncements indicated that this trend continued. The Soviets regarded the "correlations of forces" (*sootnoshenie sil*) as the key concept behind their views on international relations.[10] This concept roughly correlates with the Western concept "balance of power."[11] It is true that "force" (*sila*), according to the Soviet concept, involves more than simply military power; it also includes political, economic, social, scientific-technological, and mental powers.[12] Yet, Soviet authorities regarded the military component as the most vital.

The late Soviet Defense Minister Andrei A. Grechko stated directly that military might was one of the most potent means for increasing the voice, role, and influence of the USSR in the international arena. He bluntly noted: "The military might of the USSR is . . . one of *the most important factors* assuring foreign conditions favorable for the building of communism in our country and the development of all socialist countries" (emphasis added by H.K.).[13] Iurii Andropov also emphasized the role of military might immediately after he became the CPSU General Secretary on November 12, 1982:

> We know well that one cannot get peace by begging the imperialists for it. It can be upheld *only by relying on the invincible might* (*tol'ko opiraias' na nesokrushimuiu moshch'*) of the Soviet armed forces. [emphasis added by H.K.)[14]

The Soviet explanation of what compelled the United States to approve détente with the USSR in general, and to conclude the SALT (Strategic Arms Limitation Talks) I agreement in particular, illustrated this point. According to the Soviets, the United States under President Richard Nixon had to sign the SALT I agreement with Moscow because Nixon recognized the cold reality that "the correlation of forces was changing in favor of the socialist camp headed by the USSR."[15] In the Soviets' eyes, American leaders' reluctant recognition and agonizing reappraisal of the situation was compelled by "the power—the social, economic, and *ultimately, military power* [*nakonets, voennaia moshch'*] of the Soviet Union and the socialist countries" (emphasis added by H.K.).[16] Georgii A. Arbatov, director of the Institute of USA and Canadian Studies (ISKAN), of the Soviet Academy of Sciences, noted the following in his article "Soviet-American Relations at a New Stage," which summarized President Nixon's May 1973 visit to Moscow: "The growth of Soviet *defense power* made it impossible for the United States to succeed in attaining the military superiority that would enable them to achieve their objectives with the threat of use of military power" (emphasis added by H.K.).[17]

The marked contrast between the Japanese and the Soviets outlined above reminds us of two types of European diplomacy that Sir Harold Nicolson identified in his classic work, *Diplomacy* (1939): the British "shopkeeper-type or mercantile" conception and the German type of diplomacy based on a "warrior or military conception."[18] In the former, the foundations for good business—"credit, confidence, consideration and compromise"[19] also serve as the foundation for good diplomacy. In the latter, it seems more important to "inspire fear than to beget confidence," and "force or the threat of force" is considered the main instrument of negotiation.[20] This classification, though made more than 50 years ago, is still helpful to our understanding of the disparity between Japanese and Soviet foreign policy orientations during the postwar period. This contrast also reminds us of the two modes of organizing international relations that Richard Rosecrance has differentiated: a trading system and a military-political and territorial system.[21]

One small note is warranted. Despite the sharp contrasts in lessons learned from their separate World War II experiences, one common aspect in these two nations' attitudes toward the past can still be identified: both the Japanese and Soviets, exaggeratedly speaking, are prisoners of their immediate past experiences, and as such, probably learned "overgeneralized lessons" from history (in Robert Jervis's words).[22] While the Japanese, haunted by their traumatic experience in the war, attempt as much as possible to avoid the folly of repeating their mistakes, the Soviets attempted to stick to the policy that brought them such great "success" in the past. Both nations shared a tendency to apply the axioms gained by their recent experiences to the present changed circumstances, without careful examining whether the crucial dimensions of the present resembled those of the past.[23]

2. Basic Views on National Security

If I were asked to summarize in a single word the basic concept governing the Soviet view of national security, I would not hesitate to pinpoint their idea that "security is indivisible." Without a doubt, the Soviets upheld this position in terms of time, geography, means, and efforts involved in achieving national security. Japanese views of security contrasted sharply with those of the Soviets in these four areas, as we will examine below.

Different Philosophies of Life

Security is, defined by Arnold Wolfers, "in an objective sense, the absence of threats to acquired values; in a subjective sense, the absence of fear that such values will be attacked."[24] The first important feature in the Soviet view of security was the assumption that it was possible to assure security only through *constant* efforts. No doubt this Soviet perception of security as a constant challenge stemmed from one of the basic tenets of Marxism-Leninism—i.e., class struggle. It was also reinforced by the tremendous physical stress of the Russian environment—the severe climate and the unyielding demands of the land. Due to the near absence of natural borders, the Russians must always maintain a state of vigilance against possible invasions. If we carry this train of thought a little further, we see that the Russian *Weltanschauung* teaches that endless struggle is not abnormal; rather, it is a basic human condition.

As a result, the Soviets did not clearly distinguish between the conditions of war and peace. It is usually believed that the Bolsheviks were faithful disciples of Carl von Clausewitz, who said that "war is a mere continuation of policies by other means."[25] In my view, however, their true beliefs were a reversal of this famous axiom, as illustrated by the words of Maxim M. Litvinoff, foreign minister under Stalin: "The Soviet diplomat tries in peacetime to perform the task that the Red Army would have to perform in wartime."[26] The Soviets viewed diplomatic negotiations as part of the same continual political process of incessant struggle toward a final objective.

The Japanese *Weltanschauung*, and hence the Japanese view on security, contrasts markedly with the Soviet view. Living in an amazingly homogeneous and harmonious society,[27] the Japanese are neither accustomed to nor fond of direct confrontation or conflict. In contrast to the Soviets, for whom conflicts of interest (or "class struggle") were a normal part of life, the Japanese consider hostile conflicts of interest, or struggle, as the exception and regard peace, harmony, and stability as life's norm.[28] When faced with natural disasters or military conflicts, the Japanese either accept them with fatalism or do their utmost to counter the crises. Generally speaking, the Japanese are quite good at coping with and even solving such critical situations and often do so more promptly and efficiently than other nations. Masao Maruyama, late professor of the University of Tokyo, accurately described the Japanese as a "problem-solving" or "goal-achieving" nation rather than a "goal-setting" nation. Today, however, given the extraordinary development of weapons technology, once military crises start, it would be too late to do anything in most cases.

What further makes the Japanese unique is that once crises have passed, the Japanese tend to forget them quickly and to take peace and stability for granted once again—until the next imminent crisis. In his 1971 book, *The Japanese and the Jews*, Isaiah Bendasan (reportedly the pseudonym of the late well-known Japanese social commentator Hichihei Yamamoto) made the often-quoted remark: "Japanese take it for granted that security and water are obtainable without paying a price."[29] Though this sounds a bit obsolete for today's Japanese, it still holds some validity.

Is Security Indivisible?

Second, Soviet strategic theorists considered security to be *geographically* indivisible; that is, the security of one sector of the globe is closely linked with that in other places. V. Pavlovskii, a Soviet commentator on international relations and in particular on Asian affairs, regarded this "principle of indivisibility of the globe" (*printsip nedelimosti mira*) as a "guiding principle of the foreign policy of the Soviet Union and socialist states."[30] Based on this principle, the Soviets viewed events taking place in one part of the world in close interconnection with developments occurring in other parts. Ivan I. Kovalenko, a Deputy Chief of the CPSU Central Committee's International Department, who is well-versed in Japanese affairs, emphasized the basic Soviet conception that "the world is indivisible" (*mir nedelim*)[31] by linking developments in Asia, for example, with those in the rest of the world:

> The problems of war and peace in Asia at the present time affect not only the people of this region but touch upon the interests of all states, because stormy events developing in Asia directly or indirectly exert influence upon developments in Europe and upon the political atmosphere throughout the whole world.[32]

D. Petrov, another Soviet specialist on Japan, likewise stated:

Asia is no longer the remote periphery of world politics. Owing to developments in contemporary means of transportation and in communications media, the Asia-Pacific region has increasingly been influenced by happenings in other parts of the globe and in turn has exerted greater influence upon the international climate.[33]

The Soviet view noted above carried with it several important implications. More than anything else, it meant that we should eschew dichotomous ways of thinking, such as asserting that the USSR is either an Asian or a European power. One must also attempt to discern the directions toward which Soviet concerns are moving—toward Europe, the Middle East, Africa, or the Asia-Pacific area.

In my opinion, the prevailing views in the West and the PRC were inaccurate due to their attempt to define the USSR as *either* a European *or* an Asian power. The real point is that the Soviet Union was and intended to be *both* a European *and* an Asian power.[34] The Soviet position was determined quite flexibly and even opportunistically in accordance with such variables as risk-benefit calculation and Soviet capabilities in a given situation, not by any fixed design or list of priorities reflecting geographic boundaries.

This Soviet way of looking at world events, combined with the self-confidence they gained as a result of achieving strategic "rough parity" with the United States,[35] prompted Kremlin leaders to boldly assert at the threshold of the 1970s that the USSR was entitled to have a major say in all questions or events taking place anywhere in the world.[36] Soviet Foreign Minister Andrei A. Gromyko espoused this view in his 1969 declaration that "the Soviet Union, which, as a major global power, has extensive ties, cannot take a passive attitude toward events that may be geographically remote but affect our security and the security of our friends."[37] General Secretary Leonid I. Brezhnev was also quoted as saying a year later, on March 14, 1970: "At the present time, the world's single largest problem cannot be decided without our participation or without the consideration of our economic and military might."[38]

In striking contrast to the Soviets, the Japanese rarely approached security matters from a global perspective. Postwar Japanese policymakers have adopted and nurtured a unique concept of self-defense, or "exclusively defensive defense" (*senshu bōei*).[39] This concept limits the use, level, and geographical scope of the Japanese Self-Defense Forces (SDF) to a minimum. First, Japan will not put its SDF into action "until she herself comes under armed attack."[40] Second, Japan cannot possess the kinds of troops and weapons that have offensive capacity, such as ICBMs and long-range strategic bombers.[41] Third, and most important to the present discussion, the geographical scope of the SDF will be the minimum required for Japan's self-defense.[42]

This does not necessarily mean that Japan would strictly confine use of its military power to Japanese territorial land, sea, and air. As Prime Minister Eisaku Satō stated, "The security of Japan could not be adequately maintained without international peace and security in the Far East."[43] In fact, the Japan–United States Mutual Treaty of Security and Cooperation (MTS) has closely linked the security of Japan with "international peace and security in the Far East " (Article IV). By the same token, however, the Japanese consider it totally inappropriate to send their own SDF to any foreign territory for the purpose of using force.[44] The MTS obligates the United States to take military action to defend Japan and the Far East but does not require Japan to reciprocate in the same manner: Japan's sole obligation is to provide military bases and facilities for the United States.

It is true there is increasing awareness among more and more Japanese that the security of Japan is linked with the rest of the world. A series of shocks and crises in the Middle East in the 1970s, such as the oil crisis of 1973, and the political crises in Iran and Afghanistan since 1978 and 1979, respectively, contributed greatly to Japan's new consciousness of this kind of linkage. Yet, it is noteworthy that even these shocks did not change the basic attitude toward security that prevailed among the majority of Japanese. For instance, in the wake of the Soviet military invasion of Afghanistan, a high official in the Japanese Foreign Ministry stated in a speech to the Diet that the "Far East" referred to in the MTS includes the Middle East. The justification he provided at that time was that "any region which affects the security of Japan is to be regarded as the 'Far East' stipulated in the MTS." His argument is partially right; one can no longer separate the security of Japan from affairs in other regions of the world. The question is, however, why did he not say so more directly, instead of making such a convoluted and contradictory justification? He simply lacked the nerve to do so, because he was well aware of the fact that such a position would not yet be supported by the majority of Japanese.

It is also a fact that Prime Ministers Zenkō Suzuki and Yasuhiro Nakasone committed Japan to the so-called 1,000-mile sea-lane defense. From this commitment, one is likely to get the impression that Japan may expand the geographical scope of its military operations far beyond its own territory. It is inappropriate, however, to identify this commitment as a clear manifestation of change in the principal concept of Japanese security, for this commitment was made more as a compromise to alleviate the pressure exerted on Japan by the United States than as a statement of change in underlying principles in Japanese policy.

It is difficult, and even dangerous, to simplistically generalize about Japanese views on security, since Japan is a pluralistic society in which all kinds of opinions exist. On the one hand, there surely are Japanese who clearly associate the security of Japan with that of the globe (the "globalists"). As far as they are concerned, no disparity exists between the Soviet Union and Japan concerning the geographic element of security. However, it is safe to say that such thinkers do not yet constitute the majority of Japanese. On the other hand, there were and are still strong voices—which seem to express the majority view—arguing, rightly or wrongly, that as a medium-sized power without much military strength, Japan must remain outside any Soviet power confrontation on a global scale and must avoid unnecessary involvements that would endanger Japan's security. In July 1978, Henry Scott-Stokes, the Tokyo correspondent of the *New York Times*, reported with great amazement that the Japanese were not intimidated by the Soviet military buildup in the Far East. As one Japanese official explained, this was because in the eyes of most Japanese, "they [Soviet actions] are not directed specifically at Japan. They are part of their [Soviet] worldwide competition with the United States."[45] The late Vladimir Petrov, a Russian-born American professor at George Washington University, observed quite accurately that in 1981 "few Japanese share our [American] global vision."[46]

Hisao Maeda, a former professor at the National Defense College in Tokyo, provided a typical example of this Japanese attitude in his best-selling book (in Japan), *Defense Theory Full of Errors* (Machigai-darakeno Bōei-ron) (1981). For the April–June 1982 issue of *Japan Quarterly*, he summarized the gist of his argument: "Not one of the military conflicts *in the world* has anything to do with Japan."[47] For, in his view, "the military conflicts in the world" were nothing but "the conflict between the United States and the Soviet Union, or the United States and Western Europe [on the one hand] and the Soviet Union and Eastern Europe [on the other], and conflicts among individual states *in other regions of the world.*"[48] According to him, "the two superpowers may have reasons to deploy their respective military forces *all over the world:* mutual distrust, struggle for power and superiority in nuclear missiles."[49] The NATO and Warsaw

Pact member countries may also had historical and geographical reasons to confront each other. However, in Maeda's judgment, the situations in which Japan found itself were "entirely different from those of the United States or Western countries."[50] He concluded: "What is important for the security of Japan, therefore, [is] to be neither dragged into the military conflicts of *other countries*, nor to create any new military issues with *other countries*" (all emphases added by H.K.). Maeda's view serves to show that the Japanese blurred the geographic (but not the political) distinction between self-defense and global affairs. To rephrase it in a slightly different way, the Japanese tended to separate rather distinctly two levels of security problems, as best illustrated by Maeda: issues directly affecting the defense of Japan itself (some of which happen to have regional origins and relations) and security issues of a global scope that indirectly affected the security of Japan.[51]

Means to Achieve Security

As we examine the third area in which the Soviets expressed their concept of security—i.e., *in the sphere of human activities*—we see that their approach was again indivisible, or holistic, in that they did not set up priorities among political, economic, military, and other fields that support national security. An example of this concept is the Soviet conviction that economic strength and mass resilience are as important as active military forces.

The Soviets were always prepared to mobilize all conceivable *means* available to them—political, military, economic, and other—that would help insure their security. Lenin once taught that "all and everything" (*vse i vsia*) should be exploited to achieve the goal.[52] Put succinctly, the end justifies the means. As Soviet literature on international relations conceded: "In order to achieve their own purposes in international fields, the classes and their political organizations utilize in a planned and goal-oriented manner *all* arsenals of political, economic, ideological, military, and propagandistic means and methods that will assist them in their attempts to influence the development of international processes and foreign policy activities of other states in the direction desired by them" (emphasis added by H.K.).[53] Consequently, it is a mistake to think that Kremlin leaders solely or exclusively exploited military means. The pursuit of "détente" is a good example of how far the Soviets went to buttress their security interests using nonmilitary means such as diplomacy.[54]

However, as the facts show, the Soviet Union often had no other choice but to resort to military might due to the declining ideological appeal of communism, the nation's failure to provide the world with an exemplary economic model, and the sterility of Soviet culture.

The second unique feature of the holistic Soviet approach to security lies in the quite unique way in which it connected or disconnected one field of human activity (e.g., politics) with or from another (e.g., economics). The Soviets were not at all disturbed by their own conceptual inconsistencies in or de-linking various activities, as long as their actions served to fulfill their goals at a given time.

Let us illustrate the Soviet way of arbitrary linkage by quoting a public statement made in their government organ *Izvestiia* regarding Soviet-Japanese relations. One commentator there wrote in 1979: "The Soviet Union has consistently advocated and continues to advocate the all-round *(vsestoronnii)*, mutually advantageous development of commercial, economic, cultural, and other relations with Japan.[55] Having said this, however, he immediately noted one important exception: "The anti-Soviet campaigns surrounding the imaginary 'territorial problem' are interfering with the development of such bilateral relations."[56] Here we see that while advocating improved "all-round" bilateral relations with Japan the author, in almost the same breath touched on one of the major stumbling blocks to the achievement of these relations with Japan. This appears to be an attempt to tie Japan's hands. On other occasions, seeking to justify and strengthen their own position in the face of criticism, the Soviets did not hesitate to use volatile issues such as the territorial question to gain an edge over their critics. For example, in a 1979 article, *Izvestiia's* Tokyo correspondent connected the territorial issue with the Soviet military buildup on the island of Shikotan, against which the Japanese were vigorously protesting. He wrote: "The first casualties of such a hostile position toward the Soviet Union could be *cultural, scientific, and technical links, and mutual relations in the fishing, trade, and economic spheres"* (emphasis added by H.K.).[57]

Since no territorial problem existed between Japan and the Soviet Union according to official Soviet pronouncement, the above quotations provide only a limited explanation of the manner in which the Soviets arbitrarily linked such matters. Let us therefore look at the relation between politics and economics as another example. As expected from the above discussion, the usual Soviet rule was to link politics with economics. The Kremlin undoubtedly considered the promotion of close economic relations with other countries as one of the best means for improving political relations with those countries. TASS correspondent Nikolai A. Golonin acknowledged on November 4, 1979 that "mutually advantageous *economic* cooperation is an important means of cementing relations between states with different social and *political* systems" (emphasis added by H.K.).[58] With regard to Soviet relations with Tokyo, the Soviets make no secret of their intentions to let joint economic projects with Japan serve as a catalyst for improving political relations. N.N. Nikolaev, a commentator on Japan, noted that "[the] gain [of such projects] will be not only economic but also *political*" (emphasis added by H.K.).[59] In a similar manner, Pavel D. Dolgorukov, another Japan specialist, conceded that "with the increase in the magnitude of [Soviet-Japanese] joint projects, not only their economic but also their *political significance inevitably has been growing*" (emphasis added by H.K.).[60] Dolgorukov further disclosed that one of the important reasons why the Soviets persistently pressed Tokyo to sign a long-term intergovernmental economic agreement lies in the political function that such an agreement was expected to play: "A long-term intergovernmental *economic* agreement [between the Soviet Union and Japan] will bring together huge economic benefits and a big *political* responsibility" (emphasis added by H.K.).[61]

A clear arbitrariness or inconsistency came to the fore, however, when the Soviets demonstrated their unwillingness to let other countries adopt the same approach or strategy toward the relationship between politics and economics. In other words, while closely linking these two human activities to one another themselves, the Soviets did not like Japan to view economic matters in terms of political functions. This attitude was exemplified by strong Soviet opposition to Japan's participation in economic sanctions against the USSR due to the Soviet military presence in Afghanistan. The sanctions evoked strong protest and criticism from the Soviet side, which considered the Japanese linkage of economics with politics "an ugly thing." The criticism aired in Japanese on October 26, 1980 by Alekseyev, a Moscow Radio commentator, suffices as an example:

> In the middle of the 1970s, Japanese leaders extensively advertised their intention to uphold the principle of separating political matters from economic matters, but now they have suddenly become believers in the principle that economic matters cannot be separated from political matters. The Japanese side has framed a political demand as a condition to resuming normal economic ties with the Soviet Union. . . . To use trade as a tool of political intimidation is an ugly thing.[62]

It is quite evident that a comprehensive approach to national security is not solely a Soviet phenomenon. Both Japan and the Soviet Union have shown an inclination to approach national security in this manner. In fact, it is more or less a universal tendency, given the increasing interdependence of the two spheres of human activities. In practice, a disparity does exist, however, in terms of the relative weight that each nation assigns to the means of attaining national security. According to Arnold Wolfers, nations differ widely in pursuing their separate policies of security, with some standing close to the pole of complete reliance on nonmilitary means and others close to the pole of complete reliance on coercive power. It is not completely inconceivable that Japan and the Soviet Union were at quite distant positions from one another on Wolfers's spectrum, which stretched "in diametrically opposed directions."[63] In any event, Soviet thinking placed military might in the overriding position—even to an excessive degree. In sharp contrast, the postwar Japanese notion holds that national security is best attained not by coercive measures but by nonmilitary means—for instance, promotion of mutual trust among nations, skillful diplomatic measures, economic prosperity of one's own nation, and financial assistance to other nations.

More than anything else, the Japanese emphasis upon "mutual trust" makes Japan's view of national security particularly unique. Japan's postwar Constitution, commonly and affectionately called the "Peace Constitution" by the Japanese,[64] declares that "we have determined to preserve our security and existence, *trusting in the justice and faith of the peace-loving peoples of the world*"(emphasis added by H.K.). Postwar Japan's so-called "peace diplomacy" or "omnidirectional diplomacy" (*zenhōigaikō*)—a foreign policy posture that strives to make Japan a friend to all countries of the world—embodies this spirit of mutual trust. It is evident that Japanese leaders' current security and foreign policy orientation is conditioned both by peace-oriented and idealistic determination stemming both from the traumatic Japanese experience of World War II and from a realistic view of current circumstances in Japan. Postwar Japan is a typical example of the "trading state"[65] (Richard Rosencrance). As an extreme case of a trading nation, whose 110 million people survive by depending upon the import of 88 percent of their energy resources from abroad (including 99.8 percent of oil) and by exporting manufactured products overseas, Japan has no alternative but to pursue an "all-directional diplomacy." As Kunio Muraoka, a Japanese diplomat, put it:

The failures of the last century argue strongly that diplomacy should play a leading role in Japan's security policy; the dependence of her economy on trade, and the vulnerability of transport routes, makes military protection inimical to both. Japan must rely upon the peace and friendship of the world—she will never be able to survive its active ill will—and for this purpose diplomacy is the only valid tool.[66]

The majority of Japanese believe as Muraoka does, and they advocate using extra financial resources for economic aid to developing countries and troubled areas in the world rather than spending huge amounts on military affairs as other powers do. This alternative approach is intended to reduce tension and enhance stability in those areas, and ultimately help assure the security of Japan. Even such a conservative political figure as former Director General of the Japanese Defense Agency Shin Kanemaru of the Liberal Democratic Party (LDP) stated:

I am of the opinion that it constitutes good security policy [for Japan] to pursue a peace-diplomacy, with the aim of promoting coexistence and economic cooperation with, at least, neighboring nations. I consider it one of the fundamentals of our defense policy to spend a huge amount of money for economic cooperation rather than simply increase our defense capability.[67]

The well-known *Report on Comprehensive National Security* promoted in 1980 by Prime Minister Masayoshi Ōhira's private advisory group provides another example of Japan's approach to national security.[68] A superficial glance at the title gives the impression that the "comprehensive" approach finally has gained legitimacy in Japanese political culture. A closer examination, however—as will be demonstrated below through an investigation of various interpretations and criticisms of the Ōhira approach—reveals that the Japanese concept of "comprehensive" security is still different from that of the Soviets. According to the Ōhira group's report, Japan's security must be comprehensive, because "our fields of interest and kinds of threats are diverse and not limited solely to the military sphere."[69] The *Report* explains further:

[Previously,] the problem of security was considered essentially as a question of coping with a military threat. . . . The oil crisis, however, demonstrated that there are other problems . . . that could threaten people's life. Furthermore, from a medium- or long-range perspective, the possibility of a food shortage is being pointed out. Given these serious threats other than those in the military sphere, it is necessary to formulate a comprehensive policy encompassing all areas.[70]

Likewise, the *Report* draws our attention to the fact that a security policy must be based on a mix of various measures:

> One must not ignore nonmilitary means, such as to ease or eliminate confrontation through "peace diplomacy" or to remove causes of conflict through economic cooperation. Such observations are true to some extent, but still show a lack of complete understanding. This is because the dynamism of international relations is governed by an all-encompassing mix of both military and nonmilitary means, and because every country, as a matter of fact, gives weight to military security. . . . Military capability is a major factor governing the foreign policy of every country.[71]

National security is an ambiguous and elusive term,[72] and yet in the Soviet Union, as well as in the West, it seems to have been roughly equated with military security. It is evident, however, that the Ōhira *Report* obviously broadened the term beyond the military field, inevitably giving rise to some confusion. One reason why the group broadened the concept of national security to include not only military defense but also a variety of political, economic, and energy fields, is the Japanese public's strong psychological aversion to a military presence and military action. This aversion made it difficult to rapidly increase Japan's military defense spending above 1 percent of the GNP. A broadened concept of comprehensive security would make it possible to increase defense expenditure by allocating a budget for nonmilitary economic assistance to vital places from which oil and other needed natural resources are imported into Japan.

Not surprisingly, this redefinition of security in more comprehensive terms brought criticism both from leftists and from rightists in Japan. The leftists charged that the redefined concept was nothing more than a cunning device that could be used to manipulate the attitudes of the general public toward military security issues when it became expedient to do so. The rightists, along with some Americans, criticized the concept for concealing the fact that no substantial increases in the defense budget had actually been made. Moreover, they were concerned about the risks of publicly diluting the critical role that military security occupies in the maintenance of national security. Others have put forth yet a third criticism namely: that this concept of comprehensive security is nothing but a tautology, since the essence of the concept of national security is its compre-hensiveness.

Self-Reliance or Alliance?

In general, national security policy is inherently comprehensive in the following sense as well: it must contain efforts in three areas—(1) strength-ening self-reliance; (2) pursuing a more peaceful order in the overall in-ternational community; and (3) attempting to create a favorable environment on a more limited scale, e.g., through alliances or coopera-tion with countries sharing common political ideals and interests.[73] In practice, each nation wittingly or unwittingly resorts, in varying degrees, to a combination of all three efforts. From this perspective, no one strongly disagrees with the characterization of Japan's postwar policy as one that uniquely placed greater weight upon forming an alliance with the United States than upon increasing Japan's self-reliance. Shigeru Yoshida was instrumental in orienting Japanese national security along these lines. Justifying his policy, Yoshida stated in his *Memoirs*:

> Japan is an island nation in which a population in excess of ninety-one million must be provided with a civilized standard of life. This can only be accomplished through an expanding volume of overseas trade. We should, to that end, pay special regard to our relations with Great Britain and the United States—two countries which are economically the most advanced nations on earth, and with whom our dealings go back deep in history. This is a matter of prudent national policy unconnected with any considerations of political ideology. It is neither a policy of subordination nor depen-dence. It is the most prompt, effective means and a shortcut to promoting the interests of the Japanese people.[74]

The so-called Yoshida Doctrine,[75] which emphasized Japan's economic growth and development primarily by means of diplomatic and military alliance with the United States, has been carried out for three decades without significant modifications by Yoshida's successors. According to one American observer's view,[76] scholars who form "the mainstream of Japanese strategic thought" have also inherited the Yoshida strategy. Op-posing the development of an autonomous defense (*jishu bōei*), these scholars wrote in a report to the Ōhira government in 1978:

> A policy of so-called autonomous defense would necessitate fairly enor-mous outlays. It would also lower the level of Japan's security by provok-

ing the aversion of other countries and thereby increasing the possibility of inducing threats that exceed Japan's ability to defend herself. Such a policy, therefore, should not be adopted.[77]

The report leaves no doubt whatsoever concerning its support of Japan's basic, long-standing defense policy—a policy that supports the possession of minimum self-defense capability as a "denial force"[78] and total dependence upon the United States, not only for nuclear deterrence but also "for aid in the case of large-scale military aggression even with conventional forces." The report contains the following:

> Japan's defense policy has been based on the stance that Japan *totally depends* [*zenmentekini izon*] *on the United States* for nuclear deterrence and that, against aggression with conventional forces, Japan possesses defense capability as a "denial force" in the case of small-scale, limited military aggression to make such aggression costly and to prevent invasion of Japan from easily becoming a fait accompli, and it *waits for the United States forces to come to Japan's aid* in the case of large-scale aggression. [emphasis added by H.K.][79]

One may argue that the stance taken by Yasuhiro Nakasone, a strong advocate of Japan's efforts toward greater self-reliance, is unique or even unprecedented in postwar Japanese history. For instance, Nakasone outwardly advocated *jishu bōei* of Japan. By *jishu bōei*, Nakasone meant the autonomous and independent defense of Japan, provided primarily by the Japanese themselves.[80] In *My Life in Politics* (1982), Nakasone wrote that he believes "true independence is impossible as long as a nation chooses to depend in large measure on the military power of another country for its territorial security."[81] In this English-language work obviously intended for American readers, Nakasone boldly revealed his long-cherished dream in a concrete proposal for Japan to pursue *jishu bōei*: "To attain Japanese independence in national defense, the security treaty with the United States should be revised to put equal responsibility on both parties, and U.S. military forces should be gradually removed from Japan."[82] The concept of *jishu bōei* is nothing new to Soviet and Western specialists on security. Yet, given Japan's excessive dependence on U.S. security arrangements in the past, Nakasone's proposal appeared extraordinary.

Nakasone's personal political conviction does not indicate any intention on his part to completely replace the United States alliance with Japanese self-reliance. On the contrary, Nakasone is one of those Japanese political leaders who has demonstrated an eagerness to "continue,"[83]or even "revitalize,"[84]the alliance with the West, particularly the United States. Identifying the Japan–U.S. Security Treaty as "essential for attaining Japan's peace and security" and highly applauding "the contribution of the United States military troops stationed in Japan to this objective," Prime Minister Nakasone declared in the Diet (Japanese Parliament) that his "government is not in any way considering the revision of the Japan-U.S. Security Treaty, but on the contrary, is going to make further efforts to let that system [be] exercised more smoothly and effectively."[85]

Nakasone's intentions in the security field can be characterized as twofold: (1) to exert a more positive effort toward military cooperation with the United States, and (2) to increase Japan's efforts at self-reliance. In each of these efforts, Nakasone seemingly was determined to do far more than any of his predecessors. Nakasone apparently saw no serious contradictions in his attempt to simultaneously pursue these two goals. Nakasone, it seems, views these two efforts as complementary rather than mutually exclusive, as indicated by his remarks: "Japan must fulfill its international responsibilities. Its excessive dependence on others serves only to injure its international credibility."[86] He himself summarized his security efforts in one phrase: "the establishment of an autonomous defense [*jishu bōei*] capability linked with the United States."[87] Nakasone seems quite convinced that Japan can and should contribute more to the Western community—specifically to its major ally, the United States—through greater efforts to increase its own defense capability, thereby inevitably reducing the defense burden on the United States.

Though the Soviet notion of national security is comprehensive or indivisible in nature, as indicated in the above discussion, it must be emphasized that the Soviets did not always treat security affairs as comprehensive in actual practice. As for Soviet efforts to attain national security, we detect a kind of discrepancy between what the Soviets' own theory of comprehensive security states they should do, on the one hand, and what they actually did in practice, on the other. While the Soviet Union should have attended to all three efforts outlined above, it emphasized efforts at self-reliance rather than efforts at forming alliances with other states. In this, it contrasts markedly with Japan, which put the greatest emphasis upon the nuclear umbrella and similar deterrence capabilities of other nations (e.g., its major ally, the United States), thereby minimizing its own capability.

Of course, the Soviet Union never hesitated to form alliances with other states; in fact, the USSR maintained security arrangements or relations with quite a number of countries on a multilateral or bilateral basis (e.g., the Warsaw Pact, and bilateral security relations with Iraq, Afghanistan, etc.). It is also true that such arrangements greatly served the national security interests of the USSR, either defensively as a buffer zone between the USSR and potential adversaries or offensively as a springboard for further expansion of the Soviet sphere of influence. Apart from these positive functions and services, however, the Soviet Union's alliances with other countries did not seem to bring it much benefit. On the contrary, these alliances seemed burdensome to the Soviet Union in terms of economic cost and security responsibilities. The power the Soviet Union exercised over its allies and the obligations it fulfilled toward them closely resembled those of the United States (rather than those of Japan) in the Japan–U.S. Mutual Security Treaty. According to the Brezhnev Doctrine, any attacks from the outside or any changes from within that threatened the "socialist achievements" of any member of the socialist bloc were to be considered an attack on the "socialist" community as a whole and would trigger a response from the USSR.[88] On the other hand, the countries allied with the Soviet Union seemed neither terribly capable nor reliable as allies.

The emergence of new political and military elites among Soviet allies, often characterized by virulent nationalism, raised questions concerning the validity of security arrangements with the USSR —arrangements derived mostly as a result of the USSR's insistence. One systematic attempt at estimating the reliability of armies in the event of an East-West military confrontation concluded that of all East European armies, only the East German army could be relied upon to carry out Warsaw Pact military operations: the remaining East European armies were viewed as not totally reliable.[89] Admittedly, as Andrzej Korbonski, professor of political science at the University of California, Los Angeles, wrote, the evidence used in support of the above contention tends to be impressionistic and intuitive, yet at the same time, it did correspond to the popular perception of the role played by individual countries in the overall activities of the Warsaw alliance.[90] Perhaps Kremlin leaders themselves realized the nature of the situation better than anyone else and for this reason did not place much expectation in or rely heavily on their allies. They were convinced that they had to depend exclusively upon their own powers to defend not only the USSR but its allies as well.

The Soviet proclivity to place greater emphasis on self-reliance than on an alliance system with other nations to attain national security was not solely derived from the realities that Soviet allies happened to be very weak and unreliable. It was also derived from a long tradition of Russian xenophobia and "almost pathologically mistrustful behavior" (S. Kertesz),[91] the root of which is not too hard to trace. Having lived in the defenseless steppes and "lacking natural geographical barriers, the Russians have had to deal principally with fierce hostile neighbors."[92] They have never experienced a permanently peaceful coexistence with neighboring states. Both prior to and since the October Revolution, the Russians have endured unhappy and bitter experiences associated with invasions, ruthless rule, and isolation—the "Mongol Yoke," Napoleonic War, Russo-Japanese War, interventions during the Civil War (1918–1921), containment by Western powers in the Cold War period, and Sino-Soviet conflicts—to mention just a few examples.[93] According to many analysts, these geographic and historical factors, combined with Marxist-Leninist doctrine,[94] which teaches uncompromising struggle against enemies, provided major reasons for Soviet suspicions, hostility, and distrust of foreign nations, and hence for their inclination to rely heavily on their own power. For instance, George F. Kennan, former U.S. Ambassador to the USSR and professor emeritus of Princeton University, remarks that "the Russians therefore have no conception of permanent friendly relations between states."[95] "Russian diplomacy," he continues, "is concentrated on impressing an adversary with the terrifying strength of *Russian* power" (emphasis added by H.K.).[96] Louis Halle reaches much the same conclusion, noting that "the Russians learn at an early stage to trust no one, to be suspiciously alert," and instead "to keep their *own* counsel" (emphasis added by H.K.).[97]

3. Contrasting Views on Military Forces

Owing to the provisions of its security treaty with the United States, Japan need not completely arm itself; however, Japan does maintain its own coercive instrument—the Self-Defense Forces (SDF)—as an effort at minimal self-reliance. A 1982 Japanese *white paper on defense* justifies the SDF, proclaiming that "Japan as an independent sovereign nation has the inherent right to maintain minimum military strength necessary to exercise the right of self-defense."[98] What is surprising, and particularly noteworthy, is the relatively small scale of the Japanese SDF. In terms of its size, budget, and equipment inventory, the Japanese SDF is disproportionate to Japan's political role and economic capabilities.

The imbalance becomes even more striking when one compares the Japanese military with the Soviet equivalent—the Soviet Armed Forces. In terms of gross national product, Japan and the USSR occupied second and third place, respectively, in the world. In the military domain, however, a vast disparity existed between these two countries—one that sometimes has been described as the difference between a mouse and a lion,[99] or a dwarf and a giant. Whereas Japan ranked only eighth in the world in terms of total military expenditures, the USSR ranked first. Whereas Japan allotted less than 1 percent of its national budget for military expenditure, the Soviet Union spent 12–14 percent of its budget on the military.[100] Whereas the Japanese SDF has maintained a military staff of less than a quarter-million, the USSR boasted a total force of 3.7 million—15 times more. Table 2.1 shows how large were the asymmetries between the USSR and Japan in military and defense areas. What was at the root of these differences? In the previous discussion on the legacy of World War II and on basic Japanese and Soviet views of national security, we have already answered this question in part, but not sufficiently. It seems quite reasonable to suspect that underlying such uneven military figures were fundamental differences in views on and attitudes toward the use of a coercive physical instrument. Again, we assume that Japanese and Soviet perceptions, this time of the military, were quite dissimilar. The quantitative imbalance between the Japanese SDF and the Soviet Armed Forces was nothing but a reflection of their divergent views. Let us try to confirm this assumption by examining Japanese and Soviet views on the military along three lines.

Maximize versus Minimize

The concept of national security is relative to each particular nation. To begin with, absolute or total security is unobtainable unless a country is capable of world domination.[101] In fact, Professor Hedley Bull reminds us that "absolute security from war and defeat has never been enjoyed by sovereign states living in a state of nature and is foreign to all experience of international life."[102] One can even agree with Dimitri K. Simes's conclusion that "total security is impossible in the nuclear age."[103] Even in the cases of countries that have seemingly achieved absolute or total security, the fact of the matter is that insecurities and fears are simply "internalized" rather than eradicated. Thus, as Professor Arnold Wolfers advises, nations must, to some extent, "live dangerously"[104] and remain content with a level of "relative" security.[105]

Table 2.1

Asymmetries between the USSR and Japan in Military and Defense Areas

	USSR (1978)	Japan (1980)	USSR/ Japan
Military spending			
Total (billion US$)	148	8.96	16.5
Per capita (US$)	574	75	7.7
Percentage of GNP	11–13	0.9	12.2–14.4
Armed forces (number)			
Total	3,705,000	245,000	15.1
Army	1,825,000	155,000	11.8
Navy	450,000	45,000	10.0
Air Force	475,000	45,000	10.6
Strategic nuclear forces (number)			
Forces	1,398	none	—
ICBMs	606	none	—
IRBMs: MRBMs	989	none	—
Aircraft (number)			
Long-range bombers	150	none	—
Medium-range bombers	925	none	—
Combat aircraft	6,730	314	21.4
Navy (number)			
Submarines	273	14	19.5
Major surface combat ships	290	49	5.9
Army (number)			
Tanks	100,000	890	112.4

Sources: Shimizu Hayao, Nissokan no 'shinrai-kyōka-sochi' no kiso o kakuritsu seyo (Establishing a Basis for "Confidence-Building Measures" Between Japan and the USSR), unpublished paper read at the Japan-Soviet Specialist Symposium held in Tokyo on December 4–6, 1982, p. 13; *The Military Balance, 1982–1983*, pp. 13–17, 87.

The amount of military strength a nation needs to defend its interests and achieve a level of "relative" security is also highly debatable. No one can provide definitive and categorical figures to this effect, because the amount of military power necessary depends on how a nation perceives the capabilities and intentions of its adversaries at a given moment. Judging from Japanese and Soviet practices, however, we can safely conclude that the two nations addressed this issue of military strength quite differently. It seems that the Soviets felt secure only when they possessed far greater military resources than might be expected of them given their circumstances; in contrast, the postwar Japanese have considered it sufficient to maintain a minimal level of defense capability.

Why did the Soviet Union consistently attempt to maximize its military might—often to a level unnecessary for merely defending its own interests—at the great expense of gains in other fields? In this section we will address this question, which long puzzled many Western "Soviet" observers. The following is a list of speculations made by Western specialists of the Soviet Union on the possible reasons for the Soviet emphasis on military strength:

1. Geographical features of Soviet Russia—e.g., lack of natural geographic barriers; lack of warm ports; sterile land, which forced the Soviets to expand in order to feed the population.
2. Historical experiences—e.g., recurrent foreign invasions (by the Mongols, Napoleon, Hitler), intervention, encirclement, and containment by Western capitalist powers.
3. "Russian national character," which includes a distrust of foreigners and a high regard for and reliance on power.
4. Marxist-Leninist ideology based on class struggle, which aims ultimately at world revolution and the final victory of socialism over capitalism.
5. The existence and growing influence of a Soviet military-industrial complex.
6. Apprehension of scientific-technological breakthroughs in the West, which forced Soviet adversaries to develop new weaponry.
7. Less reliable allies and less available bases overseas compared with those available to Western powers.
8. Potential conflict with the People's Republic of China, which gave rise to the possibility of a "two-front war."
9. The lack of other available means with which to pursue their foreign policy goals.

While Western specialists continue to debate which of the above factors constitutes the most important driving force behind the growth of Soviet military forces,[106] they have reached a consensus on one fact: the Soviet Union made persistent efforts to increase its military capabilities. Even George F. Kennan, who has contended that the West exaggerated the notion of a "Soviet threat," admitted, "That the Soviet leaders overdo in this respect [i.e., the inordinate and relentless growth of military capabilities] and that this presents a serious problem for the rest of us . . . I do not dispute."[107] The Soviets themselves never denied the need to possess extensive military might to counter imperialist aggression. One textbook on military doctrine published by the Soviet Defense Ministry, *The Philosophical Heritage of V.I. Lenin and Problems of Contemporary War* (1972), states: "If the imperialists start a war against a country of the socialist bloc, the Soviet Union must take measures to respond with *overwhelming power*" (emphasis added by H.K.).[108] Although we cannot be certain what is meant by "overwhelming power" (*prevoskhodiashchaia sila*), it is not unreasonable to equate it with "superiority" (*prevoskhodstvo*) over rather than "parity" with the United States.[109] One thing that is clear from both official Soviet pronouncements and Soviet practice is that the Soviet Union was interested in "incessant growth" (Brezhnev) of its military forces. The speeches and statements of Defense Minister Dmitrii F. Ustinov, for example, were permeated with such phrases as "constant" (*neuklonnoe*) increase, "all-round" (*vsestoronnoe*) growth, "daily" (*povsednevnoe*) strengthening, and enhancement "by all means" (*vsemernoe*) of the fighting capability of the Soviet Armed Forces.[110]

In sharp contrast, Japan has tried to limit its defense level as much as possible. The *White Paper on Defense* (1982 edition) states, "The self-defense capability that Japan is allowed to possess under constitutional limitations is a *necessary minimum for self-defense*" (emphasis added by H.K.).[111] "A necessary minimum for self-defense" is, of course, dependent upon factors such as technological development of weaponry, international circumstances, and so on. Japan, rather surprisingly, however, has adhered strictly to self-imposed limitations. For instance, the task (assigned to) the Japanese SDF is limited strictly to the defense of the homeland; Japan will not send military personnel overseas. Japan renounces long-range strike capabilities and neither exports nor transfers arms.[112] Last, but not least, Japan abides by the "Three Non-Nuclear Principles" of not possessing, not manufacturing, and not introducing nuclear weapons into Japan. It is no wonder that Japan ratified in 1976 the Treaty on Nonproliferation of Nuclear Weapons (NPT). Most noteworthy in Japan's approach to the military is the effort to restrict it financially, thus making the above-mentioned measures at self-restraint effective. On November 5, 1976, the Japanese government decided that total defense-related expenditure for each fiscal year was not to exceed a sum equivalent to 1 percent of Japan's GNP.

There are numerous reasons for the Japanese determination to keep military capabilities at a disproportionately low level despite Japan's economic capacity. The following are the major factors contributing to Japan's desire to minimize its military strength:

1. Very deep-rooted pacifism and anti-military sentiments exist in Japan as a reaction to the rampant militarism of the 1930s and 1940s and the consequent trauma of World War II.

2. Consideration is given to the psychological impact a strong Japanese military would have upon peoples of other Asian nations, who still have bitter memories of Japanese militarism and worry about its resurgence.

3. Geographical factors make Japan hopelessly vulnerable to nuclear attack: (i) Though separated from its adversaries by water, Japan is located close enough to the Asia mainland to put the entire Japanese archipelago within range of any Tu-22M *Backfire* supersonic bombers or SS-20 intermediate-range ballistic missiles launched from the continent; (ii) Japan is a small, insular land lacking so-called "strategic depth"; and (iii) Both population and industry are concentrated in a few metropolitan areas (approximately 40 percent of the population and roughly 70 percent of Japanese industry are concentrated in the Tokyo-Yokohama and Osaka-Kobe areas).[113]

4. There is strong doubt concerning Japanese nuclear deterrence capability. Strategic deterrence makes no sense for a country with the geopolitical vulnerabilities described above: the first nuclear strike by an adversary would probably destroy Japan's population and industry to such an extent that hitting back would become pointless.[114]

5. There are many practical difficulties in producing large numbers of nuclear weapons. For example, Japan has neither secret access to uranium ore nor sites to set up a nuclear plant or to test bombs. And there is insufficient contact and cooperation among scientists, engineers, and university specialists, who fear, among other things, student protests.[115]

Whatever the underlying reasons for Japan's self-imposed limitations, the resulting "low standard of the [Japanese] military forces"[116] was recognized even by Soviet specialists on Japan. For example, D. Petrov observed in his 1973 book:

In terms of numbers of military forces, quality of military technology, amount of military spending and all other indices, Japan cannot be compared to the U.S.A. or "Common Market" countries. Japan has no atomic weapons of her own and *is unable to independently solve strategic tasks.* [emphasis added by H.K.][117]

Even ten years later, Petrov held a basically similar view. In the article "Militarization of Japan: Threat to Peace in Asia," which, as its title indicates, is critical of "growing militaristic tendencies" in Japan, Petrov revealed his true feelings when he noted that "today and in the near future Japan *will be unable to independently solve strategic tasks* or conduct offensive large-scale operation" (emphasis added by H.K.).[118] In an article written after Andropov assumed the leadership of the USSR, two Soviet commentators on Japan, N.N. Nikolaev and A. Aleksandrov, asserted that Japan's failure to realize its military potential made Japan "strategically vulnerable": "Since Japan lacks military capabilities and is strategically vulnerable, the view is held in Tokyo that problems confronting the country . . . can be solved only by strenthening the [Japanese] alliance with the United States.[119]

Outward-Thrusting versus Inward-Looking

Discrepancies between Soviet and Japanese views on "what level of military power is sufficient" indicate the existence of yet other disparities in their views on the military—concerning, for instance, questions of *for what purpose* and *where* military forces are to be utilized. The Soviet Union's insistence on maintaining "overwhelming power" suggests that the USSR assigns to its military forces missions that are more extensive than the ordinary task of defending the nation. In fact, the Soviet Armed Forces are responsible not only for the somewhat passive and minimal task of protecting Soviet achievements and vested interests but also for the more active task of expanding Soviet influence whenever and wherever an opportunity presents itself. In pursuit of this latter goal—extending its influence—the Soviet Union has shown no hesitation in sending Soviet military forces beyond its national borders.

From a careful study of Soviet strategic military newspapers, periodicals, and other writings, such as *Krasnaia zvezda* and *Kommunist vooruzhennykh sil*, Kuniko Miyauchi, a former professor at the National Defense College (Tokyo), ascertained that in the late 1960s the Soviet Union made a decision to convert its military-strategic policy orientation from an "introverted" system to an "extroverted" system.[120] Miyauchi's assertion reinforced similar observations made by Western specialists on Soviet military affairs, such as William F. Scott and Carl G. Jacobsen.[121] These Western observers also noted that when the Soviet Union attained strategic parity with the United States at the start of the 1970s, it considered itself a global power and in turn used this newly attained position to justify expanding its military power to other parts of the globe.

The book *Military Power and International Relations* (1972) edited by Soviet Colonel V.M. Kulish justifies the Soviet military presence "in various regions of the world" by clarifying the additional tasks assigned to the armed forces of the Soviet Union. In particular, the tasks of preventing local wars and supporting national liberation struggles are discussed:

> Greater importance is being attached to *a Soviet military presence in various regions of the world*, reinforced *by* an adequate level of *strategic mobility for its armed forces.*

> In connection with *the task of preventing local wars* and also in those cases in which *military support must be furnished to those nations fighting for their freedom and independence* against the forces of international reaction and imperialist interventions, *the Soviet Union may require mobile, well-trained, and well-equipped forces.* . . .

> *Expanding the scale of Soviet military presence* and military assistance furnished by other socialist states [is] being viewed today as a very important factor in international relations (emphasis added by H.K.).[122]

In an article entitled "Historical Mission of the Armies of Socialist States," which appeared in the May 1972 issue of *Kommunist*, Aleksei A. Epishev, Chief of the Central Political Administration of the Armed Forces of the USSR, also clearly outlined the tasks of the armed forces of "socialist" nations. First, he classified the functions of the military into internal and external functions. According to Epishev, with the maturation of socialist society in the Soviet Union, the domestic function of the military had faded away, leaving only the external function for the Soviet Armed Forces to fulfill.[123] Epishev then claimed that the external function entailed not only defending the country and the entire socialist bloc against outside threats but also preventing the export of imperialist counterrevolution and assisting "the struggles of the international working class and national liberation movements *in any part of the world*" (emphasis added by H.K.).[124] In an article appearing in the May 1974 issue of *Prob-*

lems in the History of the CPSU, former Soviet Defense Minister Andrei A. Grechko more explicitly discussed the responsibilities of the Soviet Armed Forces "in whatever distant region of our planet":

> At the present stage, the historic function of the Soviet Armed Forces *is not restricted* merely to their function in defending our Motherland *and other socialist countries*. In its foreign policy activity, the Soviet state actively [and] purposefully opposes the export of counterrevolution and the policy of oppression, supports the nationa-liberation struggle, and resolutely resists imperialist aggression *in whatever distant region of our planet it may appear*. [emphasis added by H.K.][125]

The decision to send Soviet tanks and expeditionary forces to any remote place on the globe actually depended upon many considerations, such as their capabilities at the time, cost-benefit analysis, and so on. For example, the Soviets refrained from intervening in the "Sino-Vietnamese War" in the spring of 1979, whereas they actively intervened in Angola, Ethiopia, and Afghanistan.

In striking contrast to the Soviet Union's extroverted, outward-looking, and expansive attitude toward defense, Japan adopted an introverted, "quite inward-oriented"[126] attitude with regard to security and military matters (an attitude that differs markedly from Japan's expansive approach to economic activities). Most importantly, postwar Japan refrained from deploying military forces overseas. As noted previously, the Japanese government has insisted that the Japanese SDF be retained, as its name indicates, exclusively for self-defense; any action exceeding this purpose—such as attacking a foreign nation or sending troops overseas for possible military action—is prohibited by the Japanese Constitution.

In their very strict and faithful interpretation of the Japanese Constitution, Japanese government officials have contended that even the exercise of "the right to collective self-defense" exceeds the limits of self-defense permissible under the Constitution.[127] Several unique situations have resulted from this strict interpretation. One is Japan's possible denial of the United Nations Charter. Article 51 of the U.N. Charter proclaims the right of collective self-defense as an inherent right of any nation. Yet, even this international charter is not powerful enough to change Japanese government officials' position on this subject. In an interview with *Newsweek* magazine in September 1979, Ganri Yamashita, then Director General of Japan's Defense Agency, gave an apparently contradictory answer when explaining Japan's position on this matter:

Japan supports United Nations' diplomacy, and therefore we would endorse any peacekeeping efforts by the United Nations. However, we cannot participate in them by sending our own troops. There will be absolutely no change in basic policy; i.e., the defense based on *self*-defense. [emphasis in original][128]

Japan's white paper on defense published the same year also made the Japanese position clear:

Even regarding the right of collective self-defense—recognized internationally by Article 51 of the United Nations Charter—the Japanese Constitution does not permit the dispatch of the Japanese SDF abroad to counter aggression against the territory and people of a foreign nation, even one that has relations with Japan.[129]

Another outcome of the Japanese Constitution's denial of the right to collective self-defense is the unique arrangement stipulated in the current Japan–United States Mutual Security Treaty (MTS). While the Treaty obligates the United States to defend Japan, it does not require Japan to reciprocate. Unlike other Asia-Pacific area a signatories of similar treaties with the United States, Japan has no obligation to act in the event of an attack on U.S. territory. All this treaty requires of Japan is to grant the United States use of bases and facilities "for the purpose of contributing to the security of Japan and the maintenance of international peace and security in the Far East." (Article VI)

Indeed, some specialists in international affairs have recommended that the Japanese government opt for a "slightly relaxed interpretation" of the collective self-defense concept.[130] In light of the fact that, publicly, the Japanese government has strictly interpreted the Constitution on this issue, there seems to be little possibility for change, unless the Constitution itself is first changed.

Political Functions

For the third contrasting point between Soviet and Japanese views on the military, we will examine the functions that the two nations assign to their respective military forces. Undoubtedly, no difference whatsoever exists between Japan and the Soviet Union in terms of the basic function assigned to the military; i.e., the function of physical coercion. (It is this function, after all, that constitutes the *raison d'être* for military forces.)

Herein, however, lies the contrast: The Japanese do not permit their Self-Defense Forces (SDF) to play any role other than this basic coercive function, while the Soviets also highly value other functions—e.g., the political-diplomatic functions of the military.

The Japanese SDF, the existence of which is regarded by most Japanese as a "necessary evil" required by current international circumstances, is under strict civilian control. It is expected to perform a solely military, or more precisely, an exclusively defensive role. Only one other *minor* function is assigned to the Japanese SDF—to carry out "disaster rescue" operations in any area of the country when the situation demands.[131] This minor function, however, is neither political nor diplomatic in nature.

The lack of a political role for the Japanese SDF is the point that distinguishes it most from the prewar Japanese Imperial Army. Osamu Kaihara, formerly the secretary-general of the Japan Defense Agency, noted that "while the Japanese Imperial Army was a means to carry out the national policy, today's SDF has nothing to do with such a policy."[132] This distinction has also been noted by Soviet specialists on Japan. D. Petrov accurately notes the limited influence of the Japanese SDF in contemporary Japanese society:

> The [Japanese] Constitution imposes a clear obstacle against [such] rampage of the military clique as was prevalent in Japan near the end of World War II. [Even] the commanding officers of the SDF have not played any significant role whatever in the political life of Japan. In terms of quantitative size and position in the socioeconomic structure, the military assumes a remarkably smaller role in today's Japan than in any of the imperialist countries of Western Europe, not to mention in the United States.[133]

Petrov also underscores the lack of a political-diplomatic role for the SDF in the international arena: [Postwar] Japan has been deprived of the so-called "special service" of robbing neighboring nations, which was characteristic of Japanese militarism both before and during the war years."[134]

By contrast, the role the Soviet armed forces was expected to play for the Soviet state was not restricted to the truly military function. In the USSR, where the concept of "separation of powers" was rejected as a Western bourgeois subterfuge, the legislature, the executive, and the judiciary were viewed not as three independent powers but simply as three functions of one single power—the proletariat. The Soviet notion of a single state power representing the interests of the working class rejected yet another Western concept—the "division of labor." Such a division would separate politics and economics, or politics and the military, from one another to some degree. Instead, under the Soviet system, all branches of government and all institutions and groups were expected to work for whatever the interests of the state were determined to be, regardless of their respective group functions or interests. The Soviet armed forces were expected to contribute in this manner as well. In other words, they must be ready to perform whatever tasks may be assigned to them in conjunction with the overall task of enhancing the power and influence of the Soviet Union.

Just before he was deprived of his Soviet citizenship, Nobel laureate Aleksandr I. Solzhenitsyn wrote a letter to Kremlin leaders in which he criticized their desire to maintain excessive military strength. Solzhenitsyn blamed this excess on the psychological factors of "vanity, prestige, and conceit":[135]

> For peacetime we are armed to excess several times over; we manufacture vast quantities of arms that are constantly having to be exchanged for new ones; we are training far more than we require. . . . We maintain this army solely out of military and diplomatic vanity—for reasons of prestige and conceit.[136]

Solzhenitsyn's observation was only partially correct; it seems that he did not fully comprehend the weight of the political-diplomatic tasks that Soviet leaders placed upon the military even in peace time. The following public statement on the significance of the Soviet military's political function was made by a Soviet spokesman, Admiral G.S. Gorshkov:

> To ensure solution of the military-political tasks of the state, efforts have always been made to have armed forces, including a navy, and to keep them modernized. As part of the country's armed forces, the fleet fulfills *an important role as an instrument of state policy in peacetime* and is *a potent means of achieving the political ends of* armed struggle in wartime. [emphasis added by H.K.][137]

It was this firm Soviet conviction of the political utility of the military in combination with a traditional Russian sense of insecurity (which caused them to be "over-defensive") that motivated the incessant Soviet interest in military buildup.

One of the most important political functions of the Soviet armed forces was a *demonstrative* function. V.M. Kulish, a Soviet strategist, candidly admitted the significant utility of this political function:

Attainment of serious strategic superiority [*prevoskhodstvo*] has always been one of the most important preconditions for conducting an active foreign policy, because the very recognition of this superiority by other states has frequently forced them to make certain, often significant, concessions and has mitigated the demands of our more powerful adversaries.[138]

The aim of this demonstrative function was to exert psychological pressures on potential adversaries and achieve national goals by merely demonstrating the presence of armed forces without resorting to their direct, active employment. This technique, almost as old as human history, has gained greater significance since the advent and development of nuclear weaponry. As the risks involved in actually deploying weapons on the battlefield have increased in recent years, the demonstrative function of the armed forces—previously a subsidiary function—has become more important. One Western specialist in international politics aptly describes this trend:

In the nineteenth century there was not much room for maneuver between verbal communication and full-scale violence. But, since World War II, states have been extremely inventive in developing a varied ensemble of physical maneuvers and "uses of force short of war" to communicate and test resolve in crises. Military force, in general, has been somewhat transformed from an instrument of direct physical coercion to one of psychological or political influence.[139]

The Soviet Union clearly valued and practiced the demonstrative function of military power. Admiral G. Sergei Gorshkov, a typical Soviet proponent of this function, firmly believed in utilizing the armed forces, particularly the navy, for their demonstrative value, stating: "The navy, as a constituent part of the armed forces of the state, has one more distinctive feature; namely, the ability to demonstrate (*demonstrirovat'*) graphically the real fighting capability of one's state in the international arena."[140] The Soviet fleet, however, was not the only outfit used for demonstrative purposes of this kind. Indeed, the Soviets seemed to grasp all available opportunities for demonstrating their military might, from military parades on May Day and October Revolution Day to massive naval exercises such as *Okean*-70 and -75. At least partially, one can also detect similar motivation behind the Soviet military buildup in the Far East (e.g., deployment of the *Minsk*, *Backfires*, and SS-20s), particularly in the vicinity of Japan (e.g., deployment of a military division in the disputed Northern Territories).

In sum, during the postwar period, Japan and the USSR were aimed in directly opposite directions in their approaches to the military forces. First, and foremost, Japan had minimized its military power to a level disproportionate to its economic strength, while the Soviet Union attempted to maximize its military power. Second, Japan strictly limited the use of its Self-Defense Forces to the defense of the Japanese homeland from outside invaders, while the Soviet Union dispatched its armed forces far beyond Soviet borders. Third, Japan has limited the role of the SDF to a strictly military mission: defense of Japanese territory. The Soviet Union, on the other hand, highly valued the political and demonstrative functions of its military presence. These three striking contrasts are due to the fundamental differences that existed between the two nations with regard to *Weltanschauung*, national security, and means for solving international conflicts, all of which were analyzed in the previous section.

Chapter 3
Japanese and Soviet Views on Territory

1. Territorial Dispute as a Symbol

In the previous chapter I examined in detail the divergency in views on national security held by the Japanese and the Soviets, which constituted, in my judgment, the most significant *a posteriori* determining factor in Soviet-Japanese relations. Another important *a posteriori* determinant that created a gap between Japan and the Soviet Union was each nation's distinct view of national territory. Popular argument suggests that the Northern Territories issue constituted the major stumbling block to the development of harmonious relations between the Soviet Union and Japan.[1] This view seems to me to be superficial for various reasons presented earlier and for additional reasons to be addressed in this chapter. As presented in chapters 1 and 2, fundamental differences in the Japanese and Soviet *Weltanschauungen* and their divergent approaches to national security, particularly conflicting opinions concerning the use of military means in solving international disputes, constituted, in my judgment, more serious stumbling blocks to smooth bilateral relations. Perhaps the obstacle was best *symbolized* by the Northern Territories issue. The Northern Territories issue was only the visible tip of the iceberg; it was the underlying attitudes of both nations toward territory that formed the greater stumbling block. In this sense, the point to be made here is a continuation of the discussion in the previous chapter.

Both the Japanese and the Soviet governments seemed to consider the issue of the Northern Territories (as referred to by the Japanese; the Southern Kuriles by the Russians—the Habomai group of islets and the islands

55

of Shikotan, Kunashiri, and Etorofu off the northeastern coast of Hokkaido (see Map 3.1) to be the biggest thorn in their bilateral relations. The Japanese Ministry of Foreign Affairs firmly declared that resolving the Northern Territories issue, i.e., "the only remaining unsettled issue left over from World War II,"[2] was a precondition for the conclusion of a peace treaty and the development of friendly, stable relations between the two countries.[3] No Japanese prime minister, since World War II, has failed to make public that until the Northern Territories are returned to the Japanese, there will be no further improvement in Soviet-Japanese (or Russian-Japanese) bilateral relations.[4]

In contrast, the Soviets did not officially identify the territorial question as the major stumbling block because, according to their view, it was "nonexistent."[5] Public denials notwithstanding, they were well aware that the territorial issue was the *de facto* obstruction to concluding a peace treaty with Japan. (In private conversation, various Soviet spokesmen acknowledged the existence of a *territorial* problem between the two countries.[6]) Their argument did not identify the territorial question per se; rather, they identified "the obstacle artificially elaborated"[7] by the Japanese—more precisely by the Tokyo government connected with and supported by what the Soviets termed "Japanese reactionary *revanchists*"—as that which prevented the two neighboring nations from signing a peace treaty and developing friendly relations. The Soviets accused the Japanese of stubbornly maintaining "unfounded [*neobosnovannye*], unlawful [*nezakonnye*], and artificially created territorial claims" (Leonid Brezhnev)[8] to the USSR, which were described as "the principal hindrance" [*glavnoe prepiatstvie*] (S. Modenov, I. Latyshev),[9] "brake" [*tormoz*] (A.P. Markov),[10] or "barrier" [*pregrada*] (N. Nikolaev)[11] to the development of good relations.

Various other Soviet spokesmen indicated that the Soviets indeed viewed the territorial dispute as a major obstacle between Moscow and Tokyo. For example, Soviet Foreign Minister Andrei A. Gromyko revealed: "In relations between our countries [the USSR and Japan], like those between any countries, problems requiring time and patience to solve can certainly exist. The important thing is not to let the positive development of our relations be conditioned by these problems."[12] Aleksander Bovin, a political commentator for *Izvestiia*, proposed shelving the territorial question in order to help develop bilateral relations, thus acknowledging the existence of a territorial issue as "the obstacle." When asked by a Japanese journalist, "What is impeding the improvement in Soviet-Japanese relations?" Bovin replied: "In my opinion, the first political obstacle is Japan's demand for the return of the Southern Kuriles. All Japan has to do is to shelve the question of the Southern Kuriles."[13] In answer to the same question by an American interviewer, William Oltmans, Georgii A. Arbatov, the Director of the Institute of USA and Canadian Studies (ISKAN) at the Soviet Academy of Sciences, conceded, "I do hope that in time this question [the Northern Territories question] will lose some of its present acuteness for the Japanese and cease to be an *obstacle* to positive development of Soviet-Japanese relations" (emphasis added by H.K.).[14]

I must, however, disagree with these Japanese and Soviet assertions that directly or indirectly ascribe primary blame for the poor relations between Japan and the Soviet Union to the territorial issue. The territorial problem, in my judgment, is simply a reflection of a more profound cause for the stalemate. Let us surmise that, for some reason, the Kremlin were to immediately decide to return the Northern Territories to Japan. This would certainly improve Russo-Japanese relations to a great extent and lead to a great improvement in Moscow's reputation in Japan. Yet, it would have been overly optimistic, even naive, to presume that Soviet-Japanese relations would have become rosy simply as a result of this, or that all friction, conflict, and problems between the two countries could have been solved automatically. To begin with, any "Soviet fever" that resulted in such action would not have lasted long, as was the case with Japan's "China fever," which reached its peak with the signing of the 1978 Sino-Japanese Peace Treaty and subsided shortly afterward. Moreover, there is even a chance that many Japanese would not have particularly appreciated a Soviet decision to return the islands. Such a decision might have been interpreted by some Japanese as just being a matter of course; i.e., the Soviets had simply done what they were supposed to do sooner or later, just as the Americans had with the reversion of Okinawa. It is conceivable that Kremlin anticipation of such short-lived or unenthusiastic appreciation for Soviet "favors" to the Japanese might have been partially responsible for Soviet determination not to give the islands back to Japan.

At any rate, what must be emphasized here is that the return of the Northern Territories would neither have solved all the problems nor mended the friction that existed between Japan and the Soviet Union. The main obstacle to improvement in Soviet-Japanese relations was, as discussed in chapter 2, the great disparity in ways of life and in the principles that guided the two nations since the end of World War II—especially their attitudes on national security and the means they chose for solving international conflicts. The Northern Territories issue is merely a spin-off from these more fundamental differences. It is crucial that we pay more attention to what lies behind these differences. Only then can we understand why the Tokyo government ranked the return of the Northern Territories in second place in its prioritized list of demands on the Soviet Union in December 1979, and in third place at a later time. In addition to the pre-existing demand for the reversion of the Northern Territories, Japan at that time insisted on the withdrawal of Soviet troops from Afghanistan and the removal of Soviet SS-20s from the Russian Far East before any improvement in relations could occur. These three demands had the same origin: Japan's concern for its own national security. Without an appreciation of this, it is difficult to understand why the Japanese adhered so insistently to the reversion of these small islands at the expense of other potential gains.

2. The Concept of "Inherent" Territory

The first divergent point between Japanese and Soviet views in regard to territory concerns the concept of so-called "inherent" territory. The concept of "inherent," "indigenous," "inalienable," or "integral" territory involves an assertion that each nation possesses land that is regarded historically and legally as part of that particular country alone, due to the fact that it has belonged to that nation from ancient times without becoming the possession of any other nation. The Japanese firmly believe in this concept, whereas the Soviets seem not to believe too strongly in such a notion.

Tokyo has consistently justified its demands for the reversion of the Northern Territories on the basis of the core concept of "inherent" (*koyūno*) territory.[15] According to the Japanese, the disputed Northern Territories are an example of such "inherent" territory. Japanese maintain that the four northern islands were discovered, settled, cultivated, and permanently populated by the Japanese and that they had "always been under Japan's sovereignty and jurisdiction," until the Soviet army seized them by force in the period of August 28–September 5, 1945, soon after Japan surrendered on August 15, 1945.[16] The Japanese further argue that they did not take islands from any other country "by violence and greed" (the Cairo Declaration). Moreover, the Northern Territories were described as areas rightfully claimed by Japan in a series of international legal documents from the Treaty of Commerce, Navigation and Delimitation between Japan and Russia (1855), all of which testify to the legitimate Japanese ownership of the islands.[17]

The foregoing has been the Tokyo government's official position from the start of diplomatic negotiations with Moscow in 1956 until now. For example, "The Government's View on the Northern Territories," an official document issued in 1961, stated: "Foreign Minister Mamoru Shigemitsu made it clear during the Soviet-Japanese negotiations of 1956 that the islands of Etorofu and Kunashiri (not to mention the islands of Habomai and Shikotan) are our *inherent* territories. This view has undergone no change to this day, nor shall it undergo any change in the future" (emphasis added by H.K.).[18] The U.S. Department of State officially endorsed this Japanese government position with a statement made on September 7, 1956: "The United States has reached the conclusion after careful examination of the historical facts that the islands of Etorofu and Kunashiri (along with the Habomai islands and Shikotan, which are part of Hokkaido) have always been part of *Japan proper* and should in justice be acknowledged to be under Japanese sovereignty" (emphasis added by H.K.).[19]

Likewise, virtually all governmental, semi-governmental, and privately run organizations in Japan that have been sponsoring and promoting the movement for the reversion of the Northern Territories take it for granted that the Soviet Union was bound to return the islands on account of this concept of "inherent" territory. Pamphlets, brochures, bulletins, posters, and leaflets that they have issued are permeated with expressions and slogans reflecting their own firm convictions based on this concept: "Kunashiri and Etorofu, where our ancestors lived and were buried";[20] "The Soviet Union illegally occupies Japan's inherent territory";[21] "These islands were ours in peacetime; we never acquired them by violence or greed, so we must campaign perpetually [to regain our possession]";[22] "Let's go ahead for the all-embracing reversion of the Northern Territories—our forefathers' land!";[23] and so forth.

By examining a few background factors, it is easy to understand why most Japanese have become firmly committed to the concept of "inherent" territory. First, there is a major geographic factor, an "ideal" natural border (i.e., the sea), separating Japan from other countries. This factor has nourished the notion among Japanese that natural, racial, linguistic, and cultural boundaries must always coincide with political and administrative borders. In cases where, for some reason, they do not coincide, Japanese feel uneasy and insecure, or even frustrated, and they want badly to rectify the incongruence. On this subject, Taizō Yamagata, a Japanese

Map 3.1

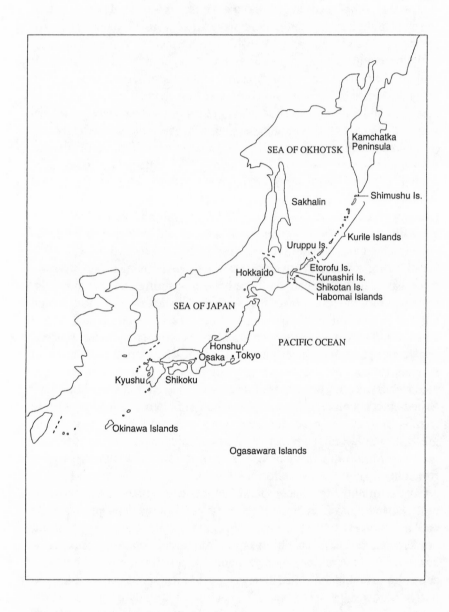

Source: Ministry of Foreign Affairs, Japan.

specialist on the Northern Territories question, correctly writes: "Geographic insularity and homogeneity in race and language are at the root of Japan's unique concept of borders."[24] Second, the unique historical experiences of the Japanese have further ingrained their concept of "inherent" territory." Primarily because Japan has not undergone any fundamental changes in territory during its long history, the Japanese have failed to develop the notion that "political boundaries are, after all, of an artificial kind."[25] Furthermore, the Japanese have always fought their wars abroad, and they have experienced neither prolonged international conflict on their own land nor occupation of their own land by foreign powers until the 1945 United States occupation. Yamagata makes similar observations:

> Fortunately or unfortunately, unlike European countries, until World War II, we Japanese had neither the tragic experience of being deprived of our own territory by other nations nor the disgraceful experience of being invaded by foreign troops.[26]

The following can be said in summary of the Japanese view: (1) most Japanese are convinced that the disputed Northern Territories are Japan's "inherent" territory; (2) few Japanese appear to doubt the Soviet Union's obligation to return the islands immediately to Japan (in other words, most Japanese are inclined to *equate* the concept of "inherent" territory with the Soviet obligation to return the islands to Japan); and (3) many Japanese felt for long this line of argument should be sufficient to persuade the Soviets to carry out their obligation. (Few Japanese tended to ask what would happen if such thoughts were not shared by their counterparts in the negotiation.)

It would be incorrect to state that the Russians do not possess a concept of "inherent" territory.[27] Soviet scholars also asserted a Soviet right to the "Southern Kuriles"—which the Japanese call the "Northern Territories"—because the Russians were the first to discover, develop, and permanently settle on Sakhalin and the entire Kurile archipelago—an area which, according to the Soviet view, includes the disputed "Southern Kuriles."[28] Soviet spokesmen insisted that Sakhalin and the Kuriles belong to the Soviet Union by right of prior discovery and settlement.[29] Based on this conviction, Pavel A. Leonov, then First Secretary of the Sakhalin Regional CPSU committee, wrote:

> Sakhalin and the Kurile Islands have long been part of Russia. There are numerous historical documents proving indisputably our country's prior-

ity in the discovery, incorporation, exploration, and development of Sakhalin and the Kurile Islands. Russia began to develop these lands when other countries either did not know they existed or had only vague ideas swathed in mystery and legend.[30]

According to Professor John J. Stephan of the University of Hawaii, perhaps the most informed historian on the subject, this Soviet conviction had a relatively recent origin. "Before the revolution, [Russian] writers readily accorded Japan her due in the southern Kuriles while affirming their own preeminent role in the northern portion of the arc."[31] One Soviet book entitled *The Kurile Islands*, published in June 1945, before the Soviet seizure of the Northern Territories, similarly conceded that Japan had discovered "the island of Kunashiri and the small Kuriles [i.e., Shikotan and the Habomai islets],"[32] although the remaining islands, from Etorofu north to the Kamchatka peninsula, were discovered by the Russians.[33] However, Professor Stephan found this passage deleted in a revised 1947 edition of the book,[34] which appeared after the Soviets had occupied the islands and incorporated them into USSR territory.

An exhibit at the Regional Museum in Iuzhno-Sakhalinsk, capital of Sakhalin Province, quotes from a book by Yoshi S. Kuno, a Japanese-American professor at the University of California: "Even in the middle of the 19th century, not only Sakhalin and the Kurile Islands but even Yezo (now called Hokkaido) were not regarded as an integral part of the Empire of Japan."[35] Japanese scholars, including Toshiyuki Akizuki and Akira Takano,[36] however, have refuted these and similar Soviet assertions based on one-sided citations from the writings of foreign scholars without consideration of context, and other arbitrary interpretations of this kind, which do not correspond to the historical facts.

The Soviets, however, did not adhere to the concept of "inherent" territory as strongly as the Japanese. Instead, they justified their rights to the Northern Territories by other means, as will be examined in the next section. Namely, they believed in *their* own concept of "inherent" (*neot'emlemaia* or *iskonnaia*)[37] territory, which is not exactly identical to the Japanese concept. One may, in fact, conclude that the Soviet view of "inherent" territory was quite different from the Japanese one. This difference helps account for the Soviets' categorical refusal to discuss this subject with the Japanese for the purpose of clarifying which country has a right to the islands on the basis of "inherent" territory. How, then, did the Soviet concept of territory differ from the Japanese, and why?

As in the case of the Japanese view, the Soviets' view of territory was also partially a product of their own geographic and historical backgrounds. The Soviet view, of course, was the product of very different—even quite opposite—backgrounds. Though Russia embraces territories over a wide area, unlike Japan, it is not blessed with any natural barriers. The Russians have survived only through constant vigilance against the incursions of foreign enemies. When they failed to protect themselves against foreign invaders, they were forced to forfeit territory; and when they succeeded, they usually managed to expand their territory. It is only natural that a people reared under such circumstances share neither the Japanese concept of "inherent" territory nor the Japanese respect for an unchanging, immovable map. For the Soviets, national borders were in constant flux and were subject to frequent change according to circumstances. Soviet borders embodied the results of conflicts with neighboring countries. Thus, Soviet territory naturally expanded and contracted according to what George F. Kennan calls the "elastic"[38] nature of territory.

3. What Determines Boundaries?

The last point made in the above discussion lends itself to the second disparity between Japanese and Soviet views on territory—the disparity in their answers to the question "What determines national boundaries?" The quite different responses that would be evoked from the Japanese and from the Soviets were closely related to, or even originated from, their respective attitudes toward the more general question "How are international conflicts solved?"

The Japanese believe that national boundaries can be changed only when the nations concerned reach a consensus through peaceful discussion and negotiation based on international law. This position, based on pure legal theory, emphasizes dialogue and respect for treaties and international principles. Throughout the postwar period, Tokyo has adhered to this legal and peaceful approach in its efforts vis-à-vis Moscow and the return of the Northern Territories.

The Japanese government has emphasized that the Northern Territories, and even the entire Kurile Archipelago, legally became its integral territory by treaties reached through a process of peaceful negotiations with tsarist Russia in the nineteenth century, i.e., the so-called Shimoda Treaty (1855)[39] and the Treaty for the Exchange of Sakhalin for the Kurile Islands (1875). The Tokyo government has also stressed that, in accordance with the Potsdam Declaration (1945), Japan was required to surrender only those territories that were described in the Cairo Declaration (1943) as having been "taken by violence and greed." Moreover, the Tokyo government points out that Japan is not legally bound by the Yalta Agreement (1945), in which Allied leaders agreed that the Kurile Islands should be handed over to the Soviet Union, because the agreement was merely a declaration of common Allied objectives, without Japanese participation or knowledge.

Firmly convinced that Japan has a legal right to the Northern Territories and that the issue can and should be resolved according to international law, the Tokyo government has made many attempts to raise this territorial issue in the international arena. For example, while the Soviet Union refused to sign the San Francisco Peace Treaty (1951), Japan long asserted a willingness to conclude a bilateral peace treaty with the USSR and resolve the territorial issue. Successive Japanese foreign ministers of late have never failed to mention this territorial issue in their speeches to the United Nations General Assembly. Some Japanese politicians have proposed to bring the matter to the International Court of Justice.[40] Various opposition parties[41] have proposed that Japan continue to request the return not only the four northern islands but also of the entire Kurile Archipelago "through international conferences in which the countries concerned participate."[42]

Soviet spokesmen attempted to rebut the Japanese view on legal grounds as well. The Soviets maintained that a series of works by Soviet scholars clearly showed that "Japanese territorial claims are historically and legally unfounded."[43] Semen I. Verbitskii, for example, cited the writings of Leonid N. Kutakov and Dmitrii V. Petrov, who, in turn, referred to a *series* of international treaties and agreements, such as the Yalta Agreement and the San Francisco Peace Treaty, and other historical incidents and events. They contended that by having capitulated, Japan had accepted all the provisions laid down by the Allied powers, including the Yalta Agreement. Soviet specialists also cited the San Francisco Peace Treaty, in which Japan renounced all rights to southern Sakhalin and the Kuriles.

They tried to reinforce their argument by saying: "By the very conduct of its own one-sided aggression, Japan deprived itself of all the moral and legal legitimacy and reasons to cite the treaties of 1875 [i.e., the Sakhalin-Kurile Exchange Treaty] and 1905 [i.e., the Treaty of Portsmouth]."[44] They also contended that by signing the revised Japan-U.S. Security Treaty (1960) directed against the Soviet Union, Japan had lost its right to ask the Soviet Union the benevolent favor of transferring the Habomais and Shikotan islands to Japan when a Japanese-Soviet peace treaty is concluded. In conclusion, the Soviets regarded the Japanese claim to the Northern Territories as "[historically] unfounded and unlawful."[45]

From a purely legal viewpoint, however, the Soviet arguments lose their persuasiveness when juxtaposed with the Japanese counterarguments touched on previously: (1) Japan does not regard the Yalta Agreement as legally binding; (2) the USSR is not entitled to cite the San Francisco Peace Treaty, which it refused to sign; (3) a signatory nation is not entitled at a later date to unilaterally invalidate a treaty previously formally agreed upon (i.e., the 1956 Soviet-Japanese Joint Declaration) due to the unpleasant behavior of the other concerned party (i.e., the Japanese agreement to renew the Japan-U.S. Security Treaty); and (4) the Soviets cannot satisfactorily answer the question, At what exact point in time and precisely by what legal document did the disputed Northern Territories cease to be Japanese and become Soviet?

Without pinpointing any single legal document, Soviet scholars usually replied that a *series* of international and bilateral agreements and treaties led to the present situation. When questioned further, they reluctantly identified one or two treaties, though those identified vary from one spokesperson to another. In part as an effort to avoid an awkward situation, Soviet writings and speeches began to put less stress on *individual* legal agreements and treaties signed at the close of World War II and more stress on the war *as a whole*. The Soviets asserted that the stability of the international order would not benefit from any changes in the *status quo as it stood at the end of World War II*. In so doing, they emphasized their belief that national boundaries as they stand should not be subjected to alterations, a line of logic that justifies their view that "the *result of the war* is irreversible and inviolable." This rationalization was first made public by former Soviet Premier Aleksei N. Kosygin to Japanese Foreign Minister Kiichi Aichi in September 1969 and thereafter became an official Soviet view. In 1969, the Soviet Premier said, "To maintain *the realities that have developed as a result of World War II* contributes to the maintenance of international order" (emphasis added by H.K.).[46] Repeating the same view, CPSU General Secretary Leonid Brezhnev stated on June 5, 1977 in his interview with Shōryū Hata, editor-in-chief of the *Asahi Shimbun*: "Only if the Japanese side more seriously considers *the realities that have developed as a result of World War II*, will other countries [the Soviet Union and Japan] solve the question [of concluding a peace treaty between them]" (emphasis added by H.K.).[47] Similarly, on June 12, 1977, *Pravda* bitterly criticized the Japanese Communist Party for its request that the USSR return the Northern Territories, regarding the request as an attempt to alter *the results of World War II*.[48]

Despite the fact that the Soviet argument for the inviolability of the results of World War II can be refuted by contemporary international law and practice—which distinguishes between *de facto* seizure of land as a result of military battle and ultimate *de jure* sovereignty, the Soviets continued to cling to these views. The reversion of Okinawa by the United States to Japan provides one recent example of contemporary practice. It is doubtful, however, that the Soviets truly believed in the righteousness of their position, especially in light of behavior they exhibited toward others that contradicted their position toward the Japanese. Let us take as an example the way in which the Soviet Union regained Bessarabia from Romania. Moscow totally disagreed with the Romanian assertion that the "Bessarabia dispute" was "solved once-and-for-all" either by the Romanian army's seizure of the area or by the residents' vote to unite with Romania (1918). Nor did Moscow recognize the decision of other powers of the Union in the Treaty of Paris (1920). Moscow continuously criticized Romania of violent aggression and finally succeeded in convincing Bucharest under pressure to cede the area to the Soviet Union (1940).[49] This past record of Soviet diplomatic behavior leads us to doubt whether the Soviets possessed a distinct principle with regard to the issue of territory. Instead, it seems that they quite arbitrarily employed different principles at different times. Other examples of the Soviet double standard regarding territorial claims are provided by the Soviet Union's strong support of Arab and Argentine irredentist claims against Israel and Great Britain (on "the Falkland issue"), respectively, which was in marked contrast to, and clearly contradicted, its own insistence on the argument that no territory it has ever annexed can ever be transferred to others. The Soviet Union greatly increased its own territory after World War II by taking land away from about a dozen other nations. This particular experience and the circumstances it engendered must be partially responsible for the Soviets' firm assertion that the frontiers established as a *result of World War II* should not be altered.

A close look at the Kremlin's argument on *the inviolability of results* of World War II reveals that it boils down to one simple fact: the Soviet Union took the Northern Territories as war spoils from the defeated Japan. As long as World War II enters into the situation, the Soviet position may be summarized by the axiom of a German geopolitician, Karl Haushofer, who once said: "Boundaries are places of combat rather than legal norms of decision."[50] Indeed the writings and statements of Soviet spokesmen reveal the accuracy of such an assumption. For example, Khaim T. Eidus, supposedly one of the Soviet authorities on Soviet-Japanese history, wrote simply, yet definitively, in his book, *The USSR and Japan: Diplomatic-Political Relations after World War* (1964): "The victory of the Soviet Army returned Sakhalin and the Kurile Islands to the hands of our people."[51] Other Soviet specialists on Japan, such as Stanislav S. Modenov, N.N. Nikolaev, Igor' A. Latyshev, and Iurii N. Bandura, unanimously emphasized that due to Japan's past defeat, it presently has no say concerning *the results of the war*. Modenov, for example, wrote:

> The Soviet Union restored its historical rights to Southern Sakhalin and the Kurile Islands as *a result of the defeat of Japanese militarism in the Second World War*. That is why no "territorial" issue exists. Resolved once and for all, it is not to be revised [emphasis added by H.K.].[52]

Likewise, a Soviet high official under the Andropov government was reported as saying to Leslie H. Gelb of the *New York Times* that "Like Germany, Japan will have to accept the idea of 'lost' territory."

The Soviet view that the territorial question had been resolved *by the war* logically led to a dreadful conclusion. If the Japanese were unhappy with the situation resulting from the war, there was, unfortunately, only one alternative left: another war. As a matter of fact, one Soviet politician boldly disclosed such a conclusion. In the summer of 1973, Iadgar S. Nasriddinova, then chairman of the Soviet Nationalities of the Supreme Soviet, was quoted as saying to a Japanese delegation headed by Hirohide Ishida, one of few pro-Soviet Diet representatives: "Those who want to alter the present boundaries, which the Soviets gained by the sacrifice of the blood of 20 million people, must be ready for the 'Third World War.'"[53]

4. The Value of the Northern Territories

The third and most important contrast between Japan and Russia concerns the value and significance each nation attaches to the Northern Territories. Why is it that the two countries cling so tenaciously to these tiny, barren islands of less than 5,000 square kilometers (1,930 square miles) in the northern seas, even sacrificing other benefits that might otherwise be gained? There are probably political, economic, and other reasons for their perseverance. Let us elaborate on the most significant of these possible reasons for each nation.

It is doubtful that for the Japanese, the value of the Northern Territories lies in their military-strategic importance. In fact, it is likely that most Japanese would agree to a ban on the military use of these islands by both the Japanese themselves and the Americans, if this were a Soviet condition for reversion.[54] Fishing may be *part* of the reason, but it is hard to imagine that it would have been a major driving force behind such a long-lasting movement for reversion supported by the majority of Japanese. Former Japanese inhabitants of the islands, repatriated to Hokkaido after the war, want the islands returned so that they can expand their fishing operations, but they would probably not return to live again on the islands.[55]

In my opinion, *psychological* and even *symbolic* reasons[56] are at the core of the Japanese request for the return of the Northern Territories. First, the Japanese wish to see "inherent" territory returned as a final token of the end of the war.[57] Ichirō Suetsugu, one of the most enthusiastic activists in the movement for reversion of the islands, explained his motive once to an interviewer, saying simply: "I just want to tie up the loose ends from the war."[58] Additionally, former Prime Minister Eisaku Satō was fond of asserting that "for Japan, the postwar period will not end until the Northern Territories have been returned." By repossessing these islands, the Japanese seek to wipe out, once and for all, the last trace of defeat from a disgraceful war. This desire has become more intense since 1978, when Tokyo succeeded in *Vergangenheitbewältigung* (overcoming the past)[59] in relations with China, by concluding the Japan-China Peace Treaty (see chapter 7). Satō's appeal indeed serves as a reminder to the Japanese that one more task still remains.

Second, through the return of the Northern Territories, the Japanese hope to confirm the universal validity of the guiding principle of their postwar foreign policy. As noted previously, postwar Japanese foreign policy may be summarized by such terms as "omnidirectional diplomacy" or "diplomacy of trust and peaceful negotiation." Japan's hope is to conduct foreign policy in a spirit of even-handed friendliness with all nations, with the expectation that these nations will respond in kind. This policy, aimed at solving international disputes by means of peaceful talks at the negotiation table, has been fairly successful, *except* in the case of the USSR.

Third, the Japanese would interpret reversion of the islands as a much desired sign that friendly relations with the Russians are indeed possible.

The Japanese attitude toward the Soviet Union was very ambivalent. The majority of Japanese feared and intensely disliked the USSR after the Soviets violated the Japanese-Soviet Neutrality Pact of 1941. At the same time, the Japanese were well aware of the fact that their national security demanded good relations with their number-one potential adversary. For Japan, security was incomplete as long as it did not get along with its neighboring "communist" giant. Yet, the situation could not be settled by unilateral efforts on Tokyo's part. The Japanese were hoping that the Soviet Union—which in their minds was not only the stronger nation but also the initiator of the poor bilateral relations of the postwar period—would act first and in a manner that would foster Japan's trust, thus leading to the establishment of cooperative relations. As an editorial in the *Asahi Shimbun* put it:

> If the Soviets desire friendly and closer relations [with Japan], a change in their adamant stand on the Northern Territories is indispensable and should come first.[60]

Only when the Soviet Union had provided clear evidence of goodwill would the Japanese have felt relief from the threat to the north of them. The Japanese hoped to see visible proof[61] of such good intentions by the Soviet action of returning the Northern Territories, an action that would have served as a symbol of the dawn of good-neighborly relations between Japan and the Soviet Union.

Fourth, the Japanese government's uncompromising stance on the Northern Territories issue represents to both the Japanese and the Soviets a symbolic gesture of Japan's firmness on the issue of territorial sovereignty, thus contributing to the security of the rest of Japan. From a politico-military perspective, it is doubtful that Japan would have benefited greatly from yielding these small islands to the Soviet Union. There is no guarantee that Japan's shelving of its claim to these small islands would have assured the security of the four main islands comprising Japan proper. Some Japanese were afraid that the reverse might even be the case: they feared such action might have mistakenly given the Kremlin the idea that the Japanese were not very persistent in their political principle and were easily subject to a *fait accompli* for practical, short-range benefits. Such a message certainly would not have contributed to the national security of Japan. Japanese concerns evoke the warnings of the famous German legal philosopher, Rudolf von Jhering, who wrote in his book *The Struggle for Rights*:

From the nation that allowed itself to be deprived of one square mile of territory by its neighbor, unpunished, the rest would also be taken, until nothing remained to it to call its own and it had ceased to exist as a state; and such a nation would deserve no better fate.[62]

In contrast to the Japanese motives, we assume that the major reasons for the Kremlin's unwillingness to return the Northern Territories lay in the more visible, concrete, and practical value the region holds in terms of Soviet military strategy.[63] Although this region is known as one of the most fertile habitats for a rich variety of fish, it is its geopolitical and hence military-strategic role that made the area particularly important and made the Soviets reluctant to return the islands. (It should be noted that the Japanese Imperial Navy used one of the ports there, Etorofu's Hitokappu Bay, as a staging point for Japan's attack on Pearl Harbor.)[64]

Located at the southwesternmost exit to the Pacific, the geopolitical and military significance of the islands was great, particularly for the USSR, which badly needed access to ice-free ocean routes from the Sea of Okhotsk. On September 2, 1945, the day Soviet forces seized Shikotan and the Habomai Islands, Joseph V. Stalin proudly declared that "henceforth, the Kurile Islands shall not serve as a means to cut off the Soviet Union from the ocean or as a base for a Japanese attack on our Far East."[65] On May 26, 1964, during his visit to Japan, Anastas I. Mikoyan, at that time the USSR's First Deputy Premier, told then Japanese Prime Minister Hayato Ikeda that Etorofu and Kunashiri were small islands, but due to their importance as a gateway to Kamchatka, they could not be abandoned.[66] Similarly, on two occasions (in July and September of 1964), Nikita N. Khrushchev unintentionally revealed the Soviet Union's real interest in the area. To a delegation of Japanese socialists and later to various members of the Japanese Diet, he declared: "It should be kept in mind that, for us, these islands are of small economic value but of great strategic and defensive [*strategicheskoe, oboronnoe*] importance. We are concerned with our own security."[67] L.N. Kutakov, a Soviet authority on Soviet-Japanese diplomatic history, also writes:

Extending as a continuous chain from the southern tip of Kamchatka toward Hokkaido, the Kurile Archipelago closes the key to the Sea of Okhotsk. It prevents access to the Far Eastern Russian maritime province. Its geographic position as a frontline for the defense of the Far Eastern maritime province attaches very important significance to the Kurile Archipelago.[68]

There were even signs that the Soviet government was making plans to construct a huge military-industrial complex along the Sea of Okhotsk, spanning the Far Eastern part of the USSR, Sakhalin, Kamchatka, and the Kurile Islands, including the "Northern Territories."[69] There were also signs that this project had indeed progressed under both the Brezhnev and Andropov administrations, and the military-strategic significance of the Sea of Okhotsk increased, largely because of the new Soviet bastion strategy.[70] Submarine-launched ballistic missiles (SLBMs) based in the Sea of Okhotsk region had a range that covered almost every part of the United States. The American radar fence, in turn, was fully equipped to track all Soviet submarines equipped with SLBMs; therefore, in order to prevent such tracking, it became more vital for the Soviets to turn the Sea of Okhotsk into "both a closed and internal sea" (Sergei G. Gorshkov)[71] for themselves alone. Above all else, it was with this aim of making the Sea of Okhotsk a military sanctuary that the Soviet Union deployed almost 10,000 ground troops, including a coastal defense division, and built bases on three of the islands (Etorofu, Kunashiri, and Shikotan), all of which was confirmed in 1979. It was unimaginable that the Kremlin leaders would, of their own accord, discard territory of such great military-strategic importance. As Lilita Dzirkals, a specialist on Soviet conduct of foreign policy at the RAND Corporation, put it:

> The military factor thus could well account for the rigid Soviet position on the islands in the face of Japanese claims. . . . The Soviets indeed consider the Southern Kuriles essential for their security and are willing to incur heavy political costs for the sake of retaining these forward deployment bases.[72]

Part Two

SOVIET POLICIES TOWARD JAPAN
Why Were They Counterproductive?

Chapter 4
Soviet Policy Toward Asia

Regrettably, there is no generally accepted formula or simple methodology for defining Soviet conduct in foreign affairs. Soviet international behavior, like that of any other state, was inevitably shaped by various domestic and international factors, and based on considerations such as perceptions, goals, priorities, principles, capabilities, means, opportunities, risks, and leadership at any given moment. To complicate matters further, the combination of these factors is "not consistent but in continuous flux."[1]

However, despite such complexities in Soviet foreign policy, there was one predominant feature in the USSR's policy toward Japan: a tendency to view Japan from a global perspective, which means that Soviet policy toward Japan was a natural outgrowth of policy toward the rest of the world. Thus, the Kremlin's policy toward Japan can be correctly understood only by looking beyond the narrow scope of bilateral relations to the much broader context of Soviet global and regional considerations.[2] The USSR's confrontation and competition with the United States on both global and regional levels carried such tremendous weight that certain political scientists are tempted to conclude that Moscow was unaware that it needed to formulate a policy oriented strictly toward Japan. (For discussion of this point, see chapters 1 and 2.)

This provides sufficient justification for opening this chapter with an examination and identification of the main features that characterized Soviet views on U.S. strategy in Asia before analyzing Soviet policy toward Japan per se.

1. Soviet Perception of the Changing U.S. Policy Toward Asia

Soviet observers of international affairs discerned a pattern of both continuity and change in U.S. policy toward Asia in the 1970s. On the one hand, from the Soviet perspective, the United States continued to adhere to one of its basic foreign policy orientations, that of regarding the USSR as its principal enemy. Genrikh A. Trofimenko, head of the U.S. foreign policy department of the ISKAN, wrote in 1979: "The United States considers the Soviet Union not only the central opponent in global conflicts but the major foe in the Asia-Pacific region."[3] Trofimenko was undoubtedly suggesting that, for its part, the Soviet Union also must continue to view the United States as its major adversary in Asia. In other words, Moscow perceived the United States as being quite determined to remain the major power in the Asian theater, if only from a military standpoint, regardless of any gestures Washington might make toward withdrawal.[4] In 1979, another Soviet specialist on Asia, Vladilen B. Vorontsov, editor-in-chief, *Far Eastern Affairs*, wrote: "The demonstration made in the form of the 'Nixon doctrine' on the question of the withdrawal of military forces has not meant at all, of course, the weakening of the U.S. army-navy forces in Asia and the Pacific Ocean basin."[5]

On the other hand, the Soviets professed to see some significant changes occurring in the basic U.S. orientation toward Asia in the late 1970s. They noted, for example, the shift of emphasis made by U.S. administrations— in particular, the geographic shift of U.S. interests from continental Asia to Northeast Asia and to the Pacific region proper. Vladimir P. Lukin, head of Asia-Pacific affairs at ISKAN, wrote in 1979:

> The reduction of U.S. military involvement in continental Asia . . . with respect to long-term strategy was . . . linked to a tendency to shift the center of the regional policy of the United State to Northeast Asia and the Pacific basin proper. . . . The decrease in the American military presence in continental Asia was accompanied . . . by serious measures aimed at strengthening the American Pacific Fleet—the principal U.S. military force in the region.[6]

Judging from such Soviet writings, it would not be incorrect to infer that the Soviet Union accurately assessed the "selective commitment" policy of U.S. administrations toward Asia.

Furthermore, Soviet Asia watchers were also quick to draw attention to what they saw as a "division of labor" policy,[7] in which the United States (1) worked toward improving its relations with its strongest and most viable allies, i.e., Japan, Australia, and New Zealand;[8] (2) gave Japan an "extraordinary,"[9] or exceptional,"[10] role in the region; and (3) raised the People's Republic of China (PRC) to the position of "quasi ally."[11]

As the Soviets saw it, this shift in U.S. strategy in Asia reflected the changing vantage points of both the United States and its Asian allies, especially Japan. In his book *American Policy of "Partnership" in the East Asian Region* (1980), Andrei V. Krutskikh emphasized that Washington had come to realize that Japan and other Asian countries could now play significant roles as its "partners."[12] As a result, several U.S. leaders felt that it might be acceptable—perhaps even desirable— for Japan and other Asian allies to assume broader responsibilities for maintenance of security on their home turf—an approach favored, the Soviets contended, by the American government's calculation that as long as the United States retained military superiority over Japan and its other allies, particularly in the field of nuclear weapons, it was able to retain sufficient means to draw these countries into the diplomatic and economic relationships it desired.[13]

As for Japan, Soviet observers noted the Japanese government's awareness of the decline of a U.S. commitment to Asian security in the wake of the Vietnam War and its growing comprehension of U.S. demands for Japan to carry its weight in the resulting "power vacuum."[14] With these developments, they speculated, Japan was once again presented with an opportunity to expand its influence in its own "backyard." As Lukin commented:

> The present activization of Japan's Pacific policy is of essential significance for the further evolution of the situation in the Pacific Ocean basin. . . . In the early 1970s it became clear that Japan, the economic giant, although it remains cautious and hesitant, and maintains a careful watch on its "senior partner," is, nonetheless, definitely and persistently seeking its own, specifically political course, one that would reflect greatly increased Japanese capabilities for economic and other influences in the international arena, and above all, in the traditional zone of Japanese foreign policy activity—the Pacific region.[15]

It does not require much "reading between the lines" to decipher how the Soviets perceived the strategy orientations of the United States and its partners in Asia, nor is it hard to detect that the Soviets sized up the situation with an astute eye to the effect that any changes might have on their own global interests.[16]

2. Soviet Approach to Asia

What, then, was the Soviet approach to Asia and the Pacific, and what impact did it have on the region?

To begin with, the Soviets did their best to drive home their contention that their country was not only a European power but also an Asian power. Despite the obvious pitfalls, however, many Western and Chinese specialists on Soviet foreign policy were likely to decide that the USSR strongly resembled a European rather than an Asian power. To support their views, these observers frequently cited that the majority of the Soviet population and most of the country's strategic political activities, industries, and other important human activities were heavily concentrated in European Russia.[17] This was also the case militarily. The Pacific Fleet, the Far Eastern Military District, and the Frontier Guards were all tightly controlled by their respective headquarters located in Moscow and commanded by European-oriented Great Russians or Ukrainians.[18] Consequently, according to these Western and Chinese specialists, Moscow was inclined to consider Europe as more vital to the country's interests, with Asia as secondary and even subordinate to more important concerns in Europe and elsewhere. Furthermore, these same observers sometimes contended that the Soviets simply expected unchallenged stability in Asia at least a maintenance of the status quo, which would permit more activist Soviet policies elsewhere. This view led some scholars to the one-sided conclusion that Soviet behavior in Asia had become largely defensive rather than offensive in character.

The Soviets themselves, however, sought to refute such views. They underlined, above all, the geographical composition of the USSR, which, they believed, provided sufficient reason for the USSR to assert itself as an Asian state. They never failed to cite Lenin's words:[19] "Geographically, economically, and historically, Russia belongs not only to Europe but also to Asia."[20] After quoting this, one Soviet writer further elaborated that "two-thirds of Soviet territory is situated in Asia"; or, looking at it differently, "more than one-third of Asia, or the whole northern part of Asia, is included in the makeup of our fatherland—the USSR."[21] The geographical element did not necessarily give the USSR the status of an Asian power, as I shall explain later. However, the Soviet justification that the USSR was not only a European but also an Asian state is not totally without substance.

Furthermore, although the exact date cannot be pinpointed, in the early or mid-1970s, the USSR began to define itself as an Asia-*Pacific* power, not simply as an Asian power. This point was brought home clearly to the late Osamu Miyoshi, professor of Kyoto Sangyo University, at the Japanese-Soviet conference of security specialists held in Kyoto in 1976, when the Soviet representative declared that the USSR was a "Pacific power."[22] To demonstrate this point, for example, the Soviets presided over the 14th Pacific Science Congress at Khabarovsk in the summer of 1979.

Beyond this general claim, the Soviet Union appeared to have several political objectives in Asia and Pacific. It consistently sought to weaken and, if possible, to eliminate U.S. political and military influence in the region. It attempted to isolate the PRC, and particularly to prevent it from entering into an anti-Soviet military alliance with the United States and Japan. It apparently wished to preserve the status quo on the Korean peninsula and made every effort to defend the territorial status quo regarding its borders with the PRC and Japan.[23] At the same time, it tried hard to coax Japan into cooperation, both political and economic.

To consolidate these claims and objectives, in the early 1970s the Soviet Union began to take concrete actions in the Asia-Pacific region. One example was Brezhnev's bold proposal, made first in June 1969[24] and again in March 1972,[25] to create an Asian Collective Security System. Although, in theory, this system was designed to promote friendly relations between the Soviet Union and Asian countries, most observers suspected that the Soviets envisaged some sort of military alliance aimed at isolating the PRC and undermining the Western position in Asia. Received coolly in Asia from the outset, even after ten years the plan did not win acceptance, and it passed "quietly into oblivion."[26] Japan, potentially the most important member of the proposed organization, displayed no interest in this proposal. (For more details, see chapter 9.)

Another manifestation of the new attention that the Soviets were devoting to the Asia-Pacific region was the plan[27] to build a second trans-Siberian railroad, the Baikal-Amur Mainline (BAM),[28] with the intention of expanding the country eastward, which had been the tsar's goal in constructing the first Siberian railroad. Naturally, the Soviet Union under Brezhnev wanted Japan's cooperation in executing the project, but it was unsuccessful in obtaining it to the desired degree.[29]

The third important indication of the USSR's interest in the Asia-Pacific region is the massive military buildup it undertook there in the mid-1970s and the early 1980s. There is evidence that the Soviets' strategic concerns about the region were increasing. A joint command headquarter was reestablished at Chita for the four military districts of Central Asia, Siberia, Transbaikal, and the Far East, as well as for the units stationed in Mongolia and for part of the Pacific Fleet.[30] Moreover, a very high-ranking military leader of Soviet ground forces, Army General

Vladimir L. Govorov, former commander of the Moscow military district, was assigned command of these new headquarters of the Far Eastern Troops. The Soviet Pacific Fleet became the largest in the Soviet Navy, surpassing the other three fleets (the Northern Fleet, the Baltic Fleet, and the Black Sea Fleet). It included about one-third of all Soviet submarines and about one-third of all Soviet surface-combat ships, notably the *Kiev*-class anti-submarine warfare aircraft carrier *Minsk* and the amphibious assault transport dock vessel *Ivan Rogov*. Approximately one-third of the Soviet Union's arsenal of SS-20 mobile medium-range missiles were deployed and targeted at the PRC, Japan, and South Korea. Moreover, there were reports that the Kremlin was making preparations that could lead to the virtual doubling of the number of its SS-20s targeted on Asia.[31] The Soviet Union also deployed *Backfire* bombers (about 70 in 1983) in the Soviet Far East. The newly established military headquarters on Sakhalin, which directs the troops stationed in the disputed Northern Territories and controls approximately 100 new military aircraft, including MiG-23 fighters, authorized frequent military exercises in the Sea of Japan. Finally, Soviet ground troops were deployed in large numbers (ten thousand men, almost the size of an entire Soviet division) on three of the disputed Northern Islands, as was disclosed in 1979.

3. Unsuccessful Outcome: Its Reasons

We have presented above a broad outline of Soviet intentions and policies. There is one important addendum: while the Soviets publicly expressed these goals, few were realized. This disparity between policy objectives and their achievement was nowhere more apparent than in the Asia-Pacific region. To put it more bluntly, a considerable number of Soviet policies in the region met with no success. The following is a description of some of these unsuccessful Soviet policies, with some possible reasons for their failure.

Without doubt, the greatest failure in Moscow's policies in the Asian and Pacific region was its inability to make significant headway in improving its relationship with the PRC. Mao Zedong's death (1976) did not result in any breakthroughs in resolving the long-standing Sino-Soviet feud. There were even developments to the contrary: the deterioration of bilateral relations; the signing of the Sino-Japanese Treaty of Peace and Friendship (August 1978); the normalization of Sino-American relations (January 1979); and the Chinese unilateral termination (April 1979) of the Sino-Soviet Treaty of Friendship, Alliance, and Mutual Assistance (1950). We must be wary, on the other hand, of becoming prisoners of the myth of eternal Sino-Soviet conflict, as we were for quite some time blind believers in a perpetual Moscow–Beijing alliance.[32] As Leonid Gudoshnikov, deputy director and China specialist at the Institute of Far Eastern Studies (IDV) said during an interview with the Kyodo News Service in February 1979: "The state relations between the Soviet Union and the PRC will unmistakenly be improved. Improved relations will be possible even by the late 1980s."[33] This view, however, was interpreted at that time as a typical Soviet trial balloon, put out to test the reactions of the West and Japan. Since the last years of the Brezhnev regime, Russian-Chinese relations, particularly in trade and in personnel and cultural exchange, have shown signs of rapid improvement. Yet early in the 1980s, it seemed premature to predict that such a rapprochement would extend into the politico-diplomatic realm in the immediate future, particularly in view of the fact that the preconditions Beijing attached to normalization with Moscow would be difficult for the Kremlin to accept.[34]

In the mid-1970s, the USSR was stymied by the same low measure of success in its policy toward Japan. Indeed, as the Soviets themselves officially admitted,[35] Soviet-Japanese relations had never been cooler. The events that contributed to the decline in Soviet-Japanese relations are: the MiG-25 incident (1976); the 200-nautical-mile fishing zone negotiations (1977); Japan's signing of the Treaty of Peace and Friendship with the PRC (1978); Soviet redeployment of troops in the Northern Territories (1979); the Soviet military invasion of Afghanistan (1979); Tokyo's participation in the U.S.-sponsored "sanctions" policy against that action (1980); continued Soviet military buildup, and decisions made by Prime Minister Zenkō Suzuki, including his statements to undertake the so-called "1,000-mile sea-lane defense" and to establish the "Northern Territories Day," and his inspection tour of the Nemuro, closest point to the disputed islands (1981); Tokyo's acceptance of the deployment of U.S. advanced F-16 fighters at Misawa (1982); the Soviet threat to transfer its SS-20s from Europe to Asia (1982–83); Prime Minister Nakasone's statement on Japan being an "unsinkable aircraft carrier" as a bulwark against Soviet military attack (1982); and the Soviet shooting down of Korean Air Lines Flight 007 (1983). Detailed discussion of these events is provided in Part Three of this book.

If the best foreign policy entails winning as many friends as possible while preventing the adversary from doing the same, then the Soviet Union was clearly losing ground in the Asian and Pacific region. In the late 1970s and the early 1980s, the Soviet policy actually resulted in a strengthening of the alliance between Japan and the United States and the establishment of a loose anti-Soviet triangle that included Washington, Tokyo, and Seoul or Beijing. Thus, Soviet efforts to prevent alliances between the West and countries in the Asia-Pacific region actually resulted in a consolidation of alliances—a typical example of the "self-fulfilling prophecy," defined by Robert Merton as "a false definition of the situation which makes the originally false conception come true."[36] The major reasons for the Soviet failure in the Asia-Pacific region are identified below.

First, the Soviet Union had neither sufficient experience nor sufficient prestige to claim to be a full-fledged Asian power.[37] Historically, it was a latecomer to the region, and it had little convincing justification for its claims to regional influence. The fact that the Soviet Union became a global power with global reach did not automatically guarantee it the ability to decisively influence developments, either in Asia or around the globe. Soviet inaction during the Sino-Vietnamese War in the spring of 1979 is a good illustration.

Second, the Soviet Union was handicapped by its lack of close cultural ties and other means upon which to build enduring relationships with the states and peoples of Asia. Aware of this handicap, it resorted to the only means it had at its disposal for influencing Asian countries: the military. As Richard H. Solomon put it, the Soviet Union "projects . . . its influence in the region almost exclusively through military means."[38] However, the people of Asia viewed such military actions not only as a serious security threat to themselves but as a reflection of the Soviets as formidable aggressors.[39] Since the end of World War II, the Japanese people had been for many years extraordinarily naive, and even insensitive, to the problem of national security and external military threats from other countries. However, in observing the heavy-handed attitudes and coercive policies of the Soviets and, in particular, their reliance on military force to achieve their ends, the Japanese gradually came to suspect Soviet motivations and to look for ways to maintain their own security.[40] The threat of Soviet "countermeasures" against the signing of the Sino-Japanese Peace Treaty and the buildup of military forces in the Northern Territories awakened the Japanese consciousness to the Soviet threat.

Third, the Soviets did not make any realistic or constructive proposals for mutual cooperation to nations in the Asia-Pacific region. The proposals they did offer—such as the Asian collective security scheme and the

Soviet-Japanese Treaty of Good-neighborliness and Cooperation—were unrealistic and one-sided. Basically, the Soviet policies for Asia were reactive in character, presenting as *faits accomplis* situations created by their military might. Thus, Soviet efforts to prevent alliances among other countries frequently resulted in their consolidation.

In summary, many Soviet policies toward Asia ended in failure because, first, the Soviets did not recognize the gap between their objectives and capabilities and, second, they overestimated the usefulness of military power. The last, but certainly not the least, of the reasons that account for the Soviets' failure in Asia is ascribable to their poor record of relations with Japan, one of the most important countries in the region.

Chapter 5
Soviet Strategy and Tactics Toward Japan

1. The Importance of Japan

The Soviet Union could not afford to underestimate Japan as a vital neighbor if it was to achieve any measure of success in Asia and the Pacific. First, it had to consider Japan's great geopolitical significance: the bow-shaped archipelago blocked Soviet access to the Pacific Ocean. Both Soviet navy and merchant vessels were able to go in and out of Pacific waters only by passing through one of three straits—i.e., Soya (La Pérouse), Tsugaru, or Tsushima (see Map 5.1)—all of which are either completely or partially controlled by Japan.[1] If these strategic straits had been closed for any reason (for example, by mining), Soviet ships would have been confined to the Sea of Okhotsk or the Sea of Japan, and passage into the Pacific would have become difficult, if not impossible—a scenario that reveals how crucial it was for the Soviet Union to have the route kept open and navigable. It can therefore be said that if Kremlin leaders wanted to expand the Soviet Union's interests and influence in Asia and the Pacific, then, bearing in mind this geopolitical and strategic significance of Japan, they should have made every effort to maintain good relations with Japan.

Second, the Soviet Union had to consider the significant diplomatic position that Japan occupied in Asia and the Pacific and Japan's increasingly influential voice in the management of that region's affairs. Japan's diplomatic and strategic position in Asia and the Pacific is of such great importance that high officials in the U.S. State and Defense departments have long considered Japan the "cornerstone" of Washington's policy in the Asia-Pacific region.[2] Historically, Tokyo has been closely allied with

Map 5.1

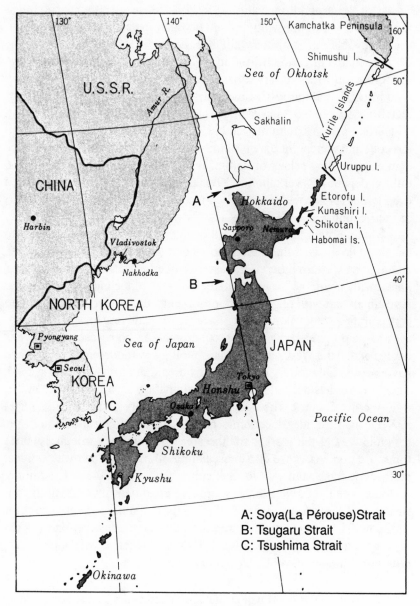

A: Soya(La Pérouse)Strait
B: Tsugaru Strait
C: Tsushima Strait

Source: Northern Territories Issue Association (Tokyo).

Washington through the Japan-U.S. Security Treaty since the end of World War II. Furthermore, Japan has been able to establish good relations with the PRC, particularly as a result of the conclusion of the Japan–China Treaty of Peace and Friendship in 1978. Tokyo seemed to have no intention whatsoever of allowing diplomatic relations between the two countries to evolve into a military alliance, despite strong pressure from the Chinese in that direction. If, for any reason, Japan had decided to join in the formation of a military alliance against the Soviet Union, together with the U.S. and the PRC, Soviet strategy would have been greatly affected not only in the Asia-Pacific region but throughout the entire world.

Third, Japan was of immeasurable importance to the Soviet Union from an economic standpoint. Japan's industrial and technological performance demonstrated that a lack of natural resources was no handicap for 116 million Japanese "workaholics." Japan's economic importance loomed even larger for Soviet leaders when the development of the eastern part of their country became a major necessity for expanding their economy as a whole. Soviet leaders revealed openly that they could not afford to develop two areas at the same time—i.e., the west European part of the country and western Siberia, and eastern Siberia and the Soviet Far East.[3] Faced with an almost insurmountable shortage of technology and capital investment and with ongoing labor problems, the Soviets were forced to concentrate on redeveloping the first area, while relying on Western countries to help them develop the second area.[4] In both cases the Soviets badly needed the West's advanced technology, without which they would have been unable to redevelop the first area, not to mention the second. Then, the Soviets needed the active participation of Japan more than that of any other country. The geographical proximity of the two countries makes Japan the ideal economic partner for providing the capital, the technology, and the market for the area's resources, particularly since transportation costs rose due to escalating oil prices. Japan was an ideal partner and the best market for Sakhalin offshore oil and gas. In addition, it would take the Soviets many years to recoup their investment in construction of the BAM railroad if the Japanese did not actively use it for transport. The Soviets made it no secret that their construction of BAM presupposed an increase in Soviet economic exchange with Japan, *inter alia*. For example, Pavel D. Dolgorukov observed:

> Construction of BAM will create new opportunities for the Soviet Union to expand its ties with Japan and other countries of the Pacific basin. If

before building the mainline, the transportation problem was a serious obstacle to cooperation on a massive scale, then its building will fundamentally change the situation.[5]

In sum, Japan was of vital importance to the USSR in the Asia-Pacific region in both inputs (capital and technology) and outputs (market). As Allen Whiting notes in his book *Siberian Development and East Asia: Threat and Promise* (1981):

> Japan must weigh heavily in Moscow's decisions on the development of East Asian Siberia. Japanese capital and technology are essential to attaining the desired goals of resource extraction and economic expansion. Japan also offers the only market of significance for exports like timber, coal and gas. Without that market the products of East Asian Siberia have little chance of earning foreign exchange to serve the overall Soviet economy. Japan thus occupies a central position in Moscow's calculations, in inputs as well as outputs.[6]

2. Decision-Making Structure

If Moscow had really appreciated the geographic, economic, and diplomatic importance of Japan for the Soviet Union as noted above, there would have been many ways by which it could have done a much better job vis-à-vis Tokyo. Yet, the Kremlin kept doing precisely what it should not have done; and Soviet leaders often ended up seeing exactly what they did not want to see take place. Tokyo's signing of a peace treaty with Beijing, awakening of the "Soviet threat" and defense-consciousness among Japanese, the revitalization of the movement for the return of the Northern Territories, the "remilitarization" trend and increasing military cooperation with the United States—these are some examples of Japanese behavior which were, at least in the Japanese view, either directly caused, or at least accelerated, by Soviet conduct toward Japan.

"Puzzling," "inept," "inflexible," "rigid," "very unimaginative if not stupid," "almost a total disaster," and "a diplomatic failure" are labels that were frequently used to describe Soviet conduct of foreign policy toward Japan. Part of the possible answer to the question of why Soviet policy toward Japan was counterproductive or self-defeating seemed to lie in the structure for making Soviet foreign policy. As a result of private conversations with Soviet specialists on Japan, many Japanese and Americans concluded that some Soviet specialists were aware of the fact that

Soviet actions toward Japan were not intelligent and effective. Official denials notwithstanding, they knew, for example, that there *was* territorial problem in Japan's claim to the Northern Territories. Moreover, they recognized that the impasse on this issue served Chinese and American objectives insofar as it inhibited a Japanese-Soviet rapprochement.[7]

The problem was, however, that Japan specialists in the USSR did not have much influence on the Kremlin's policy toward Japan. Many of these specialists worked at various research institutes in the USSR's Academy of Sciences, such as the Institute of Oriental Studies (IVAN), the Institute of Far Eastern Studies (IDV), the Institute of World Economy and International Relations (IMEMO), and the Institute of the U.S.A. and Canadian Studies (ISKAN). Referring in general to area specialists or "*mezhdunarodniki*" (internationalists)[8] or "*institutniki*" in these Soviet Academy of Sciences research institutes, Dimitri K. Simes, formerly himself a researcher at the IMEMO, provided an answer to the question of why their influence on policy making remained severely constrained in the future: "First, these research institutes are somewhat outside the institutional decision-making process. Most of the staff in these institutes are not cleared for classified work. . . . Second, while many key officials at the Institute [IMEMO] have come from the Central Committee apparatus, the Foreign Ministry and the KGB, there are few instances of scholars moving to important party and government jobs."[9] Simes concluded that "those institute personnel . . . are . . . used as advisors rather than as policy-makers. The bureaucratic distinction between consultants and *apparatchiki* is much more marked and important in the Soviet Union than in America."[10]

From her own experience as a specialist on Japanese affairs, Galina Orionova, a defector from the ISKAN, recounts an intriguing episode that helps us understand how the Party disregarded information from academic sources: "In 1978, scholars from several institutions met in great secrecy to examine the threat posed by Sino-Japanese rapprochement. They all agreed that it was a mistake to continue treating the Japanese as inferiors and that they [the Japanese] were not militarists and could not be denied their right to deal with China on their own terms."[11] However, "the Party took no notice."[12] Orionova continued: "I think we were lucky if more than two percent of what we wrote was read by anybody who mattered."[13] Through one of her colleagues who was married to a man who worked for the CPSU Central Committee, Orionova learned that "the documents that constantly flood in from all the rival academic institutions find their way straight into the wastepaper basket."[14]

Ivan I. Kovalenko, a deputy chief in the International Department of the CPSU's Central Committee, occupied the highest position in the CPSU held by a Japanologist. He was identified as the "commander-in-chief" of Soviet policymaking toward Japan.[15] However, as John I. Stephan has written, there is no means of detecting to what extent Kovalenko influenced the Soviet top leadership's policy decisions toward Japan.[16] Kovalenko's influence on Soviet Japan policy was clearly less than that of Mikhail S. Kapitsa, Sinologist and one of the Soviet Vice-Foreign Ministers,[17] on Soviet policy toward China. If Kovalenko did exert an influence, many Japanese were afraid that it was not of a positive kind for Japan. Kovalenko was in charge of public relations and communist education of Japanese prisoners-of-war in Siberia, and he appears to Japanese who have met him to hold the notion that Japanese are easily intimidated. This is an out-of-date notion, because the Japanese have fully recovered from World War II and have regained a national sense of confidence, having terminated the status of war with China with the signing of a peace treaty and having achieved the status of economic giant, second only to the United States. Yet, many Japanese shared the pessimistic feeling that as long as Kovalenko or someone who held such outdated views occupied an important position in Soviet policy-making with respect to Japan, the possibility of improvement in bilateral relations was slim.

3. Perceptions, Objectives, and Strategy

Whoever the decisionmakers of Soviet foreign policy toward Japan, the mind-set of individual decisionmakers was an important variable that influenced Soviet foreign policy behavior. Mind-set is an amorphous, elusive amalgam of many elements: values, beliefs, images, and even psychological dispositions. Nobody knows exactly how or why Soviet leaders made particular decisions. In fact, Soviet decisionmakers themselves probably did not know the complete answer to this question. The answer undoubtedly varied over time, depending on issues and circumstances. Judging from what Soviet leaders said and did, however, it is not entirely impossible to detect what mattered most to Soviet decisionmakers and to imagine what kinds of operational codes[18] they had in their minds.

The Soviets perceived Japan[19] as: (1) a capitalist nation ruled by a conservative regime; (2) an anti-Soviet state, which being one of the United States' basic allies, together with the U.S. and NATO member countries, formed part of the anti-Soviet encirclement system; (3) an Asian nation that was likely to lean toward China rather than the Soviet Union; (4) a relatively weak country, from a military perspective, which had no nuclear weapons and relied upon the United States for national security but which, given the decline in American strength, would assume greater responsibility for defense in the future; (5) an economic power with capital and advanced technology that would prove very useful for Soviet development in Siberia and the Far Eastern part of the USSR; and (6) a country in which reactionaries and "revanchists" were attempting to block a peace treaty with the Soviet Union by making "unfounded and unlawful" territorial demands.[20]

Soviet policy objectives toward Japan followed almost inevitably from the above mentioned perceptions: (1) to prevent Japan from forming closer ties with the United States, especially in the field of military security; (2) to stop Japan's "globalization" process, its growing consciousness of its responsibilities as a member of the "Western community"; in particular, to stop the "NATOization" of Japan; (3) to prevent Japan from cooperating closely with the PRC in diplomatic, economic, and technological spheres, and above all, to keep the Sino-Japanese Peace Treaty (1978) from turning into a military pact; (4) to stifle security consciousness or, in Soviet words, the "resurgence of militarist tendencies" in Japan; (5) to encourage Japan to separate its political differences and disagreements with the USSR from its economic goals, so as to gain Japan's more active participation in trade with the USSR in general and joint economic development in Siberia and the Soviet Far East in particular, on a much larger scale and a longer, more stable basis; and (6) to contain what the Soviets termed the "unfounded and unlawful" Japanese demands for the Northern Territories, and keep them from hindering favorable Soviet-Japanese relations.

Clearly, these objectives were quite arbitrary and represented the maximalist program. The first error in the Soviet Union's foreign policy toward Japan lay in attempting to pursue all these goals at once, disregarding the fact that some were mutually exclusive. A simultaneous and uncompromising pursuit of aims that were far too ambitious, and a failure to envision any trade-off among these objectives—these were the salient characteristics of Soviet policy toward Japan. For example, the Soviet Union's hard-line position on the territorial question was counterproductive to its achievement of other objectives; i.e., of drawing Japan away from the United States; discouraging military cooperation among Japan, the United States, and the PRC, and encouraging economic cooperation with Siberia.

How did the Kremlin policymakers view Japan in their global strategy? In the Soviet *Weltanschauung* and in the Soviet list of foreign policy priorities, the United States occupied the most important position—so much so, that Moscow did not seem to realize the need to develop a specific policy oriented toward Japan. The basic strategy of Soviet foreign policy could be thus summarized as follows: "Let us do business with the United States first, leaving the others to later stages." In a list of Soviet foreign policy priorities, the global confrontation with the U.S. occupied the primary and highest place. Relations with Japan, in contrast, took a secondary place in that list, subordinated to the primary objective of struggle with the United States. The Soviets seemed to believe that the USSR's success vis-à-vis the United States on the global level more or less would determine its interactions with other countries in other regions. More concretely, if the USSR happened to lose the battle with its major adversary, the United States, this would almost mean that there would no longer be any use in the Soviets' exerting much effort elsewhere. Conversely, if it could win the major battle with the United States, this would make its victory or success in other areas a lot easier or even automatic. Only within such a framework of Soviet perceptions—and concomitant strategies in international affairs—can we explain why the Soviet Union kept taking a counterproductive position toward Japan, as has often been described in this book. The Soviet leaders firmly believed in, or expected, final victory over their arch opponent, the United States, so they did not care much in the meantime about their temporary losses or failures in diplomacy toward Japan.

However, this Soviet strategy toward Japan was based on premises that were unrealistic or increasingly outdated, including the belief that the role of military strength carries extraordinary weight in assessing the "correlation of forces" and the belief that the United States is the major and almost exclusive concern of Soviet diplomacy. As a result of these premises, the Soviet Union for a long time neglected formulating a distinct policy toward Japan, a policy that was not simply an extension of its U.S. policy but one independent enough to be distinguishable from it. This seems to provide another reason for the unsuccessful record of Soviet foreign policy toward Japan. If the Soviets wanted to be successful in their conduct of Soviet foreign policy toward Japan, it was necessary that the Soviets undergo, above all, a kind of mental "reprogramming"—for instance, a transformation from their obsession with military strength to a more nonmilitary (economic, scientific-technological, psychological) mentality. Having undergone such a mental transformation, the Soviet leaders would have realized the urgency of forming a distinct foreign policy toward Japan that fully took into account the specific conditions of Soviet-Japanese relations. Such a transformation or modification of traditional perceptions, values, and images is, of course, difficult to effect and cannot be completed overnight. At the same time, without this transformation, however, the success of Soviet foreign policy toward Japan seemed remote.

4. Separation of Japan from the United States

One might expect Soviet politicians and diplomats to have applied their own peculiar kind of tactics, quite different from those employed by their non-Soviet counterparts. This was not necessarily the case, however, for the Soviets used more or less the same methods as those practiced by Western politicians and diplomats. It was in the following areas that the real differences lay. First, the Soviets were ready to utilize every possible means of achieving their goals. As Stephen Kertesz, a former Hungarian diplomat, noted, any means that promoted Soviet objectives was regarded as good and legitimate.[21] Second, the Soviets employed these techniques "methodically and regularly,"[22] while non-Soviet countries used them unsystematically and infrequently. Third, there remained certain tactics and gambits for which the Soviets evinced a special fondness and which they used with greater frequency than others. Because the Soviet Union used numerous techniques vis-à-vis Japan, it is necessary to limit this discussion by examining only those that appear most relevant.

One of the tactics that the Soviet Union rarely failed to apply in dealing with Japan was to attempt to drive a wedge between Japan and the West, particularly the United States.[23] The technique of divide and conquer was adopted by Vladimir Lenin, who expressed the view that the practical task of Communist policy is "to incite one [enemy power] against the other." Emphasizing again the tactics of utilizing and sharpening conflicts between enemies, Lenin wrote: "Our policy is to utilize exclusively discord (*rozn'*) of imperialistic powers."[24] Quoting these words of the founding father of the Soviet Union, Valerian A. Zorin wrote in his book *The Fundamentals of Diplomatic Service* (first edition, 1964; second edition, 1977): "Our party has been practicing this very tactical line also in its guidance of the foreign policy of the Soviet state, successfully utilizing contradictions among the adversaries and drawing to the side of the USSR those who are not necessarily consistent."[25]

Besides this Bolshevist tradition, there is another, perhaps more important reason why Soviet leaders, no matter who they may have been, repeatedly applied the tactics of divide and conquer with regard to Japan. Soviet leaders did not perceive Japan by itself to be a significant power in military terms. However, if Japan's foreign policy were closely combined with U.S. global strategy, then, the Soviets considered, Japan would suddenly emerge as a formidable power. Dmitrii V. Petrov still considered in 1981, as he had done almost ten years earlier, in 1973,[26] that "today and in the near future, Japan will be unable independently to solve strategic tasks and conduct offensive large-scale operations."[27] Having said this, however, Petrov hastened to add, "The militarization of Japan has been indissolubly linked with U.S. military-strategic doctrine and American foreign policy, which assigns a major role to the military alliance with Japan in achieving its regional and global ends."[28] Aleksandr I. Bovin stated even more clearly, during his trip to Japan in 1983:

> I want to say that we are not frightened by the Japanese military forces as such. What I am saying is that a Japanese military alliance with the United States makes us uneasy. We are well aware that Japan will never attack the Soviet Union, but the United States can do so, using its bases in Japan, which are located near the USSR, and this does alarm us. We are not frightened of Japan.[29]

As one of the best means of applying the tactics of divide and conquer to Japan, the Soviets frequently pointed out the possible or actual contradictions between Japan and the United States. It was the basic Soviet perception that, although both the American and Japanese ruling classes and elites had found common interests to justify close relations across the Pacific, they had found and would find their fundamental differences increasingly difficult to bridge. The gap between these two states would continue to grow,[30] as Japan challenged the United States not only in the economic sphere but in almost all other fields. Particularly serious contradictions were likely to surface, according to the Soviets, when "Tokyo starts to obtain more independence than it has had within the framework of its military alliance with the United States."[31] With Yasuhiro Nakasone's ascent to power, this process appeared to have started. The Soviet Union also encouraged Japan to become less dependent on the United States. To be precise, however, the Soviet position on this matter was an ambivalent one: On the one hand, the Soviet Union did not want to see Japan grow into an overly independent and militarily powerful state in the future, as we will examine shortly, but on the other hand, the USSR certainly did not welcome a Japan that was wholly dependent on the United States.

Unlike America's Western European allies, which "have claimed more or less independence [from the U.S.] and freedom of action for the protection of their national interests," Japan, in Soviet judgment, "has not even tried to do that."[32] Japan appeared to the Soviets "to be too content with the status of an obedient junior partner,"[33] always "blindly copying the U.S. position"[34] and "at the disposal of its overseas patron's instructions."[35] According to the Soviet judgment, Japan was excessively exploited as a very convenient, most faithful "partner" or "ally" by the United States, in exchange for "an honorary membership card of the Western community."[36] No matter how often American politicians described Japan in flattering terms like "equal partner," "a vital cornerstone," and so on,[37] Japan was—the Soviets warned—simply being used by the Pentagon as "a territory for accommodating [U.S.] air forces and naval bases"[38] and relied upon because of its "material and productive capability from the viewpoint of securing military actions in Asia."[39] The Soviets thus warned that in the case of an emergency the United States would not necessarily come to help Japan, which enjoyed "less support among American citizens than does Western Europe."[40] Consequently, the Soviets advised that the Japanese should abrogate the unreliable and unnecessary alliance relationship with the United States.

Whatever the reason behind its tactics of divide and rule, the Soviet Union attempted to do its utmost to drive a wedge between Japan and the United States by resorting to persuasion, bluffs, encouragement, entreaties, and all other means at its disposal.

In an effort to persuade Japan to reconsider its position, Moscow explained to the Japanese what the new U.S. global strategy was and how dangerous the role was that Japan was expected to play in that American scheme. In the Soviet perception, American's ultimate goal of world domination would never change in the future. What would change was the method. Due to increasing U.S. awareness of the decline of American power and also its realization of the fact that Japan and other allies had grown strong enough to be able to assume more of a military burden than before, Washington decided, in the Soviet view, to rely more heavily upon new methods, the principal one of which was "division of labor." Based on this principle, Moscow warned, Japan's role as a partner or "accomplice,"[41] especially in the Asia-Pacific region,[42] was increasing significantly. Concretely speaking, Washington was, in the Soviet prediction, going to convert the Japan–U.S. security arrangement from a mostly uni-lateral configuration into a NATO-type, more equal, bilateral form, a pro-cess the Soviets describe as "NATOization,"[43] so that a bridge between these two allied military blocs could be created.[44] The Soviets were also greatly concerned about U.S.-Japanese cooperation in developing defense-related applications of science and technology, such as "micro-electronics, computers, lasers, and other advanced technology necessary for the de-velopment of future weaponry."[45] Soviet leaders believed that such coop-eration would definitely increase in the near future.

With the aim of alienating Japan from the United States and other coun-tries, the Soviet Union attempted to play the role of benevolent judge. Soviet leaders tried hard to let the Japanese know that the Soviets accu-rately grasped what really was going on in the world: it was not the inno-cent Japanese but rather the American imperialists (and Chinese expansionists) who were primarily responsible for pushing Japan onto the dangerous course of "remilitarization" and "anti-Sovietism." The Sovi-ets thus advised the Japanese not to succumb to but rather to persistently resist "the pressures" and "demands" exerted on Tokyo by Washington (and Beijing).[46] Constantly and carefully avoiding the risk of directly assailing and thus diametrically opposing Japan, Brezhnev criticized instead the United States and the PRC, as best illustrated in his speech at the 26th CPSU Party Congress (1981), when he stated: "In Japan's foreign policy course, negative factors are becoming stronger—playing second fiddle to the dangerous plans of *Washington and Beijing* and a tendency toward militarization" (emphasis added by H.K.).[47] Having said this, the general secretary was cautious enough to add: "However, we do not think that these are Tokyo's last words, so to speak, and we hope that foresight and understanding of the country's inter-ests will prevail there. As before, the USSR favors lasting and genuine good-neighborly relations with Japan."[48] It is interesting to note, however, that after Beijing responded positively to Soviet overtures for normalization be-tween the USSR and the PRC during the latter part of Brezhnev's regime, Soviet leaders stopped criticizing the PRC for applying pressure and concen-trated exclusively on "American" pressures on Japan.

5. Prevention of Japan's "Globalization" and "Remilitarization"

The Kremlin also made strenuous attempts, both through criticism and through action, to block Japan's trend toward "globalization" and "remilitarization." Japan's trend to "globalization" involves a growing awareness of its membership in the world, or to be more exact, the Western community, and a readiness to accept responsibility for defense commensurate with its economic capability. As the Soviets perceived it, Japan's intention was to become a world power with interests throughout the world.[49] The transition of Tokyo's principles of foreign policy conduct from the "Yoshida Doctrine," which concentrated on the economic welfare of the Japanese people, to the "doctrine of globalism" (D. Petrov)[50] was regarded by the Soviets as a "very substantial qualitative change" (Iu. Bandura).[51] The Kremlin had good reason not to welcome such a "transformation" of Japan.[52] Tokyo's transition to a position of "global diplomacy" was, according to Soviet judgment, dictated "not so much by Japan's individual national interests as by its 'membership in the club' of imperialist states,"[53] and positioned Japan on "a course of confrontation with the Soviet Union."[54]

With the hope that Japan would forever remain in its immediate post–World War II status, in which its concern was confined strictly to its own narrowly defined interests and particularly to the defense of its own territories, Moscow tried hard to persuade Tokyo not to become interested in the affairs of "other countries such as Afghanistan and Poland," which, in the Soviet view, "have nothing in common with the interests of the Japanese people."[55] It was also unnecessary, and even dangerous to the security of Japan, according to the Soviets, for Japan to participate in such joint naval maneuvers as the Rim of the Pacific Exercises (RIMPAC), joint U.S.–Australian–New Zealand exercises conducted in the Pacific Ocean basin, "thousands of miles away from the Japanese coast and far beyond the boundaries of the Far East."[56] What was likewise intensified was the Soviet campaign against the Japanese plan to undertake the so-called 1,000-mile sea-lane defense. Referring to these exercises, Dmitrii V. Petrov opined: "This means an essential expansion of the function of the Japanese 'Self-Defense Forces.' It would mean that Japan's navy is going to act thousands of miles away from the coast of its own country."[57]

One of the major reasons why the Kremlin was concerned about Japan's "globalization" tendency is that this would, in practice, be almost inevitably accompanied by what the Soviets refer to as the "remilitarization" of Japan. Except for the unlikely case in which Japan would move away from the United States and/or closer to the USSR, the Soviets naturally did not welcome at all what they termed "remilitarization" of Japan.[58] This proved to be the case, particularly since Japan's effort to increase its defense forces was targeted almost exclusively against the threat from the Soviet Union. As the Soviets saw it, "Anti-Sovietism and militarism [in Japan] were intertwined in a single mass."[59]

On the other hand, the Soviets also understood that the United States did not wish to see Japan become too strong militarily. What the United States wanted was for Japan to forever be its faithful junior partner, with a reasonable, but never exceedingly large, amount of armaments, and more importantly, for Japan to support the framework of the American global strategy. For example, Leonid P. Pinaev noted in his book *Evolution of the Military Policy of Japan* (1982): "It would be dangerous to encourage Japan to rearm beyond this scale, because it would yield consequences contrary to the interests of the United States. From the vantage point of American global military strategy, Japan should play not an independent but an auxiliary role."[60]

However, it seemed to Soviet observers that Japan would inevitably accelerate its rearmament drive in the future toward the development of independent military forces. Factors driving Japan in that direction were, in the Soviet view, the "weakening of the American guarantee for the security of Japan and U.S. credibility as perceived" and "a shift in the focus of American attention to Western Europe and the Middle East."[61] Whatever the reasons are, according to D. Petrov, "The [Japanese] proponents of militarization state that Japan should rely on her own forces and build up her 'defensive capabilities,' i.e., her military potential."[62]

A salient feature of the Soviet campaign against the "remilitarization" of Japan is its *preventive* character. What Moscow was concerned about was clearly not the current level of the Japanese Self-Defense Forces—which was insignificant compared with the Soviet Armed Forces in terms of budget, size, and kinds of weaponry—but the *potential* that Japan had, unless prevented, to grow into a strong military power in the future. I.I. Ivkov (a.k.a. Ivan I. Kovalenko) candidly admitted in 1978 that the process of militarization of Japan had not yet become all embracing.[63] Having said this, however, Ivkov, like other Soviet security and Japan specialists, hastened to call attention to the fact that Japan commanded "the newest [*noveishii*], most advanced, up-to-date technology,"[64] which, in his judgment, could be "quickly and easily switched, converted or re-equipped to serve military purposes."[65] In short, Japan had, in the Soviets' view, "a powerful military-industrial *potential* [*potentsial* or *vozmozhnost'*], which could have made it possible for the Japanese ruling circles, whenever necessary, to build up a multi-million-man army and equip it with advanced military technology" (emphasis added by H.K.).[66]

While stressing the potential power of Japan,[67] the Soviets did not place much trust in the intentions of the Japanese government[68] to keep its military potential within a reasonable, limited scale. To the Soviet mind, the existence of potential capabilities was almost identical to an actual threat. What worried the Soviets was the *direction* in which Tokyo was moving and the traditionally rapid *speed* of transformation in Japan once Japan set its course. Worried that they might find themselves in a position in which it was too late to counter such a transformation of Japan, the Soviets were determined to nip in the bud what they refer to as the "resurgence of Japanese militarism."

One clever way of discouraging Japan from moving in the direction of "globalization" and "remilitarization" was the Soviet contention that "the Japanese are forgetting the lessons of history."[69] This theme was characteristic of a campaign initiated in the late Brezhnev era, in which the Soviets called attention to the fact that "Japanese ruling classes in the 1930s and 1940s dragged the otherwise peaceful and innocent Japanese people into the dangerous path of militarism, which finally culminated in the disaster of World War II." Ivkov reminded the Japanese of the devastating consequences of the war:

> The World War took a toll of two million Japanese lives, and another eight million Japanese were seriously injured. About one-third of the country's national wealth was destroyed. Japan was the first, and so far the only, country to experience atomic bombings, which took 300,000 lives.[70]

Having perhaps sympathetically underlined the misery that the Japanese public suffered from World War II, the message that the Soviets really wanted to convey to the Japanese was a warning that it was foolish and potentially devastating for the Japanese to forget such a traumatic experience. Dmitrii F. Ustinov, Soviet Minister of Defense, for example, stated, "[Yet] revanchist forces [in Japan] are trying to bury in oblivion the tragic lessons of World War II and to persuade their country's people to support the idea of reviving Japan as a 'mighty military power.'"[71]

What is interesting to observe in this campaign is that the Soviet Union was warning that "lessons of the past" must be remembered not only by the Japanese but also by the Soviets, the Americans, and all other nations of the world. While demonstrating that "the Soviet people remember well the lessons of the last war [of Japanese militarism],"[72] the Soviets warned Americans, who also would not like to see a militaristic Japan, that "the

United States cannot ignore the history of Japan's militarism in the 1930s and 1940s, which led to Pearl Harbor."[73] Of course, the circumstances of Japan and the world in the 1980s were quite different from those in the 1930s and 1940s, and it is difficult to say to what extent lessons of the past could be applied to the present. However, such comparisons and analogies did not prevent the Soviets from warning against the revival of Japanese militarism. What the Soviets were trying to exploit is obvious: the human propensity to "overlearn from traumatic events" or to "learn too much from what happens to themselves" and to apply the "lessons of the past to [the] changed context" (Robert Jervis).[74]

6. Attempts to Improve Relations Through Bargaining ("The Carrot")

Another of the Soviet tactics in dealing with Japan was to reinforce efforts to improve its relations with Japan through bargaining. The Soviets perceived Japan as an increasingly important country and were revising somewhat their previous inclination to underestimate Japan, an assessment caused by their proclivity to evaluate a nation primarily in terms of military capability. What means were available to the Soviet Union to try to improve its relations with Japan? This question seems quite relevant, as what the Soviets were able to do with regard to Japan was greatly influenced by the instruments at their disposal. It is appropriate, therefore, to identify and examine Soviet policy options toward Japan in terms of resources accessible to them. Let us start by examining those instruments that could be used as a "carrot," leaving the "stick" for later discussion.

Trade and Fishing

There were few powerful and effective instruments available to the Soviet Union to improve its relations with Japan. One conceivable instrument was economics. Generally speaking, the Soviets did not hesitate to use economic tools for noneconomic, political purposes. In other words, they often linked political and economic issues. There appeared to be good reasons for the Soviets to believe this tactic of linkage could have worked particularly well vis-à-vis Japan, given Japan's dependence on foreign sources for energy and raw materials.

In practice, however, these tactics had serious limitations, largely due to Soviet international adventures and poor economic performance. Consequently, it became the USSR and not so much Japan that needed more active trade and economic relations between the two countries.[75] It was not Japan but the Soviet Union that persistently proposed the conclusion of a long-term economic agreement with the purpose of stabilizing trade relations.[76] A Soviet call[77] for a joint meeting of the Japan-Soviet Economic Cooperation Committee and Soviet-Japanese Economic Cooperation Committee, which had been suspended by Japan since 1979, was another illustration. Furthermore, it is appropriate to recall at this juncture that Japan froze its economic relations with the USSR as a part of the sanctions against the Soviet invasion of Afghanistan. True, this policy caused some losses to Japanese businesspeople. However, unlike in West Germany, where enterprises engaged in trade with the USSR were relatively small and hence the problem of unemployment was more threatening, in Japan, comparatively large corporations were dealing with the Soviet Union.[78] This meant that Japan did not necessarily need extensive business relations with the Soviet Union. Undoubtedly, the Soviet Union suffered more from the sanctions than Japan did. Having made the unusually candid remark that "the Soviet Union now finds itself in an economically difficult situation due to, among other things, the sanctions imposed by the United States and its allies," Nikolai S. Patolichev, Soviet Minister of Foreign Trade, was quoted in February 1983 by a Japanese business delegation to Moscow, headed by Mr. Shigeo Nagano, as asking that Japan cooperate in promoting improved trade relations with the USSR.[79] In this case, instead of pursuing the tactic of linking politics with economics, the Soviet Union was advocating to Japan a policy of separating politics from economics.

Another instrument that appeared to serve as a "carrot" tactic was fishing rights. Fishing issues had previously been manipulated skillfully by the Soviet Union with the aim of inducing diplomatic concessions from the Japanese government and influencing Japan's positions on other matters in favor of the Soviet Union. With the advent of the so-called 200-nautical-mile fishing zone era around 1976–77, however, fishing rights ceased to play a significant role. To begin with, the USSR was adversely affected (to a greater degree than was Japan) by the implementation of the 200-mile fishing zones, as will be discussed in greater detail in chapter 7. As a result, the Soviet Union was not able to adopt a generous policy toward Japan regarding the question of fishing quotas in its coastal waters. Based on the so-called "principle of equal quotas," what Moscow and Tokyo agreed upon in 1979 were total fishing quotas of 750,000 and

650,000 tons for Japanese and Russian fishermen, respectively, within each other's 200-mile zone. This new agreement meant a large reduction (by about half) in the Japanese quota from the previous level of 1,220,000 tons, while the Soviet catch quota remained the same as, or slightly higher than, the earlier level of 500,000–600,000 tons. Furthermore, in exchange for the 100,000-ton difference between the two sides' quotas, the Japanese paid the USSR a fee in foreign currency, which the Soviet Union badly needed. As these quotas became a stable standard acceptable to both the USSR and Japan, the Japanese-Soviet negotiations on fishing rights became very brief and almost ceremonial, lasting only about ten days.[80] The fishing issue ceased to be a serious source of dispute or a resource for manipulation by the Soviets.

Northern Territories

The territorial issue was and continues to be the most effective political instrument exploited by the Kremlin. The Northern Territories, i.e., the four islands just off Hokkaido seized by the USSR at the end of World War II but claimed by the Japanese as their sovereign territory, constitute an obstacle to any improvement in relations between Japan and the Soviet Union. In fact, the Japanese government regards the reversion of these islands to Japanese control as a *sine qua non* of any meaningful rapprochement and appears persistently determined to undertake almost any sacrifice or inconvenience this stand might entail. Japan's very persistence and determination provided the Soviet Union with substantial bargaining leverage. Besides, the Soviet Union, as we have already seen and will see more clearly, had little to offer the Japanese, beyond these four islands. Consequently, although the Soviet government took the position in its official pronouncements that the territorial question was already resolved once and for all, it is highly probable that the Soviet Union was simply waiting for the time when it could utilize its bargaining card most effectively.

The Soviets' ultimate goal with regard to Japan was to change Japan into a close and reliable ally in Asia, even to such an extent that Moscow could manipulate Japan's domestic and foreign policy decisions and utilize fully its advanced technology and knowhow to assist the Soviet economy. In exchange for such a transformation (what may be roughly labeled "Finlandization" of Japan), the Kremlin would readily have returned the islands to Japan: an exchange of Japan's four *big*, industrialized islands for four *tiny* and barren islands would certainly have been an attractive deal for the Soviet Union. The next-best scenario the Soviets hoped for was one in which Japan moved away from the United States and pursued an "equidistance" diplomacy vis-à-vis Washington and Moscow. In order to encourage Japan to move in a diplomatically neutral or nonaligned direction, the Soviet government might have agreed to the return of two, if not all, of the islands. It may be useful to recall in this connection that in 1955 the Soviet government under Nikita S. Khrushchev agreed to withdraw Soviet military forces from Austria on the condition that, among other things, Austria would become a neutral state. To be sure, historical analogies must be drawn very carefully, as Ernest R. May warns in *"Lessons" of the Past* (1973),[81] but this scenario cannot be completely ruled out, given the Soviets' increasing awareness of the significant role Japan plays in the world in general and in Asia in particular.

The third, but less important, objective of the Soviet Union's efforts in regard to Japan was to encourage Japan to stop, or reduce the magnitude of, its anti-Soviet campaign and increasing military cooperation with the United States. In order to achieve this goal, the Soviet Union was willing to sign a peace treaty with Japan, giving Japan only *two* islands (the Habomai Islets and the island of Shikotan), as stipulated in Article 9 of the Soviet-Japanese Joint Declaration of 1956.[82] The Soviet government officially denied the validity of Article 9 after Japan renewed its security treaty with the United States in 1961. The Soviets were so displeased by Japan's commitment to the Western camp that they took the position that the Japanese side could no longer expect the USSR to fulfill its pledge to transfer the two islands.[83] However, chances were that the Soviet Union would go back to this compromise formula again, because it needed a peace treaty and good relations with Japan more than it had in the past. As a matter of fact, the Brezhnev government did propose in 1972—according to the memoir of Mikhail C. Kapitsa, Soviet deputy foreign minister—to the Japanese government under Prime Minister Eisaku Satō, to return to the two-island formula.[84] However, it can be concluded that there was little possibility that the Soviet Union could use the islands as diplomatic leverage in the ways outlined above, because the Japanese side was not willing to pay such a price.

7. Accommodation with China

In his *Politics Among Nations*, Hans J. Morgenthau suggested that nations have three choices in order to maintain their relative power positions:[85] (1) they can withhold the power of other nations from the adversary; (2) they can add their own power to the power of other nations; or (3) they can increase their own power.[86] We have already discussed the Soviets' resort to the first method, i.e., their increasing efforts to separate Japan from the United States and other members of the "Western community" (section 1). However, the Soviet Union was not very successful in its attempt to divide and conquer, and it was therefore tempted to resort to the second or third choice listed here.

One objective that the Soviet Union considered both desirable and feasible was to form an alliance with the People's Republic of China (PRC). Evidently, Japan was another, perhaps even better, candidate to become a Soviet ally. In fact, during his last years in office, Brezhnev made almost identical appeals to China and Japan, apparently believing that either country's acceptance of the invitation would be a great achievement. These appeals were best illustrated by Brezhnev's overtures at the 26th CPSU Party Congress in February–March 1981[87] and at Tashkent in March 1982.[88] As could readily be predicted, however, Japan categorically turned down these overtures. China, in contrast, showed a positive reaction.[89] Encouraged by the far more receptive responses from Beijing, it appears that the Soviets decided to work first with China and leave Japan until later, as was indicated by Brezhnev's speech at Baku in September 1982.[90] The Soviet strategy appeared to be one of making a breakthrough first with the PRC, and then to do the same with regard to the more difficult Soviet neighbor, Japan.[91] Brezhnev's successor, Andropov, demonstrated that he would not only continue but would also pursue with greater boldness and at a quicker pace than his predecessor this strategy of normalizing relations with China, with the aim of breaking the so-called anti-Soviet encirclement and perhaps even isolating Japan and the United States.[92]

The reconciliation of Soviet differences with the PRC brought a number of benefits to the Soviet Union. In the field of diplomacy, it greatly improved the Soviet position in the world and particularly in the Far East. A complete Sino-Soviet rapprochement would have ended the possible or actual formation of a Washington–Tokyo–Beijing axis targeted against Moscow, thereby providing Moscow with a way out of its awkward isolation in Asia. In addition, it would have enabled the Soviet Union to increase its bargaining power vis-à-vis Japan and the United States. In the military-strategic field, accommodation with Beijing would also provide Moscow great relief and help. If the presence of all or some of the "one million Soviet troops" (in the words of China's paramount leader, Deng

Xiaoping) along the Sino-Soviet border ceased to be necessary and the number were reduced, it would have helped the USSR lessen its military burden as well as financial costs.[93] The Soviet Union could have threatened the West, including Japan, since its troops[94] and SS-20s stationed on the Sino-Soviet border could have been transferred to Asia. It is possible that a Sino-Soviet détente would have deprived Japan of economic profit and that the USSR could have used this possibility as a threat.[95] It is a well-known fact that trade between the USSR and the PRC was growing at a rapid pace in the early 1980s. According to Vladimir N. Sushkov, a Soviet Vice-Minister of Foreign Trade, these two countries were expecting an increase in two-way trade to about the equivalent of US$1 billion in 1983—a threefold increase over that in 1982—and to $1.6 billion in 1984.[96]

At the same time, however, rapprochement between the PRC and the Soviet Union did not bring to Japan (or the United States) solely adverse effects. In other words, one should not view the accommodation of Sino-Soviet relations as a "zero sum game" in which the reduction in Sino-Soviet tensions was accomplished at the United States's expense; instead, one must regard it as what Robert G. Sutter, a senior specialist at the Congressional Research Service of the U.S. Library of Congress, called an "expanding sum game" in which the rapprochement brought to the West, including the United States and Japan, certain benefits as well.[97] Rapprochement, or normalization, is a relative term,[98] and the following three variants may be distinguished:[99] (1) a limited détente or repair of state-to-state relations; (2) further accommodation, with some substantial breakthrough or compromise formula on disputed issues; and (3) genuine rapprochement, with the resurrection or establishment of a Sino-Soviet alliance. In each of these variants, the impact of improved Sino-Soviet relations upon Japan (and also upon the United States) was not as severe as one might have expected.[100] Let us consider each of these three alternatives in more detail.

To begin with, a limited degree of relaxation in Sino-Soviet tensions was a normal, inevitable, and even desirable development. In April 1980, one year after China publicly announced its intention to abrogate the 1950 Sino-Soviet Treaty of Alliance, the PRC and the USSR were in an abnormal and even dangerous state, with no treaty agreement whatsoever existing between them. It is therefore quite natural and understandable for these two powers to make efforts to achieve the normalization of state-to-state relations, with the aim of reducing tensions between them. Otherwise, there would be the ever-present possibility that frictions and clashes along the disputed borders might have triggered an all-out Sino-Soviet war, from which no one could have profited.[101] In this regard, a minimal reduction in tensions between the Soviet Union and China was necessary and beneficial to all nations of the world, not only the United States and Japan.

Even if Sino-Soviet relations went beyond rapprochement, such a development would have still brought some benefits to Japan. Namely, if the Soviet Union and China stopped antagonizing each other to the extent that neither of them would criticize the other's conduct of foreign policy, Japan would be able to return to a policy of even-handedness between the USSR and the PRC. Then, for example, should Japan desire, it would be able to assist further with the construction of the BAM through financial and technical cooperation, which was at least partially obstructed by opposition from the PRC. Likewise, Japan would have been able to extend more economic and technological assistance to the PRC without worrying about reactions or interference from the Soviet side. Moreover, if talks on the disputed borders between the USSR and the PRC had in some way found a formula for "adjustments," it might have helped the Soviets become more flexible with regard to the Japanese request for negotiations on the Northern Territories dispute, which the Soviets adamantly refused to talk about.[102]

It is well-known that the Chinese side repeatedly stated that three "obstacles" had to be cleared before China's relations with the Soviet Union could be normalized: (1) the presence of Soviet troops along the Sino-Soviet border and in Mongolia, (2) the Soviet occupation of Afghanistan, and (3) Soviet assistance for the Vietnamese troops occupying Cambodia. Should a compromise formula have been found on any one of these sensitive issues, the positive outcome not only would have benefited the two countries concerned but undoubtedly would have benefited many other nations, including the United States and Japan. A removal of Soviet troops from Afghanistan, and a Vietnamese withdrawal from Cambodia, which the West was unable to achieve despite its strenuous efforts (sanctions, boycotts, declarations, maneuvers) certainly would have been also in the interests of the West as well as of the countries concerned.[103] Suggesting that future Sino-Soviet détente could have had an overall positive effect on U.S. interests, U.S. Secretary of State George Shultz said at a press conference following his return from Brezhnev's funeral in November 1982: "If, through their discussion, [China] can persuade the Soviet Union to get out of Afghanistan and, in effect, get out of Cambodia, so much the better."[104] Reduction of Soviet forces facing China also would have been helpful in reducing international tensions, providing they were not redeployed against Japan, Europe, or the Middle East.

The final point to be discussed is the implication of a Sino-Soviet military alliance for U.S.-Japanese relations. Any step in the direction of such an alliance certainly would have been met with deep and profound suspicion and fear by other countries. It could have possibly restored a sense of Western unity and caused the United States to refocus its attention on the Asian region. Viewing itself as being unable to control the possible formation of a Sino-Soviet alliance in Asia, the United States would have pressed Japan harder to rearm substantially so as to serve as a partner in the common defense against the Soviets and Chinese.[105] As a result, Japan would have become a very strong military power, which would have been counterproductive to Soviet interests, at least in part offsetting those benefits that accommodation with China would have brought to the Soviet Union.

8. Military Buildup and Bluff ("The Stick")

The final choice for the Kremlin is the third in Morgenthau's classification: to increase its own power capability, particularly its military potential. Almost without regard for the kind of foreign policy orientation Japan may take for the future, it appeared that the Soviet Union was unlikely to stop its military buildup in the Far East and in the vicinity of Japan. The Kremlin's tactics in blackmailing Japan were a combination of a warning of the dangerous situation in which Japan would find itself and "retaliatory measures" (*otvetnye mery*)[106] the Soviet Union would take should its warnings be ignored by Japan. It was impossible to dismiss their words as mere bluffs, for, though they might appear to be purely verbal threats (since, of course, there was no actual aggression by the Soviet Union), there was increasing military deployment and buildup by the Soviets.

Why were the Soviets doing so? To begin with, the Soviets appeared to be firmly convinced that there was a need for them to undertake military measures to cope with the possible formation of an anti-Soviet *military* alliance by the United States, Japan, South Korea, and the PRC in the Far East. Second, it is also worth recalling that the Soviets (as noted in chapter 2) seemed to feel that the military was the most effective instrument for achieving almost any goal. They were unconcerned by the difficulty of converting military strength into *political* gains. Possibly based partially on their experiences in dealing with Japanese prisoners-of-war in

Siberia, some CPSU *apparatchiki* and high government officials in charge of Japanese affairs appeared to still adhere to the notion, inapplicable to contemporary Japanese, that the Japanese could be easily intimidated. If the Japanese were pressed hard and frequently enough, they would—in the Soviet view—ultimately capitulate and come to Soviet terms. The third, and perhaps most important, reason why the Kremlin continually relied on threat tactics (the "stick") in dealing with Japan may be that no other effective instrument of influence remained at the Soviets' disposal. Marxist-Leninist ideology and the Soviet system had long since ceased to hold any appeal for the majority of Japanese. Neither geographic proximity nor economic complementarity provided, as illustrated in the foregoing sections, particularly in chapter 1, a convincing basis for improvement of Soviet-Japanese bilateral relations. Furthermore, as examined in this chapter, almost none of the Soviets' tactics in dealing with Japan produced any positive results. Consequently, the only means left for the Soviets to exploit in their attempt to influence Japan was the continued buildup of their military and the threat of its use.

Yet, military threats also proved particularly ineffective in dealing with Japan. The Japanese were not easily impressed or influenced by the demonstration of naked military might. They concluded from their own defeat in World War II that military means do not lead to the achievement of national goals. Accordingly, for better or for worse, they were extraordinarily insensitive as well to Soviet bluffs with military might.

The Soviets, unaware of such sentiments in Japan, continued to rely on coercive tactics that usually adversely affected Soviet objectives. The "*Okean-75*" demonstration of the Soviet Navy in 1975, the MiG-25 incident in 1976, the heavy-handed Soviet tactics in negotiations on fishing rights in 1977—all of these worked against Soviet objectives concerning Japan. The climate of threat helped persuade the Japanese government to purchase the Lockheed U-3C anti-submarine patrol planes, despite the bribery scandal in 1975. Moscow likewise proved unable to prevent Japan from concluding a peace treaty with the PRC in 1978, because the Soviet Union relied exclusively on the instrument of bluff from beginning to end. This took the form of Soviet military maneuvers conducted in May–June 1978 around the island of Etorofu and frequent verbal threats by the then Soviet Ambassador to Japan, Dmitrii S. Polianskii, who spoke of Soviet readiness to introduce "certain correctives into its policy toward Japan" if Japan concluded the treaty.[107] However, Soviet policy seemed to have backfired.[108] The USSR maneuvered militarily to deter

Japan from entering an alliance with China, yet it was these maneuvers that at least partially reinforced Tokyo's determination to promote normalization of its relations with Beijing. The signing of the Sino-Japanese peace treaty led in turn to an intensification in the Soviet military buildup, especially in the Northern Territories. This buildup provoked Japan into taking further measures to cope with "the Soviet threat."

We will return to this chain of action and reaction on the part of the Soviets and Japanese in the chapters dealing with the late 1970s and early 1980s (Parts Three and Four). It is sufficient to note here that the threat of growing military power, the Soviets' last resort, was ultimately self-defeating. We can thus conclude that, together with the incompatibility and unrealistic nature of Soviet objectives with regard to Japan, the inappropriate means employed by Moscow to achieve these goals, particularly the stress placed on military leverage, accounts for the Soviet Union's failure to deal effectively with Japan.

9. Interaction of the Determinants

In the preceding pages I have sought to identify and examine individually those variables that I personally regard as the principal factors influencing Soviet foreign policy toward Japan. What, then, was the relationship among these variables? *How* and *to what degree* did each of these factors exert an influence on Soviet policy toward Japan, and under *what* conditions and during *which* time period were these factors influential?[109] These are naturally the last, and probably more important, questions to be asked.

Unfortunately, however, we may become "frustrated" to learn that these are questions that can never be answered accurately and convincingly.[110] Professor Alexander Dallin, who has written a most authoritative article on the subject of domestic determinants of Soviet foreign policy, has concluded that there is "no technique or methodology that permits us to assign weights to the ingredients in the mix."[111] The interrelationship among the ingredients remains by definition in a state of constant flux,[112] varying over time and contingent upon issues and circumstances. If there is no methodology for defining the interconnection among variables, probably the best we can do is to speculate, or attempt to "intuitively" and "impressionistically"[113] make some assessments and judgments that might be subject to later revision.

It has often been pointed out that foreign policy in the Soviet Union, as elsewhere, was not purely an exercise in rational choices.[114] According to

Dallin, Marxism-Leninism does not validate resort to a rational actor model.[115] Soviet conduct of foreign policy toward Japan seems to me to provide perhaps the best illustration to reinforce this general observation: Moscow's foreign policy toward Tokyo perplexed and puzzled the Japanese as well as many outside watchers with its inscrutable repetition of self-defeating behavior. As noted previously, for example, there were obvious incompatibilities among Soviet foreign policy objectives toward Japan. Moreover, there were contradictions between the goals and means to achieve them. The point is that, despite their possible awareness of these incompatibilities and contradictions, the Kremlin leaders showed no sign whatsoever of changing policy toward Japan—leading us to consider that, among other things, Soviet foreign policy was not made and conducted rationally, with careful calculation of gains and losses.

What does this mean for our present concern of assessing the relative weight of each of the variables in terms of its explanatory power in affecting Soviet foreign policy behavior toward Japan? It may mean that: (1) economic variables did not weigh heavily in the determination of Moscow's policy toward Tokyo; (2) such "intangible" factors as the Japanese sentiment toward the lost Northern Territories and anti-Soviet feeling played far less significant roles; and (3) such intangible and nonrational elements as the Soviet inclination to view the power of a nation in military terms, the optimistic Soviet view concerning the convertibility of military power into political influence, and hence the tendency to underestimate the power of Japan as a state and a nation—the inertia of the Soviet decision-making process—weighed quite heavily.

Part Three

THE DETERIORATION
IN JAPANESE-SOVIET RELATIONS

Relations between Russia and Japan have remained cool since the end of World War II. The period from the late Brezhnev era to the Andropov era (1976–1983) could be described as the coldest and most difficult in the entire postwar history of Russo-Japanese relations. During this period, except for the attendance of Japanese Prime Minister Zenkō Suzuki at Leonid Brezhnev's funeral, no official visits were made to either country by the top leaders of these two neighboring countries. During the same period, Japanese Foreign Minister Sunao Sonoda paid only one visit to Moscow, and his Soviet counterpart, Andrei A. Gromyko, long refused to come to Tokyo, making his visit in 1976 his last one. The Soviets later officially recognized this deterioration in their relations with Japan, which they claimed was primarily caused by Japanese misconduct. In the Soviet yearbook *Japan: 1981*, O.V. Vasil'ev wrote: "Since the mid-1970s, unfavorable tendencies have begun to develop, through no fault on the Soviet side, in relations between the USSR and Japan."[1]

First, let me simply identify the series of incidents and events that contributed to make this period the lowest ebb in bilateral relations between these two neighboring countries:

- the MiG-25 incident (1976)
- the 200-nautical-mile fishing zone negotiations (1977)

- Japan's signing of the Treaty of Peace and Friendship with the PRC (1978)
- Soviet redeployment of troops on Japan's Northern Territories (1979)
- the Soviet military invasion of Afghanistan (1979)
- Japan's participation in the U.S.-sponsored sanctions policy against the USSR (1980)
- Zenkō Suzuki's decisions to undertake the "1000-mile sea-lane defense" and to establish "Northern Territories Day" (1981)
- Tokyo's acceptance of deployment of U.S. advanced F-16 fighter-bombers at Misawa (1982)
- The Soviet threat to transfer their SS-20s from Europe to Asia (1982–83)
- Yasuhiro Nakasone's statement on Japan being "an unsinkable aircraft carrier" (1983)
- The Soviet shooting down of KAL 007 (1983)

Why did Japanese-Soviet relations deteriorate to such a low level in this period? Before trying to answer this important question, it is worthwhile mentioning an interesting attempt by the Soviet Union to discern two stages in this period of deterioration. Some Soviet specialists on Japanese affairs divided this period of deterioration into two stages, one stage being the latter half of the 1970s and the other the early 1980s.[2] According to these specialists, the difference between these two periods is as follows. In the mid to late 1970s, Soviet-Japanese relations began to worsen due to "isolated, individual actions."[3] However, attempts were made in these years not only to prevent relations from deteriorating further but also to normalize and even improve relations.[4] In the early 1980s, however, Soviet-Japanese relations steadily worsened, and neither country showed any willingness to make efforts to improve them.[5] The difference between these two stages, in the view of Soviet specialists, can be summarized by the following words: "While in the mid-1970s, signs of decline were apparent only in isolated, or individual actions carried out by the Japanese ruling circles, in the early 1980s, the cooling of relations with the Soviet Union seems to stem from "a political line," which has taken on a "systematic" character.[6]

Leaving this "systematic" deterioration process in the early 1980s for later discussion in Part Four, I will focus in Part Three on three events[7] that took place in the latter half of the 1970s: (1) the negotiations over fishing rights in the newly established Soviet and Japanese 200-nautical-mile fishing zone (1977) (chapter 7); (2) the Sino-Japanese Peace and Friendship Treaty, which contains an "antihegemony" clause, apparently inserted by the Chinese to counter Soviet expansionism (1978) (chapter 8); and (3) the repeated Soviet proposal for confidence-building measures, and Japan's refusal (chapter 9). In each case, the main thrust of the discussion will not lie in providing a historical description of the development but in analyzing how the Soviets and the Japanese behaved toward each other.

Chapter 6

Japanese and Soviet Negotiating Behavior

The Spring 1977 Fisheries Talks

The spring 1977 Japanese-Soviet fisheries negotiations, conducted mainly in Moscow from February to May, turned out to be one of the most protracted (ninety days), heated, and difficult bilateral talks in the postwar history of the two participating states. It was above all an economic battle for fisheries rights between the world's two top-ranking fishing nations. The rivals found it necessary to make up for the fish catch that each had suddenly lost in other fishing areas when several maritime countries adopted a 200-nautical-mile exclusive fishing zone. To make matters worse, there was also the dispute—under the surface, yet ever present— over the Northern Territories question, helping to make both sides inflexible and uncompromising. It seemed impossible to draw a demarcation line for fishing without creating problems related to territorial boundaries. In fact, the Soviet and the Japanese 200-mile zones both include waters surrounding the four islands just north of Hokkaido, whose ownership is hotly contested. Moreover, differences and similarities in "national character"—culturally conditioned patterns of behavior and thought—played a large role in making the negotiations unnecessarily prolonged and exasperating. The first and second factors are quite well known and easily understood, but this last element has received much less publicity and emphasis. Consequently, it is the cultural aspect that is analyzed here. First, however, some background on the spring 1977 fisheries talks will be helpful.

1. A Chronicle: December 1976–May 1977

On December 10, 1976, the Presidium of the Supreme Soviet of the USSR decreed without warning that the Soviet Union intended to establish a 200-nautical-mile fishing zone, within which the Soviet state would exercise exclusive control over all fishing.[1] Two and a half months later, the Soviet government made it clear in a Council of Ministers resolution dated February 24, 1977 that the decree of the Supreme Soviet was to take effect on March 1, 1977.[2] What is more significant, the resolution expressly mentioned the four Soviet-held islands claimed by Japan.

The Japanese were shocked by these Soviet actions. In the first place, the promulgations were made without any consultation with, or even a warning to, the Japanese side. Second, Japan had traditionally been getting more than 17 percent of its entire catch from an area within the newly established Soviet fishing zone. Last, and certainly not least, it did not take long for the Japanese to understand that the Kremlin leaders intended to apply their new principle to the Northern Territories and so to consolidate Soviet sovereignty over the islands, which were occupied by the USSR at the end of World War II but have been claimed by Tokyo as Japanese territory. Japan's acceptance of the 200-mile fishing zone around these islands, then, would have killed virtually all hope that the Northern Territories might be returned to Japan.

When Soviet intentions became public knowledge, the Japanese government sent Minister of Agriculture, Forestry, and Fisheries Zenkō Suzuki to Moscow both to protest and to negotiate. Suzuki's five-day talks (February 28–March 4, 1977) with his Soviet counterpart, Alexander A. Ishkov, however, failed to bring about any agreement. Early in April, Japanese Prime Minister Takeo Fukuda dispatched his chief cabinet secretary, Sunao Sonoda, to Moscow in order to break the impasse. Sonoda was to impress upon the Kremlin leaders the importance of bringing the fisheries feud to an early resolution if a full-scale diplomatic row was to be avoided. The April 7 talks between Sonoda and Soviet Premier Aleksei N. Kosygin, however, did not bear fruit. When the second round of the Suzuki-Ishkov talks (Moscow, April 7–16) also broke down, it became obvious that there would be no easy way to separate the territorial issue from the fisheries problem.

To "separate the fish from the islands," of course, was not necessarily impossible. Japan, for instance, proposed a joint fishing area in the disputed zone, transcending the question of territorial sovereignty. Japan also favored a joint declaration that the fishing zone would have nothing to do with the territorial zone. Yet, neither of these compromise solutions was accepted by the Soviet Union, which saw no need for such measures. In the Soviet view, the territorial question had already been settled—at the end of World War II. The Tokyo government decided not to go further on these compromise proposals for fear that it would weaken Japan's position on the Northern Territories issue. The negotiations were deadlocked.

Meanwhile, although somewhat belatedly, the Japanese decided to take retaliatory action, rushing through both houses of the Diet two bills extending Japan's territorial waters from 3 to 12 miles offshore and setting up a 200-mile exclusive fishing zone of their own. The Japanese zone was, for the time being, to apply only in relation to the USSR, not to the People's Republic of China or to South Korea. Without a doubt this action greatly strengthened the Tokyo government's bargaining position vis-à-vis the Soviet Union, whose fishermen had traditionally been catching 500–600 thousand tons of fish (particularly sardines, the Russian favorite) within Japanese waters, between 3 and 12 miles off the shores of Japan. The Soviets may have realized, too, that if they continued to pursue their strategy of exploiting the fishing talks in order to undermine Japan's long-standing claim over the disputed territory, the exercise might prove counterproductive: the Japanese were standing quite firm and were showing no signs of yielding on the territorial issue, even if it were to mean a considerable loss of fish. Indeed, anti-Soviet feeling among the Japanese began to run unexpectedly high.

Thus, at the end of the third round of the Suzuki-Ishkov talks, held in Moscow from May 3 to 24, 1977, both sides finally "agreed to agree." They were able to initial the Japanese-Soviet Interim Fishing Agreement by sidestepping the territorial issue and limiting the scope of the bilateral agreement to fishing problems only. Article 8 summed up this maneuver, stipulating that no provisions of the agreement could "be construed so as to prejudice the positions . . . of either government . . . in regard to various problems in mutual relations."[3]

2. Negotiating Behavior and Cultural Differences

Throughout the Japanese-Soviet negotiations just outlined, one can isolate three sharply contrasting aspects of the two parties' behavior: (1) their *basic attitude* toward the talks, (2) the *tactics and instruments* employed, and (3) the *behavioral pattern* during the entire negotiation process. I believe these three points of contrast are to a remarkable degree nothing more or less than a reflection of the two countries' "cultural differences." In other words, these negotiating differences are not solely systemic (ideological, political, or economic); rather, they stem from differences in culturally conditioned patterns of thought or behavior. In short, conflicts between the Soviets and the Japanese, as seen in the negotiations, can and must be considered as deriving from a mix of two basic systemic and cultural components,[4] although it is sometimes very difficult to distinguish one component from the other. In this chapter, against the general tendency to emphasize the first component, I will deliberately stress the importance of the second.

"Negotiation from Weakness" vs. "Negotiation from Strength"

In the 1977 fisheries talks, the Japanese side negotiated from a peculiar position of weakness, whereas the Soviets constantly pursued their objectives from a position of strength.[5] The Japanese method of negotiating, in fact, was labeled by the Japanese press at the time "a petition, or beggar or kowtow diplomacy,"[6] while the Soviets pursued "diplomacy by intimidation."[7]

It should be noted here that Japan perceived itself as a victim of selfishness on the part of maritime superpowers (the United States, the USSR, and Canada) that wanted to gain exclusive control of waters in their proximity by unilaterally establishing 200-mile fishing zones—without waiting for the conclusion of the Third United Nations Conference of the Law of the Sea. An article in *Asahi Shimbun* accused those three states of "bigpowerism" at sea, noting that the history of ocean law was nothing but "the history of power, which shows that big countries have encircled the sea by force for themselves. No wonder that advocacy of the principle of international law by Japan has been completely disregarded."[8] In such an atmosphere, very few Japanese saw any fault on the part of Japan, which, having the world's largest fishing industry (bringing in one-seventh of the world's total catch), was of particular concern to countries wishing to conserve fishing resources.

It cannot be said that the Japanese perception of the Soviet position on fishing was completely fair or well-balanced. It was not Japan but rather the USSR that was most severely hit by the wave of 200-mile fishing zones claimed by various maritime countries in late 1976 and early 1977.

While in 1976 the Japanese catch within those 200-mile zones constituted about 36.5 percent of its total (9.6 million tons), more than 60 percent of the Soviet total (9 million tons) was affected. This fact received
little attention in Japan and, indeed, was almost totally disregarded. What
was stressed instead was that on the bilateral (Japanese-Soviet) level, it
was not the Soviet Union but Japan that would suffer the most serious
damage from the imposition of 200-mile zones. It was pointed out that,
while the USSR had been taking 500–600 thousand tons of fish within
Japan's 200-mile zone, Japan's catch within the Soviet zone was twice
that amount (i.e., 1.22 million tons)—or nearly three times as much, if
the waters around the disputed islands were included.[9] An editorial in
Asahi Shimbun was typical of the one-sided Japanese view: "We fully
understand that the Soviet Union has a difficulty as a distant-water fishing state, but the situation of Japanese fishing, having no way out, is more
serious than that of the USSR."[10]

No negotiator can be perfectly fair. It is natural for a negotiator to
manipulate the facts to his or her own advantage, stressing certain aspects
and neglecting others. Granted this general principle of negotiations, it is
still of interest to know why in the fisheries negotiations in 1977, the
Japanese side tended to, or pretended to, perceive itself as the weaker
partner, while the Soviets insisted on regarding themselves as the stronger one. One reason the Japanese behaved so, consciously or otherwise,
seems to be a Japanese conviction that a "low profile" (posing as victim)
might work to their advantage.

As Professor Takeo Doi, one of Japan's leading psychiatrists, has pointed
out most eloquently,[11] the concept of *higaisha-ishiki* ("sense of being victimized") clearly derives from the unique psychology of *amae* ("dependence upon the leniency of others") in the Japanese mentality. More
specifically, those who are totally engrossed in *amae* develop an attitude
of *higaisha-ishiki* when they feel rejected.[12] In essence, *amae* refers to
the attitude and expectation of the inferior or weaker party in a relationship with, or a dependence upon, a superior party. It involves an assumption that the stronger party will be indulgent toward the weaker party, that
he or she will recognize an obligation to act favorably toward the weaker
party without demanding a reciprocal obligation, since the strong can
afford to be generous, while the weak cannot.[13]

An editorial in *Asahi Shimbun* provides us with a good example of
Japanese *amae*, this time vis-à-vis the rich and powerful Americans. Appealing for American understanding of the misery of Japanese fishermen,

now expelled from the U.S. 200-mile zone, the author wrote: "We do hope that President [Jimmy] Carter will not disappoint the Japanese, who are allied with the United States and have profound trust and friendly feeling toward the American people."[14] The same kind of *amae* was used by Japanese Prime Minister Takeo Fukuda when he addressed in October 1977 the Soviet delegation to Japan, headed by Minister of Merchant Shipping, Timofei B. Guzhenko and Soviet Ambassador to Tokyo, Dmitrii S. Polianskii: "The islands that Japan has been requesting from your country occupy only a minor, insignificant portion of your huge, vast country."[15] Fukuda thus disregarded, purposely or unwittingly, the fact that the disputed islands were not insignificant to the Soviets, especially from a military-strategic point of view.

In marked contrast, the foremost feature of Soviet negotiating behavior in the 1977 fisheries talks was a heavy-handed attitude of superiority toward Japan. Though the Soviet Union, second only to Japan in distant-water fishing, must have been aware that the new restrictions on fishing hurt Japan just as much as they hurt the USSR, the Soviet negotiators nonetheless showed absolutely no sympathy toward the Japanese. For example, they showed no sign of understanding the Japanese position that since the questions of licenses, fees, and legal jurisdiction could not be dissociated from the question of Japan's sovereignty, Japanese negotiators would require the approval of the Diet. (The American negotiators had understood this point fully and decided not to press the Japanese.) Indeed, the Soviets constantly reminded the Japanese side of Soviet strength vis-à-vis Japan and sought to take full advantage of this purported superiority.

Basically, the Soviets took the position that the fishing negotiations were more necessary to the Japanese than to them—indeed, the talks came about at the request of Japan. For instance, Iurii Bandura, *Izvestiia* correspondent in Tokyo at that time, wrote in April 1977, "The talks were begun at the request of the Japanese side,"[16] and again in May, "As is well known, these talks were held at the wish of the Japanese side and would have ended successfully long ago if Tokyo had displayed a constructive approach."[17] Iurii Afornin, a commentator for Moscow Radio, went out of his way to demonstrate the Soviet position of strength, stating on May 11 that "in today's world, Japan has no alternative but to adjust to good-neighborly relations with the Soviet Union."[18] Using the same logic, the Soviets threatened the Japanese negotiators: if the talks were to become protracted, it would be Japanese fishermen, not Soviets, who would suffer most. A Soviet broadcast to Japan (in Japanese) on May 8, 1977 went as follows: "A large number of Japanese fishermen now find themselves in great difficulty. It is natural that they feel regret and dissatisfaction over the protracted fisheries talks."[19]

Taking full advantage of the fact that Japan's need to operate a fishing fleet within the Soviet 200-mile zone was greater than the Soviet need to fish within the Japanese zone, Soviet representatives demanded that fishing vessels of the Soviet Union be allowed to fish even closer—within Japan's 12-mile *territorial* zone. Tokyo rejected the demand, calling it totally unreasonable and without precedent. Soviet Fisheries Minister A. Ishkov, however, insisted that "the Soviet Union should be given the right, on the basis of reciprocity, to continue its traditional fishing operations off Japanese shores."[20] Even after admitting that the request could not be considered legitimate, the Soviet minister did not give up. For instance, on May 11 Ishkov remarked to a Japanese labor delegation then visiting Moscow:

> We have learned that the Japanese government intends not to admit Soviet ships into their traditional fishing grounds within Japan's 12-mile zone of territorial waters. It is the legitimate right of the Japanese government, but we would hope for a more friendly attitude to the settlement of questions of fishing near the coasts of Japan, as it is precisely such a stand, taking into account mutual interests, that is being taken by the Soviet delegation at the current talks in Moscow.[21]

The Soviets' high-handedness toward the Japanese is illustrated also by the former's bad manners[22] in ignoring generally accepted diplomatic rules and customs. The Soviets unilaterally promulgated their two decrees on the 200-nautical-mile fishing zone; they at first refused and then delayed issuing visas to Sunao Sonoda, the special envoy designated by Prime Minister Fukuda, and to other members of the Japanese delegation; and they frequently, very often at the last minute, went back on mutually accepted agreements and wordings. Other examples abound.

The Soviet attitude contrasted sharply with that of the Japanese, who tried their utmost to please their counterparts. Thus, when the Japanese Diet passed the new law establishing a 200-mile fishing zone and a 12-mile zone of territorial waters, Suzuki went out of his way to explain the law to Ishkov, providing the text in both Japanese and Russian. In contrast, the USSR never officially informed Japan of Moscow's two decrees on the Soviet Union's 200-mile fishing zone; the Japanese learned about them through the Soviet news agency.[23] Gerald L. Steigel, an American specialist on negotiating with Communists who has conceptualized an ideal Soviet negotiating model (wherein Soviet aims are fully realized), writes that the Soviets wanted the adversary, or adversaries, "to come to a place selected by the USSR and at the time designated by it."[24] As the former British ambassador to Moscow, Sir William Hayter, advised, "Western delegations ought not to be at the mercy of their timetable."[25] Yet, despite this advice from Western experts, the Japanese negotiators in 1977 turned out to be the ideal adversary for the Soviets—being precisely at the mercy of the Soviet timetable. That is to say, the Japanese allowed the Soviets, quite one-sidedly, to decide, postpone, and reschedule the date and place of the Suzuki-Ishkov talks at the convenience of the USSR. In Japan, the *Sankei Shimbun* reported: "Suzuki, Minister of Agriculture, Forestry and Fisheries, was waiting patiently all day for a meeting with his Soviet counterpart Ishkov in the Japanese embassy."[26]

Next, we shall examine the cultural and psychological roots of this kind of arrogance and high-handedness in Soviet negotiating behavior. Almost all Western experts agree that Russian society is far more "rank-and-hierarchy-conscious" than Western societies—strange as that might seem for a state that prided itself in being the protagonist of the classless society. In Russian society, power determines rank from top to bottom, and a sense of subordination or superiority seems inescapable in Russian life.[27] To begin with, the Russian cult of power may derive from Russia's physical, political, and religious heritage. The vastness of the land and the cold, cruel climate have taught the Russians how powerless they are before nature.[28] A long tradition of authoritarianism, tsarist and Bolshevist, has also contributed to a feeling of powerlessness in the face of the political system. Likewise, the teachings of Orthodox Christianity have helped strengthen the belief that the unlimited power of the secular ruler should be accepted as absolute. Excellent reports on life in Russia such as Hedrick Smith's *The Russians* and Robert Kaiser's *Russia: The People and the Power*,[29] have offered abundant evidence that the cult of power and the belief in gigantism are strong among the Russian public. Smith, for example, writes that in Russia "bigness and power are admired almost without qualification. Size inspires awe—huge Kremlins, cannons, churchbells . . . huge dams, missiles. . . ."[30]

Psychology teaches us that masochism and sadism are two sides of the same coin.[31] So, too, is the submissiveness of Russians to the stronger or the superior quite easily converted into aggressiveness against the weaker or the inferior, especially since they also need an outlet for their long-pent-up psychological frustration. This is one reason why the Russians, having identified themselves with a strong leader (e.g., Stalin) or organization (e.g., the Communist Party) or state (e.g., the USSR), are sometimes very demanding and ruthless vis-à-vis the weaker party (e.g., Japan). Smith expressed his surprise upon hearing a Swedish diplomat talk about this Russian character trait and vent his bitter frustration at the short shrift given Sweden and other small nations by Moscow: "The Russians respect power. They deal with you Americans with respect because you have power, because there is something behind your words. But they don't deal with us [the Swedes] that way. We're not powerful. We're a 'little' country."[32]

"Nontactical Approach" vs. "Every Available Means"

Also significant during the 1977 fisheries negotiations was the difference in tactics used by each side. Whereas the Japanese rejected manipulative tactics as unnecessary or even counterproductive, the Soviets made full use of every possible device that might help them achieve their goal. I will elaborate.

Generally speaking, the Japanese are sensitive to a certain Machiavellian connotation attached to the term *tactics* and to other terminology familiar in the West, such as *maneuvering, leverage, manipulation*, and *bargaining*. This does not mean, of course, that the Japanese completely reject the concept of tactics in itself or deny the usefulness of tactics as a means to achieve objectives, as we shall see. It does imply, though, that Japanese are quite skeptical of the effectiveness of tactics employed in negotiation, especially those of a manipulative kind, which are perceived as risky, dangerous, or even self-defeating.[33] One Japanese saying goes like this: "He who likes to gamble is often defeated by his own cards [tactics]." Indeed, one frequently hears in Japan, "No better tactics than no tactics." Likewise, during the Japanese-Soviet fisheries talks in 1977, the comment was frequently heard on the Japanese side that Japan did not have any card to play against the Soviet Union. Japanese newspapers at the time were writing that "while the USSR has numerous cards in her hands, Japan has none,"[34] that "all the trump cards are held by the Soviets,"[35] that Japan had "no bargaining material whatsoever of any significance,"[36] and that "since Japan [is] without a trump card . . ."[37]

The Japanese prejudice against the use of tactics is at least partially derived from a conviction that when their demands are proper and reasonable, they should be accepted by the other side without any need to resort to tactics. In other words, few Japanese understand very well that diplomacy and negotiation are not matters of goodwill or good intentions. Negotiation is, in the words of Stanley Hoffmann, "a performing art"[38] that necessarily requires highly specialized skills and techniques. Philip E. Mosely, among the most experienced of U.S. negotiators, testified that "the Soviet negotiator does not believe in 'goodwill.'"[39] The Japanese negotiator, on the other hand, thinks that "goodwill" or a "just" position will eventually prevail simply because it is "good" or "just."[40] For many Japanese, right is might; not *vice versa*, as the Soviets seemed to believe. The Japanese negotiator's concern, then, is to let the other party in the negotiations know exactly where the Japanese stand; it boils down simply to a technical matter of accurate translation and transmission.

Japanese are also quite optimistic (or naive) on the matter of communication, holding the view that one's true intentions can eventually be correctly conveyed if one is ready to make every possible effort to explain one's position sincerely, patiently, and persistently.[41] The Japanese—who have long lived in a geographically very small country with a uniquely homogeneous people and language, enjoying a surprisingly free and swift flow of information—do not perceive language and other cross-cultural differences as very serious obstacles. Many Japanese believe that such barriers can be scaled if the negotiators try hard enough and talk frankly with their counterparts. "Where there is a will, there is a way"—so believe more than a few Japanese. Once, in 1956, Ichirō Kōno, one of the most powerful leaders in the Liberal Democratic Party (LDP), insisted on conducting direct, personal negotiations without an interpreter. His rationale was that the language barrier could be overcome by the mutual trust generated by sincerity and openness.[42] Some twenty years later, in 1977, both of Japan's chief envoys to Moscow, sent by the government to negotiate on fishing, expressed precisely the same belief. In interviews given before their departure from Tokyo, both Suzuki and Sonoda said: "Ishkov and I are old friends. He will surely understand Japan's position if we talk to each other straight from the shoulder."[43]

In practice, though, whether consciously or unwittingly, the Japanese undoubtedly do employ tactics. Otherwise they could never win. Tactics are necessary in negotiations, and, if one is attempting to carry out a specific policy or strategic objective, the choice of tactics may be the critical variable. As noted by another most experienced U.S. negotiator with the USSR, George F. Kennan, "It is axiomatic in the world of diplomacy that methodology and tactics assume an importance by no means inferior to concept and strategy."[44] Yet, even here one discerns a uniqueness in the kinds of tactics favored by the Japanese, compared with those preferred by other nations.

The favorite "tactics" employed by the Japanese are national solidarity and national sentiment. In Japan, a pluralist society, there are naturally those, especially fishermen, who maintain that today's fish are more important than territorial claims on the islands that might, in their judgment, never be satisfied anyway. In 1977, therefore, the Kremlin tried very hard to play Japanese fishermen against what the Soviets called "territorial irredentists," and the Ministry of Agriculture, Forestry, and Fisheries against the Ministry of Foreign Affairs. This Soviet strategy proved unsuccessful, however. The Japanese government was able to maintain solidarity and cohesion among the Japanese people, who remained firmly united behind the call, first, for both fish and islands and, in the final stage, for islands even at the cost of fish. Even the fishermen, reluctantly or not, agreed to follow the general policy, considering the territories more important to their national interest. Japan's political parties also united on this issue. Even the Japanese Communist Party (JCP) supported the ruling LDP[45] in its move to establish quickly both a 200-mile fishing zone and a 12-mile territorial sea limit. This kind of national solidarity in an emergency might be related to Japan's thousand-year-old rice-farming culture, requiring close cooperation by all during the growing and harvesting seasons.

The Japanese negotiators in 1977, striving to cope with strong Soviet pressure, also made a very interesting appeal to "national sentiment," summed up well by *Asahi Shimbun*: "There exists a Japanese national feeling in Japan, as there exists a Soviet national feeling in the USSR. If we badly hurt each other's national feeling, we cannot possibly establish genuine good-neighborly and friendly relations. The Soviet decision on a 200-mile exclusive fishing zone would inflict a long-lasting injury to the heart of the Japanese people. . . . We wonder what the Soviets think of, and how they evaluate this spiritual damage brought to bear on the Japanese ?"[46]

One might expect Soviet negotiators to apply their own peculiar kind of tactics, quite different from those employed by their Western counterparts. This was not the case. The Soviets used more or less the same methods as those practiced by Western diplomats, the real difference being that the former employed these techniques more methodically and regularly, while the latter use them unsystematically and infrequently.[47]

To put it another way, the Soviets were ready to utilize every possible means of achieving their goal, whereas their counterparts in the West were not. Soviet representatives were totally uninhibited in their tactics. The end justifies the means. Repetition, accusation, bluffing, warnings, threats, ultimatums, innuendo, "stonewalling," patient probing,[48] package deals, time limits—these are only a few items in the seemingly unlimited list of Soviet tactical devices. Still, there were certain tactics and gambits for which the Soviets seemed to have a special fondness and which they used with greater frequency. Bluffing—that is, the threat or display of force—is one of these. The Soviets seemed to be fascinated by this tactic, even in its brutal form, untouched by shame or remorse, simply because it appeared to them to be the most successful means of achieving their ends.

Soviet "force tactics" appeared to stem from a deep-rooted Russian tradition of inordinate respect for force. According to Richard Pipes, "The instant the Russian peasant leaves the familiar environment of personal contacts and becomes a stranger among strangers, he is likely to view the world as a ruthless fighting ground, where one either eats others or is eaten by them, where one plays either the pike or the carp and where force is one of the surest means of getting one's way." Thus, a Russian proverb says, "*Bei russkogo, chasy sdelaet* (Beat a Russian and he will make you a watch)."[49] Explaining how Russians and Americans differ sharply in their attitude toward power, but not necessarily because of their ideological differences, Hedrick Smith quotes the following from the Soviet dissident Pavel Litvinov: "You should understand that the leaders and the ordinary people [of the Soviet Union] have the same authoritarian frame of mind, Brezhnev and the simple person both think that 'might is right.' That's all. It's not a question of ideology."[50]

Several examples have already been cited to illustrate that the Soviets were particularly fond of displaying their powerful position and, in fact, made full use of that tactic throughout the 1977 fisheries negotiations with Japan. It was also during those negotiations that then Soviet Premier Aleksei N. Kosygin suggested to Sonoda that Soviet relations with Finland were a quite appropriate example for Japan. The implication was clear to the Japanese: the Soviets expected Japan to follow a neutral policy and to defer to the USSR, both in foreign and in domestic affairs, in the same way that Finland had been doing since the end of World War II.

Another favorite Soviet tactical weapon was the efficient use of "time" during the negotiating process. A special significance was attached to the time element by Lenin, who wrote "gaining time means everything"

(*Vyigrat' vremia—znachit vyigrat' vse*)."[51] One hardly need add that this Soviet conviction was ultimately based on the precepts of Soviet *Weltanschauung*, according to which the "correlation of world forces" was continually shifting in favor of the socialist states, led by the USSR.[52] It stemmed, too, from the Soviet political system, in which political leaders (and negotiators) were free both from parliamentary timetables and from public pressure to get things done by a certain date.[53] Still, the notion also seems to be heavily culture-bound. The same geographic and historical heritage (the long, hard winter and the long history of totalitarianism) that produced the Russian cult of power also yielded an astonishing endurance and patience. Whatever the background may be, observers sometimes wonder whether the Russians have a different concept of time from that prevailing in Japan and the West.[54] Unlike Japanese and Western representatives, who generally are eager to get things done as quickly as possible, Russians rarely seem to be in a great hurry. They do not appear to mind when negotiations drag on for months or years. A Russian can sit through meeting after meeting without getting anywhere, persistently repeating lines that others at the table already know by heart. Ambassador Hayter observed, for example: "They [the Russians] seem prepared to sit about indefinitely. . . . The Russians are prepared to go on, at meeting after meeting, producing again and again proposals that the West has repeatedly declared to be unacceptable."[55] Russians seem to consider this time-consuming procedure most useful, as if they believe the passage of time can work only to their advantage.[56]

During the 1977 fisheries talks, the Soviets tried hard to exploit the characteristic impatience of the Japanese people to complete a task once it was identified.[57] In the third round of the Suzuki-Ishkov talks, in April 1977, the Japanese side, in the face of interminable Soviet reiterations of the selfsame inflexible positions, finally submitted three proposals to the Soviets and asked the Soviets to choose the one that pleased them most. This impatience was criticized even in Japan as playing into the hands of the Soviets.[58] Yet, it cannot be denied that the Japanese side was then greatly pressed for time—if by May Japan had failed to reach agreement on the catch quota for salmon, Japanese fishermen would have completely lost their opportunity to catch salmon, for by then the salmon would have migrated into the Soviets' 200-mile zone.[59]

Another tactic that the Soviets almost never failed to apply in their negotiations was "divide and conquer." This tactic was also one of Lenin's favorite techniques, for he taught the Bolsheviks:

The more powerful enemy can be conquered only by exerting the utmost effort, and by the most thorough, careful, attentive, skillful and obligatory use of even the smallest "rifts" [*treshchiny*] between the enemies, any conflict of interests among the bourgeoisie of the various countries and among the various groups or types of bourgeoisie within the various countries, and also by taking advantage of any, even the smallest, opportunity of winning a mass ally, even though this ally is temporary, vacillating, unstable, unreliable and conditional. Those who do not understand this do not understand even the smallest grain of Marxism, of scientific modern socialism in general.[60]

Quoting the paragraph above in its entirety, Valerian A. Zorin emphasized in *The Fundamentals of Diplomatic Service* (1964 and 1977), a textbook that all Soviets in the foreign service were required to read: "V. I. Lenin's proposition on tactics for political battle also forms the basis for diplomatic tactics and all the activities of the [Soviet] Ministry of Foreign Affairs, and the [Soviet] embassies in various countries are based on this diplomatic provision."[61]

This Soviet tactic of "divide and conquer" may be profitably contrasted with the Japanese notion of national solidarity. In their tireless effort to undermine Japanese solidarity on the issue of the Northern Territories, for instance, the Soviets constantly repeated the theme that the Northern Territories movement was supported in Japan only by a handful of anti-Soviet reactionaries and revanchists. The Soviets also made full use of this technique during the 1977 fisheries negotiations. Soviet Minister of Fisheries Ishkov told representatives of Japan's major trade union federations, who were visiting Moscow, "There are *forces* in Japan that are trying to impose a political complexity on the talks about fishing" (emphasis added by H.K.). [62] "*Certain Japanese circles,*" Afornin noted, "have used difficulties as an excuse to wage a hysterical anti-Soviet campaign" (emphasis added by H.K.).[63] The Soviets stressed, however, that "the propagandist ballyhoo in the press and in certain Tokyo political circles over the Japanese-Soviet fisheries talks naturally reflects neither *the true interests of the Japanese people nor the true feeling of the broad strata of the Japanese public*" (emphasis added by H.K.). [64] "*The Japanese people,*" concluded the Soviets, "want to have true neighborly friendship with the Soviet Union."[65] *Pravda* correspondent Igor' A. Latyshev wrote:

Japan's fundamental interests demand the further broadening of good-neighborly ties and friendship with the Soviet Union. Wisdom is being shown by those representatives in Japan of the political and business worlds and also by public organizations who, in contrast to the bellowing anti-Soviets, are in favor of a persistent quest for mutually acceptable solutions and the preservation of an atmosphere of business-like cooperation. And the sooner these feelings predominate among the Japanese representatives at the talks, the sooner the way to their successful conclusion will be found.[66]

In their attempts to divide and conquer, the Soviets demonstrated a special interest in setting Japanese fishermen against those Japanese who were interested in the reversion of the Northern Territories. Indeed, Latyshev went out of his way to visit the city of Nemuro, in the easternmost part of Hokkaido—only a few kilometers from the disputed islands—to report that Japanese fishermen there were more interested in fish than in the territorial question. Latyshev's article of April 22 included the following account, which subsequently was strongly refuted[67] by the people of Nemuro:

> During long conversations with groups of fishermen from Habomai, Tomoshiri and Raos, none of them mentioned territorial claims against the Soviet Union. Instead, they all expressed a desire for good-neighborliness and the widening of day-to-day interaction with Soviet people living on the Kurile Islands and fishing alongside them in the waters of the Pacific Ocean and the Sea of Okhotsk. "We are interested in fish, not territory." This is the standard way many of the fishermen expressed their thoughts.[68]

Reactive vs. Initiatory Behavior

There is a great difference between the Russians and the Japanese in the way they proceed with negotiations once under way. The Russians often start by launching a strong offensive action; then they tend to retreat gradually in the face of strong resistance by the other side, frequently ending up with what amounts to a substantial compromise. The Japanese, on the other hand, follow almost the opposite behavioral pattern. They start reactively, unite themselves slowly, and then manage the crisis fairly well. Let us elaborate on this difference of approach.

Living in an amazingly homogeneous and harmonious society, the Japanese are neither accustomed to nor fond of direct confrontations or conflict resolution through argument. In contrast to the Russians, for whom conflicts of interest (or class struggle) are a normal part of life, the Japanese consider hostile conflicts of interest or of divergent viewpoints, except in an emergency or crisis, to be undesirable. Japanese usually try to postpone negotiations as long as possible, frequently deceiving even themselves with the excuse that the time is not ripe yet. It is no exaggeration to say that very often the Japanese do not start negotiations at all but, rather, are thrown into them.

The Japanese-Soviet fisheries talks in 1977 provide an excellent illustration of this conscious or unconscious unpreparedness on the Japanese side. Although some had already warned that it was only a matter of time before the great powers would declare their own 200-mile fishing zone, when the USSR declared its zone in December 1976, the Japanese were shocked by the news. They were totally unprepared. The headlines of Japan's newspapers bore witness to the national shock: "New Soviet Demarcation Line—A Life-and-Death Crossroads for Japanese Fishermen"; "Serious Shock"; "Heavy Damage to Fishing Industry"; "Out of Business and into Inevitable Bankruptcy"; "Everything Is Finished"; and so on.[69]

For a few months after the Soviet announcement, the Japanese government persisted with a quite passive attitude. In February 1977, the Ministry of Agriculture, Forestry, and Fisheries was reported to be still hesitant to send its minister Zenkō Suzuki to Moscow, on grounds that it would be dangerous for Japan to take action without being certain of the steps the Soviet Union would take next.[70]

The Japanese, however, do their utmost to solve a problem once that problem is faced. The late Masao Maruyama, professor of political science at the University of Tokyo, was quite right when he described the Japanese as a "goal-achieving nation" rather than a "goal-setting nation."[71] As an "open society,"[72] Japan—as was then emphasized by the powerful LDP leader Kiichi Miyazawa—enjoys an advantage that the Soviet Union did not have. The Japanese public can apprehend quickly and correctly the situation facing them. In the public learning process, the following were among the issues considered by the Japanese: "The efficient Japanese way of fishing is seriously threatening to deplete fishery resources throughout the world's oceans,"[73] and "the historical fishing quota does not guarantee much in today's 200-mile [limits]."[74] Positive proposals were also made. For example: "The Japanese should stop thinking that they are being one-sidedly victimized"[75] and "It is necessary to look at the other side's point of view and position in order to make the negotiations a success."[76]

This kind of gradual and free learning process among the Japanese culminates not infrequently in national unanimity and unity.[77] In 1977, as noted above, differences in emphasis between the Ministry of Agriculture, Forestry, and Fisheries and the Ministry of Foreign Affairs were gradually overcome. It is important to note that very few Japanese fishermen argued that their making a living by fishing was more important than the territorial claims of the whole nation—despite the excruciating cuts in catch quotas that they suffered, particularly the loss of high-priced salmon and trout, as a result of the prolonged negotiations on the territorial issue. Remember, too, that on April 18, the chairpersons of all the political parties, including the Japanese Communist Party, put aside their partisan differences for the moment in order to achieve national unity. These characteristics—most notably the voluntary sacrifice of personal interests for the sake of the national interest—are uniquely strong in Japan, where a long tradition of rice cultivation has required near-unanimous and complete cooperation at specific times of the year. Such total unity may be not necessary, for example, in wheat-growing or hunting cultures. This is not to deny that similar characteristics are common in Western liberal democracies. In contrast to the totalitarianism of Nazism, Fascism, and Communism, the voluntary amalgamation of individual wills into a national consensus permits pluralist democracies to make up later what they might have lost initially through surprise.

I would be remiss, however, if I did not add one final Japanese characteristic: Once negotiations are over, the Japanese tend to forget quickly the valuable lessons that were paid for at high cost. Instead, they tend to become preoccupied with the newest tasks immediately at hand, once again leaving themselves unprepared for the next round. One perceptive Japan watcher, Professor Bernard Gordon, thus observes rightly that, while known for their skill at devising immediate responses to immediate problems, Japanese foreign policymakers have not been very successful in developing long-term strategy.[78] This "unpreparedness–unity–forgetfulness" cycle may be ascribed, at least in part, to the Japanese national character, which has been shaped by the aforementioned rice agriculture and by seasonal natural disasters, particularly typhoons and earthquakes.

In contrast to the Japanese tendency to see harmony as the norm, the Soviets seemed to perceive constant struggle as a basic fact of life, as noted in the previous chapter. No doubt the origin of this Soviet *Weltanschauung* was closely related to one of the basic tenets of Marxism-Leninism, the class struggle, but it also stemmed from the Russian physical environment. Whereas the Japanese enjoy an ideal border (the sea) and the beauty and comfort of a mild climate with four marked seasons, the Russians lack such natural boundaries and are engaged in constant battle with a severe climate, especially with long, cold winters. If they relax for a moment, they might well lose not only their fortunes but their very lives.

It is not difficult to carry this logic a little further and suggest that the Russian *Weltanschauung* taught the Soviets that good offense was the best defense. Indeed, the Soviets tended to initiate unilateral surprise attacks against competing states, especially weaker ones. The purpose of such an offensive was to disorient the opponent, to intimidate him, and, through the *fait accompli*, to extract the maximum advantage at the lowest possible price.

The 1977 fisheries talks were no exception to this virtually immutable pattern of Soviet behavior. The USSR surprised Japan several times with its unilateral offensive actions. There was no better example of this than the abrupt announcement on February 24, 1977 of the Council of Ministers resolution that a 200-nautical-mile fishing zone would be put into effect in a week? Announced only four days before the scheduled arrival in Moscow of the Suzuki delegation, the resolution was a calculated Soviet move, intended to strengthen the Soviet position vis-à-vis Japan and to force Tokyo to negotiate with Moscow on the basis of this *fait accompli*.

Without a doubt, the best possible protection in such instances is sound preparedness—easier said than done. The next best defense is to show no sign of yielding. Only in the face of immediate counterattack does Russia resign itself to lesser demands and gradually take a more pragmatic view of things. Otherwise, the Russians most certainly take it for granted that their initial high demands are being accepted without major opposition or revision. True, the initial stance appears very firm—even final—but it must be realized that the Russians try to measure the opponent's determination and patience and to ascertain the exact point at which a real fight becomes inevitable. If they do not encounter strong resistance, the Russians will push their demands relentlessly in order to achieve maximum gain.

The Russian Way of Compromising

It is debatable that the Russians regard "compromise" or "concession" as a key concept in negotiation, or that in practice they make any compromises or concessions. They do not appear to attribute the same importance to these concepts as do Anglo-Americans, who view compromise as natural and even inevitable in negotiation, in which the central tenet is to reach an agreement by "accommodation of [conflicting] interests on particular matters."[79]

Strictly speaking, the concepts of "compromise" and "concession" did not exist in the Soviet vocabulary, as Philip E. Mosely wrote in his pioneering essay entitled "Some Soviet Techniques of Negotiation" (1951): "One of the difficulties of Soviet-Russian vocabulary is that the word 'compromise' is not of native origin and carries with it no favorable empathy."[80] "To the Russians, who traditionally think that in negotiations, whether commercial or political, sheer power will always prevail and the weaker party must perforce submit," compromise, says Hedrick Smith, "is an Anglo-Saxon concept that assumes a rough equality. It does not arise instinctively in the soul of Russian officialdom. For the Russians, the instinctive question is: who is the stronger and who is the weaker. Inherently, any relations become a test of strength."[81] The Bolshevist doctrine of the class struggle reinforced this traditional Russian way of thinking. Thus, Russian doctrine is noted for its "distaste for compromise,"[82] and, as Mosely further reported, the word "compromise" is "alien to the Bolshevist way of thinking . . . habitually used only in combination with the adjective 'putrid.'"[83] For the Russians, concessions, especially appeasement, are "signs of weakness."[84] In fact, Lenin condemned concessions as "tributes to capitalism."[85] Nikita S. Khrushchev once stated: "They [the West German politicians] say: 'With the USSR one must negotiate as follows: concession for concession!' But that is a huckster's approach! . . . We do not have to make any concessions because our proposals have not been made for bartering. We act on the principle that sensible solutions must be found. . . . Those who really strive for peace must not use methods of petty bargaining in talks."[86] Confirming the former Soviet First Secretary's attitude, Arthur M. Schlesinger, Jr., who had been engaged in negotiations with the Soviets in the capacity of advisor to President John F. Kennedy, cited the words of Khrushchev in his memoirs: "He [Khrushchev] objected to the language of commercial bargaining so often used in dealing with the Soviet Union— 'you give this and we'll give that.' What was he supposed to concede?"[87]

Yet Soviet history and writings also reveal many cases in which Soviet negotiators altered substantially their original positions and entered into the adjustive and accommodative process of compromise.[88] Otherwise, there would have been no purpose in negotiating with the Soviets. Moreover, the extraordinary development of nuclear weapons made the Kremlin realize that to stop an endless arms race it must negotiate seriously with the West and hence make the compromises or concessions necessary to reach agreement. Consequently, the negative Soviet view of compromises and concessions pointed out by Western Soviet watchers during the Cold War period (of which Mosely's article is a typical example) no longer colored Russian public pronouncements. Instead, around the late 1950s, Soviet spokesmen suddenly started to argue that compromise was inevitable in diplomatic negotiations. O. V. Bogdanov, for example, wrote in his book *Negotiations Are a Basis of Peaceful Settlement of International Problems* (1958):

> Negotiations presuppose a mutual search for solutions acceptable to both sides, mutual concessions and compromises, because only by way of such methods is it possible to eliminate disagreements between sovereign, independent states. In the process of international cooperation, states have to enter mutual concessions and compromises. But these must be reciprocal, of mutual advantage, and voluntary.[89]

The Soviets' change of attitude toward compromise in diplomatic negotiations coincided with their adoption of "peaceful coexistence" as the general foreign policy line in 1956. Almost equating the necessity of making compromises in negotiations with the policy of peaceful coexistence itself, some Soviet spokesmen at that time went so far as to state: "Without such compromises, there can be no peaceful coexistence. He who denies compromise, denies peaceful coexistence as well."[90] Thus, one may consider that the concept of compromise then obtained a legitimate place in Soviet vocabulary. For instance, in his textbook, Zorin declared that *"the use of a variety of compromises* in the course of international negotiations is the most important method of socialist diplomacy, guaranteeing peaceful solution of the disputed problems" (emphasis in original). [91] The General Secretary Brezhnev is quoted in Strobe Talbott's *Endgame: The Inside Story of SALT II* (1979) as having said on the evening before the signing of this agreement: "Of course, [the treaty] is a compromise. It could not be otherwise. Each side would like some parts of the text to be somewhat different, more suitable from its own standpoint. But each side has had to yield something, taking into account the legitimate interests of the other side."[92]

Granting that Russian diplomacy in the post-Stalin era[93] not only approves of and justifies the concept of compromise but makes use of it in practice, one should not fail to discern certain specific features of the Russian approach to compromise. First, the Russians regard compromise simply as a means, or to put it more bluntly, a tactic of their foreign policy conduct. The following passage, usually cited by Russian spokesmen in an effort to justify their argument that Lenin taught them the importance of compromise, revealed above all else their tactical approach to the concept. The founding father of Bolshevism wrote in *"Left-Wing" Communism—An Infantile Disorder* (1902):

> In the question from the Frankfurt pamphlet, we have seen how emphatically the "Lefts" have advanced this slogan ["No Compromises!"]. It is sad to see people who no doubt consider themselves Marxists, and want to be Marxists, forget the fundamental truths of Marxism.

> It would be absurd to formulate a recipe or general rule ["No compromises!"] to suit all cases.

> After all, the German Lefts must know that the entire history of Bolshevism, both before and after the October Revolution, is *full* of instances of changes in tactics, conciliatory tactics and compromises with other parties, including bourgeois parties! [emphasis in original]

> To carry on a war for the overthrow of the international bourgeoisie . . . and to renounce in advance any conciliation or compromise with possible allies. . . is that not ridiculous in the extreme? Is it not like making a difficult ascent of an unexplored and hitherto inaccessible mountain and refusing in advance ever to move in zigzags, ever to retrace one's steps, or ever to abandon a course once selected and to try others?[94]

Because such writings have not made any secret of the fact that Russia views compromise (*kompromiss*) or concession (*ustupka*) as a "diplomatic tactic" (*diplomaticheskaia taktika*),[95] some Western observers rightly observe that in reality Russians "do not regard any compromise as a permanent solution."[96] Two Western observers, Bryant Wedge and Cyril Muromchew, wrote that since principles are inviolable for the Russians, no concessions are permissible. Therefore, the Russian equivalent for compromise is to be found in bartering, especially when quantitative values are involved. Any concessions have to be on a *quid pro quo* basis.[97] In conclusion, Wedge and Muromchew wrote, "When the Soviets do seem to make a concession they make every attempt to point out that their basic position has not changed and all the correct principles have been preserved."[98] To illustrate their point, they quote the following statement made by a Soviet representative, Semen K. Tsarapkin: "We deem it necessary to stress that the Soviet proposal is in no case a departure from the Soviet Union's fundamental approach to the question."[99]

Second, it is not very useful to discuss in abstract form whether Russia makes compromises. Rather, a more appropriate way of addressing the question is *when, under what circumstances,* and *in what fields* of negotiations the Russians are willing or likely to make compromises. It has been reported that in negotiations dealing with such matters as strategic nuclear weapons; space programs; trade and other economic exchanges; science; technology; ecological and environmental well-being; and cultural, academic, and athletic exchanges, Russia is, relatively speaking, more likely to make compromises and concessions than in other areas.[100] In these fields the Russians frequently emphasize such words as "mutuality" (*vzaimnost'*), "mutual benefit" (*vzaimovygodnost'*) or "mutual interdependence" (*vzaimozavisimost'*).[101] On the other hand, regarding subjects that touched upon the legitimacy of the Soviet system and the fundamental interests of the Soviet Union, the Kremlin seldom agreed to yield to any degree whatsoever. Examples of such subjects are the political security of the Soviet system, dissident issues, the strategic security of the Soviet Union, and East European affairs. Criticizing the Western understanding that "détente" was, or ought to be, of a "comprehensive" nature, Dimitri K. Simes, a former member of the Institute of World Economy and International Affairs (IMEMO), at the Soviet Academy of Sciences, drew our attention to the Soviet conception of compromise and détente with the West:

> It does not seem, however, that from the Soviet standpoint there can be any compromise when the most fundamental security interests are involved. In this sense, détente is widely perceived as a shield to protect the Soviet states and Soviet clients. In no way does the Kremlin interpret detente as authorization for the West to interfere in Soviet domestic affairs or to exert greater influence in Soviet-dominated Eastern Europe.[102]

The Russian approach varies also according to the country the Russians are dealing with; they demonstrate a relatively flexible and compromising posture toward the United States but take a different line with less powerful nations, including Japan, with which Russia has often negotiated from a position of strength.

A third characteristic of Russian compromise is to take this course only at the last moment, when there is no other alternative. Michael Blaker, former professor at the University of Southern California, wrote: "Because the Soviet diplomats have fewer perceived nonvital and therefore expendable interests, concessions are made reluctantly and grudgingly, only when all else has failed."[103] According to a painstaking study by Lloyd Jensen, professor of international relations at Temple University, in the postwar disarmament negotiations with the United States, the USSR made 75 percent of its concessions *during the last third* of the seven rounds of negotiation under scrutiny, while the United States made 82 percent of its concessions *in the first third* of the same talks.[104] Some Western students of Russian negotiating behavior call this trait a "departure time decision."[105]

Fourth, the Russians surprisingly have been known to alter their position after protracted negotiations—making a 180-degree turnabout from their previous stand—with no concern that they might be accused of inconsistency. This feature of Russian behavior has been pointed out by many Westerners who have negotiated with the Russians. Foy D. Kohler, a former Ambassador to Moscow, wrote: "More than once, lengthy, laborious, acrimonious, and seemingly hopeless negotiations [which had spanned] months and years without any sign of progress *ended in sudden agreement within a matter of hours*" (emphasis added by H.K.).[106] Hayter pointed out that the Soviets did not mind changing their position drastically because of their "lack of inhibitions about consistency."[107] Similarly, another former U.S. Ambassador to Moscow, Charles Bohlen, was quoted as saying that the men from Moscow were never troubled by consistency and "close their books at the end of every day."[108]

Finally, in contrast to Japanese "forgetfulness" after the event, the Soviets by no means thought that the agreement with which the 1977 negotiations culminated meant an end to the struggle for their best interests. This should come as no surprise, since, according to the "Soviet bible," negotiations with capitalist countries could lead only to temporary agreements.[109] The Soviets might sometimes "withdraw," but they must never "yield."[110] They would continue to fight by searching for opportunities to alter the agreement or to make it a dead letter.

3. Negotiating Behavior and Cultural Similarities: Non-Western "Rules of the Game"

Japan and Russia also share similar attitudes and behaviors with respect to negotiations. I will limit myself to mentioning just a few of them.

First of all, neither Russian nor Japanese negotiators are necessarily inclined to perceive the other party as an equal. Yet, to negotiate as equals is a fundamental starting point in the Western concept of negotiation. As has been most clearly shown by Professor Emeritus Chie Nakane at the University of Tokyo in her book *Japanese Society* (1972), Japanese are most accustomed to ranking other people as either seniors or juniors, and only very rarely as equals. When it comes to dealing with other nations in the international arena, Japanese seem to find it difficult to free themselves of this "ranking consciousness," to use Nakane's phrase.[111] Projecting their national structure of human relations onto the international stage, the Japanese tend to regard themselves either as inferior, and thus weaker (e.g., vis-à-vis the Western nations and the USSR), or as superior and stronger (e.g., vis-à-vis the smaller Asian countries). As discussed above, the Russians are also extremely conscious of rank and hierarchy, tending to regard others, both individuals and nations, as either inferior or superior to them.

Second, neither the Russians nor the Japanese show much interest in the give-and-take bargaining so common in Western, primarily Anglo-Saxon, negotiating practice.[112] The Russians and Japanese tend to let their demands or concessions escalate almost without limit, depending upon the leniency or toughness of the opposition. Philip Mosely, from his personal experience with Russian negotiators, told us that Russian representatives are incredulous when told that "an agreement is reached through a give-and-take of views, by which no side gets its full position and each gets a part of it."[113] Similarly, Sir William Hayter, observing that "the Russians always negotiate for victory," added that it never seems to occur to them that "the proper objective of a negotiation is not to defeat your opposite side but to arrive at an agreement with it which will be mutually beneficial."[114] Nor do the Japanese seem to have become accustomed to the rules of a game that were developed mainly in the Western diplomatic world. They tend to perceive negotiations as a sort of war, which they must either win or lose, as indicated by the titles of two of the few Japanese books published in 1977 on the subject of the Japanese-Soviet negotiations: "The 200-Mile Fish *War*" and "The 200-Mile *War*."[115]

Third, the Russian and Japanese approaches toward compromise are similar. Since each side is firmly convinced of the righteousness of its own position,[116] neither party is disposed to compromise at all.[117] In practice, however, they have no choice but to strike a compromise, and a favorite technique employed by both in order to save face is what the Japanese call *tamamushi-iro*,[118] which refers to the insect *Chrysochroa elegans*, whose color changes depending on the angle of the observer. By analogy, *tamamushi-iro* is a diplomatic solution reached through a vague, ambiguous, and generalized agreement that can be interpreted quite differently by each side. The Western expression that comes closest in meaning to *tamamushi-iro* is the notion of a "gray area."[119] Typical of such a solution is the famous passage in the October 1973 Japanese-Soviet Joint Communiqué stipulating that "the two sides realize that unsolved problems have existed since the end of World War II."[120] Japan interpreted this passage as including the territorial problem; the USSR did not. Again, in the 1977 fisheries talks, Moscow and Tokyo agreed to a *tamamushi-iro* solution. The article inserted into the Soviet-Japanese Interim Fishing Agreement, finally concluded on May 24, 1977, is worth quoting again: "No provisions of this agreement can be construed so as to prejudice the positions . . . of either government . . . in regard to various problems in mutual relations." By limiting application of the agreement to fishery problems, both sides sidestepped differences over the disputed islands.[121] With the inclusion of this article, both Tokyo and Moscow managed to separate fishing problems from the territorial issue. Acknowledging this, Andrei P. Markov, a Soviet specialist on Japanese affairs, conceded: "These agreements maintain the position that none of the provisions should impair the position of the Soviet Union or Japan with respect to the *territorial* status of the four Kurile islands" (emphasis added by H.K.).[122]

To sum up, neither the Japanese nor the Russian people have yet adopted the Western notion of negotiation, the rationale of which is "accommodation of conflicting interests through realization of a common interest" based on the principle of "mutuality at any level."[123] This, of course, does not mean that the Japanese or the Russian way of negotiating is necessarily inferior to the Western approach. Such a conclusion would be premature. Rather it must be stressed that quite a few countries in the world have been negotiating, and will continue to do so for quite some time, in a different way from that of Western nations. It is important that these non-Western sociocultural patterns be further studied and better understood.

Chapter 7

The Conclusion of the Japan-China Peace Treaty (1978)

1. The Significance of the Treaty for the Soviet Union

On August 12, 1978, after six years of frequently interrupted negotiations, the Treaty of Peace and Friendship was finally concluded between Japan and the People's Republic of China (PRC). Moscow had opposed the treaty, particularly because it contained the so-called "antihegemony" clause, which in Beijing's parlance was directed against Soviet hegemonism and expansionism.[1] The treaty itself—a general statement of five broad principles—did not constitute a serious threat to Soviet security.[2] Yet, both the symbolic and, hence, the political significance of the treaty signing at that time should not be underestimated. Its negative impact upon the Soviet Union was significant. Let us start this chapter by briefly discussing this.

First, from the international perspective, or at least the perspective of the Asian regional power constellation, the rapprochement of the two powers, the PRC and Japan, accompanied by the blessing of another power, the United States, meant almost automatically a tremendous blow to the remaining fourth power, the USSR. The impact upon the USSR was more than doubled by another diplomatic blow immediately thereafter—the Sino-U.S. normalization in January 1979. A Western observer on Asian affairs, Professor John J. Stephan at the University of Hawaii, suggested that neither the Sino-Japanese nor the Sino-American normalizations came necessarily as a surprise to the Soviets, but conceded that Soviet analysts did not envision "a simultaneous Sino-Japanese and Sino-American rapprochement without any corresponding attenuation of Japanese-American ties."[3]

One theory argues that the conclusion of the Beijing–Tokyo peace treaty in 1978 was a part of the U.S. global strategy, particularly promoted by the Carter-Brzezinski team. If we accept such a theory, as do some Western observers and Soviet spokesmen,[4] we must also admit that the Soviet Union fell victim to this ploy.

Second, the treaty clearly signaled a Chinese victory over the Soviets in their bitter rivalry to court the Japanese.[5] Japan and China had begun efforts to improve their relations far later than Japan and the USSR, but they had been able to move ahead quickly. Relations between Japan and China were normalized in 1972, and only six years later, the two nations concluded a peace and friendship treaty. In contrast, Japan and the USSR, despite their early normalization of relations in 1956, had not yet concluded a peace treaty, largely because of Moscow's highly inflexible and insensitive attitude toward Japanese feelings about the recovery of the "Northern Territories." Japan's signing of a peace treaty with China also signaled a manifestation of Tokyo's decision of "let us do first what we can do now, leaving other matters until later," but by the same token meant that the Tokyo government *de facto* had discarded one of its diplomatic principles—its "equidistance policy" toward the two Communist rivals. In an attempt to justify the shift in Japan's major foreign policy line, Sunao Sonoda, at that time Foreign Minister of the Fukuda government, replied in the Diet (Japanese parliament): "We will seek an understanding from the Soviet Union of Japan's intention to pursue a policy toward China separate from that toward the USSR."[6] The Fukuda government was reported by *Asahi Shimbun* to be according the PRC a priority in policy second only to the United States. As the paper stated under the headline "The New Starting Point of Japanese Diplomacy":

> Although it is based on the principle that Japanese-U.S. relations constitute the basis of Japanese foreign policy orientation, the Fukuda diplomacy has revealed that it gives first priority to its relations with the PRC in Asia. That is, the "all-dimensional diplomacy" advocated by Prime Minister Fukuda does not mean an "equidistance policy" to all countries but rather presupposes that there naturally exists a difference in the degree of closeness with regard to relations with different nations.[7]

Furthermore, the conclusion of the peace treaty contributed to closer and friendlier relations between Japan and China. Previously, being a neighboring communist giant, the PRC had been regarded as one of the sources of threat to the security of Japan, but, with the signing of the peace treaty, it almost ceased to be a potential adversary to Japan. This meant that Japan no longer had an excuse for not cooperating with China in many areas. While Japan was still trying very hard not to let improved bilateral relations turn into a military alliance, despite strong pressure from China, it nevertheless found it difficult, even in the defense area, to decline a minimum level of exchange and contact, such as the exchange of personal visits and information. In economic fields, where Japan and China were no less complementary than were Japan and the Soviet Union, trade and other economic exchange between Japan and the PRC gained further momentum the signing of the peace treaty, which provided a legal, public, symbolic endorsement and encouragement of stable and developing economic relations. In their efforts to woo Japanese capital, technology, and management knowhow for the development of their less-developed economies, China and the Soviet Union were in the position of competing against each other in a manner which was not necessarily completely, but was at least partially mutually exclusive, particularly given the fact that Japan's capital and other economic capabilities were not unlimited. In this regard, China's success meant a loss for the Soviet Union.

Last, the signing of the Treaty of Peace and Friendship helped to enhance Japan's diplomatic and economic position. In the postwar period from 1945 to 1978, Tokyo's diplomacy faithfully followed Washington's lead,[8] and Japan sometimes found itself in the awkward situation of being compelled to abruptly alter its policy line after encountering a "shock." (The best example of this was the "Nixon shock" in the early 1970s—the U.S. failure to inform Tokyo in advance of U.S. President Nixon's impending visit to Beijing despite repeated assurances to Tokyo by successive U.S. administrations that the United States would support the Taiwan regime and not the Beijing regime.) By concluding a treaty with China before Washington could, however, Tokyo must have derived a silent satisfaction that this time it was not kept behind but, on the contrary, was even able to demonstrate diplomatic initiative and independence to a certain degree, although this Japanese decision and action was, according to some interpretations, endorsed, encouraged, and even urged by the Carter-Brzezinski administration.[9] In September 1978, after the signing, Prime Minister Takeo Fukuda told the Diet that "Japan has entered a new era in which it can no longer be content with reacting passively to what takes place in the world."[10] Moreover, he continued, "The time has come for Japan to play an active role in world peace and prosperity,"[11] assuming that "the conclusion of the Sino-Japanese peace treaty will contribute to peace and stability in Asia and the world."[12] The *Baltimore Sun* at that time noted that, "having finally played ball with the big boys and won an inning after a long diplomatic low profile since its defeat in World War II," Japan had found its self-confidence.[13]

The largest benefit that the signing of the treaty brought to Japan was the reduction of the military threat from the PRC. Another benefit to Japan was the Chinese pledge to abrogate the 1950 Sino-Soviet Treaty of Friendship, Alliance, and Mutual Assistance, which was directed specifically against "Japan and any states allied with it." Deng Xiaoping told Sunao Sonoda that China was ready to take the necessary steps to annul the treaty with the USSR; and within the year, in April 1979, the PRC carried out this promise. This was a milestone for postwar Japanese diplomacy, which had been aiming at rectifying the unfavorable conditions and situations created by the Allies and other countries at the end of World War II. In sum, Japan's successful rapprochement with China left the former free to concentrate on the only major diplomatic task left over from World War II—namely, improvement in its relations with the Soviet Union, resolution of the territorial dispute, and complete termination of the "state of war."

It is debatable whether the signing of the peace treaty with Beijing contributed to the enhancement of Tokyo's diplomatic leverage with regard to Moscow. Some observers of international affairs argued that compromise, or what the Soviets called "capitulation,"[14] on the Japanese side to the Chinese demand to include the "antihegemony" clause in the main body of the treaty helped make the Japanese position vulnerable vis-à-vis the Soviet Union, which sought in turn to obtain a similar compromise or "capitulation" in its own favor. Others, including the Japanese government, argued that it was China that made a concession in agreeing to insert in the treaty the so-called "third countries" clause, which states expressly that the treaty shall not affect "the position of either contracting party regarding its relations with third countries" (Article 4). Since Japan had made such a painstaking effort to include this provision in the main body of the treaty in order to mollify Soviet apprehension, the Tokyo government did not have to feel a strong sense of guilt toward one of the third countries, the Soviet Union.

What was also pointed out by some, including Soviet spokesmen,[15] was that Japan's signing of a peace treaty while shelving the issue of the Senkaku (*Diaoyu* in Chinese) Islands, which are claimed by Tokyo, Beijing, and Taipei, provided a precedent that the Soviet Union might attempt to use in Japanese-Soviet peace treaty negotiations. Others, however, pointed out that the circumstances of the two territorial disputes were so different that the same formula could not be used: First, the Soviet Union had denied even the existence of the territorial issue—a fact that made the Soviet claim to shelve the question logically contradictory. Second, the Senkaku islands were *de facto* controlled by Japan, and hence the Chinese suggestion of maintaining the status quo by shelving the issue until "a future generation has the wisdom to settle it peacefully" (Deng Xiaoping)[16] coincided with the Japanese interest, whereas the Northern Territories were *de facto* occupied and controlled by the Soviet Union and hence maintaining the status quo would benefit only the Soviet Union.

Regardless of which of these arguments may be correct, a clear byproduct of the conclusion of the Sino-Japanese treaty was the fact that, after the conclusion of the treaty, the Japanese appeared to have more self-confidence than before in their dealings with the USSR. Having done fairly well in dealing with one of the two Communist powers, the Japanese in general appeared to feel that one more *Vergangenheitbewältigung* would not be very difficult if they concentrated their entire diplomatic effort on the task. This self-confidence was a new phenomenon, in which some observers detected the birth of Japanese nationalism.

2. Soviet Attempts to Prevent the Signing of the Treaty

The conclusion of a peace treaty between Japan and the PRC became a pending issue for Tokyo and Beijing as a result of the Sino-Japanese Joint Communiqué of September 29, 1973, which stipulated that the two nations should conclude such a treaty to improve relations with each other.[17] Nevertheless, the signing of a Sino-Japanese Treaty of Peace and Friendship was delayed for six years for a variety of reasons, the major ones of which are as follows. First, given that diplomatic relations had already been normalized between the two countries, bilateral administrative agreements on such concrete matters as trade, civil aviation, shipping, and fishing were regarded as more urgent.[18] Second, both Japan and China were preoccupied with their own domestic political problems and crises (on the Japanese side, the "Lockheed bribery scandal," and the weak and unstable transitional government under Takeo Miki; on the Chinese side, the Cultural Revolution; the deaths of Zhou Enlai and Mao Zedong, and the arrest of the "Gang of Four," to mention just the most pressing), which made it difficult for them to be engaged in serious diplomatic discussion.

Third, opposition by the Soviet Union toward such a treaty made Japan reluctant to proceed with treaty negotiations until it could be assured that the signing would not impair the Japanese position with regard to the Soviet Union.

The basic Soviet attitude toward a peace treaty between Japan and the PRC can be summarized by the following propositions: (1) Both Japan and China were completely free to do whatever they wished in their bilateral relations, into which any third countries, including the USSR, had neither the right nor the intention to interfere. (2) However, if the bilateral treaty did contain something unfavorable or damaging to the interest of any third country, including the Soviet Union, that third country reserved the right to decide its attitude toward that treaty.[19] Moreover, in order to protect its own interest, the Soviet Union made it clear that it would not hesitate to take certain measures, such as: (i) changing its policy toward Japan, which might exert an adverse effect upon Soviet-Japanese relations, including the postponement of negotiations on a series of still unresolved issues between the two countries; and (ii) taking "retaliatory countermeasures." (3) Therefore, Tokyo had better think very carefully before making a decision to conclude such a treaty, so that Japanese interests would not be damaged. This was the crux of the Soviet message conveyed *prior to* the signing of the treaty. Let us examine in more detail the Soviet pronouncement containing this warning, and some practical measures taken by the Soviets to prevent the treaty, in chronological order.

When most of the bilateral administrative agreements mentioned above had been concluded by the fall of 1974, Japan and China became serious about negotiation of the peace treaty. Since Kakuei Tanaka, who had been friendly with China and was in fact, in his capacity as Japanese Prime Minister, the major architect of the 1972 normalization of bilateral relations on Japan's side, had to resign from the premiership due to his involvement in a bribery scandal, the start of the peace treaty negotiations was further delayed. The new Japanese Prime Minister, Takeo Miki, instructed Fumihiko Tōgō, Vice-Foreign Minister, in January 1975, to start preliminary talks with the Chinese Ambassador to Tokyo, Zhu Zhen; but the negotiations were immediately deadlocked, largely due to different views on the question of the "antihegemony" clause.[20] Being fully aware of the implications of the "antihegemony" clause for the Soviet Union, the Kremlin reacted promptly when Japan and China started the negotiations. On February 3, 1975, Oleg A. Troianovskii, then Soviet Ambassador to Tokyo, visited Etsusaburō Shiina, Vice-President of the ruling

Liberal Democratic Party (LDP), and urged the LDP government to hold off on concluding any peace treaty with China containing such a clause. He threatened Shiina by saying that the conclusion of such a treaty would have "undesirable repercussions" upon relations between the USSR and Japan.[21] On February 13—the eve of the third-round meeting between Tōgō and Zhu—the Soviet Ambassador visited Premier Miki himself and handed him a personal message from Soviet President Leonid I. Brezhnev. In that message Brezhnev repeated the Soviet official proposition that between the USSR and Japan there should be concluded not a peace treaty but instead a Treaty of Good-neighborliness and Cooperation.[22] The Kremlin was calculating to kill two birds with one stone. The conclusion of a Treaty of Good-neighborliness and Cooperation would enable the Soviets to make a political breakthrough in the long-stalemated relations between Japan and the USSR, while sidestepping the territorial question. It would also counterbalance the peace treaty between Japan and China.[23] Miki instantly rejected Brezhnev's offer, insisting that only a peace treaty that settled the territorial dispute would be considered.[24]

This flat refusal, however, did not deter Moscow from making further efforts to dissuade Tokyo from proceeding in peace treaty negotiations with Beijing. A decisive action came with the statement made by the Soviet Foreign Minister Andrei A. Gromyko. During his five-day trip to Tokyo in January 1976, Gromyko verbally conveyed the official Soviet position to Japanese Prime Minister Miki and Foreign Minister Kiichi Miyazawa; i.e., the Japanese demands regarding the Northern Territories were "unfounded," and that no territorial dispute existed between Japan and the Soviet Union.[25] The Soviet envoy also expressed the Soviets' concern about the ongoing negotiations on a Sino-Japanese treaty.[26] Despite Gromyko's warning, however, Miki announced in a statement made immediately after the Soviet minister's departure that his government would make an effort to conclude a peace treaty as soon as possible with China.[27] The Soviet mass media continued to warn that the conclusion of the proposed peace treaty between China and Japan would inevitably complicate "the bilateral relations between the USSR and Japan."[28] *Izvestiia*, for example, bluntly stated on both July 18 and 19, 1976 that the Soviet Union "would have to draw the necessary conclusions and amend its policy vis-à-vis Japan" if Japan entered into a treaty with China that included an antihegemony clause.[29] A few days later, *Krasnaia zvezda* (*Red*

Star) also published a similarly harsh statement that such a treaty between Japan and China "would have an adverse effect on Soviet-Japanese relations."[30]

The most threatening word, "countermeasures" (*otvetnye mery*), appeared for the first time on November 26, 1976, two days before Prime Minister Takeo Fukuda, Miki's successor, decided to have Shōji Satō, Japanese Ambassador to Beijing, investigate the possibility of resuming peace treaty negotiations with Chinese authorities. An article under a pseudonym in the Party organ *Pravda* stated that the USSR would be entitled to take countermeasures to protect its own interest should Japan conclude a peace treaty containing an antihegemony clause:

> Japan, whether she so wishes or not, will enter the path of complicating relations with third countries . . . because the latter on their side would be entitled to take *countermeasures* if China and Japan take action on the plan that Beijing has been trying to push. . . . Such action would turn out to have a negative influence upon Soviet-Japanese relations as a whole. . . . Japan would take upon itself serious responsibility for the consequences of its inception (emphasis added by H.K.).[31]

From then on, the threat of "countermeasures" was frequently used by the Soviets in their attempts to prevent Japan from signing the treaty with China. For example, on May 30, 1978, Aleksei P. Shitikov, the chairman of the Council of the Union of the Supreme Soviet, declared in his meeting with a delegation of Japanese journalists headed by Tomoo Hirooka, chairman of the *Asahi Shimbun*: "If a treaty containing an antihegemony clause is concluded, the Soviet Union will, as a *countermeasure*, change its policy toward Japan" (emphasis added by H.K.).[32] This was the first time a high-ranking Soviet such as Shitikov, who represented the Supreme Soviet, made public the Soviet position of possible adoption of countermeasures in connection with the Japan–PRC treaty. The chairman further threatened: "If things go that way, settlement on a series of pending problems between Japan and the Soviet Union will be delayed."[33] Shitikov concluded his remarks by saying: "Consequently, a major modification of the Soviet policy along this line will be inevitable, and Japan will likely be confronted with extremely severe problems in politics, economics, diplomacy, and all other areas."[34] On June 19, the new Soviet Ambassador Dmitrii S. Polianskii, handed Japan's Deputy Foreign Minister Keisuke Arita a note, which, according to TASS, warned that Moscow could not remain indifferent to the signing of the treaty.[35] A week later, on June 24, 1978, Vladimir L. Kudriavtsev, political commentator for *Izvestiia*, also warned Tokyo against signing a peace treaty with China, writing: "The Japanese must understand that in case of a further deepening of anti-Soviet tendencies in Japanese foreign policy, the Soviet Union would be obliged to take *countermeasures* for the protection of its interests" (emphasis added by H.K.).[36]

3. Japan's Responses and the Assessment of Soviet Policy

The Japanese government seemed to have reached the conclusion by June 1978 that it was unlikely that the Soviet Union would retaliate sharply against Japan if a peace treaty with China was concluded. For example, on June 23, 1978, when informed of the Soviet refusal to hold talks on Japan–Soviet joint fishing ventures, Sonoda reportedly remarked that he did not consider such a Soviet action to be a "retaliatory measure," based upon his assumption that the Soviets would not take any action whatsoever against Japan in connection with the forthcoming conclusion of a peace treaty with China.[37] The Japanese government seemed to have examined in advance all of the retaliatory measures that the Soviet Union might take to show its displeasure in practical terms.

A series of rumors had surfaced and were circulating at that time in Japan, speculating on the possible forms of Soviet reprisal against the Japanese.[38] The first of the rumors speculated that the Soviet government might have reduced or even entirely broken off its diplomatic relations with Japan. For instance, Moscow might have closed down the Soviet embassy in Tokyo or the General Consulate in Osaka or in Sapporo and might have withdrawn some or all of the Soviet diplomats from these offices, requesting that Tokyo do the same in its Soviet outposts. Another form of Soviet reprisal considered at that time was that the Soviet Union might have adopted a more menacing military posture toward Japan, stepping up maneuvers in waters surrounding Japan or overflying Japanese territory, thus creating incidents with Japanese shipping.[39] The worst possible scenario was that the Soviet military forces might have been tempted to try a limited surprise attack against Japan, for instance, by landing on Rebun and/ or Rishiri Islands off the northwestern coast of Hokkaido.[40] It was thought that the most likely retaliatory measures might be of an economic nature. The Soviet Union might have denied or restricted Japanese access to the rich fishing waters within the 200-mile fishing zone and off its Pacific coastline. Moscow might also have severely limited its trade and economic relations with Tokyo and even shut out Japan from participation in economic development projects in Siberia and the Far Eastern part of the USSR. Furthermore, if it had wished, the Kremlin easily might have frozen or reduced personnel, cultural, academic, and athletic exchanges with Japan.

After careful consideration, however, the Fukuda government came to the conclusion that none of these options should be particularly feared by Japan, on the grounds that they would certainly have backfired for the Soviet Union. Most politicians and government officials in Tokyo agreed that it would be unlikely for the Kremlin to be so foolish as to dare to undertake such self-defeating actions. If it had, they thought, then it would have been a clear example of Soviet "hegemonic" behavior, which would have only succeeded in pushing Japan further into a possible U.S.–China–Japan alliance. It was even considered that once the Sino-Japanese peace treaty was signed, the Soviet Union would be compelled more than ever to improve its relations with Japan in order to catch up with the Chinese. We shall return to this subject again later in this section in order to discuss whether or not the Japanese diagnosis was correct.

As to the question of how effectively the Soviet threat of retaliation and other coercive strategies worked to prevent Japan from signing the treaty, one may say that the Soviet results were mixed. The Kremlin was successful in three ways.

First, it succeeded in delaying the signing of the treaty. The reasons for the six-year delay between the Sino-Japanese Joint Communiqué (1972), which stipulated a continued negotiation for a peace treaty, and the signing of a Sino-Japanese Peace Treaty (1978) were, as previously noted, not to be ascribed solely to the opposition expressed by the Soviet side. At the same time, however, it is quite obvious that if the Soviets had not been so antagonistic toward the insertion of the antihegemony clause into the treaty, the treaty would have been concluded at a much earlier date. Second, Moscow was successful in getting "the third countries" clause inserted in the main text of the treaty, despite the fact that at one time the Japanese government was simply thinking of declaring verbally or in a different document the content of this clause. The clause states that "the treaty shall not affect the position of either country regarding its relations with third countries" (Article 4). In a sense, this article neutralized to a certain degree Article 2 dealing with antihegemonism—which though without explicitly mentioning the Soviet Union—which was clearly anti-Soviet in its thrust. If Moscow had not pressed so hard, it is conceivable that Tokyo would not have worked as hard as it did to insist to the Chinese that this "third countries" clause was absolutely necessary. Third, Moscow was also successful in making some, though not all, Japanese feel that Japan should next make a more serious effort to improve relations with the USSR. True, the Tokyo government's official position was that by concluding such a treaty with Beijing, Japan in no way impaired its relations with the Soviet Union. But it was also true that many Japanese felt at that time that Japan might have leaned toward China rather than the USSR through signing the treaty with the PRC, thereby deviating from its traditional even-handed diplomatic approach toward the two neighboring Communist nations—a situation that, according to some Japanese, ought to be rectified by a positive overture from the Japanese side to the Soviet Union. Such a feeling might not have been awakened if the Soviets had not waged an intensive campaign expressing their strong displeasure and opposition to the Sino-Japanese treaty. From this perspective also, the Soviet pressures proved to be both effective and successful.

On the other hand, when viewed from a different perspective, the Soviet strategy was not very successful. In the first place, the Soviet Union failed, after all, to prevent Tokyo from signing a peace treaty containing an antihegemony clause with the PRC. Though the Soviet Union was unable to block the conclusion of the treaty, it could have, as a second choice, further delayed Japan's signing. However, the Soviet Union was unable to do so because it mishandled its relations with Japan, as will be shown in the next section. Lastly, if it had managed more skillfully, the Soviet Union could have taken full advantage of Japan's signing of the peace treaty by, for example, persuading Japan to conclude a peace treaty, or some other treaty, with the USSR. The next question, then, is why the Soviets failed to achieve these objectives.

4. Why the Soviets Failed

The answer to this question seems to lie in the inappropriateness of the Soviets' basic attitude and strategy toward Japan. The Soviet approach toward Japan at that time was greatly inept, inflexible, unimaginative, and heavy-handed. Soviet strategy also proved to be the same old one, i.e., simply to keep pressing hard on Japan, with a threat of force and without, on the other hand, providing any alternative or attractive incentive whatsoever to encourage a change of policy on the part of Japan.

True, generally speaking, the Soviets found themselves in a handicapped position, compared to the Chinese, in their relations with the Japanese. To begin with, from the perspectives of race, language, religion, and cultural backgrounds, the Chinese are much closer to the Japanese. Although the affinity in these areas sometimes draws the two nations apart, as discussed previously (in chapter 1), once nations of such similar affinities start moving toward establishing closer relations, the achievement and speed of such a development is greatly accelerated compared with similar efforts by nations without such affinities. To make matters worse for the Soviet Union, the recent history during and immediately after the Second World War turned the sentiments of the Japanese public toward the Chinese, while the Soviets were regarded as an alien and potentially offensive people. Since the Japanese military invaded China and committed numerous atrocities against the Chinese people, many Japanese have retained a strong feeling of guilt toward the Chinese, which they have hoped to relieve by making overtures of kindness when the chance arises. During and even after the postwar peace treaty negotiations, many Japanese, particularly elderly citizens, held the following opinion: "In order to compensate for what Japan did to the Chinese before and during World War II, we want to do our utmost to help them now to succeed, especially in their modernization program." The Soviets were, in marked contrast, viewed by most Japanese as a nation that "stabbed Japan in the back" by declaring war against Japan in violation of the Japan–Soviet Neutrality Pact, just when Japan was about to surrender, and seizing the Northern Islands after Japan's surrender. Undoubtedly, this bitter history contributed to the Japanese ill-feeling and suspicion toward Soviet behavior and their feeling that the Soviet Union should have shown a sign of goodwill first if it wanted to improve its relations with Japan. The results of all public opinion polls conducted in Japan in the postwar period have shown clearly that the Japanese have quite contrasting feelings toward these two neighboring nations.

If the Soviets really wanted to improve their relations with Japan, great efforts on the part of the Soviet Union were necessary to overcome those handicaps mentioned above. Then, for its part, Japan, despite its different sentiments toward the two nations, had been trying hard diplomatically to maintain an "equidistance" policy toward the two states. Undoubtedly, the Soviets found this even-handed policy advantageous and useful for them and interested in having Japan continue that diplomacy. Yet, what was notable about the Soviet actual behavior toward Japan is that the Soviet Union did not show any intention whatsoever of providing any incentive for Japan to maintain such a policy.

Moreover, the Soviet Union was engaged in behavior that helped push Japan further toward China. The following steps in the Soviets' counterproductive "coercive diplomacy"[41] were taken without concurrently offering any incentives for Japan to make possible alternative decisions: (1) The Soviet Union let Japan know clearly that no conciliatory attitude could be expected from the Soviet Union on the Northern Territories issue; (2) the Soviets renewed their campaign to put pressure on Japan to accept the Soviet proposal for a Treaty of Good-neighborliness and Co-operation as a substitute for a peace treaty, the major Soviet objective being to sidestep the territories issue; and (3) the Soviets tried to harass and threaten Japan with continued military buildup and large-scale military maneuvers in the vicinity of Japan, both of which were intended not only to demonstrate Soviet displeasure but also to put pressure on Japan in its negotiations with China. Let us examine these examples.

5. No Concessions on the Northern Territories Issue

Moscow made it clear that it did not intend to make any concessions whatsoever to Tokyo on the Northern Territories issue. Whether deliberately or coincidentally, the timing of the announcement of the Soviets' renewed firm intention to refuse to participate in any talks on the Northern Territories issue coincided with the start of peace treaty negotiations between Japan and China.

After the Brezhnev-Tanaka summit meeting in Moscow in October 1973, many Japanese had nourished for some time a hope that the Soviet Union would resume negotiations on territorial questions with Japan. They hoped that after the 17-year interval since the 1955–1956 negotiations in London and Moscow, the Soviets might even decide to return the four disputed islands to Japan. This expectation was based on the Japanese interpretation of the Brezhnev-Tanaka talks, in which the Soviet General Secretary finally made a concession to the Japanese over the islands issue.

The Japanese interpretation of the Brezhnev-Tanaka summit meeting was based largely on the following three events. First, the full text of the speech given by the head of the Japanese delegation Prime Minister Kakuei

Tanaka on October 9, 1973, which included a part mentioning "the largest unresolved problem between Japan and the USSR, i.e., the territorial problem," was printed in the major Party organ *Pravda* the following morning.[42] In the previous 17 years, no such statement of the Japanese position had ever been made public in the Soviet Union. Second, upon the request of the Japanese, Brezhnev agreed to insert into the text of the joint communiqué a paragraph that read: "Both sides confirmed that the settlement of *the yet unresolved problems left over from World War II* [*nereshennye voprosy ostavshiesia so vremen vtoroi mirovoi voiny*] would contribute to the establishment of genuine good-neighborly and friendly relations between the two countries" (emphasis added).[43] Most Japanese understood the "yet unresolved problems left over from World War II" to mean the "Northern Territories problem," since, for the Japanese, there were no other unresolved problems left over from World War II between the two countries. Third, Prime Minister Tanaka himself and a few Japanese diplomats who were present and witnessed the Brezhnev-Tanaka meeting on October 10, 1973, unequivocally reported after the meeting that, when asked for confirmation by Tanaka whether the Northern Territories question, in Soviet understanding, was included in those "yet unresolved problems," Brezhnev replied twice in the affirmative. As Tanaka himself put it in an interview:

> In the last summit meeting on October 10, we focused on the question of how to deal with the territorial problem. Both sides have now finally confirmed that the Northern Territories issue constitutes a yet unsolved problem left over from the War, which is to be resolved by the conclusion of a peace treaty, as expressed by the Joint Communiqué. I asked General Secretary Brezhnev, "Can I be sure that the most important problem among the yet unsolved problems left over from World War II is the problem of the islands of Habomai, Shikotan, Kunashiri, and Etorofu?" "That is right," the General Secretary replied. "I want to confirm that," I said once more, and the General Secretary replied, "That is correct." The same reply was given twice.

With General Secretary Brezhnev's words, there had finally come a breakthrough in the position the Soviets had maintained over the past seventeen years that "the territorial question has already been solved," and negotiations on the Northern Territories issue could now be resumed.[44]

However, shortly after the Tanaka-Brezhnev summit meeting in October 1973, the Kremlin leaders seem to have had second thoughts and started to alter their position by denying the fact that it involved any concession to Tanaka. The following are conceivable explanations for this shift in policy:

(1) The Kremlin leaders may have felt that the Japanese position had been weakened by the oil crisis in late October, precipitated by the Arab-Israeli conflict, and the following worldwide economic recession from 1974 to 1976. They may have considered that a resource-poor country like Japan, which would be severely affected by the oil embargo and subsequent energy crisis, would find itself compelled to take a more conciliatory and less-demanding stance toward the resource-rich USSR.

(2) The second explanation is the Soviets' conceivable assessment of Kakuei Tanaka. It has often been pointed out by Western observers of Soviet negotiating behavior that the Soviets showed their inclination to negotiate more seriously with strong, determined political leaders, regardless of their political or ideological orientations. An illustration of this tendency is the fact that the Soviets preferred to deal with Richard Nixon or John F. Kennedy rather than with Dwight D. Eisenhower.[45] Similarly, it is conceivable that the Kremlin leaders in 1973 may have thought that they could make a deal with Tanaka, a young, dynamic and even charismatic political leader with a very strong domestic power base in Japan. Based on this assessment, the Kremlin leaders treated Tanaka very well during his stay in Moscow and even indicated that later they could negotiate more seriously on a peace treaty. However, Tanaka was unexpectedly compelled to leave the top decision-maker's position in Japan, due to the disclosure of his involvement in a bribery scandal. He was replaced by a very weak prime minister, Takeo Miki, in December 1974. With Tanaka's disappearance from the Japanese premiership, the Soviets' hope of involving Japan more actively in the development of Siberia also faded away. This expectation was once high in Moscow and, in part, accounts for some of the conciliatory political gestures shown by Brezhnev before and during Tanaka's visit to Moscow.

(3) The third interpretation argues that from the start the Soviets had no intention whatsoever of making any concessions on the territorial issue to the Japanese, including Tanaka. What the Kremlin leaders did instead was to make sporadic political gestures that they expected the Japanese to interpret as a shift in attitude. To put it in simpler terms, the Kremlin leadership was aiming to exploit the Northern Territories question as leverage to draw political, strategic, and economic concessions from Japan. These manipulative tactics on the islands issue seem to have

worked well with Tanaka, since the Japanese Prime Minister agreed that, in a sort of exchange for the inclusion of the clause "yet unresolved problems" (Article 1), the clause on Soviet-Japanese economic cooperation (Article 2) would be included in the joint communiqué. In the latter clause, the Japanese government pledged to help Japanese private enterprises to develop economic exchanges with the Soviets and to promote the development of Siberia and the Far Eastern region of the USSR. This clause in the communiqué triggered a "Siberian boom" in the Japanese business community. With the government's endorsement, in April 1974, the Japanese Export-Import Bank granted for the first time to the Soviet Union $1.1 billion in long-term credit for construction costs, machinery, and other equipment. Following Tanaka's visit to Moscow and the signing of the communiqué, large Japanese-Soviet joint economic projects began in Siberia and the Soviet Far East. The Southern Yakut coal project, the Yakut natural gas project, and the second round of the timber-resources exploitation project, were all started in 1974. It is no wonder that P. D. Dolgorukov, a Soviet specialist on Soviet-Japanese economic relations, wrote that the "direct result" of Tanaka's visit to Moscow in 1973 was of "great significance," marking a "qualitatively new stage" of development for Soviet-Japanese "*trade and economic relations*" (emphasis added by H.K.).[46] After Moscow obtained what it wanted from Japan, however, it was natural to the Soviet Machiavellian way of thinking to start to retreat from the concessions made by Brezhnev to Tanaka.

(4) The fourth interpretation is actually just speculation, due to the lack of any evidence, concerning the internal power struggle in the Kremlin. It was speculated that some members of the Politburo were critical of the concession made by Brezhnev to Japan. They may have felt that this concession was too big, or even unnecessary, and so pressed him hard to cancel it.

Whatever the background reasons may be, the Kremlin leadership decided sometime between October 1973 and September 1975 that it was necessary to resolutely dispel the interpretation entertained by the Japanese that the Northern Territories problem constituted the most important of the "yet unresolved problems left over from World War II." Writing an authoritative article in the September 1975 issue of the Party's major periodical *Kommunist*, Soviet Foreign Minister Andrei Gromyko officially called Japan's claim to the islands "unfounded" (*neobosnovannyi*). He also stated that Japan's demands would inevitably encounter their "proper rebuff from our side."[47] This flat refusal of the existence of a territorial problem became the official Soviet line, from which Moscow did not waver for a long time. Confirming his Foreign Minister's statement, the Party General Secretary himself brushed aside Japan's request to discuss the matter, thereby naturally alienating the Japanese further. In his speech addressed to the 25th CPSU Congress in the spring of 1976, Brezhnev unequivocally stated that Japan's demands concerning the "Northern Territories" were "unfounded and unlawful" (*neobosnovannye i nezakonnye*).[48] On June 5, 1977, the General Secretary repeated the same argument in his interview with Shōrū Hata, editor-in-chief of *Asahi Shimbun*: "To say that in the relations between our countries there are some yet unresolved territorial problems is a one-sided and erroneous [*odnostoronee i nevernoe*] interpretation."[49]

6. Proposal of a Substitute Treaty

During Japanese Foreign Minister Sunao Sonoda's visit to Moscow in January 1978, Soviet Premier Aleksei N. Kosygin categorically denied Sonoda's claim that there were any unsolved territorial problems between the USSR and Japan. The following day, Soviet Foreign Minister Gromyko spurned Sonoda's request for talks on the island issue, on the same grounds. In addition, Gromyko forced his Japanese counterpart to receive the draft of a Soviet-Japanese Treaty of Good-neighborliness and Friendship, which the Kremlin leaders apparently saw as a reasonable substitute for a formal peace treaty, since the former proposed to shelve the territorial question whereas the latter would not. When the Japanese government ignored the draft, the Soviets unilaterally printed the contents of the draft in the February 24, 1978 issue of *Pravda*.[50]

At least four points rendered the draft of the treaty humiliating, and hence unacceptable, to Tokyo: (1) nowhere in the draft of 14 articles was mention made of the territorial question; (2) the draft required *de facto* abrogation of the U.S.-Japanese security treaty, a condition that was, of course, out of the question for Tokyo, and one that Beijing did not request when it concluded the peace treaty with Japan; (3) an article on the so-called "security consultation in emergency cases" gave rise to both indignation and fear on the part of the Japanese, who found a similar article only in treaties that the USSR had negotiated with its "allies" in Eastern Europe or with "developing" countries like Afghanistan, Vietnam, India, Bangladesh, Iraq, and Ethiopia; and (4) there was no article referring to the possible termination of the treaty, which even Soviet-Vietnamese and Soviet-Ethiopian treaties contained.

Such a proposal, even as a simple draft for negotiation, was unacceptable to the Japanese government, which firmly maintained that a "peace treaty" that solved the territorial question and signified the real end to World War II had to be signed before further cooperation between Japan and the USSR could be discussed.[51]

The contents of the Soviet draft gave many Japanese the impression that in Soviet eyes Japan was ranked not with Western European countries such as West Germany and France but rather with Czechoslovakia or Afghanistan. A Japanese expert on Soviet affairs was reported as saying, "The Soviets are mixing up Japan with some of those East European countries, like Poland, Hungary, and Finland."[52] Haruo Okada, one of the senior members of the Japan Socialist Party (JSP) and then Vice Speaker of the House of Representatives, was furious about this draft proposal and stated the opinion that the Soviet proposal indicated an intention to "Finlandize" Japan.[53]

In his press interview after these meetings in Moscow, the Japanese Foreign Minister Sonada was quoted as saying that he was "dissatisfied" with the uncompromising Soviet position on the territorial questions. He stated that the negotiations seemed to have taken a "step backward."[54] This situation led many Japanese to the conclusion that no matter how long Japan might have waited for a flexible Soviet posture on the territorial question, it would have been a waste of time. Hence, the Tokyo government had no choice but to go ahead and conclude a peace treaty first with China, leaving negotiations with the Soviets for a later stage. Having become convinced that for the time being no further progress could be expected on the underlying territorial disputes with the Soviet Union, Sonada announced shortly after his return home from the Soviet Union that Japan would reopen peace treaty talks with China.[55]

A Reuter reporter regarded Soviet behavior at that time as "a riddle," because the Kremlin leaders must have known in advance that such an inflexible strategy would be self-defeating and would only push Japan further into Chinese hands. As he put it:

> The blunt Kremlin's rebuff of Japan's territorial claims has posed an intriguing riddle about Soviet strategy in the Far East. Against expectations, Soviet leaders took a tougher stance in rejecting the "Northern Territories" issue. The Soviet "Nyet (No)" in itself surprised no one, but the Kremlin went a step further this time by refusing even to acknowledge that there were still some unresolved problems with Japan.[56]

Many other Western specialists on Asian affairs made similar observations and conclusions. Commenting on the Soviets' counterproductive diplomatic stance, Daniel Tretiak, a professor at York University, Canada, stated: "The Russians' interest would have been better served had Moscow been more receptive to Japanese claims to the islands."[57] Mira Sinha, political scientist, also described the Soviets' uncompromising posture on the islands issue as the major cause of Moscow's failure in its attempt to obstruct the signing of the Sino-Japanese Peace Treaty containing the antihegemony clause. Sinha observed: "It [Moscow] failed principally because it was highly inflexible on the territorial issue and underestimated Japanese feelings about the recovery of the Northern Territories."[58] It is assumed that at the time even some Soviet *mezhdunarodniki* (specialists in international relations) and *institutniki* (researchers in the area research institutes attached to the Soviet Academy of Sciences) did not consider politically clever the Kremlin's policy with regard to Japan's negotiating and signing of a peace treaty with the PRC. Galina Orionova, a former Soviet research specialist in Japanese affairs at the ISKAN, for example, disclosed a very intriguing episode as follows. In 1978, Soviet scholars from several institutions met in great secrecy to examine the threat posed by Sino-Japanese rapprochement. They all agreed, according to Orionova, that it was a mistake to continue treating the Japanese as inferiors and that they were not militarists and could not be denied their right to deal with China on their own terms. However, Orionova continued, the Party took no notice. The Sino-Japanese treaty was signed, and the Japanese officially protested against Soviet intrusion into their affairs.[59]

In sum, in order to prevent Japan from concluding a peace treaty with the PRC, the Soviet Union attempted to exert great pressure on Japan in every possible way. This pressure included a warning from Moscow that the Soviet Union would take some "countermeasures" in order to protect its own interests. However, by resorting to a menacing posture without making any constructive or acceptable counterproposals, the Soviets sabotaged their own efforts to block negotiations on the Japan-China Treaty of Peace and Friendship, which was signed on August 12, 1978 in Beijing. The treaty became effective on October 23, after the exchange of the instruments of ratification in Tokyo.

7. The Soviets' Immediate Reactions

One can say, as did some observers in the West, that the conclusion of the Sino-Japanese Treaty of Peace and Friendship was indeed as drastic a blow to Soviet foreign policy in Asia as any the Soviets had encountered.

To put it more simply, the USSR was "a net loser" vis-à-vis this treaty.[60] One thing that we have to keep in mind, however, is that, as Nathan Leites repeatedly wrote in his massive work on Bolshevist psychology and strategy, *The Study of Bolshevism*, "the Soviets may retreat occasionally, but it does not mean that they yield."[61]

Once the treaty was concluded, Soviet policy had to be based on the *fait accompli*. Generally, the rapid change, or about-face, that the Kremlin leadership demonstrated on such occasions has not often been executed by other regimes. This observation supports the argument that Russian foreign policy has been oriented not so much toward a particular strategy as to the current opportunities or situational judgments.[62] The Soviets tended to change their position drastically, in the words of former British Ambassador to Moscow Sir William Hayter, "because of their lack of inhibition to inconsistency."[63] Be that as it may, the basic objectives of the USSR vis-à-vis Japan in the wake of the Sino-Japanese Treaty were to: (i) minimize the negative impact of the peace treaty on Soviet interests; (ii) obstruct any further development of Sino-Japanese relations, especially the development of the treaty into a military alliance; and (iii) take full advantage of the conclusion of the treaty to push the Japanese government to make political and diplomatic concessions to the Soviet Union, including the conclusion of certain treaties with the USSR. Let us elaborate on these three Soviet objectives.

It seems evident that, following the conclusion of the peace treaty between Japan and the PRC, the Soviet Union endeavored as much as possible to downplay the significance of the treaty. Although the USSR, on the one hand, protested officially about the Sino-Japanese treaty, the Soviet media and spokesmen on the other hand began in reality to tone down their previously sharp reactions.[64] In the words of Avigdor Haselkorn, senior strategic analyst at the Analytical Assessments Corporation, in California, the Soviets were attempting to "reduce the attractiveness of the Sino-Japanese ties to [both] signatories,"[65] or, in the words of Peggy L. Falkenheim, to "limit or minimize the damage."[66]

Concretely, Moscow found it necessary to redefine the Sino-Japanese treaty for both domestic and international audiences as actually less anti-Soviet in character. Having predicted such a diversionary approach, Kuniko Miyauchi, a professor at the National Defense College in Tokyo, had stated, prior to the conclusion of the treaty: "While emphasizing the anti-Soviet nature of the Sino-Japanese Peace Treaty prior to its conclusion, the Soviets will have to later pretend that it is not very anti-Soviet. Is it a dilemma? Yes, they will yet be drawn into the position that the treaty does not necessarily mean the formation of an anti-Soviet alliance."[67] One can easily imagine the difficulty the Soviets had in interpreting the treaty as not being a serious threat to the USSR, since they had hitherto maintained a position that a significant threat was inherent in the treaty. However, if one also recalls the startling shift or about-face of the Soviet Machiavellian adjustment to similar instances in the past—as illustrated, for example, by the conclusion of the Treaty of Rapallo and the German-Soviet Non-Aggression Pact—the harsh realities of this Russian *volte face* are more easily understood.

This does not necessarily imply that the Kremlin underwent this radical policy change overnight. The change in Soviet assessment of the efforts by the Japanese, for instance, to "weaken" (*oslabit'*) or "neutralize" (*neitralizovat'*) the anti-Soviet character of the treaty, took place only gradually and subtly. The immediate Soviet reaction was harsh. Only hours after the treaty was signed in Beijing on August 12, the Soviet official news agency TASS declared that the antihegemony clause was "of an openly anti-Soviet character," seeing that "[Japan's] illusions about the possibility of weakening the dangerous character of the Beijing version of the treaty [by including the 'third-countries clause'] have been doomed to failure."[68] On the following day, a major news organ of the Soviet government, *Izvestiia*, made a similar comment: "The Japanese government is attempting to claim that the dangerous nature of the treaty has been neutralized by the insertion of Article Four. . . . However, the Chinese Minister of Foreign Affairs himself has made it clear that Sino-Japanese antihegemonism is the very core of the treaty. Japan surrendered to the Chinese pressure to sign the treaty on Chinese terms."[69] The playing-up of the antihegemony clause continued for some time. On August 15, 1978, Iurii Bandura, *Izvestiia* correspondent to Tokyo, was still writing as follows:

> In attempting to weaken the criticism against the treaty, the Japanese government sought to include in the treaty articles envisaging that "the treaty will not influence the position of either of the contracting parties in relations with third countries". . . . However, the importance of this reservation is to a considerable extent undermined by the unquestionable fact that, yielding to Beijing's importunate demands regarding the inclusion of an article on countering hegemony in the treaty, the Japanese ruling circles are providing an opportunity for the Chinese leadership to interfere in Japan's policy in questions concerning its relations with other countries.[70]

In an article in *Novoe vremia* dated three days later, G. Krasin, a Soviet specialist on Japan, also noted: "The Japanese government declares that the treaty does not present a danger for neighboring countries insofar as it contains an article that allegedly neutralizes the provision on opposition. . . . However, these excuses are nothing more than putting a good face on the matter."[71]

The first official reaction of the Soviet government to the treaty was expressed in a note transmitted by Boris Zinov'ev, the Soviet chargé d'affaires in Tokyo, to the Japanese Foreign Ministry on August 23. (Ambassador Dmitrii S. Polianskii had left Japan, presumably with the aim of demonstrating Soviet displeasure with and protest against the Sino-Japanese negotiations and in order to have direct consultations with the Kremlin leaders.) The note warned that Japan would be held responsible for any complications that might arise as a result of Tokyo's action. It was also emphasized in the note that Moscow could not remain indifferent to Japan's signing of the treaty and would take the necessary action to protect its interests.[72] It is worth nothing, however, that this official protest by the Soviet government was conducted only in the form of a *note verbale*.

Although the USSR was not a signatory of nor a direct participant in the Sino-Japanese peace treaty, the Chinese side never hid the fact that the antihegemony clause in the treaty was directed against the "Northpole bear." The Japanese side, however, strongly hoped that the Soviets would not interpret the treaty in the same way as the Chinese did. It was exactly at this divergence of interests between the Chinese and the Japanese that the Soviet Union, despite being a third party, found a pretext to interfere and to maneuver for its own interests, employing a very thick-skinned and yet, admittedly, a very skillful policy.

8. Japan As a Victim

To begin with, particularly after the conclusion of the Sino-Japanese peace treaty, the Soviet Union increasingly demonstrated a tendency to regard the Japanese as unwary victims of the conspiratorial designs of the Chinese. Although Soviet commentators admitted, on the one hand, that the Sino-Japanese peace treaty became possible because the basic interests of the ruling classes of both the PRC and Japan were identical and hence compromises between them were possible, they also pointed out that the treaty would not have been concluded if Washington and Beijing had not exerted great "pressures" on Tokyo.[73] The conclusion of the treaty was the result of the scheme by Washington and Beijing to lure Tokyo into accepting the U.S. and Chinese diplomatic design of anti-Sovietism. The Soviets thus started to emphasize that Washington and Beijing were more responsible than Tokyo for the conclusion of this treaty directed against the Soviet Union, even implying that the Japanese merited some sympathy from the Soviets.

There was no doubt on the Soviet side that the United States played a significant role in precipitating the Sino-Japanese negotiation process on the peace treaty. The major motivations of the Carter administration in doing so, in the Soviets' judgment, were the United States's interest in: (i) "exploiting Beijing's anti-Sovietism for its own objectives,"[74] (ii) "weakening Japan's relations with the Soviet Union,"[75] and (iii) "sounding out the degree of tactical receptiveness of Beijing's diplomacy."[76] For these reasons, according to the Soviets, Washington "pushed Tokyo and Beijing toward conclusion of the treaty," thereby "saving the negotiations from collapsing."[77] Underlining U.S. pressure on Japan's final decision to sign the treaty, *Pravda* wrote on August 25, 1978: "Now it has become clear that the Japanese side has capitulated. As noted by the foreign press, Japanese diplomacy long withstood attempts to chain Japan to the anti-Soviet chariot. But the situation fundamentally changed after Brzezinski's visit to Beijing and then to Tokyo."[78] In his memoirs, entitled *Power and Principle: Memoirs of the National Security Advisor (1977–1981)*, Brzezinski wrote about the pressure that he exerted upon the Japanese government to sign the treaty:

> I was struck in the course of my conversation with Hua Guo Feng, and the issue also arose with Deng (Xiaoping) and Huang (Hua), that the Chinese were frustrated by lack of progress in negotiating the Chinese-Japanese friendly treaty. The obstacle was Japanese unwillingness to offend the Soviets by including in the treaty the so-called antihegemony clause. . . . Accordingly, and *on my initiative*, when briefing Prime Minister Fukuda in Tokyo, immediately after my departure from Beijing, on the substance of the American-Chinese talks, *I made it a point to urge both him and Foreign Minister Sonoda to go ahead with the treaty*, with the clause in it. I pointed out to the Japanese that the clause mentioned no state, and it could, theoretically, apply to China, to the United States, or anyone else. More important, I made it clear to them that the United States did not object to the inclusion of that clause and that *it favored an expeditious conclusion of the treaty. I believe this statement, including more than subtle encouragement, did impress the Japanese*, and shortly thereafter they ac-

ceded to the treaty, with the clause included in it. I subsequently reported on *my initiative* to the President, and he approved. Till then, the State Department had been leery about it"(emphasis added by H.K.).[79]

The Soviets did not fail to point out the pressure exerted on the Japanese also by China. The article in *Pravda* quoted above, for example, also criticized the PRC: "The slogan of joint struggle against hegemony has another objective: that of drawing other countries into the orbit of Beijing's foreign policy course. In this specific instance, as we can see, Japan has fallen into this snare. Japan essentially has been subordinated to Beijing's dictates."[80] Criticism of the PRC continued in the article: "Japan, intentionally or unintentionally, has found itself in the position of objectively cooperating in the implementation of the conspiracy of the Chinese leadership's foreign policy."[81] In the evening edition published that same day (August 25, 1978), *Izvestiia* concluded that the inclusion in the treaty of the antihegemony clause was, as everybody saw it, nothing but "[Japan's] yielding to pressure from Beijing."[82]

What is to be noted next is the fact that the Soviets shifted to a position of an even more positive assessment of Japan's effort to *neutralize* the anti-Soviet character of the treaty. This shift can be clearly detected in the same Soviet publications that appeared approximately a year after the conclusion of the Sino-Japanese peace treaty. In these works, written and compiled in 1979, Dmitrii V. Petrov, head of the Japan section of the IDV, tried skillfully to reverse the weight of two articles in the treaty, i.e., Article 2 ("the antihegemony clause") and Article 4 ("the third countries clause").

First, whereas Petrov simply summarized Article 2, he quoted verbatim Article 4, which stipulates: "The present treaty shall not affect the position of either contracting party regarding its relations with third countries."[83] Second, and more importantly, Petrov interpreted the wording of Article 2 on antihegemony as "a significant retreat from Beijing's original demands" for close cooperation between China and Japan.[84] Third, Petrov emphasized that "the third countries clause" was added "owing to the strong request from the Japanese side."[85] "Because of these amendments, Petrov argued, the capability of Beijing, which had attempted to form a bloc with Japan predicated on anti-Sovietism, as reflected in the antihegemony clause, was restricted to a considerable degree."[86] In an article published in 1981, Mikhail G. Nosov, another Soviet *institutnik* at ISKAN, specializing in Japan China relations, also stated that "Beijing made some concessions to Japan."[87] Completely reversing the previously prevailing Soviet view that the inclusion of the "third countries" clause (Article 4) did not neutralize the "antihegemony" clause (Article 2), Nosov concluded that Article 4 did in effect "neutralize" (*neitralizovalo*)[88] Article 2. Whether this reversal is to be ascribed to the lapse of time or to some other reason (e.g., diversity in the views of Soviet spokesmen) is hard to determine.

Concurrent with this effort to reinterpret the Sino-Japanese peace treaty in light of its lessened anti-Soviet nature, the Soviets did not fail to stress at the same time that there still existed a number of significant differences between Japan and China, despite their treaty ties.[89] Asserting that the "Sino-Japanese Peace Treaty was not successful in resolving serious contradictions between these two countries," Petrov enumerated in his book *Japan Today* (1979) the following four problem areas: (i) imbalance in economic and trade relations between Japan and China—that is to say, an inevitable deficit in China, which lacked sufficient capital, especially in hard foreign currency, to pay Japan for products, plants, and other imports; (ii) political and strategic contradictions between Japan and China, both of which were competing for influence in Asia; (iii) the still unresolved "Senkaku Islands" question; and (iv) the "Taiwan" issue.[90] It is interesting to compare such parts in Petrov's 1979 book with parts in his earlier publications, for instance, *Japan in World Politics* (1973), which also listed four points of divergence between Tokyo and Beijing. Three of those mentioned in the 1973 book are identical to those in his 1979 book: (i), (ii) and (iv).[91] However, his 1973 book emphasized the conflicting attitudes of China and Japan with regard to the USSR. It stated that while Japan had been pursuing the so-called "equidistance policy" toward the USSR and the PRC, China had been definitely opposed to such a line of policy. It is then significant that Petrov's 1979 book completely omitted this point, because the situation had obviously changed, thus making such statements in the 1973 book outdated. In his 1979 book, that part was replaced by a paragraph on the Senkaku Islands question.[92]

9. Prevention of an Anti-Soviet Tripartite Alliance

The second strategy that can be singled out in the Soviet response to the signing of the Japan-China treaty is the strategy of regarding the tie between these two states as fluid, and as checking and preventing the treaty from serving as a basis for Beijing and Tokyo cooperation against Soviet interests.

To begin with, the Soviets viewed the roles played by China and Japan in concluding the treaty as being different, which indicated another new strategy by the USSR toward Japan. Soviet spokesmen interpreted the signing of the peace treaty between Japan and the PRC as a source of only "*latent* or *potential danger*" (*opasnost'*). In other words, they were careful not to say that the treaty itself constituted any actual danger to the Soviet Union. Interpreting its significance the day after the treaty was concluded, TASS commentator Mikhail Demchenko in *Pravda* stated: "This treaty contains a great *potential danger*, particularly for peoples of Southeast Asia, who have long been the objects of aggressive tendencies of the Beijing leaders. Into this venture, aided by this treaty, Japan *might also be drawn*" (emphasis added by H.K.).[93] What Moscow appeared to be afraid of was Japan gradually "slipping into the hands of Beijing." Expressing Moscow's apprehension, *Izvestiia*, on August 25, 1978, wrote: "There is no guarantee that having made one concession, Tokyo will not take a further step dictated by Beijing."[94] The article continued: "It is precisely because of an apprehension of the danger of a similar development of events, fraught with the peril of Japan's gradual slide into the channel of Beijing's anti-Soviet policy, that many people in Japan itself condemn the government's agreement to sign the treaty."[95]

The Soviets' real intentions surfaced when they tried to manipulate the Japanese by saying that Tokyo's future actions would determine whether the potential danger would become a real one. As early as August 13, 1978, *Pravda* did not fail to warn Japan in this regard, writing that "the future will show whether Japan will pursue its own independent foreign policy, of course, by basing itself on vague formulations, which in the opinion of its government are called upon to 'weaken' the dangerous character of the document in Beijing."[96] We can regard this Soviet pronouncement as typical of the "wait and see"[97] attitude of the Kremlin. At the same time, it may be considered to be a very skillful bluff by the Kremlin for the purpose of reserving the right to interfere in Japan's future conduct of foreign affairs. G. V. Melikhov, Soviet specialist on Asian affairs, preferred to threaten the Japanese government more directly, reminding the Japanese that there was a clear limit to what Japan's foreign policy could do: "Japan prefers to keep an equidistance from China and from the USSR, without allowing any overt measure that could damage her relations with the USSR. The developments in Sino-Japanese relations have thus their own objective limits."[98]

It is quite safe to assume that the Soviet Union was concerned about the development of close security relations between Japan and China, especially the possible development of a military alliance. Only a few days after the signing of the treaty, TASS stated that "there is a *possibility* in the near future of a strengthening of the planned Washington-Beijing-Tokyo axis with a clear anti-Soviet direction" (emphasis added by H.K.).[99] The same TASS dispatch described such a tripartite alliance as "the Oriental version of NATO."[100] Moscow was also fearful that, by signing the peace treaty with China, Tokyo would become more receptive to Beijing's pressure to increase Japan's defense capability, thereby activating what the Soviets termed "revival of Japanese militaristic tendencies." Expressing such Soviet apprehension, an article in *Trud*, the Soviet labor union's organ, stated: "The fact that Japan has been drawn into the mainstream of China's great-power aspirations will undoubtedly create an atmosphere conducive to the activation of Japanese militarism."[101] Similarly linking the treaty with the revival of Japanese militarism, M. Demchenko wrote in another Soviet newspaper *Sovetskaia Rossiia:* "A great number of facts show that after the signing of the Japan–China treaty . . . Japanese military forces remarkably increased their activity."[102]

As often speculated by Western observers, the combination of the huge human resources of the PRC with the advanced economy and technology of Japan would have been a real nightmare for the Russians. It is necessary to understand in this context that each time the PRC made an overture to the Japanese Defense Agency and its senior officials, the Soviets launched a massive media campaign protesting against such contact. In September 1978, when General Zhang Caiqian, the Deputy Chief of Staff of the Chinese People's Liberation Army, visited Japan and met with Kō Maruyama, then Administrative Vice-Minister of the Japanese Defense Agency, and Takehiko Takashina, then Chairman of the Japanese Self-Defense Forces Joint Staff Council, the Soviets fully mobilized all their communications media to represent such contact as a sign of potential formation of an anti-Soviet military alliance. Such denunciatory expressions as "dangerous contact" and "unprecedented military contact" were found almost daily in *Pravda, Izvestiia,*[103] *Krasnaia zvezda, Novoe vremia,* and other organs. *Krasnaia zvezda*, for example, interpreted this visit as "a step toward fulfillment of the plan made by the U.S.A. and the PRC to combine Japan's advanced industrial and military potential with the huge Chinese population and strategic resource materials."[104] The same kind of campaign was repeated in May 1979, when Su Yu, Chinese Vice-Minister of National Defense, had talks with the highest officials of the Japanese Defense Agency. Describing this meeting as "the first official meeting between the military leaders of Tokyo and Beijing," *Izvestiia* warned, "it is nothing but a new step on the path to broadening Japanese-Chinese military contact," permitting the Tokyo ruling circles to "involve themselves in the dangerous game of playing with fire."[105]

10. Limits of Improvements in Sino-Japanese Relations

To complete the picture, we must discuss other developments that occurred after the conclusion of the treaty between Japan and the PRC, some of which might have led the Kremlin to reevaluate its view of the Sino-Japanese relationship, recognizing that there were some significant restraints or limits beyond which Sino-Japanese relations could not go.

First, it appears that the Soviets were quite impressed by the independent posture and policies that the Japanese adopted during the Sino-Vietnamese War in the spring of 1979. At that time *Pravda* carried favorable reports on Tokyo's neutral position in that war. Concerning Deng Xiaoping's trip to Tokyo on his way from Washington to Beijing, in which the Chinese leader intended to inform Japanese Prime Minister Masayoshi Ōhira of the Chinese intention to "teach a lesson" to the Vietnamese, Igor' A. Latyshev, Tokyo correspondent of *Pravda* at that time, described the Japanese responses as follows: "Prime Minister Ōhira did not yield to Chinese pressure and dissociated himself from Beijing's bellicose policy."[106] Latyshev further stressed the fact that most Japanese observers agreed that in these talks (between Deng and Ōhira) "significant differences between the two sides" were highlighted in assessing the situation in Asia, and that Japan must continue "to preserve its independence in determining its foreign policy."[107] When the Chinese "punishment" materialized, Vladimir Ia. Tsvetov, political commentator at a Moscow television service, approvingly announced: "Japan received reports of Beijing's invasion of Socialist Vietnam with great displeasure."[108] Tsvetov continued: "The Chinese invasion of Socialist Vietnam met with strong protest in Japan. Even those conservative politicians who had worked for closer Sino-Japanese ties have criticized Beijing's behavior."[109] In conclusion, Tsvetov quoted lines from *Sankei Shimbun*, such as "the invasion shattered the illusion of a 'peaceful China' held by some Japanese people."[110]

This example of Soviet reporting may be interpreted, at least in part, as an attempt to exploit the familiar Russian tactic of "divide and rule," which tries to make full use of, and even to promote, contradictions and conflicting views between nations. On the other hand, however, one must bear in mind that the Russians sometimes make relatively objective and accurate reports of what is taking place. The writing of Mikhail G. Nosov, one of the best-informed Soviet specialists on Sino-Japanese relations, was a case in point. Correctly evaluating Tokyo's self-restraint in response to pressure being exerted by Beijing, Nosov wrote in the Soviet almanac *Japan: 1980*: "Toward the development of relations with the PRC, Japan has been more cautious than the U.S.A. Whereas the question of U.S.–China military cooperation has been openly discussed in Washington, such a question [of Japan-China military cooperation] has not yet come to the official level in Tokyo."[111] Nosov concluded: "Despite the activation of American-Chinese and Japanese-Chinese relations, the possibility of transforming relations among these states into a military-political alliance cannot now be discussed with full confidence."[112]

Second, Moscow was highly gratified by the freezing, and even abrogation, of some joint Japan China economic projects and large economic contracts as announced at the end of February 1979. In early March of that year, an increasing number of reports appeared in the Soviet mass media, stressing that Japan China relations were not going well. Reporting that "the PRC deferment of contracts with Japan was a heavy blow," Moscow Radio on March 1, 1979 said that "trade and industrial circles in Japan are extremely unhappy over the PRC's decision to defer the fulfillment of contracts for imports of industrial plants from Japan" and that "sober-minded representatives of business circles in Japan have expressed serious concern about the possibility of trade with China," with their new view that "China is unable to pay for plants" or that "the Chinese market is by no means a dreamland."[113] As for the Chinese side, Moscow Radio happily reported on April 4, 1979, "The hegemonists in Beijing have been irritated by Japan's refusal to conduct trade with China on unequal and disadvantageous terms."[114] It was also reported in the Soviet media that Liao Chengzhi, then President of the Sino-Japanese Friendship Society, in addressing a mission from Japan to the PRC made a charge of decreased interest in Sino-Japanese relations on the Japanese side and urged that "Japan show more zeal in promoting Sino-Japanese relations."[115]

From these various developments between Japan and China, the Soviets, at least officially, drew the conclusion that "euphoria about China" in Japan had disappeared in Japan by April 1979. For instance, Iurii Bandura and V. Kasits, Tokyo correspondents of *Izvestiia*, reported on the "waning of the tempestuous but short-lived 'China fever.'"[116] Similarly, I. Latyshev, Tokyo correspondent of *Pravda*, noted, "All this taken together has meant that the 'China fever' in Japanese business circles not only has abated but is being replaced by pessimistic sentiments."[117]

11. Rationale for Improvement in Soviet-Japanese Relations

The third Soviet response to the conclusion of the Japan-China treaty of Peace and Friendship was an attempt to exploit this development to promote their own designs for Japan. The Kremlin urged Tokyo to make an effort to raise Soviet-Japanese relations to the same level as that of Sino-Japanese relations.

If the Tokyo government wanted to say that its "equidistance policy" vis-à-vis Beijing and Moscow did not undergo any change in spite of the Sino-Japanese peace treaty, the Soviets argued at that time that Tokyo must demonstrate its good faith not simply by lip service but in practical actions. This was what Nikolai P. Firiubin, Soviet Vice-Foreign Minister, was reported to have said to Susumu Matsubara, chargé d'affaires of the Japanese embassy in Moscow, on August 14, 1978, when the Soviet Minister was briefed about the treaty's conclusion.[118] Thereafter, the phrase "deeds rather than words" became a major part of the Soviet argument.[119] The following passage from Iurii Afornin, a Moscow Radio commentator, in Japanese, implied this:

> Then, how is Japan trying to straighten out the ramifications of its relations with the USSR? According to information made available so far, all that Japan is doing is explaining to the Soviet side that the Japan–China Treaty is not directed against the Soviet Union and that the Japanese government is interested only in developing good-neighborly ties with the USSR. In other words, Japan is only making statements, *not accompanied by deeds*. (emphasis added by H.K.).[120]

Some observers in Japan went so far as to suggest that the Kremlin welcomed rather than dreaded the conclusion of the Sino-Japanese peace treaty, because the treaty gave the Soviets an excellent excuse, otherwise lacking, to push two specific measures that were critical to Japanese-Russian relations. Whether or not this was the case, some observers considered that any actual damage caused by the treaty to the USSR could be offset to some extent by benefits that might have been derived from the conclusion of the treaty. In short, they argued that the consummation of the Sino-Japanese treaty could not be regarded as a net loss to Moscow. What, then, were the measures that the Kremlin took to pressure Tokyo after the treaty's conclusion?

The first measure concerned the Soviet position with regard to the "territorial" issue vis-à-vis Japan. As is well known, the Sino-Japanese peace treaty in 1978 made no mention of the Senkaku (*Diaoyu*) Islands, the ownership of which had long been disputed by Japan and China. It is not unreasonable to say that the signatory states implicitly shelved the territorial issue. Taking advantage of Japan's attitude in this case, the Soviets on occasion *implicitly* pushed Japan to maintain an equivalent approach vis-à-vis the USSR, namely, to set aside the "Northern Territories" question. The term "implicitly" is stressed here because the Soviets were in no position to be explicit on this subject: it was their official line that no unsolved territorial problem existed between the USSR and Japan. Anatolyev, a commentator in the Japanese language at the Moscow Radio, in October 1978, quoted China's Deng Xiaoping as stating that "since the present generation does not have the wisdom to settle the question of sovereignty over the Senkaku Islands, it would be better to leave it to our future generations, shelving it for the time being."[121] What Anatolyev implied then is too obvious for elaboration. A similar view was expressed at a meeting on June 21, 1979 between Vladimir L. Kudriavtsev and a Japanese delegation from the LDP's youth department led by Shinya Totsuka, a member of the House of Councillors. Mission members quoted Kudriavtsev as saying, "Let us affix a *comma* to the territorial problem and not a *period*" (emphasis added by H.K.).[122] Such a punctuational metaphor underlined the Soviet preference at that time for postponing the territorial question between Japan and the USSR.

The Soviets also tried to exploit the Sino-Japanese peace treaty to make Japan accede to the Soviet request to conclude a Treaty of Good-neighborliness and Cooperation between the USSR and Japan. From 1977, the Soviet Union persistently had proposed this treaty as a substitute for a Soviet-Japanese peace treaty. Justifying the Soviet proposal, Ambassador Polianskii said: "If Japan is not yet prepared [for a peace treaty], how about concluding the Treaty of Good-neighborliness and Cooperation? This can also mark a step forward."[123] During the peace treaty negotiations conducted between Japan and the Soviet Union in 1978, Moscow pressed Japan hard, as already mentioned above, to sign a good-neighbor treaty, even taking the rather unusual step of forcing Japanese Foreign Minister Sonoda to receive the Soviet draft.

Although aware of the Japanese indignation and of the arguments against this Treaty of Good-neighborliness and Cooperation, the Soviets nonetheless pressured Japan to accept the treaty as a sort of intermediary step, given that agreement on a peace treaty was so difficult to reach. Japan's conclusion of a peace treaty with the PRC seemed to the Kremlin to provide the Soviets with justification for pushing the Japanese government further to conclude a treaty of some sort with them. By concluding the peace treaty with China, the Soviets felt that Japan had deliberately violated its concept of even-handed posture toward the PRC and the Soviet Union. Soviet public opinion held that Japan should take measures to rectify the situation by making an effort to develop friendly ties with the USSR.

12. Did Moscow Really "Retaliate" Against Tokyo?

We have so far analyzed the general policy *pronouncement* of the Kremlin's practical actions and the resulting developments following the conclusion of the Sino-Japanese peace treaty. What *specific* policies did the Soviet Union apply *in practice* to Japan following the conclusion of the treaty? The answer is the "carrot and stick," varying according to the issues and circumstances.

First, let's examine the carrot (soft) approach. Despite its threats of retaliatory measures in the event of Japan's conclusion of a treaty with China, the USSR reacted actually rather moderately, much to Japan's surprise. A similar trend can be seen not only in regard to trade and economic cooperation, but also in cultural and other exchanges. This was in marked contrast to the "MiG-25 incident" (September 1976), when Moscow expressed its displeasure by postponing the Seventh Joint Conference of the Japanese-Soviet and the Soviet-Japanese Economic Cooperation Committees, by refusing visas to the Japanese team of Go (a Japanese chess game) players, and by Soviet Foreign Minister Gromyko's staging of a rather discourteous reception for his Japanese counterpart Zentarō Kosaka on the occasion of the UN General Assembly sessions in New York in September 1976. In contrast, however, when Gromyko met with then Japanese Foreign Minister Sonoda in New York in September 1978, one month after the conclusion of the Sino-Japanese Peace Treaty, their talks were conducted in an unusually cordial and cooperative atmosphere,[124] and Gromyko even intimated that a visit to Japan was a clear possibility.[125]

In the economic sphere Moscow was much more flexible. Less than a month after the conclusion of the Sino-Japanese Peace Treaty, Mikhail I. Kuznetsov, Director General of the USSR Ministry of Foreign Trade, visited Tokyo as the Soviet representative at the Third Soviet-Japanese Off-

Shore Trade Conference.[126] In October 1978, the regular annual conference on Japan-Soviet trade was held in Tokyo as scheduled.[127] A few months later, in February 1979, the Fourth Joint Staff Meeting of the Japanese-Soviet and the Soviet-Japanese Economic Cooperation Committees convened in Tokyo with Ivan F. Semichastnov, Soviet First Vice-Foreign Trade Minister and Chairman of the Soviet-Japanese Economic Committee, representing the Soviet Union. At this meeting the Soviet delegation surprised the Japanese side with its enthusiasm for promoting economic relations between the USSR and Japan. Semichastnov, who reportedly came directly from a hospital in Moscow to attend the meeting in Tokyo,[128] put forward three new joint proposals based on a "production-sharing formula"—development of copper deposits at Udokan, exploitation of an asbestos mine at Molodezhnaia in Central Siberia, and construction of a giant, full-cycle steel plant in the Soviet Far East.[129] In the Eighth Joint Session of the Japanese-Soviet and the Soviet-Japanese Economic Cooperation Committees, held in Moscow on September 24–27, 1979, the Soviets again surprised the Japanese delegation with their unprecedented enthusiasm and flexibility. This session took place after a long interval and was the first to be held since the conclusion of the peace treaty between Japan and China. The Soviets agreed to the insertion of a paragraph in the joint communiqué stipulating that "both sides will continue to discuss *the possibility of a mutually acceptable production-sharing formula with cooperation based on reciprocity"* (emphasis added by H.K.). This was interpreted as a remarkable softening in the production-sharing formula by which the Soviets proposed to repay Japan in raw materials and in goods produced by plants to be constructed with Japanese help and credit. This formula no longer interested the Japanese, mainly because there was an abundance of raw material supplies in the world market, and Japan's economy was entering a period of slow expansion with a surplus of industrial products.[130] For this and other reasons, the Japanese reaction to these three proposals was only lukewarm.

In other domains too, the Soviets' desire to improve Soviet-Japanese bilateral relations following Japan's peace treaty with the PRC became evident. Toward the end of August 1978, the Soviets received, as scheduled, a delegation of the Japanese Socialist Party (JSP) headed by Seiichi Kawamura, and in early September, they received another delegation from the two chambers of the Japanese Diet headed by Nikichi Shirahama of the Liberal Democratic Party (LDP), who met with Premier Kosygin in the Kremlin for a 70-minute talk.[131] In November, Yōhei Kōno, a representative of the New Liberal Club, a middle-of-the-road party, visited Moscow and was well received. Kazuo Asukata, Chairman of the JSP, and Shōgo Tada, Vice-Chairman of the Clean Government Party (Kōmeitō), another centrist party, followed suit, in December 1978 and in January 1979, respectively. Perhaps the most important in this series of visits was that of Kenji Miyamoto, Chairman of the Japanese Communist Party (JCP), in December 1979, a few days before the Soviet invasion of Afghanistan. The rift between the CPSU and the JCP was at last closed, but at a great price to the Soviets, who in effect made the humiliating admission that their past policy toward the JCP had contained some errors.[132]

From the Soviet side, several important *apparatchiki* and high government officials visited Japan. One was a delegation of five members of the CPSU, including Ivan I. Kovalenko, a deputy chief of the CPSU's International Department, who came to Tokyo in October 1978[133] and held *pourparlers* with almost all of the leaders of Japan's political parties, extending invitations to visit Moscow at their earliest convenience. Another was Nikolai P. Firiubin, Vice-Minister of Foreign Affairs, who, during his stay in May 1979, declared in a conference of deputy foreign ministers that an "actual possibility has been created for moving Soviet-Japanese relations on to a new phase."[134] Firiubin even went so far as to stress to Japanese Prime Minister Ōhira, "We regard the development of Soviet-Japanese relations to be very important, *despite the negative influence of a third country"* (emphasis added by H.K.).[135] A similar statement was made by Viktor Afanas'ev, editor-in-chief of *Pravda* and member of the Party's Central Committee and the Supreme Soviet, indicating that the Soviets had swallowed the shock caused by the Sino-Japanese peace treaty and had decided to take a more conciliatory approach to Japan. Afanas'ev then reportedly stated at a Press Club meeting during his visit to Tokyo in May 1979: "*The Peace and Friendship Treaty between Japan and China does not necessarily constitute a decisive obstacle to the development of good-neighborly and friendly relations between the USSR and Japan.* I consider that difficulties produced by the Japan-China treaty can be overcome"(emphasis added by H.K.).[136]

13. Deployment of Troops on the Disputed Islands

The Kremlin did not adhere solely to the "soft" approach but chose also to express both hard and cold attitudes toward Japan. These unconciliatory attitudes can be illustrated by the Soviets' uncompromising approach to the Northern Territories issue and the rapid buildup of military bases on these territories.

In late January 1979, the Japanese public learned that the Soviets had installed military forces on two of the Northern Islands, Kunashiri and Etorofu. From the islands' seizure in 1945 until about 1960, the Soviet Union maintained an entire division of about 20,000 men there. In the early 1960s the division had been completely withdrawn, leaving only a limited coast guard and garrison force—until early June 1978, when Soviet troop movements into the islands were reported to have started.[137] In September 26, 1979, it was disclosed through American sources that Soviet military bases had been established on a third island, Shikotan. The news came as a particular shock to the Japanese, who consider Shikotan a part of Hokkaido.

This disclosure (September 26) coincided with the Eighth Joint Conference of the Japanese-Soviet and the Soviet-Japanese Economic Cooperation Committees in Moscow (September 24–27) and the Gromyko-Sonoda meeting in New York (September 24). Soviet spokesmen therefore regarded the announcement as Washington's attempt to "prevent the development of Soviet-Japanese economic relations."[138] They called it a "conjecture of American origins" or "the alleged buildup."[139] On the other hand, however, the same Soviet spokesmen did not deny that the Soviet Union was conducting a military buildup on these islands. Their way of making a counterargument in itself proves that they knew the facts. For example, an article in *Izvestiia* stated that these islands were "Soviet territory" and hence that "only the USSR is entitled to decide what can and ought to be done over there."[140] Another article in *Izvestiia* "categorically rejected such attempts [by Japan] to raise the question of what the Soviet Union can and cannot do on its own territory as interference in Soviet domestic affairs."[141] Some Soviets residing in Japan attempted to justify the presence of troops and bases on the islands as being necessary for defensive purposes, saying that these forces would never be directed against Japan. Iurii Bandura, Tokyo correspondent of *Izvestiia*, for example, regarded the security of the borders along the Kurile archipelago as "not only a right but also an obligation of the [Soviet] state."[142] Responding to the Japanese protest, Iurii D. Dmitriev, Soviet Japan specialist, tried to justify the redeployment of Soviet troops on the islands: "Local change in the distribution of individual Soviet military divisions is not in any way directed against Japan and does not generate any threat to her."[143] V.L. Kudriavtsev, another political commentator for *Izvestiia*, wrote: "The Soviet Union and Japan are separated by the La Pérouse [Soya] strait, only a few dozen kilometers wide. Are we Soviet people not worried by this fact? Put yourselves in our place, dear Japanese friends."[144]

Why, then, did the Soviets decide to increase their military forces on these islands from which they had withdrawn their troops in 1961? No definite answer to this question seems to have been given. Some observers in Japan and in the West interpreted this move in terms of "retaliation" against Japan's decision to conclude the peace treaty with China. Various official Soviet statements appeared to confirm the validity of this view. Bandura, for example, in an article for *Izvestiia*, wrote, as quoted above, that the buildup of the Soviet military bases on Kunashiri and Shikotan islands was an "obligation" stemming from the fact that Japan was drawn into a course of anti-Soviet policy in connection with *Japanese-Chinese* and American-Chinese rapprochement"[145] (emphasis added by H.K.). However, this justification becomes somewhat questionable when one scrutinizes the chronology of events. According to some reports, it was not in February 1979 but in May 1978 that the Fukuda government learned of the buildup of Soviet military forces on Kunashiri and Etorofu islands.[146] The Fukuda government did not want to let the Japanese public know about this Soviet action lest it withdraw its support for the peace treaty with China. It is therefore a fair guess that the Soviet leadership's decision to build these bases had been reached at least half a year earlier, i.e., around December 1977. There is no evidence, however, that in December 1977 the Kremlin leaders were in a position to anticipate the possible conclusion of the peace treaty between Japan and the PRC. If this assumption is correct, one could say that the Soviet military reinforcement in the Northern Territories can be best interpreted as a Soviet anticipatory move and not as a direct retaliatory response to an action that the Fukuda government had not yet taken.

Personally, I am tempted to side with the view that there were *multiple* reasons behind the Soviet military buildup in the Northern Territories: (1) it was a part of general upgrading of Soviet forces in Northeast Asia which had been in progress since 1969 and part of the Soviet global strategy primarily directed against the United States and the PRC;[147] (2) it was a move that must have seriously taken into account the generally constructive ties that prevailed at that time between Japan and China. For this reason, the Japan-China Peace Treaty was "both a contributing cause and an effect" of Soviet military strengthening of the Far East;[148] and (3) it was a strategy of psychological revenge and intimidation directed against Japan. It was "preemptive defense and a demonstration to Japan that it cannot rearm or ally with the United States without incurring high cost to itself."[149] Quite a few Soviet official statements refuting Japan's protests against the militarization of the islands seem to confirm my view.

For example, Vladimir Tsvetov, in October 1979, made the accusation that (1) "Japan also showed a readiness to join in the formation of an extensive, multilateral, anti-Soviet military alliance"; (2) Japan "actually concluded with China a treaty that was directed against the Soviet Union"; and (3) "Japan was building up its military forces in Hokkaido and conducting a series of exercises with the Soviet Union as its imaginary enemy."[150] Similarly, criticizing a "provocative ballyhoo" in Japan over the USSR military presence on Shikotan island, *Pravda* asserted in September 1979 that the U.S. and Japanese ruling circles needed this kind of public indignation in order to justify (1) "the strengthening of the Japanese-U.S. military alliance"; (2) to a certain extent, "the trend of knocking together a tripartite Washington–Tokyo–Beijing alliance"; and (3) "the buildup of the might of the Japanese armed forces."[151] These examples show that official Soviet press reports were sometimes a fairly accurate portrayal of what the Soviet government was really worrying about and, then what it was aiming at and doing in practice.

Chapter 8
The Soviets Propose
Substitute Treaties

As discussed in the previous chapter, although the Soviet Union sought to take advantage of the opportunity that arose when Japan opted to conclude a peace treaty with China, the Soviets failed to persuade Japan even to negotiate a Treaty of Good-neighborliness and Cooperation. Despite the blunt Japanese refusal of this substitute for a peace treaty, aimed at shelving the territorial question, the Kremlin never ceased in its effort to conclude a good-neighbor treaty or other legal document with similar objectives. A similar case was its attempt to reach an agreement on "confidence-building measures" (CBMs) between the Soviet Union and Japan. Because of the peace oriented connotation of the term *confidence building* and because of the supposed function of such measures as a preliminary to arms control, the Japanese found it much harder to reject this Soviet proposal than the Treaty of Good-neighborliness. For this reason, the Kremlin under both Brezhnev and Andropov exerted increasing pressure on Japan to accept the CBMs proposal. In this chapter, I will examine how hard the Soviet Union tried to sell, and why Japan rejected, the idea of CBMs in the Far East. Special attention will be focused not on the legal content of the arrangements but on their political and diplomatic functions in the specific context of Soviet-Japanese relations.

1. Are CBMs Applicable to Asia?

Confidence-building measures (*mery po ukrepleniiu doveriia*) were first agreed upon by thirty-five participating states at the 1975 Helsinki Conference on Security and Cooperation in Europe (CSCE), though the idea of strengthening confidence through bilateral or multilateral arrangements predates Helsinki by many years.[1] The CBMs included in the Helsinki Final Act consisted of specific steps to reduce tensions between potential adversaries, such as prior notification of any military maneuvers and of major military movements, and inviting observers to attend maneuvers.[2]

Of interest here in our context is the applicability of European CBMs to other parts of the world. In its first resolution on CBMs in 1978, the UN General Assembly, on the initiative of the Federal Republic of Germany,[3] recommended that "all states should consider, on a regional basis, arrangements for specific CBMs, taking into account the specific conditions and requirements of each region."[4] Since that time, there have been two schools of thought on the application of CBMs to other regions: one school advocates the usefulness of extending CBMs beyond Europe,[5] while the other is more cautious about the transferability of CBMs' parameters to other regions with different "political, military and geographical circumstances."[6] The Soviet Union made it clear that it was eager for similar arrangements in the Far East, particularly on a bilateral basis with Japan,[7] whereas in marked contrast, Japan responded coolly to that idea. In this section, both the Soviet arguments and the Japanese counterarguments will be examined.

In general, the Soviets were not so original in their conduct of foreign policy as outside observers were tempted to imagine. They tended to apply automatically the same policies, methods, and tactics that had been successful in the past, in vastly different situations.[8] One example was Brezhnev's scheme of collective security in Asia, which was nothing but an Asian version of the European collective security system.[9] A Treaty of Good-neighborliness and Cooperation between the USSR and Japan[10] would have been similar in both name and content to the agreements that had been concluded by the USSR with Egypt, India, Iraq, Turkey, Iran, Afghanistan, Vietnam, and other countries.

Against this general background, it is not at all surprising to discover that the Soviet idea of CBMs in the Far East stemmed from the USSR's experience in Europe—more specifically, from the inclusion of CBMs in the Helsinki Final Act. In other words, Brezhnev's offer of confidence-building measures in the Far East at the 26th CPSU Party Congress (1981) was nothing more than a simple, mechanical application of the CBMs outlined in the Helsinki Declaration (1975). In his address at the final stage of the CSCE in Helsinki on July 31, 1975, the General Secretary of the CPSU clearly stated: "We view the CSCE as a joint success for all participants. *Its results can also be of use outside Europe*" (emphasis added by H.K.).[11] The words of the General Secretary were confirmed by the Politburo of the CPSU Central Committee, which declared on August 6, 1975: "The decisions of the [Helsinki] Conference have great meaning not only for Europeans, because the right to peace belongs to every human being on our planet."[12]

Soviet bureaucrats and specialists on Far Eastern affairs, arguing that a large portion of the Helsinki agreements could be effectively applied to Asia and the Far East, embellished the official line set by the highest authorities in the Soviet foreign policy establishment. For instance, Soviet commentator V.L. Kudriavtsev wrote in *Izvestiia* that the principles adopted at Helsinki were "universally applicable to Asia."[13] In 1977, V.N. Berezin (a pseudonym for two high-ranking Soviet Foreign Ministry officials in charge of Japan) stated: "If we closely examine the final document that was worked out at the [Helsinki] Conference, we find in it many conditions pertaining to those problems that currently confront the states in the Far East."[14] Application of CBMs to the Far East was justified by another Japan expert, N.N. Nikolaev, who wrote in 1981: "There is no need to say that the situation in Asia is particularly distinct from that in Europe. Nevertheless, the experience of European states in developing and employing CBMs may undoubtedly prove useful in Asian countries."[15]

2. Different Geographic Circumstances

Japan has publicly endorsed the idea of CBMs. A booklet issued by the Japanese Foreign Ministry states: "The CBMs may not be regarded as an arms control arrangement per se. Yet, our country considers that, provided the specific political and military conditions of each region are sufficiently taken into account, CBMs can serve as an important element in the development of arms control. CBMs have made some achievements in Europe, and now various proposals for making CBMs more effective are being discussed."[16]

However, when the Soviets approached Japan with regard to CBMs in the Far East, the Tokyo government's response suddenly took a negative turn. The reason given by Tokyo for its refusal was that "situations in the Far East are so different from those in Europe that automatic transfer of the CBMs from Europe to the Far East is unrealistic."[17] Naturally, regional disarmament and arms control should be left to the initiative of the countries concerned. Moreover, nobody expected that CBMs used in Europe could be transferred to other regions without being tailored to the "specific conditions" of a given region. This reservation was stated not only in the recommendation of the UN General Assembly cited above but even by the Soviet Union.[18] Thus, the questions to be asked are what, in the view of the Japanese government, constituted the "specific conditions" in the Far East, and whether they were unique enough for Tokyo to categorically reject the transfer of CBMs into the region.

One must also consider the geographical factors. Japan was separated from its potential adversary, the USSR, by water. This particular geographical (hence military-strategic) circumstance lessened the urgency of a Japanese-Soviet agreement on land forces, which was the chief issue covered by the CBMs in the Helsinki Final Act.[19] Toshiaki Mutō, then director general of the European and Oceanic Affairs Bureau at the Japanese Ministry of Foreign Affairs, concluded in 1981 that "differences in geographical situations make the idea of automatically bringing the CBMs in Europe to the Far East unrealistic," arguing that "even if the USSR gives prior notification of its military maneuvers in Siberia, it will not be of much use to Japan."[20]

Mutō, perhaps deliberately, overlooked the fact that the Helsinki CBMs, obviously a by-product of particular environmental circumstances, were certainly not meant to be a formula to be automatically followed by other states in different regions. In particular, he appeared to miss the point that CBMs can also be applied to naval and air forces, an idea that even predates the Helsinki Act.[21] The 1972 American-Soviet Agreement on the Prevention of Incidents on and over the High Seas[22] is one of the most relevant examples of naval CBMs. The Helsinki Final Act also covers certain "amphibious and/or airborne troops." In addition, it is worth recalling that a proposal was made at the CSCE, though it was not pursued, to include in the Final Accord measures dealing with naval and air exercises such as "maneuvers in border zones, the flying of fighter planes close to border zones, and the navigation of warships in the vicinity of the territorial waters of other states."[23] Moreover, there was no reason to assume that the CBMs in the Final Act would not be altered, and even enlarged further, in the near future. As a matter of fact, considering as "the salient anomaly"[24] the fact that the CBMs agreed on at Helsinki did not extend to naval forces, Western specialists who were in favor of extending confidence-building measures[25] strongly urged that CBMs be extended to both air and naval maneuvers.[26]

Brezhnev also promoted naval and air CBMs in his speech at the 26th Party Congress, when he contended: "We have already said that we are prepared to go further—to also provide notification of naval and air exercises."[27] Strongly endorsing Brezhnev's idea of extending CBMs to naval exercises, Timofei Guzhenko, chairman of the Japan-USSR Society and USSR minister of the maritime fleet, reminded the Japanese in an article published after Iurii Andropov became General Secretary that, precisely because of its vital dependence upon ocean communication lines, Japan must consider more seriously than any other nation the security of sea lanes, which alone "can assure the security of Japan."[28] Guzhenko continued:

> Such initiatives must be of special interest to Japan, which has been making an effort to assure security for sea transportation. Japanese leaders have already expressed more than once their apprehension that supply routes of energy and other industrial resources to Japan pass through waters that can be blocked in the fire of any military conflict, if it breaks out in the northwestern part of the Pacific Ocean or in the Indian Ocean.[29]

This statement may be dismissed as another attempt by Moscow to check Japan's effort to take on its share of the defense of the so-called "1,000-mile sea-lanes," but at the same time it helps to recall the undeniable fact that the areas surrounding Japan were made increasingly uneasy by frequent air and naval reconnaissance exercises and other military activities by the USSR, the United States, and other states. According to a White Paper on Defense published in 1982 by the Japanese Defense Agency, the number of flights by Soviet military aircraft in the area around Japan was about 240 per year, and the number of passages of Soviet warships through three straits (Tsushima, Tsugaru and Soya) was approximately 430.[30] As a result, a number of incidents took place, such as the landing of a Soviet MiG-25 at Hakodate airport, the crash of a Soviet TU-16 *Badger* into the Sea of Japan, and the breakdown of a Soviet nuclear submarine in Japanese territorial waters. In order to prevent tensions from escalating to such an extent that it might become difficult to distinguish a simple exercise from a real military action, the concerned states must have seriously discussed some sort of arrangement of CBMs. This line of argument sounds rather difficult to resist.

3. Different Negotiating Circumstances

There are other negotiating circumstances. The CBMs constituted only one aspect of the whole package deal at Helsinki. In Europe the agreement on CBMs was reached not in isolation from, but closely connected with, political and security issues in the form of "baskets," such as the affirmation of the East European status quo; nonintervention in the internal affairs of other nations; the improvement of economic, scientific, and technological cooperation; and the free movement, contact, and interchange of ideas, information, and people between East and West. In other words, the Helsinki Final Act was a product of compromise among the participating states, each of which recorded some gains in one or more areas in exchange for concessions in other fields.

The Soviet Union, for instance, agreed to Basket III, dealing with "cooperation in humanitarian issues," only reluctantly and only after it became clear that this was the necessary price for Western acceptance of the political and security commitments contained in Basket I.[31] It must be kept in mind that this was at least the official understanding of the Soviet Union on the Helsinki Final Act, although it was in fact quite selective and arbitrary about carrying out each provision of the final accord. One Soviet specialist on international affairs put forward such an official position in an article titled "The European Conference: Experience and Significance," in *International Affairs* in 1976:

> The Final Act is an *integral* document embracing the entire spectrum of questions related to the security of, and cooperation between, the participating states. This signifies that it must be put into effect *in its entirety, with all its provisions* as they have been agreed upon and formulated in the Final Act. To single out individual provisions, to oppose them to the others, or to secure priority for fulfilling some and ignoring other similarly essential provisions would mean to act in contravention of the spirit and letter of the Final Act, to break the fundamental balance of interests embodied in it [emphasis in original].[32]

Moreover, the CSCE in itself was the result of bargaining. For instance, the United States conditioned the convening of the CSCE on that of a conference on force reduction in Central Europe known as the Mutual and Balanced Force Reduction talks (MBFR).[33] Mutō of the Japanese Foreign Ministry must have been familiar with the circumstances under which CBMs were agreed upon at the CSCE, when he said: "CBMs were adopted as a result of much bargaining. Being under different circumstances in the Far East, therefore, we cannot easily say, 'Yes, indeed. We will make the same arrangement.'"[34]

Particularly disturbing to the Japanese was the inclusion in the Helsinki Final Act, together with CBMs, of the provision for the "inviolability of frontiers," by which the West gave *de facto* recognition of borders that the Soviet Red Army had drawn at the end of World War II.[35] This was the last thing the Japanese wanted. Theoretically, agreements on CBMs and a border settlement are two completely different things and, yet, can be very easily linked because, strictly speaking, the former implies the latter. It is between neighboring states that one easily succumbs to misperceptions, misunderstandings, uncertainty, and fear about military maneuvers and movements of potential adversaries. As a matter of fact, according to the existing Helsinki Final Act, it is not the entire territory but only to "an area within 250 kilometers from its *frontier* facing or shared with any other European participating State" [36] that the provision on prior notification of military maneuvers is to be applied (emphasis added by H.K.).

Therefore, it is not an exaggeration to say that without first settling borders, it is almost impossible to even discuss CBMs and expect them to work. One episode that demonstrates the necessity of having the borders clearly defined prior to discussing military affairs is provided by the following case of inconsistent behavior by the United States in 1968. When a Vietnam-bound Seaboard World Airways jet filled with U.S. military personnel was forced to land on Etorofu after trespassing into Kurile air space, Washington apologized to Moscow for infringing on Soviet territory, forgetting that the United States' officially regarded Etorofu as Japanese and not Soviet territory, thus putting itself into the awkward position of apologizing to Tokyo for apologizing to Moscow.[37]

Consequently, it is understandable that the Japanese government insisted on negotiating the territorial issue before discussing CBMs, regarding the former as a precondition for the latter. In contrast, the Soviet Union officially took the position that the territorial issue had already been resolved; but unofficially, it was well aware of the fact that a territorial problem did exist between the two countries.[38] The Soviet Union intended to exploit a possible agreement on CBMs with Japan as a useful opportunity to make the Japanese accept formally and finally the existing borders, which were drawn by the Soviet military forces at the close of World War II. The Japanese seemed very wary of this strategy, particularly because they had just experienced similar Soviet advances in a different area.

In the 200-mile fishing zone negotiations between Japan and the USSR in 1977, analyzed in chapter 7, the Japanese strongly refused to accept the demarcation line drawn unilaterally by the Soviet government, since this would have legitimized the *Soviet* view of the *national boundary* between the USSR and Japan. The Japanese correctly suspected that once they gave in on fishing rights, it would mean implicit, or even explicit, acceptance of *de facto* existing borders. After ninety days of heated negotiations—which by then were being referred to as "the 200-mile fish *war*"—the Japanese barely succeeded in winning Soviet consent to insert a compromise formula separating the fishing zone issue from other questions into a new fishing zone agreement. The most important issue from Tokyo's perspective was that of national borders, as shown in Article 8 of the final agreement, which stipulates, "No prescription in this agreement shall be taken to violate the position or opinion of either government with respect to . . . issues in the [two nations'] mutual relations."[39] The negative attitude of the Japanese government toward the Soviet proposal for an agreement with Tokyo on CBMs can be viewed against the background of this agonizing experience in 1977.

4. Psychological Factors

There were psychological factors that constituted "specific conditions." Japanese distrust of the Soviets was so deep that the proposal by the Soviets on confidence building was unlikely to be considered worth examining. Among other things, the Japanese were disturbed by the very words "confidence building," especially when uttered by the Soviets, since most Japanese regarded Soviet actions as falling far short of building confidence. The government of Prime Minister Zenkō Suzuki argued that if the Soviets ever wished to build confidence among the Japanese, there were many other things for them to be engaged in before advocating CBMs, including "a withdrawal of their military troops from the Japanese-claimed Northern Territories, or the reversion of these islands to Japan, or the removal of SS-20s from the Far East."[40] As long as the Soviets were not ready to take these actions or even to discuss them with the Japanese government, the Japanese wondered how they could possibly take the Soviet suggestion on CBMs seriously. Pointing out the sharp contradiction between what the Soviets were saying and what they were actually doing, the 1982 version of *Asian Security*, an annual report issued by the Research Institute for Peace and Security in Tokyo, stated: "We can hardly help being skeptical of Moscow's sincerity in proposing to discuss confidence building while also building up its forces in the region."[41] Thus, what the Japanese wanted to say to the new Soviet leader Andropov seemed to be similar to the message given to Brezhnev by the British weekly *The Economist* in 1982: "You can't shake hands with a clenched fist."[42]

However, the Soviets and some vigorous West European and Japanese advocates of CBMs[43] criticized the Japanese government for not trying, or perhaps not pretending, to correctly understand the preliminary and modest nature of the CBMs in the military realm, and for attaching to its acceptance of the Soviet proposal preconditions clearly unacceptable to the Kremlin. After all, they argued, the existence of mistrust and lack of confidence among states was unfortunately normal in the international system, the cold reality on which any international agreement must be based. Precisely where there was relatively little or no confidence, there was an urgent need for CBMs to be seriously considered.[44] This line of thought seems to me somewhat logical although not totally convincing.

When discussing confidence-building measures, one ought to be very careful about the meaning of the term *confidence*, a vague and subjective word that can be interpreted in various ways. As already indicated, *confidence* in the CBMs agreed upon at the Helsinki CSCE had a very narrowly defined, special meaning—confidence in the purely military field,[45] which can be obtained by the exchange of information on military activities between states. This type of narrowly defined confidence was certainly of "an initial character and of a limited scope"[46] and yet, advocates of CBMs believed it should be pursued by as many states as possible as a precedent to be followed by others later on. The advocates of CBMs firmly believed in the correctness of the so-called "gradual approach,"[47] that confidence-building is by nature a process which should be carried out on a step-by-step basis,[48] and that any positive experience may lead to the development and enlargement of measures aimed at the further strengthening of confidence. Nevertheless, the Japanese government did not seem interested in such narrowly defined CBMs, particularly when it came to concluding an agreement with the Soviet Union. By refusing the Soviet proposal to even discuss the institution of CBMs in the Far East, Tokyo appeared to be deliberately adopting a broader interpretation of "confidence," as illustrated in the above statement by Prime Minister Zenkō Suzuki.

The remarks by Suzuki and other high Japanese officials confused, whether intentionally or unintentionally, two closely related yet distinct concepts—confidence-building measures and arms control. Arms control aims at limiting military *capabilities*, while CBMs, by focusing on the parties' *perceptions* of each other's intentions, try to reduce unintended tension among neighboring states arising out of misunderstanding about their military maneuvers and movements.[49] Although the ultimate goals of CBMs may coincide with those of arms control, the immediate objective of CBMs is, as noted above, relatively modest. The preconditions attached by Suzuki to Tokyo's return to the negotiation table with Moscow, such as the "withdrawal of Soviet military troops from the Northern Territories" and "the removal of SS-20s from the Far East" fell into the category of arms control/disarmament measures, thus making Suzuki's rationale seem inappropriate.

Another precondition—the return of the Northern Territories to Japan— also did not appear to be properly linked to the issue. Only when a certain level of confidence and friendly relations had developed between the countries concerned, some advocates of CBMs in Japan argued, would the return of the islands become possible, as was the case in the reversion of Okinawa to Japan from the United States.[50] V. Dal'nev, a Soviet specialist on Soviet-Japanese relations, warned that "to push confrontational and incompatible elements to the fore is simply to further aggravate relations and make consensus-building not close but rather remote."[51] Based on this sort of "first-things-first" logic, Georgii A. Arbatov, supposedly one of the most influential advisors to both Brezhnev and Andropov on international affairs, tried hard to sell the idea to the Japanese public in his interview with *Yomiuri Shimbun* on January 3, 1983, claiming a need for "starting from the field which is possible at the present, leaving difficult problems for later."[52]

So far, the arguments of the Soviet, Western, and Japanese advocates of CBMs sounded fairly convincing, but not overly so. Among other things, one important point that they overlooked was the possibility that the initial step would not be followed up by any further measures. This was unfortunately often the case in negotiations with the Soviet Union. In other words, CBMs may at some stage give rise to further developments, but a process of continuing development cannot be taken for granted. Most likely, a process of developing genuine confidence would not only be impaired but even halted by a premature initial agreement. This seemed to be what the Tokyo government really feared. Why then should it be fearful of such a situation? What would be wrong with a Japanese-Soviet agreement on CBMs, which might fall short of arms control, or even disarmament, but would still be better than nothing as a form of preventing accidental war? The remainder of this chapter will be devoted to answering these questions.

5. Moscow Wants Legal Document

Against the backdrop of the decline in bilateral relations between the USSR and Japan after the mid-1970s, described in the foregoing chapters, it is particularly notable that Moscow seemed more interested than Tokyo in improving relations. Japan did not, of course, regard the situation as being ideal. The Japanese government, however, contended that the undesirable situation prevailing between these two countries was nothing other than a product of inappropriate policy and actions of the Soviet Union in international affairs and in its relations with Japan. This posture relieved Japan of any responsibility to take an initiative to correct the situation. "In the final analysis, what has made Japanese-Soviet relations so cold? This ought to be the basic question when one thinks about the bilateral relations,"[53] said the Japanese ambassador to the USSR, Masuo Takashima, before briefing Prime Minister Yasuhiro Nakasone in December 1982. Answering the question himself, he argued: "The cause lies not with Japan at all but only with the Soviet Union. In the postwar period, the whole responsibility lies consistently with the USSR."[54] The Japanese ambassador continued:

> Thus, only when the Soviet Union comes to regard Japan as important, respects Japan, and hence amends its current attitudes, can Japan respond. Japan is not in a position to bow to the USSR or to seek good relations with this country.[55]

Surely, the Japanese did not fail to notice the increasing Soviet military buildup in their immediate vicinity. At the same time, however, the Japanese government knew that the Soviet Union was a sort of sick giant, which apart from its military muscle, had many weak spots and problems, both domestic and international. This would make it almost out of question for the Soviet Union to become involved in another Afghanistan in the Far East. In other words, as long as Japan maintained its own "denial force"[56] to repel limited and small-scale military aggression, to make such aggression costly, and to prevent invasion of Japan from easily becoming a *fait accompli*,[57] and as long as it continued to enjoy U.S. nuclear deterrence as a means of checking Soviet aggression, Tokyo needed not worry too much about "the threat from the polar bear."

Further expansion of trade and economic relations between the USSR and Japan may still have been desirable as a possible escape from the stagnant Soviet economy. In Tokyo's view, however, such a course had to take into consideration other political and economic factors. These included Japan's international obligation as a member-state of the Western community to participate in sanctions against Soviet international adventurism; the overwhelming importance of the United States as a major trade partner, with which Japan was conducting ten times more trade than with the Soviet Union; the USSR's own economic difficulties, such as shortages of labor and foreign currency; and a possible Soviet shift in development priorities toward Western Siberia and away from Eastern Siberia and the Far Eastern region of the Soviet Union.[58] Finally, psychological elements were also relevant. It is clear that, rightly or wrongly, Japanese self-confidence was increasing markedly. This was especially the case since Japan had terminated the state of war with China by concluding a peace treaty with the PRC in 1978 and since it had achieved the status of an economic giant second only to the United States. On the whole, Tokyo seemed to have concluded that there was no particular reason for Japan to make a diplomatic overture to Moscow in order to break the deadlock in relations with the Soviet Union.

In contrast, although Moscow publicly attributed the chilled relations to the misconduct of Tokyo, Washington, and Beijing, in practice, the Soviet Union seemed to consider it necessary to improve bilateral Soviet-Japanese relations to a much greater degree than did Tokyo. The Soviets' increasing recognition of Japan's importance indeed must be regarded as a significant departure from previous Soviet attitudes and policies toward Japan. Since the end of World War II Soviet political leaders had long shown a tendency to underestimate Japan as a state and the Japanese as a people. They had retained their earlier image of the Japanese—particularly the image of the Japanese being submissive and easily intimidated—which they formulated through their experience with Japanese prisoners in Siberian camps immediately after the war. This tendency had been further reinforced by the Soviet inclination to assess the power of a state largely in terms of existing military might. However, though belatedly and still insufficiently, Soviet political leaders gradually became aware of the significance of the Japanese power-potential, which stemmed from specific geopolitical, diplomatic, military-strategic, and economic roles that Japan could play in the world, particularly in the Asia-Pacific region.

Japan's geopolitical and strategic importance increased as the USSR desired to become a more and more influential power in the Asia-Pacific region. For instance, the USSR was able to fire submarine-launched ballistic missiles (SLBMs) from its military complex around the Sea of

Okhotsk at any target in the United States except the Florida peninsula. But if its strategic checkpoints (i.e., the Tsushima, Tsugaru, and Soya straits) had ever been closed by Japan, the Soviet Pacific Fleet would have been confined to the Sea of Okhotsk and the Sea of Japan, making its passage into the Pacific difficult, if not impossible. This would also have permitted it to be easily detected by Japanese radar.

Tokyo's diplomatic posture and foreign policy greatly affected those of Moscow. The best example was Japan's decision to improve relations with the PRC. At that time, Tokyo did not have any intention whatsoever of allowing Sino-Japanese diplomatic relations to evolve into a military alliance, despite strong pressures from Beijing in that direction. Should Japan have decided for any reason to join in the formation of a military alliance together with the United States and the People's Republic of China, Soviet strategy would have been greatly affected not only in the Asia-Pacific region but in the world at large. Japan's economic potential, second-largest in the world, was certainly becoming an ever larger attraction for the ailing Soviet economy. This was essentially true since the economic development of the eastern part of the country became crucial to expanding the Soviet economy. The geographic proximity of the two countries made Japan a more natural economic partner than West European countries to provide the capital, technology, and market for Siberian resources, especially given the problems of rising transportation costs. In these respects, Tokyo had an important card to play vis-à-vis Moscow. What is to be noted here is that the role that Japan played vis-à-vis the USSR was largely of a potential nature. What Japan might or might not do (e.g., re-arm, move closer to the PRC, cooperate with the USSR in Siberian economic development, and so on) greatly affected the Soviet Union. Some Japanese political scientists argue that power in a potential form is more influential and effective.[59] At any rate, the Soviet political leaders came at last to realize, albeit to an insufficient degree, the significance of the actual and potential power of Japan.

Just because the Kremlin leaders increasingly recognized the significant role of Japan, it did not necessarily follow that they were more likely to make concessions to Tokyo. The situation was not that simple, for a variety of reasons. To begin with, perceptions and policy decisions are usually quite different things, the former being only one of many factors determining the latter.[60] Second, Tokyo's terms still seemed to Moscow too extreme to be met. The return of the territories once occupied by the Soviet Union and the removal of its military forces there were actions that the Kremlin was not willing or able to undertake easily. Above all, there was a possibility that in the perception of Kremlin leaders Japan had not yet become important enough to justify such major concessions as those requested by Tokyo. In any case, the core of the Kremlin's Japan policy appeared to lie in its stated intentions of improving relations with Tokyo on its own terms, without yielding at all.

The Kremlin was pursuing a strategy dedicated to achieving a breakthrough in bilateral relations by reaching *some sort of treaty agreement* with Japan. In contrast, Tokyo was intent on a peace treaty, which not only the Japanese but sometimes even the Soviets[61] assumed must include a clause on the settlement of the territorial question. The Kremlin would thus have been satisfied with any kind of legal document that could have somehow substituted for a peace treaty in terms of its political and symbolic functions. Both public pronouncements and private remarks made during this period by Soviet officials dealing with Soviet-Japanese relations almost always concluded with a strong assertion of the need to have such a legal document with Japan.

The conclusion of any legal document between the Soviet Union and Japan would have served four important functions. One is a legal function. V. Dal'nev believed, "the placing of their [Soviet-Japanese] relations on a firm legal basis would be an important and useful thing."[62] A legal document would have served as a useful lever to artificially build a "solid treaty basis" (*prochnaia dogovornaia osnova*)[63] on which the road to further development of Soviet-Japanese relations could be paved. Such a document could help "to bring the bilateral relations up to a higher level and render them stable."[64] The second is a creative function. N.N. Nikolaev, another Soviet specialist on Soviet-Japanese relations, did not conceal his expectations that a treaty would serve a sort of creative function, claiming that "such a document would *create* the atmosphere of deep confidence necessary for the development of good business relations between these two countries" (emphasis added by H.K.).[65]

The third is a political function. In a booklet particularly aimed at the Japanese audience, and thus safely taken as an authoritative Kremlin view on the matter, Dal'nev expressed why the Soviets needed a *political* treaty: "If we two countries can conclude an appropriate *political* treaty, it can serve not only to stabilize all positive factors that we have achieved in Soviet-Japanese relations but also to determine the basic orientation of peaceful and mutually beneficial development of long-term future relations between our two countries. A Treaty of Good-neighborliness and

Cooperation, a draft of which was given by Andrei Gromyko to the Japanese side, will be a treaty of such a *political* character" (emphasis added by H.K.).[66] A different, yet related, reason for concluding a legal document is its propaganda function. Once a treaty was concluded between Japan and the Soviet Union, it would symbolize a major breakthrough, which would be trumpeted throughout the world.

Interestingly enough, the Soviet approach provided a marked contrast to that of the Japanese in terms of what ought to be done first to improve Soviet-Japanese relations. The Soviets clearly deemed it necessary to secure a written document in order to build confidence, whereas the Japanese proceeded in exactly the opposite way. In order to illustrate this marked contrast, it is worth citing a part of the debate between Dimitrii Polianskii, then Soviet ambassador to Japan, and Nobutaka Shikanai, the president of *Sankei Shimbun*:

> Polianskii: Thus, we are proposing the conclusion of a treaty with Japan to develop friendly relations. Such a treaty can be a peace treaty, a treaty of peace and friendship, a treaty of non-aggression, or a treaty of non-use of military weapons.

> Shikanai: In the light of world history, the conclusion of a treaty does not necessarily mean that everything is then completed and solved. A treaty becomes meaningful only when it is accepted and observed by the people of both signatory nations. Accordingly, we should first make efforts to build the national feeling on both sides in order to bring about good results.[67]

6. Asian Collective Security Scheme or Any Other Treaty

Whatever function a legal document with Japan may have been intended to serve, nobody can deny the fact that the Kremlin was doing its utmost to sell the idea of such a treaty document. CPSU General Secretary Leonid Brezhnev's proposal for an Asian collective security system was obviously one of this series of attempts.

The idea of establishing an Asian collective security system was first posited in 1969 by Brezhvev, who stated that "such a system is the best substitute for the existing military-political groupings."[68] Most Western observers interpreted the Soviet proposal as a military alliance aimed at isolating the PRC and undermining the Western position in Asia.[69] Faced with indifference, coolness, and even suspicion in Asia, Brezhnev in 1972 decided to revise his scheme by making the initially vague proposal more concrete through a set of normative principles. The principles on which the proposed collective security system would be founded were renunciation of the use of force, respect for sovereignty and inviolability of borders, non-intervention in internal affairs, and the broad development of economic and other relations on the basis of full equality and mutual advantage.[70] These were almost the same principles as those incorporated into the Helsinki Final Act of the CSCE, from which the idea of an Asian collective security system was actually derived.

Japan, supposedly a principal target of a Soviet-sponsored collective security initiative,[71] ignored the Soviet proposal, mainly because of its anti-Chinese and military implications.[72] For Tokyo, an especially disturbing aspect of the Soviet scheme was that the principle calling for "respect for inviolability of national borders" would serve, as it in fact did in Europe, to consolidate Moscow's view of the territorial status quo and thereby undermine Tokyo's claims to the Northern Territories.[73] Encountering a rather cool response among most Asian nations, the Kremlin in 1973 started to emphasize that its idea of collective security in Asia could not be realized overnight but had to be approached gradually by accumulating a series of *selective* bilateral treaty arrangements between the USSR and the various Asian states as building blocks for an eventual edifice of collective security embracing the whole region.[74]

It is quite accurate to regard Moscow's 1978 proposal of a Treaty of Good-neighborliness and Cooperation to Tokyo as one of these bilateral treaty arrangements, similar to the Soviet treaties of peace, friendship, and cooperation with Egypt, India, Iraq, Outer Mongolia, Afghanistan, and Iran. It is thus clear what kind of function the newly proposed treaty was expected to have for the Soviet Union: to serve the Soviet Union as an artificial lever for breaking its deadlock with Japan, and to pave the way for new developments. This intention was clearly evident in the following statement by Iurii Vdovin, the Tokyo correspondent of *Pravda*: "The Soviet Union has in fact repeatedly demonstrated its preparedness to develop and deepen its relations with Japan. *A good basis* for this could be a Treaty of Good-neighborliness and Cooperation. . . . The conclusion of such a treaty would *elevate relations between the two countries to a new level and open the perspectives for further development* of broad relations in various fields" (emphasis added by H.K.).[75] The Kremlin unilaterally and quite arbitrarily announced the drafting of a treaty in spring of 1977,[76] just as Tokyo had finally decided to sign a peace treaty with Beijing. This was well-timed from Moscow's point of view, for it gave the Soviets a tactical advantage: the Japanese were completely free to do with the Chinese whatever they wanted, but the Soviets would demand similar treatment on the grounds that the Japanese ought to treat their two neighbors with equal fairness. When Tokyo simply ignored the draft treaty proposed by the Soviets, the Kremlin was infuriated. Expressing such feelings, an *Izvestiia* commentator, V. Kudriavtsev, wrote: "While clearing the way for a treaty with Beijing, the Japanese ruling circles did not regard it as necessary to discuss the draft of a Treaty of Good-neighborliness and Cooperation, recently proposed by the Soviet Union, even though the latter proposal would be much better in stabilizing Soviet-Japanese relations and the basis of peace and security in the Far East."[77]

In contrast, the ultimate objective of Tokyo's policy toward Moscow can be summarized as aiming to improve Japanese-Soviet bilateral relations in a comprehensive way,[78] so that all issues would be covered and linked together. This basic policy orientation stemmed from a realization by Tokyo that it could not otherwise effectively counter the customary Soviet strategy of circumventing or even completely excluding some important issues in Japanese-Soviet relations, such as the territorial question, and arbitrarily linking or separating one issue from the other. Tokyo was particularly careful not to play into the Soviet ploy of "picking a raisin out of the cake" by prematurely agreeing to start negotiations with the Soviets on relatively easy matters, with little hope of major long-term results. Tokyo's concern can easily be understood and justified by the nature of its previous experiences.

For instance, the Japanese government under Prime Minister Ichirō Hatoyama agreed to normalize relations with the USSR under Nikita S. Khrushchev in 1956 with the signing of a Japanese-Soviet Joint Declaration, which stipulates in Article 9 that "the USSR agrees to transfer to Japan the Habomai Islands and the Island of Shikotan" upon conclusion of a formal peace treaty between the two countries. A few years later, in 1960, however, Tokyo discovered that the Soviet Union under the same leadership negated the passage in the Joint Declaration concerning Soviet promises on the return of the two islands to Japan, unilaterally adding a new condition to the declaration that all U.S. troops must depart from Japanese soil before the islands would be returned.[79] This Soviet announcement naturally left the Japanese wondering how a legal agreement could possibly be nullified by the subsequent unilateral decision of one party to the agreement.

The Tokyo government had a similar experience in the mid-1970s. Japanese Prime Minister Kakuei Tanaka signed a Japanese-Soviet Joint Communiqué in 1973 that stated: "Both sides confirm that the settlement of outstanding questions left over since World War II and the conclusion of a peace treaty would contribute to the establishment of good-neighborly relations."[80] Understanding the Northern Territories issue as an "outstanding question left over from World War II," Tanaka agreed, in return for the inclusion of this wording, to a clause in which the Japanese government pledged to extend to the USSR a huge amount of Japanese bank credit and other forms of economic cooperation for the development of Siberia and the Far East. Once again the Japanese were disappointed by the Soviets' subsequent actions. While not hesitating to accept support for their Siberian development project, the Soviets failed to show any interest whatsoever in discussing the territorial question with Japan, saying that they did not regard the territorial issue as one of "the outstanding questions left over from World War II." Immediately after unilaterally reinterpreting the above-cited portion of the Tanaka-Brezhnev Joint Communiqué in 1973, Nikolai A. Tikhonov, the Soviet Premier, had the nerve to make the following proposal:

> [For Japan] to assert that the Soviet Union has admitted the existence of a 'territorial question' [in the 1973 Joint Communiqué] is to deliberately distort our position and mislead the Japanese public. In connection with the question of the treaty basis of Soviet-Japanese relations, I would like you to recall our proposal to conclude a Treaty of Good-neighborliness and Cooperation. This proposal has remained on the table to this day.[81]

At last, after these bitter experiences, Japan seems to have learned that a "step-by-step" approach or, in Soviet terms, a "let's do what we can do first" approach for improving bilateral relations did not work for Japan but only benefited the Soviets, who were interested in picking up quick gains and ultimately not keeping their word. As a result, Tokyo appears to have decided, somewhat belatedly, that its best policy stance toward the Kremlin was a firm "all-or-nothing" position. As long as Moscow continued to show no interest in a comprehensive improvement of relations with Tokyo, Japan should not conclude even a minor agreement with the USSR. More specifically, as long as Soviet proposals continued to fall short of settling the Northern Territories issue, the Japanese government had no intention to come to terms on other subjects. If, unfortunately, these conditions were not met by the Kremlin, the Tokyo government decided that it should be content with maintaining the status quo. In the face of pressure for Japan to make a greater effort to improve the bilateral relationship, Tokyo seemed ready to answer that "regrettably, this is normal for now and the foreseeable future."[82]

Given the fact that it was the *USSR* that needed improved relations more, Japan's readiness to open talks with the Soviet Union seemed to have become its most important bargaining chip vis-à-vis the USSR. Thus, if Tokyo were to respond immediately to a Soviet proposal, or even go so far as to take an initiative, it would have almost automatically lost this bargaining leverage.[83] Acknowledging that "up until now Japanese diplomacy has made many mistakes in this regard," Masuo Takashima, Japanese ambassador to Moscow, explained to the Japanese public what he considered to be the best policy for Japan to pursue toward the Soviet Union: "If our side moves closer to the Soviets, then clearly from the outset the game will be lost for us. We should wait until the Soviet Union comes to consider Japan important enough. In my opinion this would be the best posture to assume."[84]

7. Soviet Offensive and Japan's Counter-Strategy

Nearly all arms control or disarmament overtures combine a serious effort to reach some sort of an agreement with a propagandistic appeal to impress the public at home and abroad with peace-oriented intentions.[85] In the case of Japan and the Soviet Union, CBMs were designed to function as a political instrument directed at breaking a major impasse in relations. Moscow would benefit greatly from CBMs with Japan, both in symbolic terms and in a concrete political and economic sense. In this regard, the Soviet CBMs proposal ought to be viewed as just another in a series of proposals that included the Asian collective security system and the Treaty of Good-neighborliness and Cooperation.

The idea of CBMs in the Far East was first proposed by Leonid I. Brezhnev in his speech on February 23, 1981 at the 26th Party Congress, when the General Secretary made it clear that "the Soviet Union would be prepared to conduct concrete talks on CBMs in the Far East with all interested countries."[86] Despite that fact that "Beijing hastened to call the Soviet proposals propaganda,"[87] Konstantin U. Chernenko, Brezhnev's longtime protege, expressed a month later, on the occasion of the 111th anniversary of the birth of V.I. Lenin, the Soviet Union's determination to stick doggedly to the proposal. In his initial overtures, Brezhnev clearly gave the impression that the USSR was interested in having a CBMs arrangement in Asia on a collective basis. He invited "all interested countries" to discuss the proposal, particularly mentioning "the USSR, China, Japan" and even the United States, which had, in Brezhnev's words, "military bases there [in the Far East]."[88] It is, of course, hard to determine whether this was a reflection of Brezhnev's real intentions, simply rhetoric, or a sort of *ballon d'essai*, as was his earlier, Asian collective security proposal.

In any event, Brezhnev's position shifted very rapidly on the application of his CBMs proposal from a collective to a bilateral scheme. This transition was signaled in a communiqué issued after a meeting in Crimea in August 1981 between Brezhnev and the Mongolian Communist Party leader, Yumjagiin Tsedenbal, which stated: "The application of these [confidence-building] measures is possible on a collective basis, with the participation of all interested sides." The document added, "It is also possible on a bilateral basis."[89] As expected, it soon became clear that, while the Soviets continued to claim that they were advocating an application of CBMs in the Far East on a collective basis, what they were really envisioning was obviously a conclusion of an agreement on CBMs on a bilateral basis, particularly with the PRC or Japan. The well-known Tashkent speech on March 24, 1982, in which Brezhnev made diplomatic overtures to Tokyo and Beijing, marked a clear step in that direction. Emphasizing that the proposed CBMs in the Far East did not necessarily imply the immediate collective involvement of all countries in the region, the CPSU General Secretary stated that "progress along that path could also provide a good basis for a new bilateral start, for example, between the USSR and Japan,"[90] thus calling upon Japan to weigh the proposal more seriously. Vsevolod V. Ovchinnikov, a political commentator for *Pravda*, stated more articulately a month later, at the third Japan–USSR roundtable conference in Tokyo on April 20–22, 1982, that "the Soviets do not think that the establishment of CBMs will immediately have a collective character."[91]

The fact that Moscow desperately needed CBMs or an appropriate substitute is sufficiently obvious from these repeated overtures, the most notable of which was Brezhnev's letter of reply to the group of Japanese writers protesting against nuclear weapons, which read: "We see no obstacle to beginning an exchange of opinions with Japan either within the framework of the proposal . . . on CBMs in the Far East or *in any other form* [*v liubykh drugikh formakh*] acceptable to both sides" (emphasis added by H.K.).[92] Iurii Andropov renewed proposals made by his predecessor Brezhnev with regard to CBMs, saying in general that all "peace proposals since the 26th Party Congress are still valid," and particularly mentioning the CBMs proposal to Japan.[93]

Despite these strenuous Soviet efforts, the Japanese reaction was cold and decidedly negative. The Japanese government under Prime Minister Zenkō Suzuki considered the Soviet proposal on CBMs unacceptable, and so did the government under Prime Minister Nakasone. On April 29, 1981, the Japanese ambassador to the Soviet Union, Tōichiro Uomoto, conveyed to Soviet Foreign Minister Gromyko a formal message in which Suzuki noted that unless certain conditions were met by the Soviets, Japan could not discuss these proposals. This served as an official reply to the Soviet proposal advanced by Soviet ambassador Dmitrii Polianskii to Japanese Foreign Minister Masayoshi Itō[94] on March 15 of the same year. When Brezhnev repeated the Soviet CBMs proposal a year later at Tashkent, Suzuki, clearly enunciating the conditions to be met by the Soviet Union prior to any serious discussion, stated in the Diet on March 26, 1982: "We welcome some parts of the overtures made by General Secretary Brezhnev at Tashkent—for example, the part dealing with confidence building in the Far East. Yet, the Soviet Union needs to prove such intentions with its own deeds. That is to say, it must withdraw its nuclear weapons, such as SS-20s, from the Far East; return the Northern Territories to Japan; and stop its military buildup on these islands. We cannot take the Soviet words literally, inasmuch as they are only appealing verbally to us."[95]

Given the essentially modest goals of CBMs with respect to the exchange of information on military activity of neighboring adversaries, the preconditions Suzuki attached to the Soviet CBMs proposal might appear too demanding. However, it must be stressed that, although the implementation of arms control and disarmament agreements is military in character, the negotiation and signing of them cannot completely escape political realities. The same reasoning should be applied to CBMs. After all, talks on CBMs, like any other arms control and disarmament talks, do not take place in a political vacuum.[96] They are conducted in the midst of an international political environment with specific historical elements. Each participating state pursues a variety of interests by mobilizing a variety of available means. It is thus natural to assume that negotiations on CBMs, like other arms control and disarmament talks, are used to pursue objectives other than those for which they were originally convened.[97] In short, the CBMs should be viewed as an integral part of the overall Soviet foreign policy.

Tokyo's negative response to the Soviet proposal on CBMs probably can be understood only in the historical context of the bilateral efforts made by Japan and the Soviet Union to negotiate a treaty. Japan and the Soviet Union each had been promoting their respective ideas for a treaty. Based on what was written into the previously signed documents, including the Japanese-Soviet Joint Declaration in 1956 and the Japanese-Soviet Joint Communiqué in 1973, Tokyo merely wanted to extend previous lines of negotiation toward a peace treaty settling the territorial question. Tokyo wanted to adhere by all means to this track, which it regarded as the only right one. Whatever arguments or excuses the Japanese government may have been making, what really concerned Tokyo was its suspicion that once it agreed to the Soviet proposal, it would lose any chance it might have had to press the Soviets to come to terms with the Japanese peace treaty proposal.

In contrast, however, Moscow attempted to take every opportunity to lure Tokyo away from this line of thinking. Moscow admitted that the Soviet-Japanese Joint Communiqué (1973) and Soviet-Japanese Declaration (1956) were important documents, but conveniently ignored those parts of the documents that were unfavorable to the Soviet Union. Moscow argued that since Japan and the USSR had long been deadlocked in peace treaty negotiations, the time had come for them to seriously consider another type of substitute treaty arrangement. What the Soviets were proposing, as noted above, was an Asian Collective Security Treaty with Japan on a bilateral basis or a Soviet-Japanese Treaty of Good-neighborliness and Cooperation, or any other kind of legal document. Based on such an interim document, Moscow insisted that a peace treaty could be reached sometime in the future between the two countries. In 1967, Soviet Premier Alexei N. Kosygin hinted to Japanese Foreign Minister Takeo Miki during the latter's visit to Moscow that "an interim document" between Moscow and Tokyo should be concluded on the grounds that neither side was currently willing to sign a peace treaty on terms acceptable to the other. In an interview with Shōryū Hata, the editor-in-chief of *Asahi Shimbun*, on June 6, 1977, Brezhnev also stressed: "After all, the point is not the name but the content of the treaty. . . . The important thing is to promote a bilateral relationship serving the objective of establishing genuinely good relations between our two countries."[98] Judging from past Soviet behavior, Tokyo knew well that should any one of the Soviet-proposed interim accords have been agreed to by Japan, it would have been the final one, thus precluding any chance to return to the right track. More specifically, what Tokyo feared was that once Moscow had established the rapport it wanted with Tokyo through CBMs, the need for a formal peace treaty would lose its urgency for the Soviet Union. This seemed to be the real reason why Tokyo was so hesitant to discuss the Soviet proposal on CBMs.

Part Four

A CHANGING GLOBAL ENVIRONMENT

As already mentioned in Part Three, in the period from the mid-1970s to the early 1980s, which is the period examined in this book, Soviet-Japanese relations reached one of the lowest ebbs since the end of World War II. What is, however, noteworthy here is the fact that, particularly at the threshold of the 1980s, Soviet-Japanese relations dramatically deteriorated further. Official Soviet pronouncements and writings admitted this deterioration in relations. In his speech presented before the Central Committee at the 26th Congress of the CPSU (in February 1981), General Secretary Leonid Brezhnev noted that in the Soviet Union's relations with Japan "negative factors are becoming stronger."[1] Iurii D. Kuznetsov also noted the same tendency in his article, "Where Is Japan Being Pushed?" published after Iurii Andropov assumed the post of General Secretary: "Since the beginning of the 1980s, progressive Soviet-Japanese relations have been noticeably blocked."[2]

A host of factors contributed to the deterioration in Soviet-Japanese relations, including: (1) Soviet direct or indirect intervention in other countries, such as Afghanistan (1979) and Poland; (2) the buildup of Soviet military forces in the Far East, particularly in the vicinity of Japan (1979); (3) Japan's participation in Western sanctions against the USSR (1980); (4) the rebirth of a "national security consciousness" among the Japanese, including a revitalization of the campaign for the reversion of the Northern Territories (1981); (5) the arrival to the top political leadership in Japan of Yasuhiro Nakasone, who had strongly pro-U.S. and anti-Soviet sentiments (1982); (6) the Soviet threat to transfer their SS-20s from Europe to Asia (1982–83); and (7) the Soviet shooting down of KAL-007 (1983).

The above list of factors reveals the complexity of actions and reactions linking the two countries. Indeed, it was becoming increasingly difficult to distinguish causes from consequences. Notwithstanding, the official Soviet perspective ascribed full responsibility for the deterioration in Soviet-Japanese relations to the revival of nationalism in Japan and to "the growing dependence of Japanese foreign policy on the United States."[3] For example, in an article entitled "The Soviet Union–Japan: The Course of Good-neighborliness and Its Opponents," N. Nikolaev and A. Pavlov wrote:

> At the turn of the 1980s, the shaping of Japan's foreign policy as a whole, and especially its policy vis-à-vis the Soviet Union, became increasingly influenced by *external factors* and by *nationalistic circles* seeking to revive the ambitious imperial policies (emphasis added by H.K.).[4]

Ascribing the "root of that [new] phenomenon in Japan's foreign policy" to internal political and economic trends within Japan, they continued:

> The Japanese ruling circles persistently pressed the line that the national, historical and ideological specifics of Japan made it the second-most powerful economy in the capitalist world, and, moreover, gave it the right to uphold its "specific" Japanese interests in relations with other countries.[5]

The same authors also emphasized "external factors" influencing Tokyo's foreign policy:

> The United States increased pressure on Japan to contribute more actively to Washington's global anti-Soviet strategy and to undertake a larger share of the commitments in the Japanese-American alliance, especially in the military field.[6]

Nikolaev and Pavlov even directly linked the shift in Japan's Soviet policy with U.S. pressure on Tokyo:

> Japan acceded to the American policy of "economic sanctions" and curtailed official contracts. That markedly complicated the atmosphere of Soviet-Japanese relations.[7]

In even clearer words, Kuznetsov supported this view:

> It is no secret to anyone that the discriminatory measures adopted by Japan in her relations with the Soviet Union were forced upon Japan by the United States.[8]

The foregoing Soviet interpretation of the development of events concerning Soviet-Japanese relations is, of course, not immune to criticisms and counterarguments from non-Soviet specialists, particularly the Japanese. Yet, the Soviet arguments serve—however excessively—as a reminder of some subjects not covered sufficiently in the previous chapters of this book. In particular, more explanation is warranted concerning the following three important dimensions in Soviet-Japanese relations.

(1) One dimension is the significant role played by the United States in determining Soviet-Japanese relations. As indicated both explicitly and implicitly in previous chapters, Soviet-Japanese relations must not be viewed simply from a Japan–USSR bilateral perspective but within a broader global context, or at least within the regional context of East Asia and the Pacific. Any analysis of Soviet-Japanese bilateral relations would be incomplete if it does not take into account at least two additional powers—the United States and the People's Republic of China. Yet, so far I have neglected these important actors and their influences on Soviet-Japanese relations. The China factor was touched upon, though insufficiently, in the discussion on the Sino-Japanese peace treaty (chapter 8). In this last section, the United States's influence on relations between Japan and the Soviet Union must be addressed.

(2) Soviet writings also remind us of the gradual transformation process that was occurring within Japan and the impact this transformation had on Soviet-Japanese relations. The increase in Japan's self-confidence in these years (for reasons to be addressed shortly) prompted some Soviet and Western observers to declare a "rebirth of nationalism" in Japan. Moreover, an increasing number of Japanese came to agree with the Western argument that Japan, as a member of "the Western community" with shared basic values, should shoulder a more positively political responsibility than before. The Japanese attitude toward national security was indeed undergoing some changes. As a result of these changing perspectives, people were witnessing a gradual shift in Japan's foreign policy from its previously submissive and passive posture to a slightly more forward-looking and even assertive posture. Similarly, though to a lesser degree and at a slower pace, Japan's defense and security policy began to show some changes. This latter change deserves particular attention, considering my basic premise that divergent Soviet-Japanese views on national security constituted a major stumbling block between Japan and the Soviet Union. It thus becomes necessary to examine the transformations that took place in Japan and to measure the impact of these changes on Soviet-Japanese bilateral relations.

(3) An additional, third point deserving our attention in the remaining chapters is the change and continuity on the Soviet side. Assessment of

Soviet global foreign policy is a difficult task and one that is certainly beyond the scope of this book. There is a basic consensus among Japanese and Western specialists, however, that toward the end of the 1970s the USSR failed to record any significant achievements in its Japan policy. The questions to be raised, then, are: Did the Soviet Union demonstrate any signs of altering such an "abortive"—to use the word of Professor Donald C. Hellmann at the University of Washington—policy toward Japan? What impact did Soviet conduct of foreign affairs elsewhere in the world have on Soviet-Japanese relations (e.g., Soviet military intervention in Afghanistan, or Soviet political pressure exerted during the "Poland crisis")? To what extent did Soviet relations with the United States from the late 1970s (e.g., Soviet arms control negotiations over the intermediate-range nuclear forces with the United States and West European countries) influence Japan? Did any new developments within the Soviet Union (e.g., the leadership change from Brezhnev to Andropov) affect relations between Japan and the USSR? These represent a few examples of those questions which I attempt to deal with in Part Four.

Chapter 9

The Impact of the Soviet Invasion of Afghanistan (1979)

On August 4, 1980, Japanese Foreign Minister Masayoshi Itō expressed his interest in conferring with his counterpart in the USSR, Andrei A. Gromyko, should there be an opportunity when both were in attendance at the upcoming UN General Assembly scheduled for September of that year.[1] The foreign minister of the newly installed Japanese cabinet under the premiership of Zenkō Suzuki, however, did not fail to add a caveat that mutual concessions were needed if his meeting with the Soviet Foreign Minister was to be fruitful. He said that there would be no point in talking with the Soviets as long as they persisted in their self-righteous attitude about the Soviet military buildup in the Japanese-claimed Northern Territories and about their intervention in Afghanistan, and he stressed that it was the Soviet Union that had to change its attitude.[2] Anyone who is interested in international relations in the Far East is aware of the fact that the Northern Territories were a major issue in relations between Japan and the Soviet Union. The point here, however, is the fact that another prerequisite for the improvement of bilateral relations between these two countries was added by the Japanese side: the withdrawal of Soviet military forces from Afghanistan.

The Soviet invasion of Afghanistan in late December 1979 had a major impact on Japanese foreign policy—both in its general orientation and vis-à-vis the USSR. By their act of military intervention in Afghanistan, the Soviet leaders destroyed their bargaining position in relations with Japan. The Japanese government of Prime Minister Masayoshi Ōhira adopted a policy of even closer cooperation with the United States, which was exemplified by the suspension of exchanges between high officials

of the USSR and Japan and the freezing of joint economic projects with
the Soviets, together with the boycotting of the Moscow Olympics. Furthermore, the "Pacific Basin Cooperation Design" promulgated by Ōhira
and Foreign Minister Saburō Ōkita, appeared to mark a departure from
Japan's policy of balancing relations, since it excluded specific reference
to the Soviet Union. Finally, the Soviet invasion of Afghanistan resulted
in expanded concern in Japan for military security—a concern that seemed
to have superseded the territorial questions that had dominated Soviet-
Japanese relations during the entire postwar period.

Several questions arise immediately. Why did the Soviet incursion into
Afghanistan, thousands of miles from Japan, so greatly influence the orientation of Japan's foreign policy? Are all of the shifts in Japanese policy
since the end of 1979 direct results of the Soviet invasion? Did the changes
in Japanese foreign policy take place in such a clear-cut or simplified
way as described above? What were the ramifications of a continuing
anti-Soviet attitude on the part of the Japanese?

This chapter attempts to answer these questions by examining Japanese-
Soviet relations from the Soviet incursion into Afghanistan (December 1979)
until the formation of the Suzuki Cabinet (July 1980)—one of the worst
phases in postwar Soviet-Japanese relations. I will first focus on the Japanese reaction to the Soviet invasion of Afghanistan; then I will discuss Soviet
policies and strategies toward Japan in general, and, in particular, the
Soviet response to Japan's reaction to the invasion of Afghanistan.

1. Zigzagging Between Two Policy Alternatives

In order to identify the position of the Ōhira government with respect to
the Soviet Union during the period in question, it is helpful to distinguish
between the two approaches that have characterized postwar Japanese
foreign policy. Although both approaches stem mainly from the physical
environment and economic considerations of Japan (as a country poor in
natural resources, Japan is destined to depend heavily on foreign trade),
they suggest seemingly opposite foreign policy options.[3]

One school of thought has stressed that, in order to survive, Japan must
be engaged in a system of international trade from which a free flow of
goods and information can be obtained. Thus, Japan had to play a responsible role in cooperation with liberal capitalist countries such as the United
States, Canada, Australia, and the EEC (European Economic Community,
now EU, European Union) member states so as to preserve this political-

economic system. Above all, cooperation with the United States has been of vital importance to Japan's survival, because the United States is both its major trading partner and the chief guarantor of the system.

The second approach argues that because of its lack of essential natural resources, Japan must secure energy resources from any country that can provide them, regardless of the differences in political and economic philosophy that may exist. Dependence upon one country or group of countries for the supply of raw materials and demand for Japanese products may be risky in the long run. Even if a country is not a good trading partner with Japan, its capability to disturb either directly or indirectly the security of countries important to Japan, or of Japan itself, would be of great concern. Consequently, there was no alternative for Japan but to pursue a policy referred to as "omnidirectional" diplomacy, although it is often criticized as "over-mercantilistic," because it does not adhere to any specific principle other than the promotion of business.

Although the two schools appear diametrically opposed, upon closer inspection, these two views actually complement each other. The second view is an extension of the first. Where self-preservation is concerned, Japan has no other option but to seek the help and cooperation of the United States and other Western liberal, capitalist countries. In other areas, however, Japan naturally tends to demonstrate a more expansive economic and political interest in non-Western nations, including the "Communist" states. Therefore, it is not surprising to find both views held simultaneously by the same individual or group. In fact, since World War II, Japanese foreign policy has vacillated between these two differing concepts.

Against this background, I would like to describe more clearly the effects of the previously discussed views on the period covered in this book. During a six-month period from the end of December 1979 to July 1980, continuous bickering occurred among the proponents of these two schools of thought. Despite some difficulties, the first school, which emphasized a policy of cooperation with the United States, was dominant. Nonetheless, immediately before and after the death of Prime Minister Masayoshi Ōhira, who was a supporter of the first school of thought, there was a gradual resurgence of the second school.

On the level of principle, the Japanese government under Prime Minister Ōhira reacted promptly to the Soviet military invasion of Afghanistan in late December 1979. On December 29, Foreign Minister Saburō Ōkita called for an immediate halt to the invasion and, at the same time, ordered his ministry to protest the Soviet action to Soviet Ambassador to Japan Dmitrii Polianskii. On January 4, 1980, the first working day after the New Year holiday, the Ōhira government agreed to support the United Nations resolution condemning the Soviet incursion.[4]

However, although the Japanese government verbally protested the Soviet aggression, it introduced no concrete measures to back up its criticism. The Ōhira cabinet also appeared to vacillate in the extent to which it cooperated with the Carter administration's strategy of communicating to the Soviets how costly their military action would be.[5] It was not long, however, before this inaction and indecision came to an end. The Ōhira cabinet was induced to take a concrete stand against the Soviet Union as a result of firm pressure from Washington, as well as from hawks in the ruling Liberal Democratic Party (LDP), intellectuals, and other sectors of Japanese society. On January 5, after consulting with Vice-Foreign Minister Masuo Takashima, Prime Minister Ōhira decided that Japan should do something more to "express its displeasure" with the events in Afghanistan.[6] Two days later, the Foreign Ministry announced that it was considering possible countermeasures against the Soviets in two major areas: restrictions on diplomatic and other official exchanges between Japan and the USSR, and economic sanctions, including the suspension of joint economic development projects in Siberia.[7]

The first measure, the suspension of person-to-person contacts, was not difficult to implement and was put into practice soon after the announcement: on January 8, 1980, the proposed visit of Soviet Foreign Minister Gromyko to Tokyo was called off,[8] and on the same day, a planned meeting with Ambassador Polianskii was postponed indefinitely by top members of the LDP.[9] A few days later, on January 11, a scheduled visit by members of the USSR's Supreme Soviet was cancelled by the speakers of both houses of the Japanese Diet.[10]

In marked contrast, however, the countermeasure of economic sanctions against the Soviet Union was not so easily implemented. Some Japanese, especially those representing the second view of foreign policy outlined above, feared that economic sanctions would have a "boomerang effect" on Japan and inflict great damage on the Japanese economy. Pressure from within the LDP, however, caused the Ōhira administration to advocate limited economic sanctions. On January 8, top LDP leaders publicly announced their view that economic sanctions against the Soviet Union by Japan must be made "even *in the face of resistance from the Japanese business community*" (emphasis added by H.K.).[11] Pressure on the government to take more effective action against the Soviet Union continued. The LDP's Foreign Relations Committee, chaired by former Foreign Minister Zentarō Kōsaka, expressed their view on January 11 that Japan should adopt stronger sanctions against the Soviet Union.[12] Viewing the Japanese response to the Soviet invasion as lukewarm and slow, Australian Prime Minister Malcolm Fraser also insisted during Mr. Ōhira's visit to Canberra in mid-January that Japan take stronger reprisals.[13] At the same time, from January 16–18, Japanese governmental leaders were holding talks with White House special envoy Philip Habib, who reportedly insisted that Japan terminate its loans and credits to the Soviets, so as to cooperate with the U.S. policy of containment against further Soviet expansion.[14]

After his return from a six-day tour of Oceania,[15] Prime Minister Ōhira delivered a speech to the Japan Press Club on January 22, in which three important points were made: first, Ōhira stated that Japan's foreign policy was based on cooperation with the United States; second, he noted that "the Soviet Union is a defensive, cautious, diplomatically skillful and experienced country—not a reckless country"; third, concerning Japan's possible boycott of the Moscow Olympic Games, Ōhira evasively stated that, "for the time being, the government intends to observe the reactions of Western and other countries."[16]

The slow and inconsistent foreign policy stratagems of the Ōhira administration must be seen in the context of the indirect process of decision making that characterizes Japanese leaders and often involves their waiting patiently until "the last minute," when there is no alternative but to finally decide. Unlike their Western counterparts, Japanese leaders do not dictate, initiate, or discuss various plans and alternatives with the general public and others concerned. Instead, they create an environment out of which they can later insist certain policies have evolved naturally. By taking full advantage of this contrived atmosphere, Japanese leaders are able to push through their politics without much effective resistance from those who are not "in the know." We may observe at this point that, although Prime Minister Ōhira was a relatively more articulate statesman than were many of his predecessors, he did not deviate significantly from the traditional patterns of Japanese decision making.

2. Cooperative Policy Toward the United States

Keeping in mind a favorite practice of Japanese politicians, the manipulation of public opinion at opportune times, it is interesting to analyze the two incidents reportedly involving Japanese-Soviet intrigue that surfaced in mid-January 1980. The first incident, reported on January 9, occurred in the Nemuro area of Hokkaido, the northernmost island of Japan. It involved the arrest and fining of three local fishermen by Hokkaido police for having bribed Soviet coast guards with small gifts in an attempt to ease restrictions on fishing in Soviet-claimed territorial waters. Shortly thereafter, on January 18, Yukio Miyanaga, a retired major general, and two members of the Japanese Ground Self-Defense Forces were arrested on charges of espionage. Miyanaga confessed his role in passing secret military information to the Soviet military attaché in Tokyo, Colonel Iurii Kozlov. Of course, it may be contended that mere coincidence governed the occurrence of these two incidents at the very same time that the Japanese government was debating the issue of stronger reprisals against the Soviets. Nonetheless, both incidents did serve to arouse an anti-Soviet mood in the Japanese general public. This mood, in turn, facilitated the government's subsequent decisions.

On January 25, 1980, in his program speech at the plenary session of the joint houses of the Diet, Prime Minister Ōhira finally clarified his administration's general policy regarding the Soviet incursion into Afghanistan, when he declared:

> The [Japanese] government intends to make efforts suitable for Japan that are based on its policy of solidarity with the United States and that are in accordance with the stand of Western and other nations. Up to now, our country has made its stand clear through its activities in the United Nations and the suspension of personal exchanges with the Soviet Union. We will continue to consider and implement other appropriate measures, including a tightening of COCOM (Coordinating Committee for Multilateral Strategic Export Control to Communist Areas) controls on sales to Russia.[17]

Even more boldly, Ōhira continued, "I think that in doing the above our country should not hesitate to make *sacrifices*. Moreover, I would like to make it clear that our country will do nothing that will impede reprisals taken by other countries or undermine their impact" (emphasis added by H.K.).[18]

The Prime Minister reiterated this attitude in the remaining session of the Diet. On February 1, in the House of Representatives Budget Committee, Ōhira even made it a point to amend some of his former views. For example, he corrected an earlier statement that the Soviet Union was a "defensive country," which had been criticized both domestically and internationally, by saying: "It is an objective fact that recently the Soviet

Union has been greatly reinforcing its military forces, judging from the Soviet military deployment in the Northern Territories [and in other areas]. [Thus], I cannot but regard the Soviet troops [there] as a potential threat to Japan."[19] This was a sensational statement, as it was the first time in the Japanese Diet that a postwar Prime Minister had officially called Soviet forces a "threat to Japan."[20]

This shift in Mr. Ōhira's views greatly encouraged other Japanese high governmental officials, especially those with defense responsibilities. In one notable slip of the tongue, the Director General of the Defense Agency, Kichizō Hosoda, in a press interview given on February 4, commented that he personally regarded Soviet armed forces as "a *serious threat* to Japan" (emphasis added by H.K.).[21] Hosoda later qualified this statement, saying that his view did not differ much from that expressed by Mr. Ōhira at the Diet session a few days earlier.[22] More significantly, in a Budget Committee meeting in the Diet on the same day, Hisahiko Okazaki, counselor at the Japan Defense Agency, disclosed for the first time that about ten SS-20 mobile intermediate-range missiles had been deployed by the Soviet Union in the Far East.[23] Following these revelations, the issues of defense and security assumed major proportions, and, in fact, became the biggest issues in the Diet during the first half of 1980.[24] Several books and articles with such titles as "Hokkaido Next After Afghanistan," "The Soviet Forces Have Landed in Japan," and "The 11-Day War in Hokkaido" were released, some of which reached the bestseller list.

In early February, the Ōhira administration agreed to include Japan in the U.S.-sponsored drive to boycott the Moscow Summer Olympics.[25] In addition, the Japanese government began to implement economic restrictions against the USSR. By refusing an entry visa into Japan to Vice-Foreign Trade Minister Viktor Ivanov, the Ōhira government effectively suspended the following economic projects, which the Vice-Minister was scheduled to discuss in Tokyo: the coke and coal mining production projects in Southern Yakutsk; the third-stage program for timber resources development scheduled to begin in 1980; and the exportation of large-diameter steel pipes from Japan to the USSR.[26] The Japanese government followed a "two-track" policy at this time: the Export-Import Bank of Japan was forbidden to extend credits for *new* projects; on the other hand, however, project agreements that had been previously concluded would not be suspended, although additional bank loans would be denied.[27] Moreover, the Ministry of International Trade and Industry (MITI) adopted a policy of not permitting the export of goods enumerated in the so-called "COCOM List," which required special application, and of freezing two items that also required a special application for export.[28] In an effort to rally behind President Carter's embargo of U.S. grain sales to the Soviet Union, the Japanese Ministry of Agriculture decided to purchase an additional million tons of wheat from the United States.[29] One group of professors boldly suggested that Japan go even further and purchase the entire seventeen million tons of grain.[30]

On March 13, following the initiation of the economic sanctions, the plenary session of the House of Representatives finally passed a resolution requesting the withdrawal of Soviet troops from Afghanistan. The resolution was adopted by all of Japan's political parties except the Communist Party, which insisted that the Americans and Chinese also be condemned for their support of anti-government forces in Afghanistan.[31] The direction of the Japanese government's policies was further strengthened when Prime Minister Ōhira visited Washington from April 31 to May 1 and assured President Carter of Japan's continued support for the U.S. policies toward Iran and the Soviet Union.[32]

3. Economic Sanctions: Difficult Implementation

As we have seen thus far, Japan's foreign policy during the first half of the 1980s emphasized cooperation with the United States. This policy orientation had seldom before been so clearly implemented. However, it must also be noted that a different policy orientation, which emphasized cooperation with any country serving Japan's interests, especially in the economic sphere, also had its supporters during this period.

Shigeo Nagano, president of the Japanese Chamber of Commerce and Industry, was a champion of the second school of thought, which separated economics from politics. In a press interview on March 6, 1980, he stated that Japan must deal with the Soviet Union more rationally than emotionally, stressing that economic cooperation with the Soviet Union was not to be regarded as assistance but as business.[33] Mr. Naohiro Amaya, then counselor of the Ministry of International Trade and Industry (MITI), also stressed that Japan must avoid becoming engaged in what he termed "warrior diplomacy," saying that it was advisable for Japan to become more "mercantilistic," more like a successful merchant who exercises emotional and other restraints in order to increase benefits.[34]

As a matter of fact, Amaya disclosed in a press interview that his ministry was asking the U.S. government to allow Japan to make two exceptions to its policy of economic sanctions against the USSR: that the oil and gas resources project that had begun on the continental shelf off the coast of Sakhalin be resumed, and that exports of large steel pipes to the USSR be continued.[35] These projects were two of the five projects automatically suspended by the Japanese government's decision to deny an entry visa to the Soviet trade official V. Ivanov. In May the Ōhira government decided to resume the extension of credits and loans to the Soviet Union by the Japanese Export-Import Bank for those goods that "do not help the USSR increase its military strength."[36] The government decided on May 22 to provide bank loans to the third stage of the program for timber resources development,[37] regarding it as a continuation of the first and second stages of a project previously initiated. As justification for this decision, the government explained: "If Japan shelves the third stage of this project, the Japanese investment in the first and second stages will be wasted."[38]

Of course, this rather haphazard, inconsistent practice of allowing one exception after another in the economic field, while using the "survival of a resource-poor country" as a justification, did not escape the criticism of many observers, even in Japan itself. Professor Masamori Sase of the National Defense Academy (of Japan), for instance, pointed out that, whether or not it is accepted as such, Japan cannot be considered a purely "mercantilistic" state. The fact that Japan ranked eighth in the world in military might underscored its position as *both* a "mercantile" and a "warrior" state. Furthermore, Professor Sase noted that, because of its diplomatic position, Japan could not hope to be accepted by other countries merely as a "mercantile" state. This last point stressed the priority of retaining the United States as a valuable trading partner and the desirability of preventing the United States from becoming unhappy with Japan.[39]

The sudden death of Prime Minister Ōhira on June 12 temporarily interrupted the debate on the issue of whether or not Japan was to be exclusively "mercantilistic"; however, ensuing events served to highlight its dimensions. The new Prime Minister, Zenkō Suzuki, outlined his basic foreign policy in his first news conference, on July 18. He stated that he was determined to continue the policies of his predecessor and that his selection for Foreign Minister of Masayoshi Itō, formerly Ōhira's Chief Cabinet Secretary and aide, was a concrete demonstration of this determination.[40] After characterizing the Japanese-American relationship as the pivotal point of Japan's foreign policy, Suzuki stated: "Japan's relations with its neighbor, the Soviet Union, are important; however, endeavors made only on the Japanese side are not sufficient. We expect the Soviets to initiate some action with regard to Afghanistan and the Northern Territories if it really wants to improve its relations with us."[41] This can be considered a statement of the Suzuki government's basic policy orientation toward the Soviet Union.

While repeating this policy line, Foreign Minister Itō also added that he deemed it necessary for Japan to keep open lines of communication with the Soviet Union despite the Soviet aggression in Afghanistan.[42] In addition, he granted an entry visa to Nikolai N. Solov'ev, the chief of the Second Far Eastern Department of the Soviet Ministry of Foreign Affairs. This action was interpreted as a gesture by the new government to break away from the former prime minister's restrictions on personal contacts between the two countries. During his stay in Tokyo, Solov'ev strongly communicated the willingness of the Soviet Union to improve relations with Japan.[43] However, Toshiaki Mutō, Director General of the European and Oceanic Affairs Bureau of the Japanese Foreign Ministry, clearly under instructions from Foreign Minister Itō, pointed out that: "The recent Soviet military buildup on the islands off Hokkaido claimed by Japanese and the Soviet military invasion into Afghanistan are the major causes of disharmony between Tokyo and Moscow and, hence, the Soviet Union is considered to be responsible for the strained bilateral relations."[44] Foreign Minister Itō later indicated that no entry visas would be issued to any other Soviet officials (for example, to Vladimir N. Sushkov, Soviet Vice-Foreign Trade Minister) because the government wished to continue its previous policy of not honoring personal exchanges or communications with the Soviets.[45] Soviet-Japanese relations were further strained in August, when a disabled Soviet nuclear submarine was discovered in Japanese territorial waters without Japan's advance permission. The Suzuki government denounced the trespass as an "unfriendly act."[46]

It may be concluded that, with the exception of the Japanese government's hopeful pursuit of economic ties and dialogue with the Soviet Union, the general attitude and policies of the Suzuki administration toward Moscow, like those of the previous administration, remained cool and reserved.

4. Soviet Position Toward Japan

There are two schools of thought in Japan concerning the question of how the Soviets viewed Japan. One school postulated that the Kremlin leaders did not have any specific designs or policies toward Japan *per se*, while the second school believed that the Kremlin could not afford to be without such designs or policies.

Many Western observers[47] contended that, as a global power, the Soviet Union tended to view relations with Japan not only in bilateral terms, but also in a much broader, global context. When one considers the military aspect, the arguments of the first school become particularly persuasive. As a country with what Dmitrii V. Petrov, a leading Soviet expert on Japan, called a "low level of military strength,"[48] Japan did not play any significant global military role. The Soviets understood well that Japan was dependent upon the United States for its own security. With this in mind, the above-mentioned Western observers felt that the Soviets could ignore the formulation of any specific foreign policy toward Japan, and instead, simply include Japan in their global or U.S. and China policies.

On the other hand, proponents of the second school argued that Japan occupied a cornerstone position in Northeast Asia because of its geographical location and its economic and technological capabilities and, hence, represented significant military and political potential. According to this view, the Soviet Union was necessarily concerned about both the extent of U.S.-Japanese military cooperation and the extent to which Japan would cooperate economically with the PRC in the latter's modernization program. The Soviets also feared Japan's adoption of a possible "anti-Soviet" posture in conjunction with Japan's participation in the Pacific Basin Cooperation plan. It appeared to observers of the second school that, in light of these vital concerns and of recent developments in the Pacific region, the Soviet Union must make a concerted effort to formulate specific policies toward Japan.

Although these two schools appear diametrically opposed, it is the author's view that closer examination shows them to be actually complementary. Whereas the first school stressed fundamental principles, the second emphasized the conditions that prompted the Soviet Union to alter its traditional views.

During the period covered in this chapter—namely, the six-month period from the Soviet invasion of Kabul (December 1979) to around the time of the formation of the Suzuki Cabinet (July 1980)—the Soviet Union maintained a defensive and uncompromising position toward Japanese protests of the Afghanistan invasion. First, the Kremlin leadership generally considered the foreign policy of the Ōhira administration as extremely anti-Soviet. The Soviets began to take note in late January 1980 of Japa-

nese policy changes, which they viewed as indicative of a more dangerous, anti-Soviet course. Specifically, the Soviets severely criticized Ōhira's
keynote speech in the Japanese Diet on January 25, 1980. In an article
titled "Amending Policy" in the January 20 issue of *Pravda*, Iurii Vdovin
commented: "It is no longer being said, as it was a year ago, that the
strengthening of friendship with the Soviet Union is one of the goals of
Japanese diplomacy."[49] On January 24 from Vladimir Ia.Tsvetov, the Tokyo correspondent for the Moscow Broadcast Service, who pointed out
that "Ōhira's speech failed to include his views on Japanese-Soviet relations."[50] In the February 9 issue of *Izvestiia*, Iurii N. Bandura sharply
criticized Ōhira's view of the Soviet Union's posture as having changed
from defensive to "aggressive" and "potentially threatening to Japan."[51]

The Soviets perceived Ōhira as pro-Chinese because of his eagerness
to improve Japan's relations with the PRC, demonstrated as early as 1972,
when, as foreign minister, he signed the Japan–China Normalization Treaty
in Beijing. Furthermore, Ōhira returned to Beijing in 1979—the first Japanese prime minister since the conclusion of the Treaty to do so—and
extended an invitation to China's Hua Guo Feng to visit Tokyo in 1980.

More importantly, Ōhira was regarded as more pro-Western, especially
pro-American, than were his predecessors. This belief was publicized by
Vladimir Kudriavtsev in the May 27, 1980 issue of *Izvestiia*: "No postwar government leader has formulated foreign policies with such a lack
of independence and authority as Mr. Ōhira."[52] V. Tsvetov wrote: "Prime
Minister Ōhira has demonstrated Japan's total solidarity with the
adventurist United States policy. In Washington he declared that Japan is
ready to cooperate with U.S. policy at any cost."[53] Tsvetov went on to list
examples of Ōhira's complicity with U.S. policies: "The Japanese," he
wrote, "have joined in the U.S.-provoked actions against Iran; pledged
full support of President Carter's position on the Afghan issue; built up
an attitude of anti-Sovietism; meddled with the Olympics; and catered to
U.S. demands for a large-scale military buildup."[54]

5. "The Pacific Basin Concept": Three Major Soviet Criticisms

Probably no other criticism against Japan appeared so frequently in the
official Soviet media during this six-month period as that against Prime
Minister Ōhira's "Pacific Basin concept."[55] It is, of course, understandable that the Soviets would be highly concerned about this concept, be-

cause it provided competition to the Soviet-designed "Asian collective security" concept, the cornerstone of Soviet Asian policy.

Historically, the "Pacific Basin concept" was being considered even in the early 1960s;[56] however, it was Ōhira who most enthusiastically promoted it in Japan.[57] Prime Minister Ōhira organized a special advisory group to study and work on Pacific Basin cooperation and later appointed the chairman of this group, Saburō Ōkita, as his foreign minister. In a Diet session speech on January 25, 1979, Ōhira stated: "I consider it my obligation to promote further friendly and cooperative relations with the United States, Canada, Latin America, Australia, New Zealand, and other countries in the Pacific region."[58] In response, the Soviets developed three major criticisms of this concept.

First, the Soviets objected to the capitalistic aspects of the "cooperation concept." As the *Interim Report on the Pacific Basin Cooperation Concept*, submitted to Prime Minister Ōhira on November 14, 1979, stated:

> Our concept, is, in the first place, directed to *open* cooperation. . . . Secondly, it aims at the formation of a regional community based on *free* and *open* relations. In the economic sphere, the promotion of *free* trade and capital transfer is the ideal to be achieved. In carrying out this task, it is essential that the advanced countries take the lead in . . . making effective use of market-economy mechanisms and in maintaining and reinforcing the *free* international economic system (emphasis added by H.K.).[59]

From the Soviet point of view, the report was self-contradictory in its insistence upon an "open and free" system at one and the same time. According to Marxist-Leninist thinking, there are two kinds of "free" systems; one is capitalistic and bourgeois in nature, the other is socialistic. The Soviets interpreted the word *free* to have the former meaning, as indicated in the phrase, "in the economic sphere, the promotion of *free* trade and capital transfer is the ideal to be achieved" (emphasis added by H.K.).[60] According to the Soviets, the Japanese attitude toward a "Pacific Community" was self-contradictory: although it was called a "free system," it was also meant to be "closed" in the sense that membership was to be restricted to capitalist, bourgeois countries. While some Soviet observers regarded the "Community" as, in fact, antisocialist, others considered it anti-Soviet. Obviously, "antisocialist" and "anti-Soviet" had different implications, for the latter implied the participation of China in a united front against the USSR.

Regardless of the theoretical characterization of "Pacific Basin cooperation" as an antisocialist or anti-Soviet organization, Kremlin leaders were more acutely bothered by the possible practical effects of the formation of such a community. To begin with, Moscow feared the "strengthening of cooperation and interdependent relations" and the development of closer economic ties between Japan and the cooperating Asian-Pacific countries, instead of between Japan and the USSR. The Soviet Union was dependent upon Japan for credit and technology in its attempt to achieve its goal to develop Siberia and the Soviet Far East. In fact, Moscow was urging Tokyo to conclude a long-term bilateral agreement on economic cooperation. Needless to say, the Soviets were vitally concerned about the economic and geographic directions Japan might take in conjunction with "Pacific Basin cooperation." A second practical Soviet concern about "cooperation" was based on the fear that it would eventually develop into a Pacific version of the European Economic Community (EEC). Prime Minister Ōhira had made it clear that it was not feasible to create an organization such as the EEC in the Asian-Pacific region, but this assurance did not allay Soviet fears. In interpreting another of Ōhira's statements concerning cooperation, Bandura suggested that the model for Ōhira's Pacific Basin cooperation concept was the system of economic solidarity between West Germany and the EEC.

A second major basis for the Soviet mistrust of the "Pacific Community" stemmed from a fear that the community would not allow the participation of socialist governments. This fear lingered despite Ōhira's repeated assertion that "there is no reason to refuse the participation of any nation that wishes to join the Community."[61] On one occasion, the Japanese Prime Minister even indicated that he was "not opposed to the participation of the Soviet Union or the PRC."[62] Soviet doubts were well expressed by Iurii N. Bandura in the January 17, 1980 issue of *Izvestiia*, in which he criticized the Community's *Interim Report*, submitted by Ōhira's study group. Bandura commented:

> In the recommendation submitted to the Japanese government, no mention was made concerning which countries Japan would agree to have as group members. Moreover, any analysis of the *Report* leads to the conclusion that the authors of the concept leave no room for the participation of socialist countries in the Pacific Ocean Cooperation.[63]

Bandura classified the candidate countries into four groups: the first group, to which he referred to as "fixed candidates," included Japan, the United States, Canada, Australia, New Zealand, and the ASEAN coun-

tries. The second group of countries, mentioned only "occasionally" as can-
didates, were certain Latin American countries, such as Chile, Panama, and
Mexico.[64] The third group identified by Bandura consisted of "special targets" such as South Korea, Taiwan, and Hong Kong. Bandura did not discuss
how these countries were to be treated in actual practice. He considered the
PRC as the country in the fourth group. While Bandura was aware that both
Chinese and Australian leaders advocated the participation of the PRC in the
"Community," he doubted that Japan would offer the PRC membership in
the organization, at least for the time being, although "it is true that Tokyo
feeds Beijing promises of admitting China into 'the Pacific Community' *in
the future*" (emphasis added by H.K.).[65]

It appears that one reason why the Soviets so bitterly criticized Ōhira's
Pacific Basin initiative lay in their feeling that the USSR was not being
rightfully recognized as a candidate for membership. Even worse, many
Soviets felt that their country was purposely excluded. That the USSR
considered itself a major power in the Pacific region further underscored
its sense of being excluded and of being discriminated against. It is clear
that since the late 1970s, the USSR had defined itself as an Asian-Pacific
power, not simply an Asian power.[66] Thus, the omission of the Soviet
Union from the *Interim Report on the Pacific Basin Cooperation Concept*
was a significant affront to the Soviets and stimulated some of the first
criticisms of the "concept." In the *Final Report*, the USSR, with other
countries, was mentioned only in a rather insignificant section that dealt
with a direct-broadcast relay satellite system.

A third broad Soviet criticism of "Pacific Cooperation" centered around
the fear that one of its major goals was the establishment of a military
alliance. Despite Japan's continued reassurances that its interests were
cultural and economic in nature, Soviets fears were not assuaged. In a
notable speech to the Lower House Budget Committee, Ōhira asserted,
"We want to confine this idea of Pacific Basin Cooperation to economic
and cultural spheres."[67] However, Soviet commentators believed that the
primary purpose of the Japanese design of a "Pacific Community" was
military in nature. A January 4, 1980 report from Moscow by TASS International was a typical example. Quoting *Akahata* (*Red Flag*), an
organ of the Japanese Communist Party, the report insisted that "the
'Ōhira Doctrine' is inextricably linked with plans to create a new
military bloc in that region."[68] Soviet observer S.N. Nikonov also
stressed the military purpose of Ōhira's initiative, saying that the statements of Japanese state officials frequently suggested that "the pro-

posed organization will have not a political but an increasingly *military* character" (emphasis added by H.K.) [69]

The participation, for the first time, of the Japanese Self-Defense Forces in RIMPAC-80, the program of naval maneuvers in the Pacific Ocean, together with forces from ANZUS member countries (the United States, Australia, and New Zealand) in February and March 1980, reinforced Soviet suspicions that "there are military aspects in the Pacific Community design."[70] Vasilii Golovnin remarked in the February 28, 1980 issue of *APN News*: "The participants in these military maneuvers are those countries that will play a central role in the Pacific Basin Community Design envisaged obstinately by Japan." He concluded that, "although Japan has defined this design to be of a purely economic and cultural nature, we see that the Pacific Ocean Cooperation has begun actual maneuvers in the military field."[71]

It is appropriate here to point out that the Soviet Union also had plans for promoting a community of mutual cooperation in the Pacific region. The proposal for collective security in Asia was formally introduced by Brezhnev himself at the World Conference of Communist Parties, in Moscow, on June 8, 1969: "We think the course of events is also placing on the agenda the task of creating a system of collective security in Asia."[72] Even more than ten years after this announcement, however, no such system was realized. Only three neighboring countries formally endorsed the Soviet initiative: Outer Mongolia, Iran, and Afghanistan. Since the Soviet Union had considered embracing Japan as a crucial member of its proposed organization, it came as a great shock that Japan was advancing its own scheme in the Pacific region. It would not be a mistake to relate the extreme sensitivity of the USSR toward the creation of a Japan-supported Pacific cooperation system to its own unsuccessful efforts in this regard. As its name clearly implied, the Soviets' Asian collective security design was of a political-military nature. The Soviets never attempted to conceal this fact. CPSU General Secretary Brezhnev indicated as much in the above-mentioned address: "Asian collective security is the best substitute for the now-existing political-military grouping."[73] Apparently, the Soviets revealed their own political-military purposes in their criticism of the Pacific cooperation advocated by Ōhira and others in Japan. Of course, the Soviets were primarily concerned about the development of a threatening military alliance, as evidenced in Bandura's warning: "Behind these activities the intention to create in the Pacific Ocean region a huge military bloc of imperialist states is quite clearly visible, and it is already being referred to as 'JANZUS' (a combination of the first letters of the following countries: Japan, Australia, New Zealand, and the United States)."[74]

6. Soviet Tactics: Sympathy, Bluff, and Material Incentives

Although they bitterly criticized Japanese participation in, and designs for, a Pacific Basin community, as well as Japan's increasing military potential, the Soviets showed at the same time some conciliatory gestures. When faced with an international dilemma, the Soviets often adopted the well-known "carrot and stick" strategy. Let us now examine the more conciliatory side of the Soviet strategy toward Japan during the months after the Afghanistan invasion.

One example of this aspect of policy toward Japan was found in the Soviet tendency to regard Japan chiefly as a victim of the United States and China. Moscow often saw Japan as a nation turned toward anti-Soviet and militaristic attitudes by overwhelming pressures from Washington and Beijing. This perception allowed the Soviets some space for manipulation. In the article "Dangerous Metamorphoses," in the February 9, 1980 issue of *Izvestiia*, Bandura, who viewed Prime Minister Ōhira's "arm-twisting diplomacy" as an "instrument" of the White House, commented: "These metamorphoses can be explained quite simply: the independence of Japanese diplomacy, of which Tokyo is fond of talking, is beginning to show cracks under growing U.S. *pressure*" (emphasis added by H.K.).[75] Col. V. Tatarnikov, in *Krasnaia zvezda* (March 25, 1980), also argued that the "buildup of the 'Self-Defense Forces' and anti-Soviet sentiment in Japan" was "being done *under pressure from Washington*"(emphasis added by H.K.)[76]

Specifically, the Soviets felt that the United States was coercing Japan to participate in joint military plans with the United States and NATO against the USSR by joining the "RIMPAC-80"; to turn Okinawa into a base for the transfer of U.S. marines to the Persian Gulf and other regions; to prepare for a naval blockade of three straits (the Soya [La Peróuse], Tsugaru, and Tsushima straits) in case of an emergency; to take part in the "boycott" of the Moscow Olympics; to halt credits for the implementation of Soviet-Japanese economic cooperation projects;[77] and to engage in other actions.[78]

According to the Soviets, China also exerted pressure on Japan to cooperate in adventurist anti-Soviet strategies.[79] V. Ganshi, a Soviet commentator for Moscow Radio, argued that pressure from the PRC was responsible for Tokyo's abandonment of its "equidistance" policy toward the USSR and the PRC. He asserted in the May 31 issue of *Izvestiia*, on the eve of Premier Hua Guo Feng's visit to Tokyo, that China had intensified its efforts "to draw Tokyo into the stream of its anti-Soviet, hegemonistic policy and to *push* Japan away from more balanced approaches to relations with its neighbors" (emphasis added by H.K.)[80] The insinuation that the PRC was exerting pressure on Japan became more explicit in a June 7 TASS report, following Hua Guo Feng's Tokyo visit. The report stated: "The Chinese leader sought to use this opportunity to the utmost . . . *to urge* Japan to increase the might of its armed forces and to develop an aggressive military alliance with the U.S." (emphasis added by H.K.).[81] Later, Mikhail Demchenko reported Hua Guo Feng's complaint to Yasuhiro Nakasone, an influential member of the LDP, who was visiting Beijing in April 1980, that "Japan's military spending is too low."[82]

The Soviets perceived the existence of an anti-Soviet military bloc into which the United States and China had enticed Japan. The TASS report mentioned above illuminates this view: "The U.S.-Chinese rapprochement is aimed at knocking together a reactionary anti-Soviet alliance and drawing Japan into its designs as well."[83]

The Soviets' use of the "stick" is most detectable in the area of bilateral fishing negotiations. Japan's vulnerable and relatively weak position in this area became the point of attack for Soviet countermeasures and threats. One of the first threats of retaliation against Japan's participation in the U.S.-led sanctions after the Soviet invasion in Afghanistan appeared in the February 16 issue of *Izvestiia*, in which Demchenko stated: "Any sanctions against the Soviet Union can ultimately lead to only one thing— destruction of the system of Soviet-Japanese relations."[84] More specifically, Demchenko continued: "Japanese fishing circles are now concerned about whether Japan's pursuit of the U.S. anti-Soviet course will influence the Soviet Union's attitude toward the [fishing] question, since the application of 'sanctions' against the USSR is a weapon that cuts both ways."[85]

Soviet ambassador to Tokyo, Dmitri S. Polianskii indicated on February 10, 1980 that the Soviet Union could rightly impose restrictions on Japanese fishing operations within its 200-nautical-mile fishing zone if Japan implemented its proposed economic sanctions. Polianskii warned: "We have no intention of restricting Japanese fishing operations. But if Japan follows the lead of the United States in imposing economic sanctions, we will be forced to take appropriate countersteps."[86] This warning, however, turned out to be a bluff; there was no actual Soviet retaliation in this area. On the contrary, the Soviets responded fairly and even benevolently to Japanese salmon-catch quota pronouncements.

In another curious action, Polianskii, who had previously turned down all invitations to address Japanese journalists, agreed to discuss the Afghanistan affair and Soviet-Japanese economic relations at a Japan National Press Club luncheon on March 5, 1980. The ambassador utilized this occasion to describe vividly the difficulties imposed on his country by the Japanese economic sanctions, particularly the suspension of the joint development projects in Siberia and the Far East. Having expressed his country's determination to continue the projects without the cooperation of other countries, including Japan, Polianskii nevertheless added:

> I hope that Japan will act on the matter according to its own interests without giving ear to recommendations from other quarters [i.e., Washington]. Japan must ultimately decide the future course of bilateral relations between us—that is, whether to promote friendly relations or not. I myself am optimistic [in this regard].[87]

Three days later, Vladimir Tsvetov of the Moscow Broadcast Service, speaking in Japanese, expressed the view that the desires of Japanese business circles, including those of Shigeo Nagano, to continue trade and economic relations with the Soviet Union were quite reasonable. Here, Tsvetov was resorting to a favorite Soviet technique of "divide and conquer." He employed this same strategy in pointing out the rivalries and intrigues of Western countries: "Despite U.S. demands, France and West Germany have not adopted economic sanctions against the Soviet Union in connection with the situation in Afghanistan. Thus, it will be a matter of course that the orders which Japan has received thus far will all go to West Europe."[88]

As we have seen, the low ebb in Soviet-Japanese relations was deeply rooted in the Afghanistan incident of December 1979 and in the issues and developments that reverberated from it. Although long strained by the Northern Territories question, Soviet-Japanese relations had never before reached such a precariously low point. The Middle East problem awakened in the Japanese public an increased awareness of the "threat from the North." Although it was expected that trade and economic relations between the two countries would eventually resume and perhaps even be expanded, there was strong speculation that tense diplomatic relations would prevail into the 1980s. The period from December 1979 to June 1980 underscored the great influence of Soviet-Japanese political-diplomatic relations on developments in Northeast Asia and the need for sensitive diplomacy in their preservation.

Chapter 10

From Clouded to "Somewhat Crystal"

Suzuki to Nakasone

"Of all our allies, Japan has been without question the most supportive of all our shared interests and objectives [concerning the Afghanistan issue], in spite of the fact that it incurred significant economic cost as a result."[1] These words, from the speech made by U.S. ambassador to Japan Mike Mansfield at the International Symposium on Security, Peace, and Survival on December 4, 1981, cannot be dismissed as simply a diplomatic compliment. The Japanese government under the late Prime Minister Masayoshi Ōhira engaged in a vigorous, cooperative policy, though marked by much zigzagging, to support the sanctions taken by U.S. President Jimmy Carter after the Soviet military invasion of Afghanistan—a policy that was interpreted as exceptionally and unprecedentedly clearcut in Japan's postwar diplomatic history.

This policy, as rightly admitted by the American ambassador, was pursued with some sacrifices on the Japanese side (e.g., Japan dropped from second to fifth place in the ranking of Soviet Western trade partners in 1980), and certainly it dealt some significant "body blows" to the Soviet Union. Although it is difficult to say which country suffered more, it is clear that Japanese-Soviet relations deteriorated to their lowest ebb in postwar history as a result of the Afghan incident.

In this chapter, I discuss the aftermath of the foregoing policy, treating such questions as: (1) What changes occurred in the bilateral relations between Japan and the USSR after the sudden death of Masayoshi Ōhira on June 12, 1980? More concretely, (2) what were the features of the policy orientation toward the USSR of Prime Ministers Zenkō Suzuki and Yasuhiro Nakasone? Were they as clear-cut as those of their predecessors? (3) What kind of strategies or policies was the Kremlin leadership taking toward the new Japanese administration and the Japanese people? Can any change be detected?

1. Japan's Puzzling Policies

It is almost impossible for anyone to pinpoint the major policy orientation of the Zenkō Suzuki administration toward the Soviet Union. What the Suzuki cabinet did or did not do vis-à-vis the USSR during Suzuki's tenure (July 1980–November 1982) was marked by ambiguities, inconsistencies, zigzaggings, and even mysteries.

First, let's examine Suzuki's attitude toward the Northern Territories issue. To be fair, the Suzuki administration did initiate with extraordinary enthusiasm a campaign for the return of the disputed islands, which included the following measures: the declaration of February 7 as "Northern Territories Day"; incorporation of six towns and villages situated on three of the disputed islands—Kunashiri, Etorofu, and Shikotan—into the administrative district of Nemuro City, Hokkaido; financial assistance to areas adjacent to the islands for the purpose of promoting industries; and the tour of Prime Minister Suzuki himself by helicopter to view the islands from as close a vantage point as possible—the first such visit ever made by a Japanese prime minister in the postwar history of Japan.

One cannot necessarily conclude from these measures, however, that the Suzuki government was more eager than were previous Japanese prime ministers to accomplish the reversion of the Northern Territories to Japan. Three main reasons can be mentioned to support this view.

The first is that there was no major diplomatic objective left for Japan to pursue other than the conclusion of a peace treaty with the USSR, which would resolve the territorial problem. This had been the case particularly since Japan's signing of the Treaty of Peace and Friendship with the People's Republic of China in 1978. In other words, any Japanese prime minister would have done what Suzuki did in order to demonstrate that his government was seriously coping with the task of correcting the irregular diplomatic heritage left by World War II.

The second reason, closely related, is that all the measures taken by the Suzuki cabinet were the kinds of gestures that were exclusively oriented toward domestic consumption, the imperative of any top Japanese political leader. True, it is understandable and even necessary for any political leader to unite his home constituency before dealing with an external opponent. Unfortunately, however, unlike his predecessors, Suzuki stopped at this point; that is, in contrast to the measures he directed toward domestic voters, Suzuki did not do anything of consequence vis-à-vis the Soviet Union. Then what kind of plan did he have to deal with the Soviets?

This question bears directly on the third reason why I doubt that Suzuki was particularly enthusiastic about confronting the islands issue. In order to deal with the Soviets on the territorial problem, the Japanese government had to put together a comprehensive strategy toward the Soviet Union, without which it would have seemed almost impossible for Japan to undertake such an unprecedented confrontation as demanding the reversion of the Northern Territories. Such a grand strategy, in my view, must be formulated with careful consideration of such major questions as: How to secure Japan against the growing military buildup of Soviet forces on both a global and regional level? To what extent should Japan depend upon energy resources from the USSR? What kind of pressure—and how much—should Japan apply to the Soviet Union to regain the islands? Unfortunately, it seems that Suzuki never formulated a grand strategy, or possibly never even realized the need for such a comprehensive policy toward the USSR.

Also indicating a lack of decisiveness in the Suzuki administration to formulate a grand strategy toward the Soviet Union was the ambiguous attitude of Prime Minister Suzuki toward the sanctions taken by Japan to protest the Soviet incursion into Afghanistan. True, Suzuki repeated the same line of contention as his predecessor, Masayoshi Ōhira, in this regard. For instance, in his first news conference as Japanese prime minister, on July 18, 1981, Suzuki stated that he would endeavor to continue the policies of his predecessor, and that his selection as foreign minister of Masayoshi Itō, formerly Ōhira's Chief Cabinet Secretary and aide, was a concrete demonstration of this intention.[2] Suzuki maintained this position, at least verbally, stating repeatedly that "as long as the Soviet Union remains unchanged in its policy with regard to Afghanistan and the Northern Territories, any improvement in Japanese-Soviet relations will be impossible." In practice, however, the Japanese government under Suzuki gradually softened, one by one, those measures that had been initiated by Ōhira.

The Japanese government under Ōhira had decided on three major countermeasures to demonstrate its "displeasure," together with that of other Western countries, at the Soviet move into Afghanistan. These represented a direct sign of Japan's intention to be an active member of "the West," and hence, ready to make sacrifices; to let the USSR know that such military aggression in Afghanistan would cost the invader dearly. The countermeasures were the boycott of the Moscow Olympics, the freezing of those economic projects that would make use of citizens' tax revenues through the Japanese Export-Import Bank, and the suspension of official exchanges between Japan and the Soviet Union. Although Japan followed through on the first countermeasure, the other two sanctions were gradually lifted almost to the point where the situation returned to that which existed before the Afghan incident took place. Let us look at the process by which these were related.

The Japanese administration under Ōhira froze five big economic projects planned between Japan and the USSR: (1) plans for production of a plant to produce electromagnetic steel plates; (2) the third stage of a program for timber resources development; (3) the Sakhalin offshore oil and natural gas resources project; (4) the coal production projects in Southern Yakutsk; and (5) the exportation of large steel pipes from Japan to the USSR. The first project remained inoperative, mainly because of the involvement of the U.S. company AMCO. But the second, third, and fourth projects were revived even during Ōhira's administration, the rationale being that a resource-needy country like Japan could not get along without such vital natural resources as oil, gas, coal, and timber.

In contrast, however, it was difficult for Japan to settle on a satisfying rationale to justify the reviving of the fifth project, the selling of large steel tubes by several private Japanese producers to the Yamburg Gas Pipeline Project in West Siberia, for the following three reasons. To begin with, since it was engineered to provide natural gas to Western countries, the project had nothing to do with the energy question in Japan. Furthermore, the project was mainly financed by the Japanese Export-Import Bank, which was run by the government using tax revenues, thus enabling the USSR to purchase pipelines from a Japanese industry. Last, the Reagan administration was strongly opposing this project, warning that it could lead in the future to too much Western dependence upon natural gas supplied by the USSR, which was not desirable from the security perspective. Despite the weak rationale employed to promote this project further, in 1981 the Suzuki administration approved the contracts made by some Japanese enterprises and the Japanese Export-Import Bank, saying that otherwise "all the business of selling large pipelines to the USSR will be monopolized by West Germany, France, and other Western European countries."

In the wake of the Afghan incident, the Japanese government under Ōhira immediately put into effect a policy of suspending official person-to-person contacts at high governmental levels between Japan and the USSR. As a result of this policy, the following visits and meetings were called off: a planned meeting of the Soviet ambassador to Japan, Dmitrii Polianskii, with top members of the ruling Liberal Democratic Party (LDP); the scheduled visit to Tokyo by members of the Supreme Soviet; and any proposed visits to Japan by Soviet vice-foreign trade ministers. However, even this restriction underwent a gradual softening under Suzuki.

For example, in March 1981, Prime Minister Suzuki himself nearly accepted the request for a secret meeting with Polianskii, although he eventually reconsidered and permitted Foreign Minister Masayoshi Itō to meet the Soviet ambassador first, for the purpose of feeling out in advance what the Soviet ambassador wanted to discuss. Since it turned out that Polianskii did not have anything new to propose, to say nothing of offering any concession on his country's stand with regard to the Northern Territories and other issues, Suzuki did not follow through and meet the ambassador. The fact that Suzuki even considered such a meeting, however, was regarded by some government observers as unfitting, since the Japanese ambassador to Moscow was not easily given the opportunity to meet even Soviet Foreign Minister Andrei Gromyko, not to mention General Secretary Brezhnev. Nonetheless, Suzuki overlooked this because he was misled by his own wishful thinking that the Soviet ambassador might have proposed some secret concession on the occasion of Suzuki's forthcoming visit to the United States for a meeting with the new U.S. president, Ronald Reagan.

In late April–early May, 1981, ten Japanese LDP Diet members, who had once refused the visit of their counterparts, i.e., members of the Supreme Soviet, to Tokyo, initiated a week's visit to Moscow. This was not only the first visit since the Afghanistan incident, but also the first time in ten years that a mission made up only of members of the ruling Japanese party had visited the Soviet Union. Furthermore, according to the Japanese news agency Kyōdō, the Japanese emissaries, headed by former Foreign Minister Iichirō Hatoyama, went so far as to say that they would "plan to exert efforts on the Japanese government to encourage the lifting of the restrictions still imposed on Japanese-Soviet exchange" and to express readiness to cooperate in the development of Siberia.[3]

In May 1981, Prime Minister Suzuki appointed one of his closest friends, Sunao Sonoda, to the office of Foreign Minister to replace Itō, who resigned in protest against the "double-standard" diplomacy of Suzuki, as I discuss later. Sonoda was reported to have called for a return to the so-called "omnidirectional" diplomacy, which was clearly abandoned by Ōhira when the Soviet military forces moved into Kabul. Shortly after taking the post, in June 1981, the new foreign minister decided to reverse the policy of his two immediate predecessors, Saburō Okita and Masayoshi Itō, and issued entry visas to two Soviet economic delegations headed respectively by Soviet Vice-Foreign Trade Ministers Viktor Ivanov and Vladimir Sushkov. Sonoda wen⁺ a step further. Taking an opportunity afforded by a meeting of the United Nations General Assembly in New York in September 1981, which was attended by both the Japanese and Soviet foreign ministers, the new Japanese foreign minister proposed to his Soviet counterpart, Andrei Gromyko, that bilateral talks on a working or ministerial level be resumed between Japan and the Soviet Union. Needless to say, Gromyko immediately accepted Sonoda's suggestion, since this kind of high-level contact between Tokyo and Moscow had been officially suspended by the Japanese government.

To be sure, there were some calculated rationales behind this bold initiative on the part of the Japanese. The first one had to do with the change in certain international situations after December 1979. While still taking a tough posture with regard to Afghanistan and the Moscow-based political pressure on Poland, and continuing to build up military might to cope with the Soviet threat, the Western allies of Japan, e.g., the United States under President Reagan and West Germany under Chancellor Helmut Schmidt, had started to show a sign of willingness to keep the door ajar for a dialogue with the Soviet Union. Apart from the question of whether Japan could imitate these so-called Western-type "dual" or "double-track" strategies in light of its inadequate military machine, the Tokyo government under Suzuki and Sonoda seemed to have come to a similar conclusion: that the time had come for Japan to open a channel of communication with Moscow in order to avoid being left dangerously isolated. The second rationale was that the Soviets most likely would not make any changes with regard to Japanese demands for the reversion of the Northern Territories, even if working-level or ministerial-level talks were held. Such an intransigent, uncompromising attitude by the Soviets might reinforce the impression held by the Japanese general public that it was not Japan's but exclusively the USSR's side that was to blame for the cold, strained bilateral relations between the two nations at that time.

Ambivalent policies toward the Soviet Union of the Suzuki-Sonoda team were related to its inconsistent attitude toward the policy of cooperation with the United States in security affairs. No need to repeat again that Japan's Soviet policy was inseparably related to its American policy. It thus becomes necessary for me to touch upon Japanese-U.S. relations.

In the joint communiqué between Suzuki and Reagan issued on May 8, 1981, in Washington, D.C., the Japanese prime minister recognized that "the alliance between Japan and the United States is built upon their shared values of democracy and liberty." Acknowledging further "the desirability of an appropriate division of roles" between the two countries, Suzuki stated that "Japan will seek to make even greater efforts for improving its defense capabilities in Japanese territories and in its surrounding sea and air space." These words were undoubtedly interpreted by the U.S. side as a sign of Suzuki's willingness to take a very positive, cooperative posture toward Japan's security issues.

However, upon, or even before, his return to Tokyo from Washington, D.C., Suzuki showed signs of softening the words and commitments he had made in this communiqué, giving his own interpretation to, for instance, the term *alliance* to the effect that Japan did not necessarily have to bear a greater military burden than she had so far. Foreign Minister Sonoda further underscored this attitude by stating in Manila that "a joint communiqué is not necessarily binding for Japan." If this had been the end of the story, people would not have been terribly surprised, as such verbal vacillations frequently occur. What surprised and puzzled the Japanese, however, was that Suzuki changed his position once again. Partially succumbing to external and domestic criticism of his double standard in the interpretation of the term "alliance" and the other commitments he made in Washington, which resulted in the resignation of Foreign Minister Itō, Suzuki pledged complete agreement with the United States and other Western countries at the Ottawa Summit in July of the same year, particularly stressing that the Soviet military buildup was a continuing threat to international security and stability and that the Japanese government was ready to negotiate and work with the Soviet Union only from a position of strength.

Another example of the "double-talk" diplomacy, which characterized the Suzuki administration and led many to doubt the prime minister's sense of political priorities was found in the way he treated the defense efforts of Japan. As stated above, Suzuki signed the Japan–U.S. joint communiqué, in which he agreed with the notion of "division of labor" between the United States and Japan and promised "greater efforts at improving Japanese defense capabilities." In the interview at the National Press Club in Washington on the same day that he signed the communiqué, Suzuki further clarified his position, promising that Japan would take steps to bolster its defense capabilities within several hundred nautical miles of its shores and 1,000 nautical miles of its sea-lanes.[4]

These statements may be regarded as particularly significant and encouraging in view of the fact that the United States called for Japan to step up its defense efforts in the seas west of Guam and north of the Philippines. Needless to say, these promises were more easily made than kept. In particular, Suzuki's final statement concerning the defense of the nation's sea-lanes astonished even some specialists in the Japan Defense Agency, who considered such efforts to be desirable and ideal but surely beyond the country's capability. For, apart from Japanese domestic and political constraints, it was clear that it was out of the question for Japan to extend its defense capabilities. Such drastic moves would demand an almost revolutionary change in the thinking of both the general public and administrators, a change which the Suzuki government seemed reluctant to make.

2. Causes of Ambiguities

The above, I believe, are sufficient examples to demonstrate the fact that there were observable ambiguities, inconsistencies, and even puzzling aspects in the policy orientations of the Suzuki administration toward the Soviet Union. At this point, the important question that inevitably arises is: What factors were behind this inscrutable foreign policy orientation?

In order to answer this question, one cannot help but touch upon, first, the personal character of Prime Minister Zenkō Suzuki. Many observers doubt strongly that Suzuki had any clear and definite opinion of the Soviet Union. Perhaps his first and serious personal encounter with the Soviets was in the Japanese-Soviet fishing negotiations (in spring 1977), which took place as a result of the sudden Soviet declaration of an exclusive 200-nautical-mile fishing zone in December 1976. (For details, see chapter 6.) During these talks, Suzuki must have experienced mixed feelings. On the one hand, being head of the Japanese delegation, he must have felt considerable humiliation, particularly when he was kept waiting all day long, frequently in vain, for a meeting with his Soviet counterpart, Aleksandr A. Ishkov, in the Japanese Embassy in Moscow. On the other hand, as the then Minister of Agriculture, Forestry, and Fisheries and a popular negotiator for the Japanese fishing industry, Suzuki must have found himself in the position of not wishing to strongly antagonize the Soviets and risk losing the concessions desired by his supporters. It seems to me that his experience in 1977 helped to shape his perception of the Soviet Union as a country that Japan could not get along with, but one that it could not afford to antagonize, either.

Another factor that appears to have made Suzuki take an ambiguous posture toward the Soviet Union was the situation that brought him to national leadership. When Masayoshi Ōhira died suddenly in June 1980, there were three powerful contenders for the premiership: Yasuhiro Nakasone, Toshio Kōmoto, and Kiichi Miyazawa. Because these three launched such a contentious campaign for the premiership, the LDP feared that its unity would be threatened, and thus, in its attempt to avoid fragmentation, the party nominated Zenkō Suzuki as a temporary compromise. Politically speaking, thus, Suzuki was not the kind of politician who normally would have claimed the coveted prize of national leadership. Although in the past he worked behind the scenes as a moderator in the party, Suzuki had never served in the office of Minister of Foreign Affairs, Minister of Finance, or Minister of International Trade and Industry, as had his predecessors.

Seeming to recognize his limitations, Suzuki chose practically to accommodate different views of various contenders, factions, and groups rather than to assert his own personal view from a position of strong leadership. Nonetheless, he did not wish to forfeit his leadership, and thus in order to preserve his title, Suzuki became more faction-oriented than before. He perceived his domestic reputation to be of more value to him than his international one. This may explain my earlier judgment of his Northern Territories campaign as a sort of gesture aimed mainly at earning politically useful credits on the home front and also the fact that he resorted to a double standard in interpreting the Suzuki-Reagan communiqué he signed.

Some readers may be tempted to raise here the question of why the Japanese electorate tolerated a leader who did not set forth a sound and workable foreign policy of his own. In regard to Suzuki's place in Japanese politics, I am tempted to point out the truth in the saying, "A people cannot have a political leader better than themselves," or, "Political leaders are the products of their environment." More concretely speaking, what I am suggesting is that the previously cited ambiguities, uncertainties, and inconsistencies of Prime Minister Suzuki were a reflection of the way the Japanese public deals with contentious situations. The Japanese were certainly changing, and yet it was still hard to say how fast and in what direction they were moving. In a sense, they found themselves in a transitional stage, and Suzuki himself may have been the embodiment of this stage.

In order to illustrate such ambiguous, inconsistent, and even opposing attitudes and tendencies of the Japanese public at that time, let us take a glance at an opinion poll conducted by *Yomiuri Shimbun*, a widely read newspaper, in the fall of 1981.[5] According to this survey, more than half (54.4 percent) of the readers indicated their concern that Japan might become a target for some foreign enemy in the near future. Among those who gave this reply, about 70 percent pinpointed the Soviet Union as the aggressor nation. Moreover, approximately 70 percent of the respondents agreed that both the Japan–U.S. Mutual Security Treaty (MTS) and the Japanese Self-Defense Forces (SDF) were necessary for guaranteeing the security of Japan. On the other hand, the survey also showed an attitude that did not necessarily follow logically from the answers cited above; namely, that more than half of the respondents (56.9 percent) considered the present size of the SDF to be quite appropriate. Furthermore, 42 percent, the largest group of the respondents, still supported the Japanese government's basic policy of restricting defense expenditures to within 1 percent of the Japanese GNP.

It is not hard for Western observers irritated by the logical inconsistencies demonstrated above to criticize the ambiguous and contradictory stand of Japanese leaders and public toward such important matters. By way of explanation, I would like to remind these rationally minded observers that the coexistence of apparently contradictory positions side-by-side is a sort of culture-bound feature of the Japanese, with a long tradition. It would be unrealistic for Western critics to expect the Japanese to abandon this deeply entrenched cultural characteristic overnight. Shūichi Katō, Japanese literary and social critic, has described the Japanese culture, which tolerates a variety of cultures coexisting side-by-side, as a "hybrid culture" (*zassu bunka*).[6] Professor Yōnosuke Nagai at Tokyo University of Technology went so far as to regard the Japanese capability of considering complexities and even contradictions at one and the same time as an example of the marvelous political wisdom of the Japanese nation.

What has been said so far about this Japanese characteristic can be put in a slightly different way: the Japanese do not necessarily have or want to have any fixed, distinct, clear-cut principle or standard, to say nothing of ideology, according to which they can make value judgments or policy decisions. They have tended to conceive of the world or life in general as being too complicated to be judged by a clear standard that distinguishes everything as either black (injustice) or white (justice), since they feel rather that the truth lies often in an in-between, gray area.

What, instead, plays a significant role in Japanese decision making is the "air" or "atmosphere" prevailing in a situation or environment at a given moment. No one else, to my knowledge, has described more accurately the role that "air" plays in Japanese decision making than the late Hichihei Yamamoto, social commentator, in the following passage of his book, *The Study of 'Air'* (1977):

> "Air" is a monster with really great power [in decision making in Japanese society]. It can be a sort of "super-power." . . . For "air" leads top responsible persons into a situation in which they cannot explain why they did this or that. . . . Then statistics, documents, analyses or some scientific means of judging or logical arguments—all of these become useless. No matter how systematically all of these may be composed, they may simply fade away, letting "air" decide everything.[7]

If what Yamamoto says is true, then political leaders in such a society are expected only to watch closely for a change of air on the domestic and/or international scene. If we study this phenomenon in regard to Japanese administrations, we can see that there are not many observable differences in the political determinations and activities between the Ōhira and Suzuki administrations. Ōhira participated in the policy encouraged by the Carter administration to protest the Soviet occupation of Afghanistan by "carefully watching how the Western nations reacted."[8] As a result of watching the drifts and changes in the international atmosphere following the application of this policy, especially the lifting of the grain embargo and a call to Brezhnev for arms control by U.S. President Ronald Reagan, and the Western European nations' interest in the Yamburg gas pipeline project and their positive attitude to keeping a door open for dialogue with the Soviet Union, Suzuki began softening the sanctions made previously.

The "wait and see" approach of Japanese leaders clearly illustrated to Western observers that Tokyo's method of diplomacy had not yet overcome its postwar heritage of being passive or reactive rather than innovative or active in nature. At any rate, all that the best of Japanese political leaders can do is help create an atmosphere or environment in which a desired decision can be made smoothly, rather than persuade people directly and aggressively to come to a certain decision. Naturally, such an indirect, evolutionary way of making a decision takes a longer time than does the direct way, and it may, of course, be particularly irritating to the more impatient non-Japanese, who prefer to get things done in a more straightforward way.

3. Yasuhiro Nakasone and the United States

In November 1982, Yasuhiro Nakasone succeeded Suzuki as the Japanese prime minister. In the words of Kenneth B. Pyle, professor at the University of Washington, "The palpable nationalist mood of Japan at the beginning of the 1980s and the utter ineptness of Prime Minister Suzuki in handling the nation's foreign policy set the stage for Nakasone's emergence as the most imposing leader in foreign affairs that Japan had produced since Yoshida more than thirty years earlier."[9] In the 1970s and 1980s, all of the Japanese prime ministers were not only from the LDP but also served for only about two years each; for example, Takeo Fukuda (1976–1978), Masayoshi Ōhira (1978–1980), and Zenkō Suzuki (1980–1982). In this apparently routine rotation there was one exception,[10]— Yasuhiro Nakasone, who served for a total of five years (1982–1987).

In fact, Yasuhiro Nakasone, perhaps the most articulate and outspoken political leader of postwar Japan, tried harder than any of his predecessors to accelerate the process of Japan's globalization. In order to clarify this position, Nakasone repeatedly stressed that "the fundamental principle of Japanese diplomacy" lay in making efforts "to promote solidarity with Western countries, particularly with the United States,"[11] and to "fulfill her [Japan's] obligations as a member of the Western community."[12] When the previous Prime Minister Suzuki referred to Japan–U.S. relations as an "alliance," quite a sensation resulted in Japan due to the term's strong *military* connotation. The furor, however, did not prevent the much bolder Nakasone from confirming that relations between Japan and the United States indeed constituted a military alliance,[13] or from going beyond that to describe those relations as *unmei kyōdōtai* (a community bound together by a common destiny)."[14]

In addition, in regard to Japan's position on nuclear disarmament negotiations with the Soviet Union, Nakasone clearly associated Japan with the United States and NATO member countries for the first time at the Williamsburg conference in May 1983. The final joint statement of that meeting contained a sentence that declared: "The security of our countries is indivisible and must be approached on a global basis."[15] This sentence was fully endorsed by Prime Minister Nakasone, and according to some sources, was placed in the statement specifically at Nakasone's request.[16] In any case, one can conceivably interpret Nakasone's actions as a shift in policy orientation from the traditional postwar Japanese policy of "genuine self-defense" to the concept of a more active commitment and larger Japanese role in security on a global scale.

Nakasone's policy toward the Soviet Union had three distinct features: (1) more coordination with U.S. Soviet policy; (2) manifestation of more self-confidence in Japan's own position; and (3) the gradual formation of a comprehensive policy toward the USSR.

Based on its strong endorsement of solidarity with the Western alliance and its pledge of Japanese cooperation with the West on global security matters, the Nakasone administration put into effect several concrete measures and actions. The first was Japan's continued support and participation in the sanctions initiated by the United States against Soviet actions in Afghanistan and Poland.

The expulsion in June 1983 from Japan of Arkadii A. Vinogradov, a middle-level Soviet embassy official who held the rank of first secretary, for suspected activities as a KGB agent, provides another good example of the Nakasone government's firm intention to coordinate its Soviet policy as much as possible with those of governments in the Western community.[17] This expulsion came just after similar moves against Soviet officials by France, Britain, the United States, and other Western countries over a three-month period. Although Japanese Foreign Ministry officials denied any connection with these incidents in the West, they also acknowledged that the Japanese government had first studied "these other precedents carefully" before taking action themselves. Some analysts also interpreted the expulsion as a direct response of the Nakasone government to U.S. criticism that Japan had not done much to prevent the leakage of high-technology data and information to the Soviet Union. In his testimony before the U.S. House of Representatives on June 14, 1982, Stanislav A. Levchenko, a former Tokyo correspondent of *Novoe vremia* (New Times) who defected to the United States in 1979, said that "Japan is considered by the KGB to be the easiest country in which to run active operations."[18] Even calling Japan a "paradise for spies,"[19] a former KGB major identified about ten Japanese who served as his contacts when he worked as a Soviet agent in Tokyo during the 1970s.[20] It was reported that the Japanese government had been studying possible measures for restricting the flow of high or dual-use technology information to the Soviet Union.[21] Whatever motivations were behind the Nakasone government's decision, it must have been made with the full knowledge that the expulsion of a Soviet diplomat was likely to worsen Japan's already poor relations with the USSR.

In defense and military fields as well, the Nakasone administration clearly demonstrated through concrete actions its oral commitment to bring Japan closer to an alliance with the West. Resolving an issue handed down from his predecessor, Suzuki, Nakasone agreed to provide unconditionally to the United States advanced Japanese defense-related technologies. This decision, long awaited by the United States, signaled a major turnabout of Japan's strict policy of restricting the flow of weapon and military expertise to any foreign country. Tokyo's rationale for the decision was that such a transfer to the United States, with which Japan has a security arrangement, does not run counter to Japan's self-imposed principles on weaponry export.[22] The Nakasone administration also demonstrated a serious commitment toward following up the concept of a 1,000-mile sea-lane defense, which had been mentioned but never elaborated on by his predecessor, Suzuki.[23] A 1982 White Paper on Defense thus deliberately avoided use of the term "sea-lane defense."[24] Nakasone, however, put the concept in more concrete terms, explaining to an American audience during his January 1983 visit to Washington: "Our desire would be to defend the sea-lanes between Guam and Tokyo and between the strait of Taiwan and Osaka."[25] The Nakasone government agreed to a U.S.-Japanese study of joint sea-lane operations.[26] With an official endorsement, the 1983 edition of Japan's White Paper on Defense elaborated on this idea and used the term "sea-lane defense" for the first time[27] in a Japanese government official document.

Likewise, Nakasone responded more specifically than had Suzuki to U.S. requests that Japan blockade its three straits—Soya, Tsugaru, and Tsushima—in an effort to restrict the Soviet fleet in the Far East. During his January 1983 visit to Washington, Prime Minister Nakasone emphasized: "[One of Japan's] largest objectives is to have complete and full control of the three straits that go through the Japanese islands so that there should be no passage of Soviet submarines or other naval activities."[28]

4. Self-Confidence and Comprehensive Approach

A second component in the Nakasone government's attitude toward the Soviet Union was self-confidence. In his attempt to stress Japan's need to increase its defense efforts, Nakasone made a slip of the tongue in June 1983, when he stated: "If we do not do anything much for our defense, Japan will end up becoming a country like Finland, which must ask favors from the Soviet Union [to survive]."[29] Aside from the question of whether his analogy was appropriate or not,[30] one clearly sees the message that the Nakasone wanted to convey to the Japanese voters in his election campaign for the Upper House of the Diet: Put bluntly, Japan would be "Finlandized"[31] if it did not adequately prepare for its own defense. In the context of our discussion here, the implication was simple— as long as Japan took care of herself, particularly in regard to defense matters, Japan would neither have to worry about the Soviet Union nor ask favors of Moscow. This remark by Nakasone revealed the crux of his Soviet policy: There was no particular reason for Japan to take the diplomatic initiative to improve relations with the USSR.

This fundamental policy orientation stemmed from the Nakasone administration's cold assessment of the situation at that time, as well as from increasing self-confidence on the part of the Japanese. It is true that the complete normalization and improvement of relations with the Soviet Union remained the largest diplomatic task facing Japan, and it is easy to imagine that an ambitious politician such as Nakasone—who wanted to be distinguished from his predecessors—would have been tempted to tackle and accomplish this last, most difficult task in order to be remembered forever as the politician who finally broke through the long stalemate with the USSR. Yet, Nakasone seems to have been convinced that as long as Moscow did not change its fundamental policy toward Japan, Tokyo must not initiate anything. More importantly, given the situation at that time, Tokyo was able to afford to refrain from taking action. In fact, in April 1983, Nakasone instructed the Japanese ambassador to Moscow, Masuo Takashima, to adopt a "wait and see" policy for a while, during which time Japan would take no initiative or action but instead would sit back to await a Soviet initiative.[32]

While Prime Minister Nakasone himself paid visits to South Korea, the United States (twice), and to ASEAN countries within the first half of his term in office, he showed no interest whatsoever in sending cabinet ministers to the USSR for visits. Nakasone's rationale was to strictly adhere to the diplomatic principle of reciprocity. On April 23, 1983, Prime

Minister Nakasone reportedly said: "For the purpose of improving bilateral relations between Japan and the Soviet Union, Japan wants, among other things, Mr. Andrei A. Gromyko, Soviet First Deputy Premier and Foreign Minister, to visit Tokyo. We want this particularly because our foreign ministers have visited many more times than theirs have. At stake here is Japan's national prestige."[33] By the same principle, the Japanese Foreign Ministry approved a meeting between Soviet Vice-Foreign Minister Mikhail S. Kapitsa and Japanese Prime Minister Nakasone and Foreign Minister Shintarō Abe only after Japanese Ambassador to Moscow Takashima was guaranteed a meeting with Soviet Premier Nikolai A. Tikhonov.[34]

As was expected, the Nakasone administration demonstrated a firm, uncompromising stance on the Northern Territories issue. Nakasone endorsed the movement for the reversion of the islands by sending three cabinet members on individual "visual inspection tours" of the islands, conducted off the coast of Nemuro Peninsula, the closest accessible point to the disputed islands: The director general of the prime minister's office made his inspection in January 1983, the director general of the Defense Agency made his first inspection in May 1983, and the foreign minister inspected the territories in August 1983.[35]

On February 6, 1983, the eve of Northern Territories Day, Nakasone bitterly criticized the Soviet "illegal seizure"[36] of the islands: "We have a responsibility to *secure* [*kakuho suru*] the four northernmost islands as our territory" (emphasis added by H.K.).[37] The Nakasone government, indeed, regarded the solution of the territorial question as "the top prerequisite" (Foreign Minister Shintarō Abe)[38] for establishing genuinely friendly relations between Japan and the USSR. Nakasone himself stressed, however, that there was no need for Japan to "show any coquetry" (*bitai o miseru*).[39] Nor should Japan "beg" for the return of its territory. Instead, Japan should demonstrate, in Nakasone's words, "a resolute attitude in its diplomacy as an independent, sovereign state."[40]

The third feature of the Nakasone administration's policy toward the USSR under Andropov concerns the need for a comprehensive approach. Recognition of the need for a comprehensive approach came about only gradually. Under Nakasone, the Japanese government finally seems to have realized the Soviets' skill in arbitrarily linking economics with politics when convenient and disconnecting them when linkage was inconvenient. The Nakasone government considered the best way to counter this tactic was to be not only fully aware of the method but to resort to the same technique. Thus, the Nakasone government made an effort to keep Moscow from exploiting this favorite Soviet tactic of separating trade from political affairs.

The Nakasone government displayed its own intent of linking politics and economics when confronted with the so-called Nagano business mission. This large delegation of more than 200 Japanese businesspeople, headed by Shigeo Nagano, visited Moscow in late February 1983. The Nakasone government, of course, was in no position to prevent the businesspeople from visiting the USSR, but his government officials showed their displeasure rather candidly. Reportedly, Nakasone himself declined Nagano's request to issue a personal letter addressed to Soviet President Iurii Andropov; Nakasone feared such a letter might have been interpreted as the Japanese government's full-fledged endorsement of the delegation's mission. At a meeting held prior to the delegation's departure, Yoshiya Katō, director general of the Japanese Foreign Ministry's Bureau of European and Oceanic Affairs, carefully expressed the Japanese government's hope that delegation members would behave very cautiously and would not forget that Japan could not separate economics from politics.[41] Nagano and other businesspeople in the delegation considered such remarks unnecessary and were infuriated that the government would preach such a clear principle to grown-up businesspeople, who were Japanese prior to being businesspeople.[42] Kato's unusual interference in this case was rationalized by the belief at the Foreign Ministry that economic power was Japan's only effective trump card vis-à-vis the Soviet Union and the Northern Territories question.[43]

For its part, the Japanese government under Nakasone purposely attempted, as much as possible, to link the territorial question with other issues. Advocating this comprehensive approach, Nakasone said that although the solution of the territorial question was the fundamental condition for the improvement of Japan's relations with the USSR, other issues existed as well. These included fishing, the development of Siberia and Sakhalin, and scientific and cultural exchanges. "From such a *comprehensive* [*hōkatsu-tekina*] approach, I am trying to find a way out of the deadlock in negotiations on the territorial issue" (emphasis added by H.K.).[44] On the other hand, when Japan found it disadvantageous to link one field with another, the Nakasone administration did not hesitate to separate matters. For example, when his government expelled the Soviet diplomat (Vinogradov) from Japan in June 1983, the Japanese Foreign Ministry tried to separate this incident from Japan's intention to improve relations with the Soviet Union by concluding a long-term agreement on fishing rights, a tax agreement, and plans for cultural exchanges.[45]

Chapter 11
Andropov's Policy
Any Change?

1. Continuity in Basic Attitude

Soviet foreign policy under the leadership of Iurii V. Andropov would follow the same course as that set out under Brezhnev: This seemed to have been the message that Andropov wanted to convey in his maiden speech to the CPSU's Central Committee on November 22, 1982, which particularly underlined the "continuity"[1] of Soviet foreign policy. The new CPSU General Secretary stated, "Soviet foreign policy has been and will be as it was defined by the decisions of the 24th, 25th, and 26th Party Congresses [held in Brezhnev's days—H.K.]."[2] Needless to say, no serious student of Soviet foreign policy would take these official statements literally. Given the nature of foreign policy, official comments were rarely implemented in their original form; they must instead be interpreted, modified, or even abandoned, depending upon the situation. Furthermore, actual Soviet conduct of foreign affairs very frequently deviated from goals formally enunciated, at times to such an extent that one comes to think that words and deeds were two completely different things in Soviet foreign policy.[3]

Having the above caveat in our minds, however, we can still rather safely say that, regarding Soviet policy toward Japan, there was no change after the ascendance of the new Kremlin leadership. While Japan surely did not occupy a very high place on Andropov's list of foreign policy objectives, the Soviet government had to clarify its position toward Japan on a day-to-day basis. In fact, after the death of Leonid I. Brezhnev (November 10, 1982), there were significant actions and statements by Moscow toward Tokyo. Careful examination reveals that fortunately there was not a very large discrepancy discernable between official Soviet pronouncements and their actual engagements, and, more importantly, there was no indication of a shift in their foreign policy vis-à-vis Japan away from that of Brezhnev's days. In other words, the following passages in the editorial by Moscow Radio commentator Iurii Afornin entitled "The Soviet Union's Foreign Policy Toward Japan," which was aired on November 19, 1982, about a week after Andropov assumed top leadership in the Kremlin, happened to be correct in practice as well: "Statements by Soviet leaders in Moscow in the past several days [since Brezhnev's death—H.K.] have demonstrated to the world *the complete continuity of Soviet foreign policy* and the USSR's resolve to follow the path pointed to by the decision of the 26th CPSU Congress. . . . *It also reflects the keynote of Soviet policy toward Japan*" (emphasis added by H.K.).[4] Let us look at this in more detail.

Vitalii Kobysh, chief of the U.S. section, International Department of the CPSU's Central Committee, made the following remark. I have already cited this remark in chapter 1, but, since it was made in December 1982, shortly after both Andropov and Nakasone took office, let me quote it again.

> Although Japan does not belong to the category of a great power, her weight in the contemporary world is very significant and is constantly growing. . . . Toward the end of this century Japan's GNP will constitute 12 percent of that of the whole world. It is unrealistic not to take this into consideration when analyzing the correlation of forces in the world arena. . . . As demonstrated by the experience of this country, the influence of a state today is not determined by its military potential.[5]

Previously, in the Soviet concept of the "correlation of forces" and assessment of power of a nation, the military component had occupied an exceedingly dominant position, while economic capability had far less weight. This peculiar Soviet conception resulted in Moscow's proclivity to underestimate the weight of Tokyo's voices both in international politics and in Soviet-Japanese relations. In marked contrast, however, what Kobysh was then observing and arguing was: (1) the military potential of a nation does not constitute the most important component of its political influence; (2) economic capability occupies a significant place in the "correlation of forces"; and, consequently, (3) the significance of the role that Japan might play in the next decade is great and should not be underestimated. If taken literally, the comment by Kobysh signaled a revolutionary change in the Soviet mind-set in general and in the way of assessing the power of a nation in particular.

The questions to be asked are: Was such a statement by a high Party official to be regarded as an indication of a real shift in Moscow's concept of the "correlation of forces," and hence its assessment and perception of Japan? Moreover, can we consider the remark a reflection of the Andropov administration's new policy orientation toward Tokyo, a line quite different from that under Brezhnev?

The first question concerns the nature of official Soviet pronouncements and writings. As influential Soviet commentator Aleksandr Bovin once candidly admitted, the verbal expression of a policy "can play a dual role"[6]: educational or guiding, and propagandistic. The first function "reflects [otrazhaet] real political intentions"[7]—in the case of the Soviet Union, of the Kremlin's leadership—so that the Party rank and file and general Soviet public could be informed of the official Party line on a particular issue at the given moment. If we regard the remark by Kobysh as one intending to fulfill an educational and guiding role, we may say that a change in the relative weight of variables in the Soviet concept "correlation of forces," particularly with regard to the assessment of the power of Japan, was slowly taking place in the Kremlin. Conversely, the second (propagandistic) function of Soviet official pronouncements and public writings is called upon "to conceal [skryt'] the real political interests and intentions" (Bovin)[8] in order not to let the general Soviet public and the foreign observers learn what the Kremlin leadership really had on its mind. It was, of course, possible to regard the article by Kobysh as one intending to serve the second role. The article, which was written by Kobysh immediately after his visit to Japan,[9] could be nothing but a nice verbal compliment or gesture addressed to the Japanese, which does not cost the Soviets much.

The one important example of the lack of any significant changes in Soviet attitudes toward Soviet-Japanese relations was provided by the Andropov government's intransigence over the Northern Territories issue. Due to its function as a symbol of the more profound disparities between Japan and the Soviet Union, the Northern Territories issue served as the best measure for detecting any significant changes in attitudes and policy regarding national security and basic determinants for solving international disputes.

Although Andropov did not have an opportunity to publicly enunciate his position on the territorial dispute between Japan and the Soviet Union, it did not appear likely that he would alter Soviet policy on this matter. In his maiden speech at the plenary session of the CPSU Central Committee on November 22, 1982, he indicated that he rejected any possibility of the Soviets making efforts toward improving relations with Japan or making any unilateral concessions, such as the return of the Northern Territories to Japan. As the new CPSU General Secretary put it:

> The statement, in which readiness for normalizing [state] relations is linked with the demand that the Soviet Union pay for this with some preliminary concessions in different fields, does not sound serious, to say the least. We shall not agree to this. . . . I want to stress once more that the Soviet Union stands for agreement, but that must be sought on a basis of reciprocity and equality.[10]

Having quoted the above paragraph, Iurii Kuznetsov concluded in the March 1983 issue of *Kommunist* that "there is no such thing as an unresolved territorial question between the two countries."[11] This was exactly the same phrase that had been used under Brezhnev. In an article entitled "Fabrications and Truth about the 'Northern Territories,'" which appeared in the March 1983 issue of another important Soviet periodical, *Mezhdunarodnaia zhizn'* (International affairs), Soviet authors likewise categorically denied Japanese claims to the disputed islands. Criticizing remarks made by Japanese Prime Minister Yasuhiro Nakasone in his major policy speech delivered in December 1982, in which the Prime Minister stated that his government wanted to stabilize relations with the Soviet Union by concluding a peace treaty that would settle the Northern Territories question, Konstantin Andreev and Kirill E. Cherevko literally reiterated the official position of the Soviet government that Japanese demands for the islands were both "unfounded and unlawful."[12] These were exactly the same terms that had been used by former CPSU Secretary General Brezhnev during the 25th Party Congress, held in February–March of 1976.[13]

In sum, it seemed premature to detect any meaningful change in the Soviet perception of Japan from Kobysh's remark. Furthermore, even if one admitted that the Soviet perception of Japan was undergoing some transformation, one should not associate such perceptional change directly or automatically with actual change in Soviet foreign policy conduct toward Japan. For, no matter how important a component it may be, decision makers' image or perception of other nations constitutes, after all, only one of the determinants of foreign policy formation, which is formulated by many other variables, rational and irrational. It thus becomes more important for us to see what else the new Soviet government under Andropov was stating concerning Japan and, more importantly, what it was actually doing to the Japanese. Only after carefully examining these other statements and actions, can we safely say whether what Kobysh was saying was merely lip-service to the Japanese or a more serious manifestation of a real change in policy toward Tokyo.

2. More Military Buildup in the Far East

The first important thing we must draw our attention to in this regard is the Andropov government's continued military buildup in the Far East and the regions adjacent to Japan—an area roughly east of Lake Baikal, including the maritime provinces, Sakhalin, Kamchatka, the Kurile Islands, and the Northern Territories. It may be true that the Soviet military forces that had been deployed in this area were not targeted at Japan—as explained by Soviet spokesmen—but at the United States and China. However, given the geographically multitargetable missions of the military forces, together with the technological nature and mobility of modern weaponry, this explanation was not convincing to the Japanese. The majority of the Japanese regarded the Soviet military buildup in the above-mentioned area as one directed at least partially at Japan. This was exactly the reaction that Moscow wanted to have from the Japanese.

Let us now compare the last three years of the Brezhnev era—i.e., 1980–1982—with the first year of the Andropov period, 1982–1983, in order to view clearly the intensified efforts of the Soviet military buildup in the Asia-Pacific region under Andropov's leadership. As indicated in Table 11.1, Soviet ground forces deployed in the Far East increased gradually, from 34 divisions totaling about 350,000 men in 1980, to 39 divisions of 360,000 men in both 1981 and 1982, to 40 divisions comprising some 370,000 men in 1983.

The Far Eastern naval forces, under the command of the Soviet Pacific Fleet headquartered in Vladivostok, also demonstrated steady growth. The number of their warships increased from about 785, with a total displacement of 1.52 million tons, in 1980, to 820 vessels, totaling 1.62 million tons, in 1983. Furthermore, the Soviet Union under Andropov and Chernenko appeared to be particularly interested in replacing the submarines then deployed in the Sea of Okhotsk with strategic ballistic missile nuclear submarines (SSBNs). The Soviet Pacific Fleet had already

Table 11.1

Soviet Military Deployments in the Far East

	Brezhnev Era		Andropov Era	
	1980	1981	1982	1983
Ground forces				
Divisions	34	39	39	40
Men	350,000	360,000	360,000	370,000
Naval forces				
(Pacific fleet)				
Warships	785	800	810	820
Tonnages	1,520,000	1,580,000	1,600,000	1,620,000
Air forces	2,060	2,210	2,120	2,100
Bombers	450	450	420	440
Fighters	1,450	1,600	1,550	1,510
Patrol planes	160	160	150	150

Source: Japan Defense Agency, *Defense of Japan* (Tokyo: *Japan Times*, 1980, 1981, 1982, and 1983).

deployed 12-13 *Delta*-class submarines (SSBNs) there, armed with SS-N-18 missiles capable of striking the U.S. mainland. Furthermore, it seemed that the Soviet government intended to add submarines armed with more powerful missiles—*Oscar*-class with SS-N-19, and *Typhoon*-class with SS-N-20 missiles.[14]

Although the Soviet air forces showed a slight decrease in the numbers of aircraft in 1982–1983, the quality of the forces improved. In fact, improvements in the Soviet air forces in the Far East greatly exceeded any improvements made in air forces elsewhere in the USSR. For example, the main type of bomber in the Soviet Far Eastern region was being changed from the TU-16 *Badger* (with a maximum speed of mach 0.8 and an operational radius of 6,400 km) to a vastly improved anti-surface and anti-ship supersonic bomber, the TU-22 M *Backfire* (with a speed of mach 2.5 and range of about 8,800–9,600 km without in-flight refueling). About 20 *Backfires*, targeted against Chinese ground forces, initially were identified at the Belaia airfield, west of Lake Baikal in Siberia. Later, about 50 more *Backfires* were detected in the naval aviation units stationed at the Alekseiskaia airfield, close to Vladivostok in the Soviet Far East. From their base in the Soviet maritime provinces, the *Backfires* could launch an attack against the Japanese Maritime Self-Defense Forces or the U.S. Seventh Fleet and return without refueling. On September 14, 1982, eleven *Backfires* conducted an exercise in the Sea of Japan to practice an attack on a U.S. aircraft carrier, using the Soviet carrier *Minsk* as a target.[15] The deployment of *Backfires* in the Pacific theater undoubtedly added "a new dimension to the threat to sea-lanes in the area."[16]

Under Andropov and Chernenko, the Soviet Union continued to improve the combat capabilities of its forces deployed on the disputed islands. One method by which the Soviets qualitatively enhanced their military potential on the islands was through replacement of old weaponry with more modern and sophisticated weapons. In December 1982, the Soviet Union sent twelve supersonic MiG-21 fighters to the Tennei airfield on Etorofu to replace a squadron of MiG-17s. Half a year later (May 1983), however, these MiG-21s were withdrawn and replaced by about 10 MiG-23 fighters, which presumably would be stationed in Etorofu on a long-term basis.[17] Another half year later, the Soviet Union added 10 MiG-23 fighters to the airbase on Etorofu—thus doubling the total number of planes deployed there.[18] The so-called "third-generation" aircraft, the MiG-23, had greater air and surface attack capabilities than the "second-generation" MiG-21, not to mention the "first-generation" MiG-17. While the MiG-21s, with a combat radius of 650–740 km, covered only the northeastern part of Japan, the MiG-23s, with a doubled combat radius of 900 to 1,200 km, could fly to bomb Tokyo and return to Etorofu. In the middle of October 1983, an unknown number of Soviet fighters, probably the MiG-23s that had recently been deployed on Etorofu, violated Japanese airspace east of Hokkaido.[19] This action was believed to be a demonstrative flight intended to counterbalance a joint U.S.-Japanese exercise occurring at that time on Hokkaido.[20] Regardless of Soviet intentions, it was the fourteenth recorded Soviet violation of Japanese airspace since 1967.[21] Only a month later, on November 15, the fifteenth Soviet violation of Japanese airspace was recorded, when three Soviet bombers, identified as two TU-16 *Badgers* and a TU-95 *Bear*, twice violated Japanese airspace over the Sea of Japan off Tsushima Strait.[22]

3. Diplomatic Offensive with SS-20s

The second salient feature of Soviet foreign affairs conducted toward Japan after Andropov's assumption of power was the effort to use the Soviet military buildup as a diplomatic weapon. The Andropov leadership clearly revealed its intention to apply to the Japanese continuously, and even in an intensified degree, Moscow's traditional attempt to translate the Soviet physical might into political influence. Why did not the new Soviet leadership change that policy which, under Brezhnev, turned out so frequently to be counterproductive? One can only guess at the reasons for this. Like his predecessors and many of his colleagues at the time, Iurii Andropov was probably neither a very flexible nor an imaginative leader. It is even conceivable that the new general secretary himself firmly believed that intimidation was in the end the best policy to be applied to the Japanese. Even if he was a flexible and innovative political leader, what could he do? He could not afford to take a bold initiative toward Tokyo, given the political system and climate in the Soviet Union at that time. The strong inertia of the past, his unstable domestic power position, and the high cost of Tokyo's request for the improvement of Japanese-Soviet bilateral relations (i.e., the reversion of the Northern Territories) did not provide Andropov any incentive to depart from the traditional Soviet policy toward Japan. The best that Andropov was able to do was to implement the traditional method more skillfully and effectively than his predecessors. In any case, the policy that the Soviet government under Andropov in fact followed with regard to Japan was its continuous resort to coercive diplomacy, with the demonstration of the USSR's massive military might in the Far East and in the vicinity of Japan. A typical example is provided by Andropov's "SS-20 diplomacy," which will be elaborated upon below.

Although quite a number of SS-20s—mobile intermediate-range ballistic missiles (IRBMs)—had already been deployed in Asia during the Brezhnev era, it was under the Andropov regime (November 1982–February 1984), when Japan was threatened with the possible transfer of more SS-20s from Europe to Asia, that the Japanese become greatly concerned about this extremely powerful and sophisticated missile. The shock came with the report by a West German newspaper *Die Welt*, according to which Andropov told Hans-Jochen Vogel, West German Social Democratic (SPD) leader, on January 12, 1983, that the Soviet government was then considering re-deploying "in Siberia" those SS-20s that exceeded the quota for the European zone that would be established by the pending Intermediate-range Nuclear Forces (INF) agreement with the United States, "in order to counter a new military base in Japan."[23]

It is quite clear that Andropov was apparently referring to Tokyo's decision in the fall of 1982 to accept a U.S. plan to deploy F-16 fighter-bombers, starting in 1985, at Misawa airbase in northern Japan. If this was what Andropov had in mind, it was no great surprise to find another example of the Soviet Union deliberately confusing the cause with the consequence, or of the Soviets overreacting to the U.S. and/or Japan's action. For, from the perspective of Washington and Tokyo, the decision to deploy F-16 fighter-bombers at Misawa was an inevitable counter-measure on the part of the United States and Japan in order to balance what the USSR had already done to them—that is, deployment on the Northern Islands and in the vicinity of Japan of MiG-23s, MiG-27s, and Sukhoi fighter-bombers, which could carry nuclear weapons. It was regarded as an overreaction on the side of the Soviet Union to counter F-16 *fighter-bombers* with the threat of deployment of more SS-20 *missiles*, adding to the 108 already deployed in the Asian zone.

At any rate, Andropov's threat was confirmed shortly thereafter by his foreign minister. On January 17, 1983, five days after his boss's remark to Vogel and one day before Japanese Prime Minister Nakasone's sensational statement about "an unsinkable aircraft carrier" in Washington, D.C., Andrei A. Gromyko told his West German counterpart, Hans-Dietrich Genscher in Bonn that the Soviet government would move some of its European-based SS-20s to "Siberia."[24] According to the West German weekly *Der Spiegel*, the Soviet foreign minister explained to Genscher that the Soviets ought to counter the American military buildup in Asia, including the areas "around Okinawa" and "in the sea around Japan."[25]

What the Soviets later said reveals, wittingly or unwittingly, inconsistency with regard to the question as to whether the SS-20s to be transferred from Europe to Siberia would be aimed mostly at Japan. In response to Tokyo's strong protest conveyed by the Japanese ambassador to Moscow, Masuo Takashima, the Soviet foreign minister assured Takashima on February 23, 1983 that "Soviet missiles [in Asia] were directed against nuclear weapons in South Korea but not against Japan."[26] Confirming the words of Gromyko, Georgii A. Arbatov also clearly stated to *Asahi Shimbun* on March 12 that "the Soviet intermediate-range missiles are not and will not be targeted against Japan."[27] Without hesitating at all to take back his own words to the Japanese ambassador less than six weeks before, however, Gromyko, in an exceptionally rare televised news conference with Western journalists in Moscow on April 2, 1983, tried to justify the possible transfer of SS-20s from Europe to Soviet territory in Asia and the Far East on the grounds that "Japan and the waters around it are stuffed with nuclear weapons and carriers for them. Okinawa is a huge base of nuclear weapons."[28] Surprisingly, this was not the end of the story. Soviet

Deputy Foreign Minister Mikhail S. Kapitsa reversed, in Tokyo, what his boss Gromyko had told foreign newsmen in Moscow only ten days earlier. In a meeting with his Japanese counterpart Vice Foreign Minister Nobuo Matsunaga and other high officials at the Japanese Foreign Ministry on April 11, 1983, Kapitsa noted that "the Soviet Union does not have a single SS-20 directed at Japan."[29]

As is clear from the above, the Andropov administration on one occasion indicated that the Soviet SS-20s were targeted against Japan, whereas on a another occasion, particularly when addressed to a Japanese audience, it denied statements previously made by other spokesmen. How then was one to understand these two apparently contradictory Soviet pronouncements? It would of course be conceivable to regard these mixed messages as a reflection of the fact that the Soviet government under Andropov had not itself reached a unified view on the matter. One cynical observer went so far as to comment that, particularly in view of the mobile nature of SS-20s, it was not worth discussing at what targets these Soviet intermediate missiles were directed.

For all these and other critical remarks, however, it still seems worthwhile to try to understand the real reason why the Andropov leadership was sending such seemingly inconsistent messages to Japan. It seems that the Andropov government was sending a deliberately ambiguous message to Tokyo so that it could exploit the issue as one of the best political instruments for manipulating the Japanese. That is to say, the Soviet Union under Andropov conditioned the question of the targeting of Soviet SS-20s deployed this side of the Urals to Japan's behavior. As long as Tokyo behaved itself well, particularly refraining from increasing cooperation with Washington in the military field, the Soviet Union could pledge that those SS-20s would not be directed at Japan. If Tokyo did not behave as the Soviets wanted, however, the Soviet Union could not offer such a pledge because the Soviet Union would then—according to the Soviets—have no other means to protect its own national interests.

Careful re-examination of the Soviet remarks quoted above helps prove the correctness of such an interpretation. Immediately after stating that "the Soviet Union has no single SS-20 directed at Japan," Kapitsa, for example, did not fail to make the following reservation: "Unless Japan is involved in an anti-Soviet strategy, Japan has nothing to worry about."[30] Having told *Asahi Shimbun*, as cited previously, that "the Soviet intermediate-range missiles are and will not be targeted against Japan," Arbatov also did not forget to add in the same breath the following condition: "This will be the case as long as Japan remains a non-nuclear power and does not allow other powers to deploy and maintain their nuclear weapons in Japan or to use Japanese territory for launching an attack on the USSR."[31] If my interpretation is correct, the message that Moscow intended to convey to Tokyo was not inconsistent and ambiguous but quite clear-cut, articulate, and consistent—it was not up to Moscow but Tokyo to decide finally whether the Soviet SS-20s would be targeted against Japan. This, for the Soviets, was naturally a far better tactic than to declare categorically that the Soviet SS-20s in Asia were or were not directed at Japan.

4. Andropov's New Proposal

Andropov did make a "concessionary" proposal on August 26, 1983.[32] Changing abruptly the Kremlin's earlier insistence on the right to move any of the mobile SS-20 missiles now targeted on Western Europe into Asia, Andropov proposed that his government would dismantle or destroy any missiles that it removed under the agreement in exchange for concessions from the West. The Soviet Union would not redeploy them elsewhere (presumably in the Asian part of the USSR), provided that the United States would accept Moscow's terms for limiting medium-range nuclear missiles in Europe. This new offer by the top Soviet leader might have been regarded as a "positive sign,"[33] but only in the following limited sense. To begin with, from the Western perspective, the concession, if any, in the new offer was of a "peripheral"[34] kind, because it avoided addressing the central objections to the Soviet negotiating position in the deadlocked INF talks in Geneva. What Andropov was offering could be regarded as a new condition rather than a concession; for the Soviet decision to liquidate some SS-20s was contingent on U.S. acceptance of Moscow's terms—namely of Soviet missiles remaining equal in number to those of the British and French—and on renunciation of NATO's plan to deploy Pershing-II and cruise missiles in Europe. It was quite obvious that Andropov was aiming to use the question of whether or not to shift the SS-20s from Europe to Asia, as a bargaining chip in the INF negotiations.

From the Japanese vantage point, Andropov's new offer was not regarded as a one-sided favor to Tokyo, either. True, the proposal was "welcome news," as Prime Minister Nakasone reportedly commented,[35] so long as the reduction of SS-20s in Europe would not mean a redeployment of SS-20s in the Asian part of the USSR. But, quite obviously, the new proposal did not refer to and would not affect at all those SS-20s that were already in place in Asia, and were presumably aimed at China, Korea, and Japan. Furthermore, even without removing SS-20s from Europe, the Soviet Union had the means to increase the number of SS-20s in its Asian regions, if it wanted to. This was the case, because there was neither an agreement concluded, nor even negotiated, with regard to the limitation of intermediate-range nuclear forces in the Asia-Pacific theater, unlike in the European theater. In fact, on October 4, 1983, Hirokazu Arai, a counselor of the Japan Defense Agency, predicted that the Soviet Union would increase the total number of SS-20s deployed in the Far East from 108 in 1983 to 135 in the foreseeable future.[36] Only ten days later, the Japanese learned that Arai's prediction had already partially materialized.[37] The USSR, it was learned, had completed the additional deployment of 18 missiles—making a total of 126 missiles aimed at Asia.[38] Furthermore, the Soviet Union had reportedly started construction of new missile sites in four areas, which could lead to the virtual doubling of its SS-20s targeted on Asia in the future.[39] In short, by offering a or minor "concession," even if it had to be followed through, the Soviet Union would not lose much in practice. If the offer were not accepted, then the USSR could justify thereby any SS-20s deployed in Asia.

What Andropov was aiming at by his new offer on August 26, 1983 was not limited to this. It bore one more important function—to coerce as many politico-diplomatic concessions as possible from Tokyo in exchange for the "concession" of possibly refraining from redeployment of the missiles in Asia. Taking full advantage of his visit to the Japanese Foreign Ministry to formally convey to the Tokyo government Andropov's new proposal in the INF negotiations on August 29, 1983, Soviet ambassador to Japan Vladimir Pavlov made a request to Yoshiya Katō, Director General of the Ministry's European and Oceanic Affairs Bureau, that "the Japanese government give proper respect to the new Soviet proposal."[40] "Since the INF is not simply a question of Europe," the ambassador continued, "the Soviet Union is ready to respond to Japan, if the latter wants to have a dialogue with the former."[41] The message that Pavlov really wanted to convey to Tokyo is quite clear—that is, a request of a corresponding favor from Tokyo to Moscow in exchange for the "concession" that Moscow may make in the INF negotiations in Europe. More concretely speaking, what the Soviet ambassador suggested was that Japan should make some diplomatic initiative that would contribute to a breakthrough in the long-deadlocked, chilly relations between Japan and the USSR. It is thus safe to say that Andropov did not change at all his basic strategy of exploiting the question of the SS-20s as the most powerful diplomatic instrument that his government ever had for manipulating Japanese behavior toward Moscow.

5. An Agreement on Nonuse of Nuclear Weapons

In earlier chapter, I described how the Soviet government under Brezhnev tried hard to make Tokyo agree to conclude a treaty with the USSR, or rather, an agreement short of a peace treaty, which would not solve the territorial issue. A Treaty of Good-neighborliness and Cooperation, an agreement on confidence-building measures (CBMs), and an agreement on nonuse of nuclear weapons were some of the concrete proposals made, though in vain, by the Soviet president. Andropov seemed to pursue exactly the same objective as his predecessor but with more reliance on the threat of SS-20s. He appeared to argue that if the Japanese were so concerned about the deployment and/or redeployment of SS-20s, then the Tokyo government should agree to the Soviet proposal of concluding an agreement on the nonuse of nuclear weapons. Of course, Tokyo considered it unnecessary to conclude such an agreement with the Soviet Union, particularly because both Japan and the USSR, with other nations, had already signed the Treaty on the Non-Proliferation of Nuclear Weapons (NPT), which obligates states possessing nuclear weapons (e.g., the USSR) to guarantee the security of states not possessing such weapons (e.g., Japan) from nuclear aggression or intimidation.[42] Such a situation did not keep Moscow, however, from pressing Tokyo to individually conclude another, separate treaty with the Soviet Union, such as an agreement on the nonuse of nuclear weapons, and/or CBMs.

Mikhail Kapitsa, during his visit to Tokyo in April 1983, energetically and persistently brought up the idea of concluding an agreement on the nonuse of nuclear weapons between Japan and the USSR. On April 12, the Soviet Deputy Foreign Minister made the following proposal to the Japanese Ministry of Foreign Affairs:

> Let us conclude an agreement in which Japan pledges the three nonnuclear principles and the Soviet side promises nonuse of nuclear weapons against Japan. . . . *Furthermore, it would be a good idea to write also in the same agreement such basic principles regulating the bilateral relations between*

> *Japan and the Soviet Union as peaceful coexistence, good-neighborliness, and others* [emphasis added by H.K.].[43]

Letters sent by the Communist Party of the Soviet Union (CPSU) to the Japanese Socialist Party (JSP) and Democratic Socialist Party (DSP) in January 1983 contained exactly the same proposal as the one made by Kapitsa to the Japanese Foreign Ministry.[44] The letter addressed to the DSP, for instance, reads as follows:

> If Japan adheres to its self-proclaimed principles of not possessing nuclear weapons and of refusing the development of nuclear weapons on its territory, then the Soviet Union is ready to provide Japan with an appropriate guarantee, upon which Japan can rely.[45]

Of course, one reason why Moscow wanted so badly to have an agreement with Tokyo on the nonuse of nuclear weapons was its desire to make sure that Japan faithfully abided by the three non-nuclear principles of not producing, not possessing, and not introducing nuclear weapons into Japan. Soviet concern and suspicion about the possibility of Tokyo changing both *de facto* and *de jure* these self-imposed principles into the so-called "two-and-a-half principles" was particularly reinforced by the remark made by former U.S. ambassador to Japan Edwin O. Reischauer at a press interview conducted in May 1981.[46] Reischauer stated at that time that the term *introduction* was from the beginning not meant to preclude the transit and port-calls of U.S. naval vessels carrying weapons.[47] Discussion of whether the former ambassador's remark was accurate is not the point here.[48] The more relevant point in our present context is that Soviet apprehension of a military nature did not fully or accurately explain why Moscow was so persistently pressing Tokyo to negotiate and sign an agreement on the nonuse of nuclear weapons.

As the italicized part of the above-quoted argument of Kapitsa clearly revealed, the Andropov government expected such an agreement to include not only articles of a military kind but also "such basic principles as peaceful coexistence, good-neighborliness, and other principles that regulate Soviet-Japanese relations," principles that are usually written in other types of treaties, such as a peace treaty or a treaty of good-neighborliness and cooperation. Thus, what Andropov was aiming at with Japan was crystal clear to those who were familiar with Soviet-Japanese relations at the time. Since Tokyo was not interested in signing any treaty or agreement with Moscow except a peace treaty that solved the territorial issue,

Brezhnev's attempt to press Tokyo to sign a Treaty on Good-neighborliness and Cooperation and an agreement on CBMs was not successful. What Andropov was trying to do was to pressure Japan, taking full advantage of the Japanese concern about the Soviet threat of increasing the number of SS-20s, to conclude an agreement on the nonuse of nuclear weapons—an agreement that Andropov expected would play the role of a substitute or a variant of a peace treaty, thereby making a diplomatic breakthrough in the long-stalemated relations.

6. The Downing of KAL 007

The last, but certainly not the least, worthwhile discussion concerning the Andropov regime's conduct of foreign affairs with regard to Japan is the fact that it was fully ready and willing to use the Soviet physical might in practice, whenever it considered it necessary. In other words, the Soviet Union under Andropov was interested in a continuous buildup of its military forces in the Far East not simply to exploit them as a politically effective instrument to assist in the achievement of diplomatic objectives but also to employ force as a coercive physical means to fulfill genuine military purposes. Undoubtedly, the latter function is an intrinsic and far more important one, and yet it is prone to be underestimated or at times even overlooked. The shooting-down of Korean Air Lines (KAL) Flight 007 in the skies over Sakhalin on September 1, 1983[49] reminded us of the cold reality that the Soviet armed forces did exist and that they were not expanded just for appearance's sake or for solely symbolic or diplomatic functions.

It is true that this incident may not provide the best illustration to prove that the Soviet Union under Andropov intended to employ in practice its increased military forces in the Far East against Japan. To begin with, the downing of a Korean civilian airliner cannot be regarded as a military action directed against Japan. Moreover, it is still not clear whether it was an accidental or intentional move. It is also not clear whether the Andropov leadership in Moscow was consulted in advance by the local military commander about the decision to fire on the South Korean airliner. For all these and other reservations, debates, and questions, the September 1 incident still serves to reveal to us one clear thing—that the Soviet armed forces were not a facade but a physical power that the Soviets did not hesitate to resort to, when they felt it was necessary.

First, the downing of the Korean civilian plane was a 100-percent military action in the sense that it was ordered and executed by the Soviet military forces to serve a military purpose. The disaster can hardly be discarded as an accident in view of the fact that transcripts recorded by the Japanese Defense Agency revealed without any doubt that every move of the Soviet fighters and interceptors was carefully orchestrated by ground controllers. The Soviet leadership tried very hard to excuse the shooting-down of the airplane by implying that the local military commanders made a hurried, inappropriate decision in a moment of panic and confusion, but the Soviet military undoubtedly would have reacted to any such situation in exactly the same manner. Having declared that "the Soviet armed forces have discharged their duties with honor," Marshal Nikolai V. Ogarkov, the Chief of the Soviet General Staff, flatly stated in a press conference on the KAL incident held in Moscow on September 9, 1983: "In the future, if need be, the Soviet military forces will also perform their combat tasks."[50]

Even if it were true that Andropov and other top political leaders in the Politburo were not in fact informed of the attack on the South Korean aircraft until it was over, they were not in a position to be absolved of responsibility for the shooting-down of a civilian airplane with 269 passengers aboard. For it was the Andropov government that adopted the new "Law on the USSR's State Border" in November 1982, Article 36 of which specifically states that weapons may be used to stop border violators who refuse to cooperate.[51] The law makes no exception for civilian aircraft, perhaps because in the Soviet system, civilian planes and military planes were all managed on a military basis. The local Soviet military commanders and interceptor pilots in the Soviet Far East simply followed and fulfilled the standard procedures and instructions in giving the orders and firing at the aircraft that had penetrated Soviet airspace, without having any doubt about the appropriateness of their behavior and measures. Of course, the chances are that, simply in order to evade the reprimand, criticism, and other pressure exerted against Moscow from the West, the Soviet government under Andropov acknowledged some mistakes committed by its local Air Defense Forces. Thus, in a broader sense, it does not make sense to argue that the Soviet leadership bore no responsibility for the downing of the Korean civilian jetliner.

In conclusion, it is neither appropriate nor correct to regard the KAL tragedy as an accident that had nothing to do with either the Soviet regime under Andropov or with its incessant efforts to build up its military forces in the Far East. In this regard the following remark made by Arkadii

Shevchenko, former under secretary at the United Nations and the high-est-ranking Soviet diplomat ever to defect to the United States, touches the core of the subject, though in a slightly exaggerated fashion:

One of the most sinister aspects of this tragedy [the KAL 007 incident–H.K.] is that it was not an accident; it was a natural product of the standard functioning of the Soviet system.[52]

Or, as William Hyland commented, "the tragedy was that the system worked."[53]

7. Impact of the KAL Incident

The impact of the KAL 007 incident upon Japanese-Soviet relations was too great to be passed over without mention. Just before the incident took place, the bilateral relations between Japan and the Soviet Union had begun to show signs, though to a very limited degree, of improving. During his visit to Tokyo in January 1983, Soviet Vice-Foreign Minister M. Kapitsa agreed with high officials at the Japanese Ministry of Foreign Affairs to resume and even expand cultural exchanges between the Soviet Union and Japan.[54] In August of the same year, when he paid a courtesy call at Moscow's Sheremetevo airport to Japanese Foreign Minister Shintarō Abe, who was in transit on his way back to Japan from Eastern Europe, Kapitsa conveyed to Abe the Soviet message that "the Soviet Foreign Minister Gromyko himself was 'fully aware of the fact that it was his turn next to make a visit to Tokyo.'"[55] The message conveyed by the Soviet vice-foreign minister to Abe was extremely important, considering the Soviet foreign minister's poor record in the past ten years (1974–1983); despite the Soviet-Japanese agreement to exchange visits to the respective capitals with the aim of negotiating a peace treaty, Gromyko fulfilled the obligation on the Soviet side only once (in 1976). The reason for Gromyko's reluctance to visit Tokyo was quite obvious: he did not want to discuss a peace treaty which, in the understanding of the Japanese, must include a settlement of the territorial issue.

The Japanese side had also started to show some flexibility in its attitude. For instance, Foreign Minister Abe announced on August 22, 1983 the Japanese government's intention to embark upon the enlargement of economic and cultural exchanges with the USSR, "with the aim of breaking the chilly bilateral relations."[56] Abe was quoted as saying at that time that, while Japan's fundamental policy toward the USSR was to improve bilateral relations by solving the Northern Territories question, it was still desirable, and even necessary, to maintain the dialogue between these two nations. It was obvious that such a move by the Japanese government was precipitated by U.S. President Reagan's decision to conclude a grain sale agreement with the Andropov government despite his previous solicitation of Japan and other Western countries to join U.S.-sponsored "sanctions" against the Soviet Union. At any rate, the concrete measures that the Japanese foreign minister then had in mind were: (1) to resume shortly (in October) the Soviet-Japanese bilateral trade conference, which had been suspended since January 1981 as a sanction against the USSR due to its intervention in Poland; (2) to invite several leading Soviet journalists to Tokyo in 1983 in order to promote dialogue between the two nations; (3) to resume the Japanese-Soviet film festival, which had been suspended since 1978, in two Soviet cities by the end of 1984; and (4) to expand cultural exchanges on governmental and nongovernmental levels.

The shooting down of the South Korean jetliner, with 28 Japanese among the passengers, however, destroyed in one stroke the slight upturn in Soviet-Japanese relations, canceling out almost all the above mentioned concrete measures proposed by both sides. The indignation over this act among the Japanese people was undoubtedly reinforced further by the Andropov government's insensitive attitude toward world reactions, and its clumsy, inept handling of the incident. As a result, Japanese-Soviet relations were forced back to the worst stage they had ever been at in the postwar period.

First, let us examine the official governmental level. In a major policy speech delivered to the Diet on September 10, 1983, Prime Minister Yasuhiro Nakasone stated quite plainly the Japanese government position on this tragedy: "The downing of the Korean Airlines jetliner was clearly an illegal act by the Soviet Union, abhorrent on both legal and humanistic grounds, and Japan must deal firmly with such behavior."[57] Following this speech, both the Lower House and the Upper House of the Japanese Diet unanimously adopted a resolution on September 12 and 13, respectively, that demanded a Soviet explanation and formal apology for the attack, full compensation to the families of the victims, and assurance of the prevention of similar incidents in the future.[58] Yoshiya Katō, director general of the Japanese Foreign Ministry's European and Oceanic Affairs Bureau, tried first to hand over in person to Soviet ambassador to Tokyo Vladimir Pavlov, and then to send by special registered mail to the Soviet embassy in Tokyo, a diplomatic note from the Japanese government, which, among other things, requested prompt and adequate compensation for the Japanese victims. But all these protests and requests made by the Japanese were completely rebuffed by the Soviet side. Pavlov refused to even accept the note, and later he instructed his embassy to send it back to the Japanese Foreign Ministry, reiterating the Moscow government's official stand on this subject: that the Soviet Union bore no responsibility whatsoever for the incident and that the claim should rather be directed to the United States.

Faced with such an insincere Soviet attitude, the Tokyo government decided, in concert with measures adopted by other countries, to impose a package of measures against the Soviet Union that consisted of prohibition of Japanese government officials and employees from traveling aboard Soviet government-run Aeroflot; a ban on nonscheduled Soviet charter flights to Japan, and restrictions on the number of regularly scheduled Aeroflot flights and the aircraft size. Since the Soviet Union adamantly continued to shirk its responsibility for the incident despite its admission that it had shot down the aircraft, Tokyo took the second in a series of punitive steps against Moscow, including a two-week (September 15–28) suspension of civil aviation service between Japan and the USSR.[59]

Other measures and concrete actions relating to the KAL disaster taken by the Japanese government influenced Soviet-Japanese relations inclucing cancelling a scheduled meeting between the foreign ministers of both countries in New York in late September. True, this was an inevitable consequence of the Soviet decision not to send Gromyko to the UN General Assembly on the grounds that the Soviet foreign minister flying in an Aeroflot aircraft was banned from landing at a civilian airport. Still, the impact of such a cancellation upon Soviet-Japanese relations was significant, particularly in light of the fact that this foreign ministerial meeting in New York, which was a valuable opportunity for Japan and the Soviet Union to maintain dialogue, had never been canceled before, even in the wake of the MiG-25 incident (1976) or the signing of the Sino-Japanese peace treaty (1978).

Moreover, at this UN General Assembly meeting, representatives from both Japan and the USSR publicly voiced harsh criticism against each other, an action unprecedented in the history of these two countries at the United Nations. Japanese Foreign Minister Abe urged the Soviet Union to admit responsibility for the downing of the Korean airliner, describing the Soviet action as "an intolerable outrage against humanity and international law."[60] At the same time, Abe reiterated Japan's longstanding request to the Soviet Union to return the Northern Territories. For his part, Soviet ambassador to the United Nations Oleg Troianovskii condemned Japan for "recently accelerating the militarization of the country."[61]

The invitation once accepted by the Japanese Minister of Agriculture Iwazō Kaneko to Moscow was suspended *de facto*. The Japanese Defense Agency canceled its invitations to two military attachés at the Soviet embassy in Tokyo to its firepower drill at the Higashi-Fuji maneuver grounds. Likewise, the Agency decided not to invite any representative of the Soviet Union to the marching ceremony to be held the day before the Japanese SDF Memorial Day (October 1). The Japanese government informed the Soviet Union that they wished to postpone their bilateral trade conference originally scheduled for October 1983 in Moscow. The Tokyo government also strongly advised the Japanese private sponsors and organizers of the Seventh International Air show, scheduled to be held in Kakumuhara City in October–November 1983, to refuse Soviet participation in the show. As a result of the Tokyo government's decision to suspend commercial flights between Japan and the USSR for two weeks, the Soviet ballet troupe from Buriatia, which was scheduled to perform in Japan as part of an exchange program, was canceled. In the economic sphere, too, relations between Japan and the USSR reached a low point in 1983. Despite the Soviet invasion of Afghanistan and Tokyo's subsequent participation in economic sanctions against the Soviet Union, Soviet-Japanese trade relations since 1980 had remained stable and had even experienced a slight increase. In 1983, however, trade showed for the first time a decrease of 20 percent compared with the previous year.[62] In short, Japanese-Soviet relations reached their lowest ebb in the fall of 1983.

Generally speaking, the measures adopted by the Japanese government against the USSR in retaliation for the September 1, 1983 KAL incident may be considered "rather moderate or limited."[63] One reason for the mild measures lies in Tokyo's usual inclination to follow U.S. and other Western countries' reactions, which happened to be "firm, but calm and controlled" (Ronald Reagan).[64] Another reason for the mildness was the Nakasone government's basic policy orientation toward the Soviet Union, which was that Tokyo needed continued dialogue with Moscow so that the potential Soviet threat to Japanese security would not be carried out under any circumstances, and furthermore, so that Tokyo could persuade Moscow to come to the negotiation table, to make the return of the Northern Territories possible. Probably based on these considerations, Prime Minister Nakasone and other high government officials repeatedly stated that the government should handle the KAL incident in a manner not affecting what they called "the fundamental relations between the Soviet Union and Japan."[65]

Yet, it seems wrong to underestimate the strong impact that the "termination" of a Korean civil airliner had upon the mind-set of the Japanese people. It would not be an exaggeration to say that, as far as the deep psychological level of the Japanese public was concerned, the impact of the KAL incident was greater than the impact of the Soviet intervention in Afghanistan or Poland, events which, after all, took place in countries at a great distance from Japan. A public opinion poll conducted by *Yomiuri Shimbun*, the most widely read newspaper in Japan, three weeks after the KAL incident showed that 94.3 percent of those Japanese who answered the questionnaires were concerned with the incident, 85.6 percent regarded the Soviet action as impermissible, and 75.8 percent favored a request for an apology from, and sanctions against, the Soviet Union.[66]

The Korean airliner tragedy seemed to serve to clarify in Japanese minds more than any other event the cold realities that Japan faced. The major discoveries, confirmations, and lessons gained from the incident were: (1) The Soviets had an extraordinarily deep-seated obsession with secure borders. The national borders are sacred and inviolable to every state, and yet the Russian concept of borders proved to be of an exceedingly special kind, even to a paranoiac degree. They automatically regarded even an accidental violation by a civilian aircraft as a criminal act, which called for immediate preventive reaction in the form of naked physical force. When Gromyko reportedly stated in Madrid on September 7, "Soviet territory and the borders of the Soviet Union are sacred," this was correctly interpreted as indicating that the Soviets would do the same thing again under similar circumstances.[67] (2) The Soviets were a hard partner to deal with and negotiate with. The Japanese witnessed anew with their own eyes that the Soviets were not only resorting to their favorite technique of stonewalling in a bureaucratic manner but were also not hesitating to lie, hide the facts, or be inconsistent in order to evade their responsibility and to make their position more favorable. (3) The military-strategic importance and tension of the Sea of Okhotsk and the level of tension in the area was very high. Explaining the Soviet stance on the KAL incident at TASS, the Soviet news agency, Marshal Ogarkov candidly acknowledged that Kamchatka and Southern Sakhalin were "a major base of the Soviet Union's strategic nuclear forces" and "important military installations."[68]

Japanese Prime Minister Nakasone himself thus had to confess in the Diet session that "the Sea of Okhotsk has now become more important strategically and tactically than it was previously thought to be."[69]

While basing their perceptions and observations on the same Soviet mind-set, the same Soviet system, and the same military situations surrounding Japan, the Japanese tend, surprisingly or interestingly enough, to reach different conclusions. It is conceivable, with good reason, that at least two extreme views and policy recommendations appeared in Japan. One school of thought argued that Japan must increase its power, especially its military might, which alone would make sure that nothing similar to the KAL incident happened again and would allow Japan to deal and negotiate with the Soviets more effectively. This school criticized the measures taken against the Soviet Union for the KAL incident by the Nakasone government as being too mild to be effective. In contrast, however, the second school emphasized the urgent need and importance of negotiating an agreement among Japan, the USSR, and other countries concerning arms control measures in the Far East. This group ascribed the real cause of the KAL tragedy to the military confrontation and tension between the East and the West around the Sea of Okhotsk. It proposed, for example, a plan to make the Sea of Okhotsk a nuclear-free zone. The argument of this group in reality helped to solidify the long-standing Soviet offer to Tokyo of an agreement on CBMs in the Far East.

Conclusions

We have seen that Soviet-Japanese relations were strained in the period covered in this book (1976–1983). Due to the Soviet downing of a Korean Air Lines jet in September 1983, relations became even worse. From a theoretical point of view, those incidents and events that contributed to cooling of Soviet-Japanese bilateral relations in the mid-to-late 1970s and early 1980s—as enumerated at the outset of Part Three—may be divided into the following five categories: (1) those that stemmed from *global* confrontation between the Western and Eastern camps; (2) those that were related to the *regional* power configuration in the Asia-Pacific region; (3) those that were mainly an outcome of *bilateral* interactions between Japan and the Soviet Union; (4) those ascribable to *domestic* factors in either or both Japan and the USSR; and (5) those that occurred almost *accidentally* as one-time incidents or at least independently from those factors described above.

However, in practice, it is difficult and sometimes even inappropriate to make such a distinct classification; most of these incidents and events were the result of a combination of two or more factors. Let me elaborate on this.

The MiG-25 incident (1976): Can this be regarded as a purely accidental, one-time incident? To a certain extent it was, but not exclusively so. In fact, as long as the Soviet system continued to be a totalitarian one and to constrain freedom of speech and other human rights, it would have been unable to prevent other daring attempts at defection by high-ranking Soviet military officers. Moreover, without the global confrontation between the West, headed by the United States, and the East, headed by the USSR, the impact of the MiG-25 incident upon Soviet-Japanese relations would not have been so great. Because of this *global international* confrontation and Japan's association with the Western side of the two opposing camps, Japan had no choice but to let the United States completely disassemble the body of the MiG-25, which further contributed to the worsening of Japan's bilateral relationship with the Soviet Union.

The Korean Air Lines Flight 007 incident (1983) is another example that was not a purely one-time accident. As long as the Soviet system and ideology remained as they were, one could assume that Soviet frontier coastal guards would have done the same thing again under the same circumstances, as illustrated by the so-called "Murmansk incident" on April 20, 1978, the forced downing of another South Korean commercial airliner, KAL 902, by a Soviet fighter over another militarily sensitive area, the Murmansk (Kola) Peninsula. The Soviet siege mentality, and the obsessed feeling of being encircled by—and concomitant xenophobia against—the corrupted, wicked bourgeois imperialists, were so strong that the Soviets did not hesitate to resort to physically coercive means to protect their sacred, inviolable national borders. Moreover, the military-strategic value of the Sea of Okhotsk area increased in the late 1970s and early 1980s period, due not only to the Soviet deployment there of SLBMs but also to the deteriorated relations between the two nuclear superpowers.

Likewise, the Soviet military buildup on the disputed islands (1978–1979), Japan's acceptance of U.S. deployment of F-16s at Misawa (1982), and Nakasone's statements that Japan was "an unsinkable aircraft carrier" and that "[Japan's] security is indivisible [with other Western nations]" (1983) should be interpreted not only in the light of purely bilateral Japanese-Soviet relations but also of a much broader, multilateral, and even *global* framework of East-West confrontation. This was the case at least in the Soviet perception of the world power configuration, in which the United States occupied a far more important position than did Japan—so much so that Soviet leaders did not even consider it necessary for them to formulate a policy oriented specifically toward Japan, as discussed in preceding chapters.

Even the signing of the Sino-Japanese peace treaty (1978) should be interpreted not simply as a regional affair in Asia but rather as an international one. To put it bluntly, the conclusion of this treaty was a part of U.S. global strategy, promoted and encouraged by the Carter-Brzezinski team, as was discussed in detail in chapter 8. At that time Japanese Foreign Minister Sunao Sonoda made a slip of the tongue in saying that the treaty was considered to be "one facet of U.S. global strategy."[1] It is therefore understandable that Oleg N. Bykov, one of the deputy directors of IMEMO, viewed U.S.-Soviet relations as "the foundation upon which, for example, quadrilateral relations among the USSR, U.S.A., PRC, and Japan in Asia depended."[2]

The aforementioned line of logic leads us to suspect that the Soviets had a *Weltanschauung* that world affairs are basically determined by U.S.-Soviet global confrontation. I agree with the above-mentioned view, held primarily by the Soviets, that the most important reason why Soviet-Japanese relations deteriorated so greatly in the late 1970s and early 1980s lies in the further exasperation of the overall international environment, particularly confrontational relations between the two superpowers—that is to say, the situation that, some observers too prematurely concluded, was "the end of Détente" or "the arrival of a new Cold War Era."[3] This is not, however, to be taken to mean that I consider that all of the causes of deterioration in Japan-Soviet bilateral relations in this period are ascribable exclusively to the cooling of U.S–USSR relations on a global level. In other words, I believe that Japan-Soviet bilateral relations were strongly influenced, but not completely controlled, by U.S.-Soviet relations. What, then, are the other factors besides U.S.-Soviet relations that contributed to the worsening of Soviet-Japanese bilateral relations in this period? There are many factors, but the following three factors are particularly worth mention.

The first factor is the Soviet perception that Sino-Soviet relations would be improved in the foreseeable future, which in turn would in their strategic calculation help the Soviets improve their bargaining position vis-à-vis Japan. In March 1982, Brezhnev's Tashkent speech recognized China as socialist and called for talks with China with no preconditions. True, the speech also called for improved relations with Japan, but it was not Japan but China that responded positively to the Soviet overtures. Encouraged by the far more receptive responses from Beijing, the Soviets seem to have decided to work first with China, leaving Japan until later, which was clearly manifested by Brezhnev's speech at Baku in September 1982. Andropov, who succeeded Brezhnev in November 1992, also demonstrated that he would not only continue, but would also pursue with greater boldness and at a quicker pace than his predecessor, this strategy of normalizing relations with China, with the aim of breaking the so-called anti-Soviet Sino-Japanese-American entente formulated in the latter half of the 1970s, and hopefully even isolating Japan and the United States.

The reconciliation of differences with the PRC brought a number of benefits to the Soviet Union. In the field of diplomacy, it greatly improved the Soviet position in the world and particularly in Northeast Asia. A Sino-

Soviet rapprochement would end the possible or actual formation of the Washington-Tokyo-Beijing triangle targeted against Moscow, thereby providing Moscow with a way out of its awkward isolation in Asia. In addition, it would enable the Soviet Union to increase its bargaining power vis-à-vis Japan and the United States. In the military-strategic field, accommodation with Beijing would also provide Moscow with great relief and help. If the presence of "the one million Soviet troops" (Deng Xiaoping) along the Sino-Soviet border ceased to be necessary and the number were reduced, it would help the USSR lessen its military burden as well as financial costs. The Soviet Union could have threatened the West, including Japan, since the troops and SS-20s formerly stationed on the Sino-Soviet border could have been re-deployed elsewhere in Asia. It is possible that a Sino-Soviet détente would deprive Japan of economic profit and that the USSR could use this possibility as a threat.

The second factor is the Soviet mind-set or proclivity to rely on military means for solving international conflicts, as repeatedly mentioned in previous chapters. This Soviet conviction resulted in the following consequences. First, there was a further buildup of Soviet military forces in the Far Eastern part of the Soviet Union. Of particular importance was rapid modernization of the Soviet SSBNs (nuclear submarines equipped with nuclear-armed ballistic missiles) in the 1970s and 1980s, from the *Golf* and *Hotel* classes through the *Yankee* class to the *Delta* class.[4] Moreover, by the middle of the 1970s, Soviet SLBMs (submarine-launched ballistic missiles) had developed to the point where in the foreseeable future all United States targets would be within range of launch points in Soviet home waters.[5] However, U.S. advanced antisubmarine warfare technology was capable of detecting Soviet SSBNs. This engendered a "special zone (bastion) strategy,"[6] in which the Soviet SSBNs operated from relatively enclosed seas, protected from U.S. or U.S.-allied antisubmarine forces by a combination of minefields, radars, seabed sonars, attack submarines, surface warships, and aircraft.[7] The two bastions were the northwestern Barents Sea and the Sea of Okhotsk. In the late 1970s, the latter leapt from almost total strategic insignificance to being the second-most important sea area:[8] this "bastion strategy" made the Sea of Okhotsk a sanctuary for Soviet SSBNs. This strategic leap naturally applied also to the importance of the Northern Territories, that separate the Sea of Okhotsk from the Pacific Ocean. In short, such a situation in the late 1970s made the reversion of the islands to Japan almost out of the question, even at the expense of what otherwise might have been gained. Without appreciating this increased military-strategic significance of the region to the Soviet Union, one could never fully comprehend the reason why the Soviets brutally and ruthlessly shot down a Korean civilian plane that strayed into Soviet airspace over Kamchatka and Sakhalin in September 1993.

Second, there was a firm conviction among Soviet leaders that military force was the most important determinant in international affairs, tempting them to overestimate the role that military power played as an effective means for achieving Soviet political and diplomatic objectives. Based on this inaccurate assumption, the Brezhnev leadership redeployed Soviet troops on the disputed islands, and the Andropov leadership tried to threaten Japan by disclosing its possible scheme of transferring mobile SS-20s from Europe to Siberia, targeting Japan as well as China. Third, the corollary of the Soviet's excessive emphasis on physical muscle was a proclivity to underestimate other nonmilitary factors, such as Japan's economic, scientific-technological clout, and concomitant Japanese psychology.

The third important factor that contributed to the worsening of Soviet-Japanese relations in the period from the late 1970s to the early 1980s was on the Japanese side. Since their disgraceful defeat in World War II the Japanese had become doubtful of the effectiveness of military might as a tool for achieving national goals. Instead, the Japanese have become firm believers in the importance of economic-technological progress. Having achieved an economic miracle and overcome two oil crises in the 1970s, the Japanese became self-confident and even started to demonstrate a strong sense of nationalism. Gradually, the Japanese began to realize that their national security and economic prosperity are dependent on their alliance with the Western camp, particularly with the United States. In order to keep this alliance alive and workable, the Japanese began to consider the need to make their own contribution to the Western community. This process, which has been labeled by some as "Japan's awareness of its global role" or "globalization of Japan" was advancing at a very slow but steady pace.

Let me present an example reflecting this gradual change in Japanese psychology and behavior. In 1977, in fishing negotiations with the Soviet Union, the Takeo Fukuda cabinet showed a very low-profile negotiating behavior, which was labeled as "beggar or kowtow diplomacy." In 1978, however, the same Fukuda cabinet decided to ignore the strong opposition and pressure exerted by the USSR, going ahead with the Chinese to conclude a peace treaty. In 1980, the Masayoshi Ōhira cabinet showed no hesitation in joining the U.S.-sponsored sanctions against the Soviet Union for its military incursion into Afghanistan. In 1982–83, the Yasuhiro Nakasone cabinet made it clear that "security is indivisible" and that Japan was ready to become "an unsinkable aircraft carrier" for the defense of the Western community against the Soviet Union.

The change in Japanese psychology and behavior described above is illustrated best by a statement made by Prime Minister Zenkō Suzuki in 1980: "If the Soviet Union wants to improve its relations with Japan, it must fulfill Japan's two requests: a withdrawal of Soviet troops from Afghanistan and the reversion of the Northern Territories."[9] Suzuki went so far as to say: "As long as the Soviet Union remains unchanged in its policy with regard to Afghanistan and the Northern Territories, any improvement in Japanese-Soviet relations will be impossible."[10] Previously, "the Soviet return of the Northern Territories" had been the only condition, but now "the Soviet withdrawal from Afghanistan" and later "the removal of SS-20s from the Russian Far East" were added, and, as indicated by the order of listing in Suzuki's speech, the latter two demands were considered more important than the first.

In conclusion, in the period from the late 1970s to early 1980s, Japanese-Soviet relations reached their lowest ebb. The Soviet Union and Japan both became so concerned about their own national security problems that they tended to view the territorial dispute as an issue of secondary importance. In this regard, this period may be considered a unique period in the entire postwar history of Japanese-Soviet relations.

Notes

Introduction

1. *The Dictionary of Law*, edited by Hiroshi Suekawa, defines a peace treaty as "a treaty among belligerent nations to terminate war and restore peace. It is the most common form of putting an end to war. Strictly speaking, a state of war is terminated only by mutual ratification of a peace treaty." Hiroshi Suekawa, ed., *Hōritsugaku jiten* (The Dictionary of Law) (completely revised edition) (Tokyo: Nihon-hyōron-sha, 1976), p. 898. Shigejirō Tabata, a former professor of Kyoto University, writes, however, that with the Soviet-Japanese Joint Declaration, the state of war between Japan and the USSR was terminated. Shigejirō Tabata, *Kokusai-hō Kōgi* (Lectures on International Law), Vol. 2 (Tokyo: Yūshindō, 1972), p. 229.

2. Lassa Francis Lawrence Oppenheim, *International Law: A Treatise:* (Vol. 2) *Disputes, War and Neutrality* (London: Longman, Green, 1952), pp. 605–606.

3. The USSR Academy of Sciences, Institute of Law, ed., *Kokusaihō* (International Law), translated into Japanese by Kaoru Yasui et al., Vol. 2 (Tokyo: Nihon-hyōron-sha, 1963), p. 295.

4. In early 1979, the head of the Japanese Defense Agency told the Diet that the Soviet Union could be a "potential threat." Later, on April 19, 1979, Japanese Prime Minister Masayoshi Ōhira was quoted as having told a *Los Angeles Times* reporter that the Soviet Union could be a "threat" to Japan. See also Makoto Momoi, "The Balance of Power in East Asia and the Western Pacific in the 1980s: A Japanese Perspective," in Joint Working Group of the Atlantic Council of the United States and the Research Institute for Peace and Security, Tokyo, *The Common Security Interests of Japan, the United States and NATO* (Cambridge, MA: Ballinger, 1981), p. 46. The Soviets are, of course, well aware of this. See Iurii D. Dmitriev, "Antisovetizm—orudie reaktsii," in *Iaponiia 1981: Ezhegodnik* (Moscow: Nauka, 1982), p. 88.

5. *Washington Post*, January 19, 1983.

6. Ibid.

7. Viktor B. Spandar'ian, "Sovetsko-iaponskie torgovo-ekonomicheskie otnosheniia," *Problemy dal'nego vostoka*—hereafter cited as *PDV*—No. 3 [35], 1980, p. 95.

Part One. What Made Japan and the Soviet Union "Distant Neighbors"?

Chapter 1. Basic Determinants of Japanese-Soviet Relations

1. John J. Stephan, "Japan and the Soviet Union: The Distant Neighbors," *Asian Affairs*, 8, Part III (October 1977), pp. 278–284; Stephan, "Soviet Approaches to Japan: Image Behind the Policies," *Asian Perspective* (Seoul: Institute for Far Eastern Studies, Kyungnam University, Vol. 6, No. 2 (Fall/Winter, 1982), p. 134.

2. John J. Stephan, "Japan in the Soviet Mirror: The Search for Rapprochement," *Bulletin of Peace Proposals*, Vol. 13, No. 1 (1982), p. 61.

3. *Pravda*, p. 62.

4. *Izvestiia*, September 19, 1980. For a similar statement by Akagi, see, for example, *Asahi Shimbun* (evening edition), May 20, 1977.

5. *Pravda*, March 30, 1973.

6. N. Nikolaev, "Rasshirenie sovetsko-iaponskikh sviazei," *Mezhdunarodnaia zhizn'*—hereafter cited as *MZ*—No. 7 (July 1972), p. 43.

7. N. Nikolaev, and A. Pavlov, "SSSR-Iaponiia: Kurs na dobrososedstvo i ego protivniki," *MZ*, No. 7 (July 1982), p. 31; G. Krasin, "Sovetsko-iaponskie otnosheniia," *MZ*, No. 4 (April 1976), p. 36. In the article written two years later, Krasin noted: "Our countries [the Soviet Union and Japan] are neighbors. Thus, it is understandable, they are always a subject for mutual discussion." G. Krasin, "Uglubliaia doverie," *Novoe vremia*, No. 4 (January 20, 1978), p. 7; V. Dal'nev, "Chto meshaet razvitiiu sovetsko-iaponskikh otnoshenii," *MZ*, No. 1 (January 1981), p. 50; O.V. Vasil'ev, "Nekotorye problemy vneshnei politiki Iaponii v 1980 g.," *Iaponiia 1981: Ezhegodnik* (Moscow: Nauka, 1982), p. 63.

8. Former Canadian Prime Minister Pierre E. Trudeau was once quoted as having said (March 1969) that, for Canada, being America's neighbor "is in some ways like sleeping with an elephant. No matter how friendly and even-tempered is the beast, if I can call it that, one is affected by every twitch and grunt." Quoted in Louis Turner, *Invisible Empires* (New York: Harcourt, Brace, Jovanovich, 1971), p. 166; and W.H. Pope, *The Elephant and the Mouse* (Toronto: McClelland and Stewart, 1971), Preface, p. vii.

9. For writing this passage, I am obliged to Lloyd Jensen's *Explaining Foreign Policy* (Englewood Cliffs, NJ: Prentice Hall, 1982), pp. 208–209.

10. Evan Luard, *Conflict and Peace in the Modern International System* (Boston: Little, Brown, 1968), p. 111.

11. Lewis F. Richardson, *Statistics of Deadly Quarrels* (New York: Quadrangle/ New York Times, 1960), p. 176.

12. Bruce M. Russett, *International Regions and the International System: A Study in Political Economy* (Chicago: Rand McNally, 1967), p. 200.

13. Dmitrii V. Petrov, *Iaponiia nashikh dnei* (Moscow: Znanie, 1979), p. 48.

14. Ibid., pp. 54–55.

15. Dmitrii V. Petrov, *Iaponiia v mirovoi politike* (Moscow: Mezhdunarodnye otnosheniia, 1973), p. 240.

16. Spandar'ian, *op. cit.*, pp. 91–92.

17. *Pravda*, October 19, 1973, quoted in V.N. Berezin, *Kurs na dobrososedstvo i sotrudnichestvo v ego protivniki: Iz istorii normalizatsii otnoshenii SSSR s poslevoennoi*

Iaponiei (Moscow: Mezhdunarodnye otnosheniia, 1977), p. 123. V.N. Berezin is a pseudonym for the Soviet Foreign Ministry's high official in charge of Japanese affairs.

18. Spandar'ian, *op. cit.*, p. 91.

19. P.D. Dolgorukov, "Torgovo-ekonomicheskie otnosheniia SSSR s Iaponiei," *SSSR-Iaponiia: k 50–letiiu ustanovleniia sovetsko-iaponskikh diplomaticheskikh otnoshenii (1925–1975)* (Moscow: Nauka, 1978), p. 108.

20. Petrov, *Iaponiia v mirovoi politike*, p. 240.

21. *Izvestiia*, August 11, 1976.

22. Harold C. Hinton, *Three and a Half Powers: The New Balance in Asia* (Bloomington: Indiana University Press, 1975), p. 220.

23. Ibid.; Stephan, "Japan and the Soviet Union," p. 281; Stephan, "Japan in the Soviet Mirror," p. 62; Stephan, "Soviet Approaches to Japan," pp. 135–136; Allen S. Whiting, *Siberian Development and East Asia: Threat or Promise?* (Stanford, CA: Stanford University Press, 1981), pp. 66–67; Stuart D. Goldman, "Soviet-Japanese Relations and the Strategic Balance in Northeast Asia," unpublished paper at the Congressional Research Service, Library of Congress, p. 4; M.S. Kapitsa *et al.*, *Istoriia mezhdunarodnykh otnoshenii na dal'nem vostoke: 1945–1977* (Khabarovsk: Khabarovskoe knizhnoe izdatel'stvo, 1978), pp. 230–231.

24. Ole Holsti *et al.*, "Cognative Dynamics and Images of the Enemy," in David J. Finlay, *Enemies in Politics* (Chicago: Rand McNally, 1967), p. 86; Robert Jervis, *Perception and Misperception in International Politics* (Princeton, NJ: Princeton University Press, 1976), pp. 143–145, 187–195, 216–282.

25. Alexander Dallin, "The Legacy of the Past," in Dallin and Condoleezza Rice, eds., *The Gorbachev Era* (Stanford, CA: Stanford Alumni Association, 1986), p. 2.

26. Ibid., p. 5.

27. Mostafa Rejai, ed., *Decline of Ideology* (Chicago: Aldine-Atherton, 1971), p. 221; Christer Jönsson, "The Ideology of Foreign Policy," in Charles W. Kegley, Jr. and Pat McGowan, eds., *Foreign Policy: USA/USSR* (Beverly Hills, CA: Sage Publications, 1983), p. 93; Jensen, *Explaining Foreign Policy*, p. 77.

28. Jensen, *Explaining Foreign Policy*, p. 77; Alexander Dallin, "The Domestic Sources of Soviet Foreign Policy," in Seweryn Bialer, ed., *The Domestic Context of Soviet Foreign Policy* (Boulder, CO: Westview Press, 1981), p. 380; M. Rejai, "Political Ideology: Theoretical and Comparative Perspectives," in Rejai, ed. *op. cit.*, p. 25; Seweryn Bialer, *The Soviet Paradox: External Expansion, Internal Decline* (New York: Alfred A. Knopf, 1986), p. 264.

29. Michael P. Gehlen, *The Politics of Coexistence* (Bloomington: Indiana University Press, 1967), p. 22–23; William Zimmerman, *Soviet Perspectives on International Relations: 1956–1967* (Princeton, NJ: Princeton University Press, 1969), p. 289; Christer Jönsson, *Soviet Bargaining Behavior: The Nuclear Test Ban Case* (New York: Columbia University Press, 1979), p. 14; Jensen, *Explaining Foreign Policy*, pp. 72–73.

30. Morton Schwartz, *The Foreign Policy of the USSR: Domestic Factors* (Encino, CA: Dickenson Publishing Company, Inc., 1975), p. 124.

31. Bialer, *The Soviet Paradox*, p. 264.

32. N. Nikolaev, "K 50–letiiu ustanovleniia diplomaticheskikh otnoshenii SSSR s Iaponiei," *PDV*, 3 (1975), p. 55.

33. *The New York Times*, May 11, 1959, cited by Dan Caldwell, *American-Soviet Relations: From 1947 to the Nixon-Kissinger Grand Design* (Westport, CT: Greenwood Press, 1981), p. 3.

34. *Pravda*, November 7, 1984.

35. Iurii Bandura, "Soren wa nihon ni nanio nozomuka (What Does the Soviet Union Want from Japan?)," *Jiyū* (January 1982), p. 158.

36. Basil Dmytryshyn, "Current Trends in Soviet Foreign Policy," unpublished paper read at the Japan-U.S. Society in Sapporo, February 1979, p. 12.

37. D.V. Petrov, "SShA-Iaponiia: Novaia faza," *SShA*, No. 2 (February 1972), p. 25.

38. Lilita Dzirkals, *Soviet Perceptions of Security in East Asia: A Survey of Soviet Media Comments* (RAND Corporation Paper No. P-6038) (Santa Monica, CA: RAND Corporation, 1978), p. 40.

39. Ibid., p. 41.

40. Ibid., p. 40.

41. See, for example, Oleg N. Bykov, "Vneshnepoliticheskaia strategiia SShA v aziatsko-tikhookeanskom regione," in D.V. Petrov, ed., *Mezhdunarodnye otnosheniia v aziatsko-tikhoo-keanskom regione* (Moscow: Nauka, 1979), p. 53.

42. See, for example, Patrice De Beer, "Dégel entre Moscou et Tokyo," *Le Monde* (January 29, 1972), p. 1; Robert Guillan, "U.R.S.S. envisagerait de restituer quatre îles Kouriles Méridionales," *Le Monde* (April 9–10,1972), p. 3.

43. *XXV s"ezd kommunisticheskoi partii Sovetskogo Soiuza (24 fevralia–5 marta 1976 goda): Stenograficheskii otchet* (Moscow: Politizdat, 1976), Vol. 1, p. 45.

44. Dimitri V. Petrov, "Militarizatsiia Iaponiia—ugroza miru v Azii," *PDV*, No. 1 (1981), p. 51.

45. For a more detailed discussion, see Hiroshi Kimura, "The Soviet Military Buildup: Its Impact on Japan and Its Aims," in Richard H. Solomon and Masataka Kōsaka, eds., *The Soviet Far East Military Buildup: Nuclear Dilemmas and Asian Security* (Dover, MA: Auburn House, 1986), pp. 106–122.

46. Petrov, "Militarizatsiia Iaponiia," p. 51.

47. Vitalii Kobysh, "Est'vykhod iz tupika," *Literaturnaia gazeta*, No. 51 [4909], December 22, 1982.

48. Hiroshi Kimura, "Soviet Policy toward Japan," in Dan Caldwell, ed., *Soviet International Behavior and U.S. Policy Options* (Lexington, MA: Lexington Press, 1985), pp. 122–123.

49. Hiroshi Kimura, "Failure of Soviet Policies toward Japan," *Asia Pacific Community*, No. 16 (Spring 1982), pp. 1–16.

50. See I.V. Stalin, *Sochineniia*, Vol. 2 (1941–1945), edited by Robert H. McNeal (Stanford, CA: The Hoover Institution, 1967), pp. 213–215; also *Vneshniaia politika Sovetskogo Soiuza v period otechestvennoi voiny: Dokumenty i materialy*, Vol. 3 (Moscow: Gospolitizdat, 1947), p. 56.

51. For statements by Khrushchev, see *Pravda* and *Izvestiia*, September 20, 1964; *Hokkaido Shimbun* (evening edition) and *Asahi Shimbun* (evening edition), July 15, 1964. For similar remarks by First Deputy Premier Anastas Mikoyan during his visit to Japan in May 1984, see *Hokkaido Shimbun* (May 27, 1964) and Young C. Kim, *Japanese-Soviet Relations: Interaction of Politics, Economics and National Security* (Beverly Hills, CA: SagePublications, 1974), p. 46. A Soviet specialist on Soviet-Japanese relations who also emphasizes the strategic importance of the region is L.N. Kutakov; see his *Vneshniaia politika i diplomatiia Iaponii* (Moscow: Mezhdunarodnye otnosheniia, 1964), p. 298.

52. For the "bastion strategy" of the Soviet navy, see, for example, Michael McGwire, "The Rationale for the Development of Soviet Seapower," *United States Naval Institute Proceedings* (May 1980), p. 181; Derek da Cunha, *Soviet Naval Power in the Pacific* (Boulder, CO: Lynne Rienner, 1990), pp. 18, 90; and Geoffrey Jukes, *Russia's Military and the Northern Territories Issue* (Working Paper No. 277) (Canberra: Australian National University, Strategic and Defense Studies Centre, 1993), p. 7.

Chapter 2. Approaches to National Security

1. Before the end of World War II, Japan comprised a total area of 675,000 square kilometers of land area. The surrender of Japan to Allied forces deprived Japan of 256,000 km of land area and left 50,000 km to further decisions by the Allied nations, reducing Japanese territory to only 370,000 km. Yūchi Takano, *Nippon no Ryōdo* (The Territory of Japan) (Tokyo: University of Tokyo Press, 1962), p. 1.

2. Professor Okimoto at Stanford University notes, "Of all the discontinuities brought about by the end of World War II, none is more dramatic than Japan's nearly complete military about-face." See Daniel I. Okimoto, "The Economics of National Defense," in Okimoto, *Japan's Economy: Coping with Change in the International Environment* (Boulder, CO: Westview Press, 1982), p. 231. See also *Economist* (London), Vol. 268, No. 7039 (July 29, 1978), p. 15.

3. Masataka Kōsaka, *Saishō Yoshida Shigeru* (Tokyo: Chūō Kōron-sha, 1967), p. 69.

4. Ibid., p. 69; Masataka Kōsaka, "Japan as a Maritime Nation," *Journal of Social Political Ideas of Japan*, Vol. 3 (August 1965), p. 52.

5. *Yomiuri Shimbun*, October 24, 1978.

6. *Nihon Keizai Shimbun* (evening edition), May 9, 1983.

7. Robert E. Osgood, *The Weary and the Wary: U.S. and Japanese Security Policies in Transition* (Baltimore, MD: Johns Hopkins University Press, 1972), p. 23. See also Kei Wakaizumi, "Japan's Role in a New World Order," *Foreign Affairs* (January 1973), p. 316.

8. Stephen P. Gibert, *Soviet Images of America* (New York: Crane, Russak, 1977), p. 87.

9. For a discussion of the relationship between Marxism-Leninism and violence, see Alexander Dallin and George W. Breslauer, *Political Terror in Communist Systems* (Stanford, CA: Stanford University Press, 1970).

10. John Lenczowski, *Soviet Perceptions of U.S. Foreign Policy: A Study of Ideology, Power, and Consensus* (Ithaca, NY: Cornell University Press, 1982), p. 16; A. Sergiev, "Leninizm o sootnoshenii sil kak faktore mezhdunarodnykh otnoshenii," *MZ*, No. 4 (1975), p. 104.

11. Gibert, *Soviet Images of America*, p. 23.

12. Georgii Kh. Shakhnazarov, "K probleme sootnosheniia sil v mire," *Kommunist*, No. 3 [1067], (February 1974), p. 86; Dimitri K. Simes, *Detente and Conflict: Soviet Foreign Policy, 1972–1977* (Beverly Hills, CA: Sage Publications, 1977), p. 39.

13. Andrei A. Grechko, *Na strazhe mira i stroitel'stva kommunizma* (Moscow: Voenizdat, 1971), pp. 16–17.

14. *Pravda, Izvestiia,* and *Krasnaia zvezda,* November 13, 1982.

15. Vladimir Gantman, "Politika, preobrazuiushchaia mir: o roli vneshnei politiki

SSSR v sovremennykh mezhdunarodnykh otnosheniiakh," *Kommunist*, No. 7 [1953], (May 1973), p. 35.

16. *Komsomol'skaia pravda*, June 14, 1972.

17. *Pravda*, July 22, 1973.

18. Harold Nicolson, *Diplomacy* (third edition) (Oxford: Oxford University Press, 1963), p. 144.

19. Ibid.

20. Ibid., p. 147.

21. Richard Rosecrance, *The Rise of the Trading State: Commerce and Conquest in the Modern World* (New York: Basic Books, 1986), pp. 16–18.

22. Robert Jervis, *Perception and Misperception in International Politics* (Princeton, NJ: Princeton University Press, 1976, p. 228.

23. Ibid., pp. 218, 230, 232, 234, 240, 263, 275–279.

24. Arnold Wolfers, *Discard and Collaboration: Essays on International Politics* (Baltimore, MD: Johns Hopkins University Press, 1962), p. 150.

25. Carl von Clausewitz, *On War* (London: Penguin, 1968), p. 119. See also, pp. 31–34, 37–39, 48, 416–417, 434; Nathan Leites, *A Study of Bolshevism* (Glencoe, IL: The Free Press, 1953), pp. 184, 254, 370, 434, 497; Raymond L. Garthoff, *Soviet Military Doctrine* (Glencoe, IL: The Free Press, 1953), pp. 9–19, 51–57; R.L. Garthoff, "Mutual Deterrence, Party and Strategic Arms Limitation in Soviet Policy," in Derek Leebaert, ed., *Soviet Military Thinking* (London: George, Allen & Unwin, 1981), pp. 93, 96–97.

26. Arthur Upham Pope, *Maxim Litvinoff* (New York: L.B. Fischer, 1943), p. 190.

27. Edwin O. Reischauer, *The Japanese* (Cambridge, MA: The Belknap Press, 1977), p. 136; Robert C. Christopher, *The Japanese Mind: The Goliath Explained* (New York: Linden Press, 1983), p. 44.

28. Reischauer, *op. cit.*, pp. 135–137, 142.

29. Isaiah Bendasan, *Nihonjin to Yudayajin* (The Japanese and the Jews) (Tokyo: Kadokawa-Shoten, 1971), p. 19.

30. V. Pavlovskii, "Kollektivnaia bezopasnost'—put' k miru v Azii," *MZ*, No. 6 (1972), p. 34.

31. I.I. Kovalenko, *Sovetskii Soiuz v bor'be za mir i kollektivnuiu bezopasnost' v Azii* (Moscow: Nauka, 1976), p. 4.

32. Ibid.

33. D.V. Petrov, ed., *Mezhdunarodnye otnosheniia v aziatsko-tikhookeanskom regione* (Moscow: Nauka, 1979). p. 13.

34. Kovalenko, *op. cit.*, p. 4.

35. B. Zanegin, "Aziatskaia bezopasnost': Dva podkhoda," *Aziia i afrika segodnia* (March 3, 1978), p. 2.

36. For the "somewhat premature self-appointment" by the USSR as a global power, see Vernon Aspaturian, "Soviet Global Power and the Correlation of Forces," *Problems of Communism*, Vol. 29, No. 3 (May–June 1980), pp. 1–18.

37. A.A. Gromyko, *Vo imia torzhestva leninskoi vneshnei politiki: Izbrannye rechi i stat'i* (Moscow: Politizdat, 1978), p. 145.

38. Quoted from *Dvina: Voiskovye manevry provedennye na territorii belorussi v marte 1970 goda* (Moscow: USSR Ministry of Defense, 1970), p. 8.

39. Momoi, "The Balance of Power in East Asia and the Western Pacific in the 1980s," p. 46. See also *Defense of Japan: 1982* (Tokyo: Defense Agency 1982), p. 68.

40. *Defense of Japan: 1982*, p. 68.

41. Ibid., p. 69.

42. Ibid., p. 68.

43. *New York Times*, November 22, 1969, quoted from John K. Emmerson, *Arms, Yen & Power: The Japanese Dilemma* (New York: Dunellen, 1971), p. 89. For a discussion and debate on what the "Far East" means, see Emmerson, pp. 82–84.

44. *Defense of Japan: 1982*, p. 69.

45. *New York Times*, July 8, 1978.

46. Vladimir Petrov, "Dynamics of Confrontation," in *The 1980's: Decade of Confrontation?* (Proceedings of the Eighth Annual National Security Affairs Conference, July 13–15, 1981) (Washington, DC: National Defense University Press, 1981), p. 23.

47. Hisao Maeda, "The Free-Rider Myth," *Japan Quarterly*, Vol. 29, No. 2 (April–June 1982), p. 179.

48. Ibid.

49. Ibid.

50. Ibid.

51. On this point, I am particularly indebted to the illuminating analysis in an article by Joseph Bouchard, "Japanese Views on Northeast Asian Security" (unpublished paper read at the conference of Asian Studies on the Pacific Coast, held on June 25–27, 1982), especially pp. 28, 47.

52. V.I. Lenin, *Polnoe sobranie sochinenii*, 5th edition (Moscow: Politizdat, 1964), Vol. 7, p. 14.

53. A.V. Sergiev, "Marksizm-Leninizm o sootnoshenii vnutrennei i vneshnei politiki," in *Vzaimosviaz' i vzaimovliianie vnutrennei i vneshnei politiki* (Moscow: Nauka, 1982), p. 11.

54. Simes, *op. cit.*, pp. 6–8.

55. *Izvestiia*, July 3, 1979.

56. Ibid.

57. *Izvestiia*, October 6, 1979.

58. *FBIS-SOV*, October 12, 1979, p. C3.

59. N.N. Nikolaev, "K 50–letiiu ustanovleniia diplomaticheskikh otnoshenii SSSR s Iaponiei," *PDV*, No. 3 (1975), p. 58.

60. Pavel D. Dolgorukov, "Torgovo-ekonomicheskie otnosheniia SSSR s Iaponiei," in *SSSR-Iaponiia*, p. 120.

61. Pavel D. Dolgorukov. "Torgovo-ekonomicheskie otnosheniia SSSR s Iaponiei," a paper read at the Japan-Soviet Symposium jointly held by the Soviet Academy of Sciences and *Sankei Shimbun* in Osaka, in November 1979.

62. *FBIS-SOV*, October 27, 1980, p. C4.

63. Arnold Wolfers, *Discord and Collaboration: Essays on International Politics* (Baltimore, MD: Johns Hopkins University Press, 1962), p. 156.

64. John K. Emmerson and Leonard A. Humphreys, *Will Japan Rearm? A Study in Attitudes* (Stanford, CA: Hoover Institution on War, Revolution and Peace, 1973), p. 7.

65. Rosencrance, *op. cit.*, pp. 16–18.

66. Kunio Muraoka, *Japanese Security and the United States* (Adelphi Paper No. 95) (London: International Institute for Strategic Studies, 1973), p. 32.

67. Shin Kanemaru, *Waga-taikenteki Bōeiron* (Theory on Defense Based on My Experience) (Tokyo: Ēru Shuppansha, 1979), p. 21.

68. [Japan] Comprehensive National Security Group, *Report on Comprehensive National Security (English Translation)* (Tokyo: Prime Minister's Cabinet Office, 1980).

69. Ibid., p. 22.

70. Ibid.

71. Ibid., p. 23.

72. Wolfers, *op. cit.*, p. 147.

73. *Report on Comprehensive National Security*, pp. 19, 21. A similar view was expressed by Morgenthau in his classic *Politics Among Nations*. Morgenthau suggested that nations have three choices in order to maintain their relative power positions: (i) they can withhold the power of other nations from the adversary; (ii) they can add their power to the power of other nations; or (iii) they can increase their own power. Hans J. Morgenthau, *Politics Among Nations: The Struggle for Power and Peace* (third edition) (New York: Alfred A. Knopf, 1961), p. 181.

74. Shigeru Yoshida, *Kaisō-Jūnen* (Tokyo: Shinchō-sha, 1957), Vol. 1, p. 33; *The Yoshida Memoirs: The Story of Japan in Crisis*, translated by Kennichi Yoshida (Boston: Houghton Mifflin, 1962), p. 8.

75. Masashi Nishihara, "Japanese Defense and New Implications of the U.S.-Japan Security Treaty" (unpublished paper prepared for a conference, Tokyo, December 8–9, 1980, under the Joint Japan-U.S. Security Study Project of the Japan Center for International Exchange and the Council on Foreign Relations), pp. 3, 37.

76. Mike M. Mochizuki, "Japan's Search for Strategy: The Security Policy Debate in the 1980s" (Occasional Paper No. 82–01, The Program on U.S.-Japan Relations, Center for International Affairs, Harvard University, 1982), pp. 14, 43.

77. *Report on Comprehensive National Security*, p. 42.

78. The concept "denial force" is believed to have been borrowed from Grenn H. Snyder's article entitled "Deterrence by Denial and Punishment," in Davis B. Bobrow, ed., *Components of Defense Policy* (Chicago: Rand McNally, 1965), pp. 209–237, particularly pp. 209–210.

79. *Report on Comprehensive National Security*, pp. 41–42.

80. Cf. Emmerson and Humphreys, *op. cit.*, p. 135.

81. Yasuhiro Nakasone, *My Life in Politics* (private edition), 1982, p. 25.

82. Ibid., p. 26.

83. Ibid., p. 54.

84. Ibid.

85. *Yomiuri Shimbun*, January 29, 1983.

86. Nakasone, *My Life in Politics*, p. 23.

87. Ibid., p. 80.

88. Andrzej Korbonski, "The Warsaw Treaty After Twenty-five Years: An Entangling Alliance or an Empty Shell?" in Robert W. Clawson and Lawrence S. Kaplan, eds., *The Warsaw Pact: Political Purpose & Military Means* (Wilmington, DE: Scholarly Resources, 1982), p. 21.

89. Ibid., p. 11; Dale R. Herspring and Ivan Volgyes, "Political Reliability in the Eastern European Warsaw Pact Armies," *Armed Forces and Society*, Vol. 6, No. 2 (Winter 1980), pp. 270–296.

90. Korbonski, *op. cit.*, p. 11.

91. Stephen D. Kertesz, "American and Soviet Negotiating Behavior," in Kertesz and M.A. Fitzimons, eds., *Diplomacy in a Changing World* (Notre Dame, IN: University of Notre Dame Press, 1959), p. 139.

92. George F. Kennan, *Memoirs: 1925–1950* (Boston: Atlantic, Little, Brown, 1967), p. 560.

93. According to one historian, Russia endured 160 foreign invasions during the

period of Western Europe's Renaissance (1228–1462), and ten great wars with Sweden and Poland during the seventeenth and eighteenth centuries, the period of Enlightenment. The nineteenth century witnessed the Napoleonic Wars (and the burning of Moscow), the Crimean War, and the Russo-Turkish Wars; and in the twentieth century came the Russo-Japanese War and World Wars I and II. Schwartz, *The Foreign Policy of the USSR: Domestic Factors* (Encino, CA: Dickenson, 1975), p. 75. See also Bertram D. Wolfe, *Three Who Made a Revolution: A Biographical History* (Harmondsworth, Middlesex, England: Penguin, 1966), p. 19.

94. Louis J. Samelson, *Soviet and Chinese Negotiating Behavior: The Western View* (Beverly Hills, CA: Sage, 1976), p. 24.

95. Kennan, *op. cit.*, p. 560.

96. Ibid.

97. Louis J. Halle, *The Cold War As History* (New York: Harper & Row, 1967), p. 13.

98. *Defense of Japan: 1982* (Tokyo: *Japan Times*, 1982), p. 68.

99. *Shūkan Asahi* (*Asahi Weekly*) (December 19, 1980), p. 174.

100. *The Military Balance, 1982–1983* (London: International Institute for Strategic Studies, 1982), p. 12.

101. Wolfers, *op. cit.*, p. 158. Dr. Gray similarly writes: "A quest for *absolute* security must lead a country on the path of world conquest" (emphasis in original; see Colin S. Gray, *The Geopolitics of the Nuclear Era: Heartland, Rimlands, and the Technological Revolution* [New York: Crane, Russak, 1977], p. 35).

102. Hedley Bull, *The Control of the Arms Race* (London: Weidenfeld and Nicolson for the Institute of Strategic Studies, 1961), p. 26. Quoted by Makoto Momoi, "Japan's Defense Policies: Some Background Concepts in the 1970s," in J.A. Stockwin, ed., *Japan and Australia in the Seventies* (Sydney: Angus and Robertson, 1972), pp. 103–104.

103. Simes, *op. cit.*, p. 6.

104. Wolfers, *op. cit.*, p. 158.

105. Ibid. Professor Bull also concludes that "there can be 'relative security.'" Bull, *op. cit.*, p. 26; Momoi, "Japan's Defense Policies," p. 104.

106. For example, the debate between George F. Kennan, on the one hand, and Richard Pipes and Leopold Labedz, on the other, in *Encounter* magazine in 1978: George F. Kennan, "Soviet-American Relations," Vol. 50, No. 3 (March 1978), pp. 7–13; Richard Pipes, "Mr. X Revises," Vol. 50, No. 4 (April 1978), pp. 18–21; Leopold Labedz, "The Two Minds of George Kennan," Vol. 50, No. 4 (April 1978), pp. 78–86; Kennan, "A Last Warning," Vol. 50, No. 7 (July 1978), pp. 15–18.

107. Kennan, "A Last Warning," p. 16.

108. *Filosofskoe nasledie V.I. Lenina i problemy sovremennoi voiny* (Moscow: Ministerstva oborony SSSR, 1972), p.136; (English translation) *The Philosophical Heritage of V.I. Lenin and Problems of Contemporary War* (*A Soviet View*) (Washington, DC: Government Printing Office, 1972), p. 100.

109. *The Philosophical Heritage of Lenin*, pp. 103, 115.

110. Dmitri F. Ustinov, *Izbrannye rechi i stat'i* (Moscow: Politizdat, 1979), pp. 343, 439, 501, 503–4.

111. *Defense of Japan: 1982*, p. 69.

112. Makoto Momoi, "From Disarmament to Arms Control," *Trialogue* (Summer/Fall 1982), p. 15.

113. Makoto Momoi, "Basic Trends in Japanese Security Policies," in Robert A.

Scalapino, ed., *The Foreign Policy of Modern Japan* (Berkeley: University of California Press), p. 362.

114. Momoi, "Japan's Defense Policies," p. 109.

115. Ibid.

116. Petrov, *Iaponiia v mirovoi politike*, p. 42.

117. Ibid., p. 41.

118. Dmitri V. Petrov, "Militarizatsiia Iaponii—ugroza miru v Azii," *PDV*, No. 1 (1981), p. 51.

119. N.N. Nikolaev, A.H. Aleksandrov, "Iapono-amerikanskie otnosheniia: Starye problemy, novye tendentsii," *PDV*, 4 [44] (1982), p. 81.

120. Kuniko Miyauchi, "No Slowdown in Soviet Security Buildup: Why the USSR Switched From a Introvert, Economic National Policy to an Extrovert Military One," *Japan Times*, May 13, 1979.

121. William F. Scott, "The USSR's Growing Global Mobility," *Air Force Magazine*, Vol. 60, No. 3 (March 1977), pp. 57–58; Carl G. Jacobsen, *Soviet Strategic Initiatives* (New York: Praeger, 1979), pp. 15–21.

122. V.M. Kulish, ed., *Voennaia sila i mezhdunarodnye otnosheniia: Voennye aspekty vneshnepoliticheskikh kontseptsii SShA* (Moscow: Mezhdunarodnye otnosheniia, 1972), pp. 135–136.

123. A. Epishev, "Istoricheskaia missiia armii sotsialisticheskogo gosudarstva," *Kommunist*, No. 7 [1035] (May 1972), pp. 63–64.

124. Ibid., p. 66.

125. A.A. Grechko, "Rukovodiashchaia rol' KPSS v stroitel'stve armii razvitogo sotsialisticheskogo obshchestva," *Voprosy istorii KPSS*, No. 5 (1974), p. 39.

126. Marian P. Kirsch, "Soviet Security Objectives in Asia," *International Organization*, Vol. 25, No. 3 (Summer 1970), p. 461. Subsequently, one Western specialist on Japanese security affairs suggested that Japanese defense and diplomatic policy should be changed into a more "positive" and "outward-looking" one. Stewart Menaul, *Japan's Defense Policy: Economic Power and Constitutional Restraints* (London: Institute for the Study of Conflict, 1979), pp. 14–15.

127. *Defense of Japan: 1978* (Tokyo: Defense Agency, 1978), p. 56.

128. "Newsweek Interview: Ganri Yamashita: 'Japan Rejects Militarism'," *Newsweek* (September 3, 1979), p. 48.

129. *Defense of Japan: 1979* (Tokyo: Defense Agency, 1979), p. 64.

130. Nishihara, "Japanese Defense and New Implications of U.S.-Japan Security Treaty," p. 25.

131. *Defense of Japan: 1978*, p. 72.

132. Osamu Kaihara, *Watashi no kokubō hakusho* (My Personal White Paper on Defense) (Tokyo: Jiji tushjn-sha, 1975), pp. 110–111.

133. Petrov, *Iaponiia v mirovoi politike*, p. 33.

134. Ibid.

135. Aleksandr I. Solzhenitsyn, *Pis'mo vozhdiam Sovetskogo Soiuza* (Paris: YMCA Press, 1974), p. 31; English translation by Hilary Sternberg, *Letter to the Soviet Leaders* (New York: Harper & Row, 1974), pp. 35–36.

136. Ibid.

137. Georgii S. Gorshkov, *Morskaia moshch' gosudarstva* (second edition) (Moscow: Voennoe izdatel'stvo Ministerstva oborony SSSR, 1979), p. 221; Gorshkov, "Voenno-morskie floty v voinakh i v mirnoe vremia," *Morskoi sbornik*, No. 2 (1973),

p. 21; G.S. Gorshkov, *The Sea Power of the State* (Annapolis, MD: Naval Institute Press, 1979), p. 152.

138. Kulish, *op. cit.*, p. 38.

139. Charles F. Hermann, ed., *International Crises: Insights from Behavioral Research* (New York: The Free Press, 1972), p. 220.

140. Gorshkov, *Morskaia moshch' gosudarstva*, p. 365; Gorshkov, "Voenno-morskie floty v voinakh i v mirnoe vremia," No. 2 (1973), p. 21; Gorshkov, *The Sea Power of the State*, p. 247.

Chapter 3. Japanese and Soviet Views on Territory

1. Such arguments have appeared in, for example, *Wall Street Journal* (June 6, 1978); *Reuter News* (May 12, 1979); and John J. Stephan, "The Kuril Islands," *Pacific Community* (Tokyo), p. 311. Ken Ishii of the *International Herald Tribune* has gone so far as to regard "the Soviet refusal to return four small islands to Japan" as "the *only real* stumbling block in Tokyo-Moscow relations" (emphasis added by H.K.) *International Herald Tribune*, January 5, 1979.

2. For example, *Japan's Northern Territories* (Tokyo: Ministry of Foreign Affairs, 1982), p. 3; *Warera-no Hoppōryōdo* (Our Northern Territories) (Tokyo: Ministry of Foreign Affairs, 1983), pp. 2–3.

3. *Japan's Northern Territories*, p. 3; *Warera-no Hoppōryōdo*, pp. 2–3.

4. Such statements have appeared in, for example, *Hokkaido Shimbun* (evening edition), *Yomiuri Shimbun* (evening edition), February 7, 1983; and in *Yomiuri Shimbun* (evening edition), April 23, 1983.

5. *Izvestiia*, July 3, 1979; *Pravda*, February 17, 1981; Georgi A. Arbatov and William Oltmans, *The Soviet Viewpoint* (New York: Dodd, 1981), p. 170.

6. John J. Stephan, "Asia in the Soviet Conception," in Donald S. Zagoria, ed., *Soviet Policy in East Asia* (New Haven, CT: Yale University Press, 1982), p. 42.

7. *Pravda*, October 15, 1978; *Izvestiia*, July 3, 1979; D.V. Petrov, "Vneshniaia politika Iaponii na rubezhe 70–80–kh godov," *Iaponia 1980: Ezhegodnik* (Moscow: Nauka, 1981), p. 72; L. Tolkunov, "Iaponiia segodniia," *Novoe vremiia*, No. 31 (August 1, 1980), p. 23.

8. *Pravda*, February 25, 1976; L.I. Brezhnev, *Leninskim kursom* (Moscow: Gospolitizdat, 1976), Vol. 3, p. 471.

9. S. Modenov, "Pod militaristitseskimi shtandartami," *MZ*, No. 1 (1980), p. 88; Igor' Latyshev, "Tokio-Pekin: Opasnoe sblizhenie," *Pravda*, October 15, 1978.

10. Andrei P. Markov, *Poslevoennaia politika Iaponii v Azii i Kitai: 1945–1977* (Moscow: Nauka, 1979), p. 227.

11. N. Nikolaev, "Zigzagi politiki Tokio," *MZ*, No. 10 (1981), p. 43.

12. *Pravda*, October 10, 1973. See also footnote (4).

13. *Mainichi Shimbun*, April 16, 1979; for an English translation, see *FBIS-SOV*, April 20, 1979, p. 2.

14. Arbatov and Oltmans, *op. cit.*, p. 170.

15. To cite only one example, prior to Soviet Foreign Minister A.A. Gromyko's visit to Tokyo in January 1976, the Japanese government decided that as in the past, it would counter the Soviet argument of maintaining *status quo* with the concept of inherent territory (*Asahi Shimbun*, January 6, 1976).

16. George Alexander Lensen, *The Strange Neutrality: Soviet-Japanese Relations*

During the Second World War: 1941–1945 (Tallahassee, FL: The Diplomatic Press, 1972), pp. 171–173.

17. Tatsunori Kamichi, *Hoppōryōdo* (Northern Territories) (Tokyo: Kyōiku-sha, 1978), pp. 35–36.

18. Planning Section, Department of General Affairs, Nemuro Municipal Government, ed., *Nippon-no ryōdo—Hoppōryōdo* (Northern Territories—Japan's Land) (Nemuro: Nemuro Shimbun-sha, 1970), p. 97.

19. "U.S. Position on Soviet-Japanese Peace Treaty Negotiations," *U.S. Department of State Bulletin*, Vol. 35, No. 900 (September 24, 1956), p. 484.

20. Shien Yoshida, *Hoppōryōdo* (Northern Territories) (Revised edition) (Tokyo: Jiji Tsūsin-sha, 1973), p. 132.

21. Hiroshi Noguchi, "'Hoppōryōdo' no Gensō to Genjitsu (Illusion and Reality of the Northern Territories)," *Shokun!* (March 1976), p. 138.

22. Quoted from the *Christian Science Monitor*, June 10, 1968.

23. Takehisa Shimizu, *Hoppōryōdo-mondai Kaiketsu no Yon-hōshiki* (Four Formulas for Resolving the Northern Territories Issue) (Tokyo: Kasumigaseki Shuppankai, 1977), p. vii.

24. Taizō Yamagata, *Chishima wa uttaeru: ninjū no nijūkyūnen* (The Kurils Sue: 29 Years of Submission) (Tokyo: Nippon Kyōbun-sha, 1973), p. 184.

25. Hichihei Yamamoto, "Ryōdo no Kenkyū" (Study on Territory), *Bungei Shunjū* (June 1977), p. 183.

26. Yamagata, *op. cit.*, pp. 184–189.

27. For the Soviet concept of "inherent" territory, see Chūshi Ochiai, *Hoppōryōdo: sono rekishiteki-jijitsu to seijiteki-haikei* (The Northern Territories: Their Historical Facts and Political Background) (Tokyo: Taka-shobō, 1971), pp. 153–59; "Soren no ryōdo seisaku" (Territorial Policy of the Soviet Union), *Chōsa Geppō*, No. 244 (June 1974), pp. 29–31. See also notes 37 and 39, below.

28. Boris P. Polivoi, *Pervootkryvateli kuril'skikh ostrovov* (Iuzhno-Sakhalinsk, Sakhalin: Dal'nevostochnoe knizhnoe izdatel'stvo, 1982), p. 178. A Soviet newspaper, *Sovetskaia Rossiia*, carried an article in September 1982 in which it was reported that "(Soviet) archaeologists discovered fascinating evidence of how the Russians developed the Kurile Islands," *FBIS-SOV*, September 24, 1982, p. c1.

29. John J. Stephan, *The Kuril Islands: Russo-Japanese Frontier in the Pacific* (Oxford: Clarendon Press, 1974), p. 203.

30. P.A. Leonov, "Zhemchuzhina Sovetskogo dal'nego vostoka," *PDV*, No. 4 [24] (1977), pp. 17–18.

31. Stephan, *The Kuril Islands*, pp. 203–204.

32. A. Solov'ev, *Kuril'skie ostrova* (Moscow: Glavnoe ypravlenie severnogo morskogo puti, 1945), p. 6, and its 1947 revised edition, pp. 4–7.

33. Ibid.

34. Stephan, *The Kuril Islands*, p. 204.

35. Toshiyuki Akizuki, "Nichiro-kankei to ryōdo-ishiki" (Japanese-Russian Relations and Views on Territories), *Kyōsan-shugi to Kokusai-seiji* (Communism and International Politics) (Tokyo: Japanese Institute for International Affairs), Vol. 4, No. 2 [13] (July–September 1979), pp. 2–18.

36. Ibid.; Akira Takano, "Soren ni okeru Hoppōryōdo kenkyū ni yosete" (Studies in the Soviet Union on the Northern Territories), *Shikan* (Tokyo: Waseda University), Vol. 95 (March 1977) pp. 14–28.

37. *Izvestiia*, August 29, 1980 and February 29, 1982.

38. Kennan, *Memoirs: 1925–1950*, p. 560.

39. Iurii Bandura, Tokyo correspondent of *Izvestiia*, went so far as to deny the validity of the Shimoda Treaty despite Japan's "inherent right" over the "Northern Islands," asserting that Evfimii V. Putiatin, the Russian negotiator, was at that time *de facto* a Japanese hostage "and signed the treaty in violation of the instructions given to him from the tzarist government" at St. Petersburg (*Izvestiia*, June 16, 1981). This assertion by Bandura, which was made in protest of the Japanese government's decision to designate February 7—the day when the Shimoda treaty was signed in 1855—as the so-called "Northern Territories Day," contradicts the Soviet authoritative view, for instance, of Esfir' Ia. Fainsberg. For more detail, see Fainsberg, *Russko-iaponskie otnosheniia v 1697–1875 gg.* (Moscow: Izdatel'stvo vostochnoi literatury, 1960), p. 175; Hiroshi Kimura, "Kuremurin no tainichi senryaku" (The Kremlin's Strategy Toward Japan), in Hitoshi Hanai, ed., *Kuremurin no Ronri* (The Logic of the Kremlin) (Tokyo: Nihon Kōgyō Shimbun-sha, 1982), pp. 15–17.

40. For instance, Yohei Kōno, "Soren-shushō tono Hoppōryōdo ronsō" (The Disputes with Soviet Premier on the Northern Islands), *Hōseki* (March 1979), p. 170; Mitsuru Suizu, *Hoppōryōdo Dakkan no Michi* (The Way to Get Back the Northern Islands) (Tokyo: Niphon-Kōgyō Shimbun-sha, 1979), p. 238.

41. For different views in Japan on the ways to resolve this territorial issue, the process, and range of the territories which Japan should claim from the Soviet Union, see, for example, Stephan, *The Kuril Islands*, pp. 212–14; Tokumatsu Sakamoto and Shizuma Kai, eds., *Kaese Hoppōryōdo* (Return the Northern Islands) (Tokyo: Seishun Shuppan-sha, 1979), pp. 154–57.

42. Suizu, *op. cit.*, p. 238.

43. S.I. Verbitskii, "Formirovanie poslevoennogo vneshnepoliticheskogo kursa Iaponii v otnoshenii SSSR," *SSSR-Iaponiia*, p. 100.

44. Kapitsa *et al.*, eds., *op. cit.*, p. 231. Dmitrii Petrov told me that he wrote the section on Soviet-Japanese relations, including this part.

45. *Pravda*, February 25, 1976; Brezhnev, *Leninskim kursom*, Vol. 3, p. 471.

46. *Hokkaido Shimbun*, September 5, 1969.

47. *Pravda*, June 7, 1977.

48. Ibid., June 12, 1977.

49. Wayne S. Vucinich, "Bessarabia," in *Collier's Encyclopedia* (London: P.F. Collier, 1983), p. 103; Takehisa Shimizu, *Soren no Tainichi Sensō to Yaruta Kyōtei* (*The Soviet Declaration on War to Japan and the Yalta Agreement*) (Tokyo: Kasumigaseki Shuppan, 1976), p. 212 ff.

50. Quoted in Derwent Whittlesey, *German Strategy of World Conquest* (New York: Farrar & Renihard, 1942), p. 95.

51. Khaim T. Eidus, *SSSR i Iaponiia: Vneshnepoliticheskie otnosheniia posle vtoroi mirovoi voiny* (Moscow: Nauka, 1964), p. 9. Similarly, according to Professor Stephan, a tenth-grade history textbook in the Soviet Union stated the case unequivocally: "[the Red Army] ... returned to the Soviet motherland primordially Russian lands—southern Sakhalin and the Kurile Islands—which had been seized in the past by Japan," Stephan, "Soviet Approaches to Japan," p. 138.

52. S. Modenov, "Tokio v farvatere politiki Vashingtona," *MZ*, No. 4 (1981), p. 65; N. Nikolaev, "Zigzagi politiki Tokio," *MZ*, No. 11 (1981), pp. 44–45; *Pravda*, December 5, 1978; *Izvestiia*, August 29, 1980.

53. Quoted from Akio Kimura, "Sorengaiko no honshitsu—riron to jissen o megutte" (The Essence of Soviet Diplomacy: Theory and Practice), Research and

Study Section, *Asahi Shimbun, Chōsa Geppo* (The Research Monthly), No. 12 (December 1977), p. 9.

54. An editorial, for example, in *Hokkai Times* (Sapporo) declared: "If the four Northern Islands are returned [to Japan], we will take absolute responsibility for their nonmilitary control. It is hard for the people of Hokkaido to even imagine that a military base would be built on them" (*Hokkai Times,* June 12, 1977). Professor Shinkichi Etō has proposed "the return of the islands with the precondition that the islands are not rearmed as an alternative out of 11 options" (Shinkichi Etō, "Nisso-kankei Hatten no Hōto" [The Way to Develop Japanese-Soviet Relations], *Jiyū* (October 1973), p. 27.

55. Charlotte Saikowski, "Japanese Fishermen Seek Return of Northern Islands," *Christian Science Monitor,* June 10, 1968.

56. Professor Masataka Kōsaka writes: "In themselves, the four islands are not important in either a military or an economic sense, but the territorial problem has an important *symbolic value* for both powers. The Soviet Union does not want to establish a precedent for other territorial claims, while Japan wants proof of Soviet goodwill" (emphasis added by H.K.) (Masataka Kōsaka, *Options for Japan's Foreign Policy* [Adelphi Papers No. 97] [London: International Institute for Strategic Studies, 1973], p. 28). Robert Whynant, Tokyo correspondent of the *Guardian*, regards the islands as "*a symbol* of foreign conquest and Russian 'perfidy' in breaching the 1941 Neutrality Pact" (*Guardian*, October 19, 1979). See also J.B. Sorensen, *Japanese Policy and Nuclear Arms* (New York: American-Asian Educational Exchange, 1957), p. 51.

57. Public opinion surveys conducted by *Asahi Shimbun* in 1952 and 1953 revealed that those Japanese who favored a peace treaty with the USSR cited, together with the desire to maintain peace, as the basis for their answer, "the desire to finally terminate the state of war" (Donald C. Hellmann, *Japanese Foreign Policy and Domestic Politics* [Berkeley, CA: University of California Press, 1969], p. 77).

58. Quoted from Noguchi, *op. cit.*, p. 147.

59. *Der Spiegel*, August 21, 1978, p. 96.

60. *Asahi Shimbun*, October 2, 1970.

61. Kōsaka, *Options for Japan's Foreign Policy*, p. 28.

62. Rudolf von Jhering, *Der Kampf um's Recht* (Wien: Manzsche Verlags-und Universitäts-Buchhandlung, 1925), p. 18. For an English translation, see *The Struggle of Law*, translated by John J. Lalor (Chicago: Callaghan and Company, 1915), p. 27.

63. Professor Stephan also writes: "At the heart of the Soviet perspective on the Northern Territories lies a concern for security" (Stephan, *The Kuril Islands*, p. 208). For other articles and books that have emphasized the military-strategic value of the "Northern Territories," see, for example, the following: Kim, *op. cit.*, p. 46; Yoshida, *Hoppōryōdo*, pp. 196–206; Suizu, *Hoppōryōdo Dakkan no Michi*, pp. 219–227; Tatsuo Tsukushi, "Kunashiri, Etorofu no Senryakuteki Kachi" (Strategic Value of Kunashiri and Etorofu), *Gendai no Anzenhoshō* (Contemporary Security), No. 6 (June 1979), pp. 33–47; Boris N. Slavinskii, then Deputy Chief of the Research Department, the Far Eastern Branch, USSR Academy of Sciences, told the author of this book twice at breakfast on August 30, 1979, that "in my personal view, the Northern Territorial issue is not a territorial question but a *strategic* question" (emphasis added by H.K.).

64. Stephan, *The Kuril Islands*, p. 136.

65. Stalin, *op. cit.*, pp. 213–215.

66. Quoted from Kim, *Japanese-Soviet Relations*, p. 46. See also *Hokkaido Shimbun* and *Asahi Shimbun*, May 27, 1964.

67. *Hokkaido Shimbun* (evening edition) and *Asahi Shimbun* (evening edition), July 15, 1964; *Pravda* and *Izvestiia*, September 20, 1964.

68. Kutakov, p. 298.

69. Makoto Momoi, "Beiso Kyōfu no Kinkō no Jittai o Tsuku" (The Realities of the U.S.-Soviet Balance of Fear), *Chūō Kōron* (July 1977), pp. 135–136.

70. Michael McGwire, "The Rationale for the Development of Soviet Seapower," *United States Naval Institute Proceedings* (May 1980), p. 181. On the Soviet "bastion strategy" concept, I am indebted to my discussion with Dennis Ross and Frank Fukuyama, who served as commentators at the Rockefeller Foundation Conference on "Soviet Foreign Policy in an Uncertain World" held on November 12–16, 1984, at Bellagio, Italy.

71. Quoted from D.W. Given, "The Sea of Okhotsk: USSR's Great Lake?," *United States Naval Institute Proceedings*, Vol. 96, No. 9 [811] (September 1970), p. 49.

72. Lilita Dzirkals, *Soviet Policy Statements and Military Deployments in Northeast Asia* (RAND Corporation Paper No. P-6229) (Santa Monica, CA: RAND Corporation, 1978), p. 27.

Part Two. Soviet Policies Toward Japan: Why Were They Counterproductive?

Chapter 4. Soviet Policy Toward Asia

1. Leon Goure, Foy D. Kohler, Mose L. Harvey, *The Role of Nuclear Forces in Current Soviet Strategy* (Washington, DC: University of Miami, Center for Advanced International Studies, 1975), p. xi.

2. Joseph M. Ha, "Moscow's Policy Toward Japan," *Problems of Communism*, Vol. 26, No. 5 (September/October 1977), p. 66.

3. Genrikh A. Trofimenko, "Voenno-strategicheskie interesy SShA v basseine Tikhogo okeana," in V.P. Lukin et al., ed., *SShA i problemy Tikhogo okeana: Mezhdunarodno-politicheskie aspekty* (Moscow: Mezhdunarodnye otnosheniia, 1979), p. 83.

4. A. Mirov, "Aziia: Ne konfrontatsiia, a sotrudnichestvo," *Aziia i afrika segodnia*, No. 8 [242] (August 1977), p. 10.

5. Vladilen B. Vorontsov, *Kitai i SShA: 60–70–e gody* (Moscow: Nauka, 1979), p. 112.

6. Vladimir P. Lukin, "Tikhookeanskii region i protsessy razriadki mezhdunarodnoi napriazhennosti," in Lukin, *op. cit.*, p. 302.

7. Victor A. Kremeniuk, "Osnovnye vekhi amerikanskoi ekspanskii v basseine Tikhogo okeana," in Lukin, *op. cit.*, p. 37; Aleksandr B. Parkanskii, "Ekonomicheskie interesy SShA v basseine Tikhogo okeana," in Lukin, *op. cit.*, p. 122; M.G. Nosov, "Amerikano-iaponskie otnosheniia—vazhneishee zveno v strategii SShA na Tikhom okeane," in Lukin, *op. cit.*, p. 167; S. Verbitskii, "'Tikhookeanskaia doktrina' Vashingtona," *Aziia i afrika segodnia*, No. 8 [232] (August 1976), p. 5; *Izvestiia*, August 7, 1980.

8. Kremeniuk, *op. cit.*, p. 37.

9. Verbitskii, *op. cit.*, p. 5.

10. Nosov, *op. cit.*, p. 167.

11. Trofimenko, *op. cit.*, p. 81.

12. Andrei V. Krutskikh, *Amerikanskaia politika 'partnerstva' v vostochno-aziatskom regione* (Moscow: Mezhdunarodnye otnosheniia, 1980), p. 122, *passim*.

13. "Politika Iaponii v azii," in D.V. Petrov, ed., *Mezhdunarodnye otnosheniia v aziatsko-tikhookeanskom regione*, pp. 66–67.

14. Ibid., p. 67.

15. Lukin, "Tikhookeanskii region i protsessy razriadki mezhdunarodnoi napriazhennosti," p. 303.

16. *The Common Security Interests of Japan, the United States and NATO* (Cambridge, MA: Ballinger, 1981), pp. 1–17.

17. Malcolm Mackintosh, "Soviet Interests and Policies in the Asian-Pacific Region," *Orbis*, Vol. 19, No. 3 (Philadelphia, PA: Fall 1975), pp. 763–764. Taking note of the change with time, Professor Robinson argues that the USSR is increasingly becoming an Asian power. For more details, see Thomas W. Robinson, "Soviet Policy in Northeast Asia: Determinants, Options and Possible Changes," *Triangular Relations of Mainland China, the Soviet Union and North Korea* (Seoul: Asiatic Research Center, Korea University, 1978), pp. 1–24.

18. Mackintosh, *op. cit.*, pp. 763–764.

19. For instance, L.I. Brezhnev, *Leninskim kursom: rechi i stat'i* (Moscow: Politizdat, 1972), Vol. 3, p. 492.; A. Iosilevich, "Peking i bezoapasnost' v Azii," *Asiia i afrika segodniia* (July 1976), p. 9; V.M. Mazurov, *SShA-Kitai-Iaponiia: perestroika mezhgosudarstvennykh otnoshenii (1969–1979)* (Moscow: Nauka, 1980), p. 4; Kovalenko, *Sovetskii Soiuz v bor'be za mir . . .*, p. 4; V. Pavlovskii, "Kollektivnaia bezopasnost' put' k miru v Azii,," p. 30; Petrov, ed., *op. cit.*, p. 16.

20. V.I. Lenin, *Polnoe sobranie sochinenii* (5th edition, Moscow: Politizdat, 1962), Vol. 30, p. 326.

21. Petrov, ed., *op. cit.*, p. 9.

22. Osamu Miyoshi, "The Growth of Soviet Military Power and the Security of Japan," in Richard B. Foster et al., eds., *Strategy and Security in Northeast Asia* (New York: Crane, Russak, 1979), p. 78.

23. For a comparative study on Soviet territorial disputes with the PRC and Japan, see David Rees, *Soviet Border Problems: China and Japan* (Institute for the Study of Conflict, 1982), 30 pp.

24. Brezhnev, *Leninskim kursom*, Vol. 2, p. 413.

25. Ibid., Vol. 3, p. 493. See also Ibid., Vol. 4, pp. 253–54, 329.

26. Robert Scalapino has gone so far as to say that "the earlier Soviet proposal for an Asian collective security system *has been quietly dropped*" (emphasis added by H.K.). Robert A. Scalapino, "The Political Influence of the USSR in Asia," in Zagoria, ed., *Soviet Policy in East Asia*, p. 87.

27. Brezhnev, *Leninskim kursom*, Vol. 4, p. 457.

28. For the best study in the English language on the BAM, see Theodore Shabad and Victor L. Mote, *Gateway to Siberian Resources (The BAM)* (Washington, DC: Scripta, 1977).

29. The Soviets have acknowledged that "Japanese machinery and equipment was extensively used and had been a significant contribution" in the building not only of the so-called smaller BAM but of the BAM as such. V.A. Aleksandrov, "Mesto Sibiri i dal'nego vostoka v ekonomicheskikh sviaziakh SSSR i Iaponii," *PDV*, No. 1 [41] (1982), pp. 27–28.

30. Victor Suvorov, *Inside the Soviet Army* (New York: Macmillan, 1982), p. 48.

31. *New York Times*, May 8, 1983; *Asahi Shimbun* (evening edition), May 10, 1983.

32. This warning has been made persistently, for example, by Mineo Nakajima, professor of foreign languages at Tokyo University. See Nakajima, *Chūso-Tairitsu to*

Gendai (The Sino-Soviet Conflict and the Contemporary Period), (Tokyo: Chūō Kōron-sha, 1980); and *Chūso-dōmei no Shōgeki: Nihon no anzen to keizai wa dōnaru ka* (Impact of Sino-Soviet Alliance: What Will Happen to the Security and Economy of Japan?) (Tokyo: Kōbun-sha, 1982).

33. *Japan Times* and *Asahi Shimbun*, February 15, 1981.

34. For a convenient summary of various views among Western specialists in the 1980s on the prospects of Sino-Soviet relations, see Robert G. Sutter, *Future Sino-Soviet Relations and Their Implications for the United States* (Congressional Research Service Report, No. 83–10F) (Washington, DC: Library of Congress, 1982).

35. Richard H. Solomon, "American Defense Planning and Asian Security: Policy Choices for a Time of Transition," in Richard H. Solomon, ed., *Asian Security in the 1980s: Problems and Politics for a Time of Transition* (Cambridge, MA: Oelgeschlager, Gunn & Hain, 1980), p. 8.

36. Robert Merton, *Social Theory and Social Structure* (revised edition) (Glencoe, IL: Free Press, 1957), p. 423.

37. See Ernst Kux, "Is Russia a Pacific Power?" *The Pacific Community* (Winter 1980), pp. 509–510.

38. Solomon, *op. cit.*, p. 8.

39. Andrew Nagorski, "East Asia in 1980," *Foreign Affairs*, Vol. 59, No. 3 (1981), p. 693.

40. Paul F. Langer, "Changing Japanese Security Perspectives," in Solomon, ed., *Asian Security in the 1980s*, p. 79.

Chapter 5. Soviet Strategy and Tactics Toward Japan

1. According to a Japanese *White Paper on Defense*, of a total 430 passages during the previous year of Soviet naval vessels through Japanese waters, passages through the Soya Strait accounted for about half, or 205 passages. There were 165 passages through the Tsushima Strait, and 60 through the Tsugaru Strait. See *Defense of Japan: 1982* [Tokyo: Defense Agency, 1982], p. 37.

2. For example, former U.S. Secretary of Defense Harold Brown called Japan "the keystone of our security position in the Far East" in 1981, and U.S. Secretary of Defense Caspar Weinberger regarded Japan as "a major pillar of our whole forward-defense strategy in the Asian-Pacific region." Harold Brown, *Department of Defense: Annual Report: Fiscal Year 1981* [Washington, DC: Department of State, 1981], p. 50; Caspar Weinberger, *United States Security Relationships with Northeast Asia* Stanford, CA: Stanford University, Northeast Asia–United States Forum on International Policy, 1982], p. 3.

3. John P. Hardt, Ronda A. Bresnick, and David Levine, "Soviet Oil and Gas in the Global Perspective," *Project Interdependence: U.S. and World Energy Outlook through 1990* (Washington, DC: Congressional Research Service, Library of Congress, November, 1977), p. 798.

4. See, for example, Marshall I. Goldman, *The Enigma of Soviet Petroleum: Half-empty or Half-full?* (London: George Allen & Unwin, 1980), pp. 126–131; *Izvestiia*, March 1, 1981; "U.S.-Soviet Union Trade Begins Gradual Return to Normal Level," *Business America* (June 1, 1981), pp. 7, 8.

5. Dolgorukov, "Tolgovo-ekonomicheskie otnosheniia SSSR s Iaponiei," pp. 116–17. For an assessment of the future prospects of BAM, see Robert W. Campbell,

"Prospects for Siberian Economic Development," in Zagoria, ed., *Soviet Policy in East Asia*, pp. 249–251.

6. Whiting, *op. cit.*, p. 112.

7. Stephan, "Asia in the Soviet Conception," p. 42.

8. Oded Eran, *Mezhdunarodniki: An Assessment of Professional Expertise in the Making of Soviet Foreign Policy* (Ramat Gan, Israel: Turtledove, 1979).

9. Dimitri K. Simes, "National Security under Andropov," *Problems of Communism*, Vol. 32 (January/February 1983), p. 37.

10. Ibid. For the role and the degree of influence of area specialists and *mezhdunarodniki* (internationalists), see also Rose E. Gottemoeller and Paul F. Langer, *Foreign Area Studies in the USSR: Training and Employment of Specialists* (Santa Monica, CA: RAND Corporation, 1983), pp. 73–77; Eran, *op. cit.*, p. 331.

11. Nora Beloff, "Escape from Freedom: A Defector's Story," *Atlantic Monthly* (November 1980), p. 45.

12. Ibid.

13. Ibid.

14. Ibid.

15. Stephan, "Asia in the Soviet Conception," p. 31.

16. Ibid.

17. *Asahi Shimbun*, December 12, 1982; *New York Times*, December 17, 1982.

18. Nathan Leites, *The Operational Code of the Politburo* (fifth edition) (Westport, CT: Greenwood Press, 1972); Alexander George, "The Operational Code: A Neglected Approach to the Study of Political Leaders and Decision-Making," *International Studies Quarterly*, Vol. 13, No. 2 (June 1969), pp. 190–222.

19. For an excellent study on Soviet perceptions of Japan, see John J. Stephan, "Japan in the Soviet Mirror," pp. 61–66; Stephan, "Soviet Approaches to Japan," pp. 132–150; and Stephan, "Asia in the Soviet Conception," pp. 29–56.

20. Hiroshi Kimura, "The Soviet Union and Japan," *Asian Security 1981* (Tokyo: Research Institute for Peace and Security, 1981), pp. 43–44.

21. Stephen D. Kertesz. "American and soviet Negotiating Behavior," in Kertesz and M.A. Fitzimons, eds., *Diplomacy in a Changing World* (Notre Dame, IN: University of Notre Dame Press, 1959), p. 145.

22. Samelson, *op. cit.*, p. 9.

23. For a similar argument, see Adam Ulam, *Expansion and Coexistence* (New York: Praeger, 1968), p. 189.

24. V.I. Lenin, *Polnoe sobranie sochinenii* (5th edition) (Moscow: Izdatel'stvo politicheskoi Politizdat literatury, 1964), Vol. 36, p. 168.

25. Valerian A. Zorin, *Osnovy diplomaticheskoi sluzhby* (izdanie vtoroe, ispravlennoe i dopolnennoe) (Moscow: Mezhdunarodnye otnosheniia, 1977), p. 77.

26. Petrov, *Iaponiia v mirovoi politike* (1973), pp. 41–42.

27. Petrov, "Militarizatsiia Iaponii—ugroza miru v Azii," *PDV*, No. 1 (1981), p. 51.

28. Petrov, "Militarizatsiia Iaponii," p. 57.

29. "Tōron: *Izubesuchia* to *Nōbosuchi* no Ronsetsu-iin tai *Sankei Shimbun* no Ronsetsu-iin: Naze Soren wa Nihon o dōkatsu suru no ka? (Debate: Editors of *Izvestiia* and *Novosti* vs. *Sankei Shimbun*: Why Does the Soviet Union Threaten Japan?)," *Seiron* (May 1983), p. 109.

30. *Izvestiia*, May 4, 1980.

31. N.G. Fedulova, "Perestroika voenno-politicheskoi sistemy imperializma v Azii,"

in Petrov, ed., *Mezhdunarodnye otnosheniia v aziatsko-tikhookeanskom regione*, p. 226.

32. V. Dal'nev, "Chto meshaet razvitiiu sovetsko-iaponskikh otnoshenii," *MZ*, No. 1 (1981), p. 53.

33. *Izvestiia*, August 14, 1982; D.V. Petrov, "Politika Iaponii v Azii," in Petrov, ed., *Mezhdunarodnye otnosheniia*, p. 99; Modenov, "Tokio v farvatere politike Vashingtona," p. 61.

34. *Pravda*, July 28, 1979 and September 8 and December 21, 1980; *Izvestiia*, January 22, February 9, May 4, and July 20, 1980 and January 16, 1981; *Krasnaia zvezda*, June 13 and August 3, 1979.

35. *Izvestiia*, July 20, 1980.

36. *Izvestiia*, May 27, 1980.

37. *Pravda*, December 28, 1979; *Komsomol'skaia pravda*, June 4, 1980.

38. *Komsomol'skaia pravda*, June 4, 1980.

39. Ibid.

40. Bykov, *op. cit.*, p. 48.

41. Modenov, "Tokio v farvatere politiki Vashingtona," p. 60.

42. Vasilii Golovnin, "Tikhookeanskie mirazhi tokiiskikh politikov," *Aziia i afrika segodnia*, No. 7 [277] (July 1980), p. 7.

43. N. Nikolaev, "Zigzagi politiki Tokio," *MZ*, No. 10 (1981), p. 40; *Pravda*, May 16, May 25, and August 26, 1981 and January 19, 1982; D.V. Petrov, "Vozrozhdenie iaponskogo ekspansionizma," in S.N. Morozov, ed., *Gegemonizm: Sepokhoi v konflikte* (Moscow: Progress, 1982), p. 197; Iurii Kuznetsov, "Kuda tolkaiut Iaponiiu," *Kommunist*, No. 4 [1230] (March 1983), pp. 100, 102.

44. *Izvestiia*, December 20, 1982.

45. *Pravda*, August 20, November 14, and November 19, 1981 and January 19, 1982; *Krasnaia zvezda*, December 18, 1981 and August 10, 1982; Kuznetsov, *op. cit.*, p. 101.

46. *XXVI s" ezd Kommunisticheskoi partii Sovetskogo Soiuza*, (24 fevralia–3 marta 1981 goda) Vol. 1, p. 42; Vasil'ev, *op. cit.*, p. 44, 46, 54; L.P. Pinaev, *Evoliutsiia voennoi politiki Iaponii: 1959–1980 gg.* (Moscow: Nauka, 1982), p. 58; Mazurov, *op. cit.*, pp. 154–156; *Pravda*, May 28, 1980; *Izvestiia*, July 20, 1980; *Krasnaia zvezda*, December 22, 1981.

47. *XXVI s" ezd KPSS* (*24 fevralia–3 marta 1981 goda*), Vol. 1, p. 42.

48. Ibid., p. 43.

49. Petrov, "Vozrozhdenie iaponskogo ekspansionizma," pp. 186–190.

50. Ibid.

51. *Izvestiia*, August 16, 1980.

52. *Pravda*, January 19, 1982.

53. *Izvestiia*, August 16, 1980.

54. Petrov, "Vozrozhdenie iaponskogo ekspansionizma," p. 198.

55. Petrov, "Vneshniaia politika Iaponii na rubezhe 70–80–kh godov," pp. 71–72.

56. Petrov, "Vozrozhdenie iaponskogo ekspansionizma," p. 199; *Pravda*, February 2, 1982; Modenov, "Tokio v farvatere politiki Vashingtona," p. 62; Petrov, "Militarizatsiia Iaponii," p. 61.

57. Petrov, "Militarizatsiia Iaponii," p. 58; *Krasnaia zvezda*, November 25, 1979; *Pravda*, July 21, 1982.

58. I.I. Ivkov, "Iaponskii militarizm podnimaet golovu," *PDV*, No. 3 (1978), p. 46.

59. *Pravda*, May 5, 1979.

60. Pinaev, *op. cit.*, p. 32. See also pp. 31, 22–30, 148–149.

61. Petrov, "Militarizatsiia Iaponii," p. 52.

62. Ibid.

63. Ivkov, *op. cit.*, p. 46.

64. Ibid., pp. 46–47; Petrov, "Vozrozhdenie iaponskogo ekspansionizma," p. 190.

65. Ivkov, *op. cit.*, pp. 46–47.

66. Ibid., p. 48.

67. Ibid., p. 46; Modenov, "Tokio v farvatere politiki Vashingtona," p. 60; *Krasnaia zvezda*, October 25, 1981; Petrov, "Militarizatsiia Iaponii," p. 52; Paul F. Langer, "Soviet Military Power in Asia," in Zagoria, ed., *Soviet Policy in East Asia*, pp. 260–261.

68. Ivkov, *op. cit.*, p. 47.

69. Dal'nev, *op. cit.*, p. 55; *Krasnaia zvezda*, August 30, 1980, December 14, 1981, and August 27, 1982; *Izvestiia*, August 29, 1980.

70. Ivkov, *op. cit.*, p. 47.

71. *Pravda*, September 2, 1980.

72. Ibid.

73. *Krasnaia zvezda*, October 6, 1980.

74. Jervis, *op. cit.*, pp. 218, 228, 232, 234, 240, 263, 275, 276. See also Ernest R. May, *"Lessons" of the Past: The Use and Misuse of History in American Foreign Policy* (New York: Oxford University Press, 1973), pp. ix–xiii; Klaus Knorr, "Introduction: On the Utility of History," in Klaus Knorr, ed., *Historical Dimensions of National Security Problems* (Lawrence: University Press of Kansas, 1976), pp. 1-4.

75. Langer, *op. cit.*, p. 263. See also note 5.

76. For example, Brezhnev's interview with Shōrū Hata, editor-in-chief of the Japanese newspaper *Asahi Shimbun*, on June 5, 1977 (*Pravda*, June 7, 1977); N. Nikolaev, "Dobrososedstvo i sotrudnichestvo: V interesakh SSSR i Iaponii, *MZ*, No. 1 (1978), p. 54; Spandar'ian, *op. cit.*, p. 951.; Petrov, "Politika Iaponii v Azii," p. 105.

77. For example, "Patolichev Urges USSR–Japan Business Meeting," *FBIS-SOV*, July 28, 1982, p. C3; Petrov, "Politika Iaponii v Azii," p. 104.

78. Dolgorukov, "Torgovo-ekonomicheskie otnosheniia SSSR s Iaponiei," pp. 107, 110. According to Hikaru Kens, "The major trading firms handle 90 percent of Japan-Soviet trade." Hikaru Kens, "An Outfall in the East: A Gas Row Clouds Japan-Soviet Plans for Siberia," *Far Eastern Economic Review* (July 23, 1982), p. 48.

79. *Asahi Shimbun* and *Hokkaido Shimbun*, February 24, 1983.

80. *Asahi Shimbun*, December 5, 1982; *Mainichi Shimbun*, December 7, 1982. Consequently, Nikolai Kudriavtsev, First Deputy Minister of Fisheries and head of the Soviet delegation, was quoted as proposing, "Let us complete all our negotiations in a short period of time." In fact, the fishing negotiations between Japan and the USSR became very brief after 1979, *FBIS-SOV*, November 22, 1979.

81. May, *op. cit.*, pp. ix–xiii. See also Knorr, *op. cit.*, pp. 1–4.

82. For an English translation of the Soviet-Japanese Declaration, see Stephan, *The Kuril Islands*, p. 247; Rodger Swearingen, *The Soviet Union and Postwar Japan: Escalating Challenge and Response* (Stanford, CA: Hoover Institution Press, 1978), p. 225.

83. Petrov, *Iaponiia v mirovoi politike*, pp. 233–234; V.N. Berezin, *op. cit.*, p. 105.

84. Mikhail S. Kapitsa, *Na raznykh paralleliakh: Zapiski diplomata* (Moscow: kniga i biznes, 1996), p. 155.

85. Morgenthau, *op. cit.*, p. 181.

86. Ibid.

87. *XXVI s" ezd Kommunistichecheskoi partii Sovetskogo Soiuza* (23 fevralia–marta 1981 goda), Vol. 1, pp. 27–28, 46.

88. *Pravda*, March 25, 1982.

89. Donald S. Zagoria, "The Moscow-Beijing Détente," *Foreign Affairs*, Vol. 61, No. 4 (Spring 1983), pp. 854, 856–858; Robert G. Sutter, *Future Sino-Soviet Relations and Their Implications for the United States* (Congressional Research Service Paper No. 83–10F) (Washington, DC: Library of Congress, 1982), pp. 17, 19.

90. *Pravda*, September 27, 1982.

91. *Hokkai Times*, October 25, 1982.

92. Donald S. Zagoria, "Gauging the Sino-Soviet Thaw," *New Leader*, Vol. 65, No. 22 (November 29, 1982), p. 4; Vladimir Petrov, "China Goes It Alone," *Asian Survey*, Vol. 23, No. 5 (May 1983), p. 588.

93. According to Robert Sutter, it was debatable how much economic benefit the USSR would get from a withdrawal of Soviet forces along the Chinese border (Sutter, *op. cit.*, p. 11).

94. Edmund Lee (pseudonym of a scholar who emigrated from the PRC to the United States), "Beijing's Balancing Act," *Foreign Policy*, No. 51 (Summer 1983), p. 34. However, Donald Zagoria believed that the Soviets' removal of some of their troops from the Sino-Soviet border elsewhere was "highly unlikely." Zagoria, "The Moscow-Beijing Détente," p. 869.

95. As Sutter correctly points out, Japan was a much more convenient trade partner for the Soviet Union than was China (Sutter, *op. cit*, pp. 38, 39).

96. *Yomiuri Shimbun* (evening edition), March 7, March 11, 1983, and *Yomiuri Shimbun*, March 15, 1983; *Asahi Shimbun*, March 15, 1983; *Christian Science Monitor*, March 18 and March 28, 1983; *New York Times*, March 20, 1983; *Nihon Keizai Shimbun* (evening edition), October 11, 1983; *Yomiuri Shimbun*, October 29,1983.

97. Sutter, *op. cit.*, p. 8.

98. Vladimir Petrov, "China Goes It Alone," p. 593.

99. In proposing these three variations, I am indebted to a suggestion from Professor Nakajima (Nakajima, *Chūso-dōmei no Shīgeki*, p. 54).

100. Thomas W. Robinson, "Sino-Soviet Relations During the 1980s as a Factor in Northeast Asian Security," unpublished paper, p. 13.

101. Zagoria, "Gauging the Sino-Soviet Thaw," p. 5.

102. Sutter, *op. cit.*, pp. 31–32.

103. Ibid., p. 45.

104. Quoted from *Far Eastern Economic Review*, December 3, 1982, p. 37.

105. Robinson, *op. cit.*, pp. 7–8.

106. *Pravda*, November 26, 1977; *Krasnaia zvezda*, October 9, 1982; *Pravda*, November 11, 1982; *Mainichi Shimbun* (evening edition), *Yomiuri Shimbun* (evening edition), *Hokkaido Shimbun* (evening edition), February 20, 1983; *FBIS-SOV*, January 19, 1983, p. C8.

107. *Asahi Shimbun*, June 19, 1978.

108. Avigdor Haselkorn, "Impact of the Sino-Japanese Treaty on the Soviet Security Strategy," *Asian Survey*, Vol. 19, No. 6 (June 1979), p. 563.

109. Erik P. Hoffmann, and Frederic J. Fleron, Jr., eds., *The Conduct of Soviet Foreign Policy* (expanded 2nd. ed.) (New York: Aldine, 1980), p. 31.

110. David W. Paul of Princeton University writes, "Understanding the process of Soviet foreign policy-making can sometimes be a *frustrating* challenge," partly because "there is no simple approach which will immediately enlighten the policymak-

ing process" (emphasis added by H.K.) (David W. Paul, "Soviet Foreign Policy and the Invasion of Czechoslovakia: A Theory and a Case Study," *International Studies Quarterly*, Vol. 15, No. 2 [June 1971], p. 159).

111. Dallin, "The Domestic Source of Soviet Foreign Policy," p. 380.

112. Ibid.; Goure *et al.*, *op. cit.*, p. xi.

113. Ibid.; Vernon V. Aspaturian, "Internal Politics and Foreign Policy in the Soviet System," in R. Barry Farrell, ed., *Approaches to Comparative and International Politics* (Evanston, IL: Northwestern University Press, 1966), p. 286.

114. Dallin, "The Domestic Sources of Soviet Foreign Policy," p. 380.

115. Ibid., p. 343.

Part Three: The Deterioration in Soviet-Japanese Relations

1. Vasil'ev, *op. cit.*, p. 63.

2. Dal'nev, *op. cit.*, 51.

3. Ibid.

4. Ibid.

5. Ibid.

6. Vasil'ev, *op. cit.*, p. 63.

7. The three events—the MiG-25 incident, the fishing negotiations, and the signing of a Sino-Japanese peace treaty—were listed also by Soviet Vice-Foreign Minister Mikhail Kapitsa in his article "Bor'ba SSSR za mir i sotrudnichestvo v Azii," *PDV*, No. 1 [29] (1979), p. 45.

Chapter 6. Japanese and Soviet Negotiating Behavior: The Spring 1977 Fisheries Talks

1. *Izvestiia*, December 11, 1976.

2. Ibid., February 25, 1977.

3. *Asahi Shimbun*, May 25, 1977; Swearingen, *op. cit.*, p. 287.

4. See chapters 2 and 3 in John S. Reshetar, Jr., *Problems of Analyzing and Predicting Soviet Behavior* (New York: Doubleday, 1955), pp. 4–30.

5. Cf. Coral Bell, *Negotiating from Strength: A Study in the Politics of Power* (New York: Knopf, 1962); Robert J. Einhorn, *Negotiating from Strength: Leverage in U.S.-Soviet Arms Control Negotiations* (New York: Praeger, 1985).

6. Kōji Oonuma, former *Mainichi Shimbun* correspondent in Moscow, even went so far as to call the Japanese negotiating posture "*dogeza* [prostration] diplomacy" (*Gekkan Ekonomisuto*, No. 6 [1977], p. 33).

7. Dagmar Ahrens-Thiele, "Japanese-Soviet Fishing Dispute," *Radio Liberty Research Bulletin*, May 4, 1977, p. 1.

8. *Asahi Shimbun*, December 18, 1976.

9. Mitsuru Gondō, *Nihyaku-kairi Gyogyō-suiiki* (Tokyo: Kyōikusha, 1978), pp. 110–113.

10. *Asahi Shimbun*, March 5, 1977.

11. Takeo Doi (translated by John Bester), *The Anatomy of Dependence* (Tokyo: Kōdansha, 1973), p. 26.

12. Takeo Doi, "*Higaisha-ishiki:* The Psychology of Revolting Youth in Japan," in Sakie Sugiyama Lebra and William P. Lebra, eds., *Japanese Culture and Behavior: Selected Readings* (Honolulu: University Press of Hawaii, 1974), p. 453.

13. Hideo Satō *et al.*, *Managing an Alliance: The Politics of U.S.-Japanese Relations* (Washington, DC: Brookings Institution, 1976), pp. 108–109.

14. *Asahi Shimbun*, January 13, 1977.

15. Ibid., October 27, 1977.

16. *Izvestiia*, April 2, 1977.

17. Ibid., May 4, 1977.

18. *FBIS-SOV*, May 18, 1977, p. M2.

19. Ibid., May 10, 1977, p. M1.

20. Ibid., April 13, 1977, p. M1, and April 19, 1977, p. M6.

21. Ibid., May 12, 1977, p. M1.

22. See Gordon A. Craig, "Techniques of Negotiation," in Ivo J. Lederer, ed., *Russian Foreign Policy: Essays in Historical Perspective* (New Haven, CT: Yale University Press, 1962), p. 370.

23. *Sankei Shimbun*, May 18, 1977.

24. Gerald L. Steibel, *How Can We Negotiate with the Communists?* (New York: National Strategy Information Center, 1972), p. 21.

25. Sir William Hayter, *The Diplomacy of the Great Powers* (London: Hamish Hamilton, 1960), p. 68.

26. *Sankei Shimbun*, May 18, 1977.

27. See Hedrick Smith, *The Russians* (New York: Ballantine, 1976), pp. 346–349.

28. See George Feifer, *Message from Moscow by Observer* (New York: Vintage, 1971), pp. 91–95.

29. Robert Kaiser, *Russia: The People and the Power* (New York: Pocket Books, 1976).

30. Smith, *op. cit.*, p. 250.

31. See Erich Fromm, *Escape from Freedom* (New York: Avon, 1965), pp. 165–184.

32. Smith, *op. cit.*, p. 264.

33. Michael Blaker, *Japanese International Negotiating Style* (New York: Columbia University Press, 1977), p. 28.

34. *Asahi Shimbun*, February 5, 1977.

35. *Asahi Shimbun*, March 14, 1977.

36. *Asahi Shimbum*, March 15, 1977.

37. *Asahi Shimbum*, April 3, 1977.

38. Stanley Hoffmann, "The Hell of Good Intentions," *Foreign Policy* (Winter 1977–1978), p. 3.

39. Philip E. Mosely, "Some Soviet Techniques of Negotiation," in Raymond Donnett and Joseph E. Johnson, eds., *Negotiating with the Russians* (Boston: World Peace Federation, 1951), p. 296.

40. Blaker, *op. cit.*, pp. 23–24, 50–53, 213, 218.

41. Ibid., pp. 23, 26, 53, 218.

42. See Ichiro Kōno, *Imadakara hanasō* (Tokyo: Shunyōdō-shoten, 1958), pp. 23–40.

43. *Asahi Shimbun*, March 6 and April 5, 1977.

44. Kennan, *Memoirs*, p. 290.

45. See *Asahi Shimbun*, April 16 and May 19, 1977.

46. Ibid., February 26, 1977.

47. Samelson, *op. cit.*, p. 9.

48. Bryant Wedge and Cyril Muromcew, "Psychological Factors in Soviet Disarmament Negotiation," *Journal of Conflict Resolution* (March 1965), p. 35.

49. Richard Pipes, "Detente: Moscow's View," in Pipes, ed., *Soviet Strategy in Europe* (New York: Crane, Russak, 1976), pp. 11–12.

50. Smith, *op. cit.*, p. 332.

51. Lenin, *Polnoe sobranie sochinenii* (5th edition), Vol. 44, p. 50.

52. Gibert, *op. cit.*, p. 24.

53. Gordon A. Craig, "Totalitarian Approaches to Diplomatic Negotiation," in A.C. Sarkissian, ed., *Studies in Diplomatic History in Honor of G.P. Gooch* (London: Longmans, 1961), p. 123; Hayter, *The Diplomacy of the Great Powers*, p. 68.

54. Arthur H. Deane, "Soviet Diplomatic Style and Tactics," in *The Soviet Approach to Negotiation*, p. 63.

55. Hayter, *The Diplomacy of the Great Powers*, pp. 68–69.

56. Craig, "Totalitarian Approaches to Diplomatic Negotiation," pp. 122–123.

57. C. Turner Joy, *How Communists Negotiate* (New York: Macmillan, 1955), pp. 39–40.

58. *Sankei Shimbun*, May 20, 1977.

59. Dagmar Ahrens-Thiele, "Japanese-Soviet Fishery Agreement," *Radio Liberty Research Bulletin*, May 27, 1977, p. 2.

60. Lenin, *Polnoe sobranie sochinenii* (5th edition), Vol. 41, p. 55.

61. Zorin, *op. cit.*, p. 76.

62. *FBIS-SOV*, May 12, 1977, p. M1.

63. *FBIS-SOV*, May 18, 1977, p. M1.

64. *Pravda*, April 1, 1977.

65. *FBIS-SOV*, May 18, 1977, p. M1.

66. *Pravda*, April 1, 1977.

67. See *Asahi Shimbun*, April 23, 1977.

68. *Pravda*, April 22, 1977.

69. See, for example, *Asahi Shimbun* (evening edition), and *Yomiuri Shimbun* (evening edition), December 11, 1976; *Asahi Shimbun*, December 13 and 14, 1976 and February 25 and 26, 1977; and *Hokkaido Shimbun*, March 4, 1977.

70. *Nihon Keizai Shimbun*, February 10, 1977.

71. Junnosuke Kishida and Shōji Takase wrote, in *A Study of Bargaining Power* (1981): "Observing the Tokyo Olympic Games, which were organized very systematically and beautifully, without a single error or delay, Western commentators remarked that while the Japanese do not have the capability to set a goal, once a goal is set, they exert an amazing talent to achieve it (far better than any other nation). In other words, the Japanese are a nation that works hard toward an objective, regardless of its substance. They are not *a goal-setting* nation. A notable feature of Japanese diplomacy (also) is that it responds to the goal or the circumstances." Junnosuke Kishida and Shōji Takase, *Kōshōryoku no kenkyu* (Study of Bargaining Power) (emphasis added by H.K.) (Tokyo: Gakuyō Shobō, 1981), pp. 115–116.

72. *Nihon Keizai Shimbun*, May 18, 1977. For a discussion on both the strength and the weakness that an "open society" had in negotiations with the Soviets, see Foy D. Kohler, "Negotiation as an Effective Instrument of American Foreign Policy," *U.S. Department of State Bulletin*, 38 (June 2, 1958), p. 907.

73. *Asahi Shimbun*, May 31, 1977.

74. *Mainichi Shimbun*, March 25, 1977; *Sankei Shimbun* (evening edition), May 26, 1977, *Asahi Shimbun*, May 28, 1977; and *Nihon Keizai Shimbun*, May 28, 1977.

75. *Nihon Keizai Shimbun*, May 30, 1977.

76. *Hokkaido Shimbun* (evening edition), April 7, 1977.

77. *Sankei Shimbun*, May 18, 1977.

78. Bernard Gordon, "Loose Cannon on a Rolling Deck? Japan's Changing Security Policies," *Orbis* (Winter 1979), pp. 970–971.

79. Bell, *op. cit.*, pp. 197–198.

80. Mosely, *op. cit.*, p. 32.

81. Smith, *op. cit.*, p. 264.

82. Samelson, *op. cit.*, p. 27.

83. Mosely, *op. cit.*, p. 295.

84. Kertesz, *op. cit.*, p. 143.

85. Lenin, *Polnoe sobranie sochinenii* (5th edition), Vol. 44, p. 49.

86. Gordon A. Craig, "Techniques of Negotiation," in Ivo J. Lederer, ed., *Russian Foreign Policy: Essay in Historical Perspective* (New Haven, CT: Yale University Press, 1962), pp. 368–369.

87. Arthur M. Schlesinger, Jr., *A Thousand Days: John F. Kennedy in the White House* (Boston: Houghton Miffin, 1965), p. 362.

88. Samelson, *op. cit.*, p. 27.

89. O.V. Bogdanov, *Peregovory—osnova mirnogo uregulirovaniia mezhdunarodnykh problem* (Moscow: Znanie, 1958), p. 12. The English translation of the title is Professor Jönsson's (Jönsson, *Soviet Bargaining Behavior*, p. 45).

90. G.A. Deborin, "Novyi istoricheskii etap v razvitii sovetskoi vneshnei politiki i diplomatii," in V.Z. Lebedev, ed., *O sovremennoi sovetskoi diplomatii* (Moscow: Institut mezhdunarodnykh otnoshenii, 1963), p. 51.

91. Zorin, *op. cit.*, p. 35.

92. Strobe Talbott, *Endgame: The Inside Story of SALT II* (New York: Harper & Row, 1979), p. 16.

93. This is what A.I. Stepanov emphasizes. See A.I. Stepanov, "V.I. Lenin o kompromissakh vo vneshnei politike i sovremennost'" in Lebedev, ed., *O sovremennoi sovetskoi diplomatii*, pp. 101–103.

94. Lenin, *Polnoe sobranie sochinenii* (5th edition), Vol. 41, pp. 50–54.

95. Stepanov, *op. cit.*, p. 101.

96. Sir Michael Wright, *Disarm and Verify: An Explanation of the Central Difficulties and of National Policies* (New York: Frederick A. Praeger, 1964), p. 107.

97. Wedge and Muromchew, *op. cit.*, p. 33.

98. Ibid.

99. Ibid.

100. See Walter C. Clemens, Jr., *The U.S.S.R. and Global Interdependence: Alternative Futures* (Washington, DC: American Enterprise Institute for Public Policy Research, 1978), pp. 21–31.

101. Ibid., p. 24.

102. Simes, *Détente and Conflict*, pp. 7–8.

103. Michael Blaker, *Japanese International Negotiating Style*, unpublished first draft, p. 37.

104. Lloyd Jensen, "Soviet-American Bargaining Behavior in the Postwar Disarmament Negotiations," *Journal of Conflict Resolution*, Vol. 7, No. 3 (September 1973), p. 529.

105. Committee on Foreign Affairs, Special Studies on Foreign Affairs Issues, *Soviet Diplomacy and Negotiating Behavior: Emerging New Context for U.S. Diplomacy* (Washington, DC: U.S. Government Printing Office, 1979), p. 571.

106. Kohler, *op. cit.*, p. 910.

107. Hayter, *op. cit.*, pp. 30–31.

108. Joseph C. Harsh, "Moscow Loves the French Again," *Christian Science Monitor*, November 2, 1978, p. 23.

109. Kertesz, *op. cit.*, p. 146.

110. Steibel, *op. cit.*, p. 13; Leites, *op. cit.*, pp. 475–503.

111. Chie Nakane, *Japanese Society* (Berkeley: University of California Press, 1970), p. 26ff.

112. Foy D. Kohler and Mose L. Harvey, eds., *The Soviet Union: Yesterday, Today, Tomorrow: A Colloquy of American Long Timers in Moscow* (Washington, DC: University of Miami, Center for Advanced International Studies, 1975), p. 196.

113. Mosely, *op. cit.*, p. 277.

114. Hayter, *op. cit.*, p. 28.

115. Mainichi Shimbun-sha, ed., *200-Kairi Sakana Sensō* (Tokyo: Mainichi Shimbun-sha, 1977); Kiyoshi Takada, *200-Kairi Sensō* (Tokyo: K.K. World Photo Press, 1977) (emphasis added by H.K.).

116. Blaker, *Japanese International Negotiating Style*, pp. 21–23.

117. Mosely, *op. cit.*, p. 295.

118. See *Nihon Keizai Shimbun*, March 5 and April 11, 1977; *Sankei Shimbun*, April 13, 1977; *Nihon Keizai Shimbun*, April 16, 1977; and *Asahi Shimbun*, May 26, 1977.

119. *Nihon Keizai Shimbun* (evening edition), May 4, 1977.

120. *Pravda*, October 11, 1973.

121. Peggy L. Falkenheim, "Some Determining Factors in Soviet-Japanese Relations," *Pacific Affairs*, Vol. 50, No. 4 (Winter 1977–1978), p. 614.

122. Markov, *op. cit.*, p. 225.

123. See, for example, Fred Charles Iklé, *How Nations Negotiate* (New York: Kraus, 1976), pp. 3–4; Edwin H. Fedder, "Communication and American-Soviet Negotiating Behavior," *Background* (August 1964), p. 106; and William I. Zartman, "The Political Analysis of Negotiation: How Who Gets What and When," *World Politics* (April 1974), p. 388.

Chapter 7. The Conclusion of the Japan-China Peace Treaty (1978)

1. Dagmar Ahrens-Thiele, "Moscow's Opposition to Chinese-Japanese Peace Talks," *Radio Liberty Research Bulletin*, No. 48178 (March 1, 1978), pp. 1–10.

2. For the full text of the treaty, see Chae-Jin Lee, "The Making of the Sino-Japanese Peace and Friendship Treaty," *Pacific Affairs*, Vol. 52, No. 3 (Fall 1979), pp. 443–445.

3. Stephan, "Asia in the Soviet Conception," p. 47.

4. For example, Mazurov, *op. cit.*, pp. 145–147.

5. Hong N. Kim, "The Fukuda Government and the Politics of the Sino-Japanese Peace Treaty," *Asian Survey*, Vol. 19, No. 3 (1979), p. 310.

6. *Asahi Shimbun*, February 22, 1978.

7. *Asahi Shimbun*, August 8, 1978.

8. One example is Tokyo's policy toward Beijing and Taipei. U.S. Secretary of State John F. Dulles threatened Japanese Prime Minister Shigeru Yoshida that the U.S. Senate would not ratify the San Francisco Peace Treaty ending the American occupation of Japan unless the Japanese government agreed in advance that Japan would deal with Taipei rather than Beijing. Yielding to this pressure, the Japanese government signed a treaty of peace with Taipei rather than Beijing. Since that time the Japanese feared, however, that they would wake up one morning to find that the United States had changed its policy toward Beijing, leaving the Japanese out on a

limb. Morton H. Halpern, "America and Asia: The Impact of Nixon's China Policy," in Roderick F. MacFarquhar, ed., *Sino-American Relations, 1949–71* (New York: Praeger, 1972), p. 11.

9. Zbigniew Brzezinski, *Power and Principle: Memoirs of the National Security Advisor, 1977–1981* (New York: Farrar, Straus, Giroux, 1983), p. 218.

10. *Asahi Shimbun*, September 20, 1978.

11. Ibid.

12. Ibid.

13. *Baltimore Sun*, September 25, 1978.

14. *FBIS-SOV*, August 28, 1978, p. M1.

15. *FBIS-SOV*, May 31, 1979, p. C1 and June 22, 1979, pp. C1–2; *Mainichi Shimbun*, February 4, 1975; Mazurov, *op. cit.*, p. 151.

16. *Yomiuri Shimbun*, October 26, 1978.

17. Kim, *op. cit.*, p. 297.

18. Ibid.; A. Doak Barnett, *China and the Major Powers in East Asia* (Washington, DC: Brookings Institution, 1977), pp. 117–121.

19. I. Chikunov, "SSSR-Iaponiia: Strannye tolkovaniia," *Novoe vremia*, No. 8 (1978), p. 8.

20. Kim, *op. cit.*, p. 298.

21. *Mainichi Shimbun*, February 4, 1975.

22. *Asahi Shimbun*, February 14, 1975; *International Herald Tribune*, February 11, 1975.

23. *Asahi Shimbun*, February 14, 1975.

24. Ibid.

25. Andrei A. Gromyko, "Programma mira v deistvii," *Kommunist*, No. 14 (September 1975), p. 16.

26. *Asahi Shimbun* (evening edition), January 13, 1976.

27. *Asahi Shimbun*, January 14, 1976.

28. Joachim Glaubitz, "Anti-Hegemony Formulas in Chinese Foreign Policy," *Asian Survey*, Vol. 16, No. 3 (March 1976), p. 211.

29. *Izvestiia*, July 18 and 19, 1976.

30. *Krasnaia zvezda*, July 21, 1976.

31. *Pravda*, November 26, 1976.

32. *Asahi Shimbun*, May 30, 1978. For an English account, see *FBIS-SOV*, June 7, 1978, pp. 3–4.

33. *Asahi Shimbun*, May 30, 1978; *FBIS-SOV*, June 7, 1978, p. 3.

34. *Asahi Shimbun*, May 30, 1978; *FBIS-SOV*, June 7, 1978, p. 3.

35. *Asahi Shimbun* (evening edition), June 19, 1978; *UPI*, June 19, 1978; see also *Asahi Shimbun*, June 20, 1978.

36. *Izvestiia*, June 24, 1978.

37. *Asahi Shimbun*, June 23, 1978.

38. *New York Times*, July 8, 1978.

39. *Christian Science Monitor*, August 15, 1978.

40. *Christian Science Monitor*, August 10, 1978.

41. For a detailed definition and usages of the term "coercive diplomacy," see the monumental work by Alexander George, "The Development of Doctrine and Strategy," in A.L. George, David K. Hall, and William E. Simons, *The Limits of Coercive Diplomacy: Laos, Cuba, Vietnam* (Boston: Little, Brown, 1971), pp. 1–34, particularly pp. 18–19.

42. *Pravda*, October 10, 1973.

43. *Pravda*, October 11, 1978.

44. *Tanaka Sōri wa Kataru: Nisso-shunō kaidan ni tsuite* (Prime Minister Tanaka Speaks on the Summit Meeting) (Tokyo: Hoppōryōdo Mondai Taisaku Kyōkai, 1974), p. 16.

45. See Schwartz, *op. cit.*, pp. 108–110; *Khrushchev Remembers: The Last Testament*, trans. and ed. Strobe Talbott (London: Andre Deustch, 1974), p. 487.

46. Dolgorukov, "Torgovo-ekonomicheskie otnosheniia SSSR s Iaponiei," pp. 120–121.

47. Gromyko, "Programma mira v deistvii," p. 16.

48. *XXV s"ezd KPSS* (23 fevralia–3 marta 1981 goda), Vol. 1, p. 45.

49. *Pravda*, June 7, 1977.

50. *Pravda*, February 24, 1978.

51. In making this summary I am indebted to the article by Hayao Shimizu, "Zenrinkyōryoku-jōyaku," *Sankei Shimbun*, March 21, 1978.

52. *Baltimore Sun*, September 25, 1978.

53. Haruo Okada, "Sonichi zenrin kyōryoku jōyaku no nerai wa nanika? (What Are Soviet Intentions Behind the Proposed Treaty of Good-Neighborliness and Cooperation Between the USSR and Japan?)," *Chūō Kōron* (May 1978), p. 130.

54. AFP, January 10, 1978.

55. Peggy L. Falkenheim, "The Impact of the Peace and Friendship Treaty on Soviet-Japanese Relations," *Asian Survey*, Vol. 19, No. 12 (December 1979), p. 1210.

56. Reuter, January 17, 1978.

57. Daniel Tretiak, "The Sino-Japanese Treaty of 1978: The Senkaku Incident Prelude," *Asian Survey*, No. 12 (1978), p. 1237.

58. Mira Sinha, "The Sino-Japanese Peace Treaty: Moscow Loses Round One to Peking," *China Report*, Vol. 14, No. 4 (July–August 1978), p. 5.

59. Nora Beloff, "Escape From Freedom: A Defector's Story," *Atlantic Monthly* (November 1980), p. 45. In two interviews with the author of this book in London, on October 25 and November 2, 1984, Orionova confirmed this episode.

60. *Christian Science Monitor*, September 15, 1978.

61. Leites, *The Study of Bolshevism*, p. 498.

62. Malcolm Mackintosh, "Soviet Interests and Policies in the Asian-Pacific Region," *Orbis*, Vol. 19, No. 3 (Fall 1975), p. 765.

63. Hayter, *The Diplomacy of the Great Powers*, pp. 29–30.

64. Robert Rand, "Tokyo and Moscow: Still in Search on Accommodation," *Radio Liberty Research Bulletin*, No. 210/78 (September 28, 1978), p. 1.

65. Avigdor Haselkorn, "Impact of the Sino-Japanese Treaty on the Soviet Security Strategy," *Asian Survey*, Vol. 19, No. 6 (June 1979), pp. 564–565.

66. Falkenheim, "The Impact of the Peace and Friendship Treaty on Soviet-Japanese Relations," pp. 1215–1222.

67. Kuniko Miyauchi et al., "Shumireishon Nippon Gaikō" (Similations of Japanese Foreign Policy), *Shokun!* (April 1978), p. 47.

68. TASS, August 24, 1978.

69. *Izvestiia*, August 13, 1978.

70. *Izvestiia*, August 15, 1978.

71. G. Krasin, "Iaponiia-KNR: V farvatere gegemonizm," *Novoe vremia*, No. 34 (August 18, 1978), p. 8.

72. Robert Rand, "Official Soviet Protest Against the Signing of the Sino-Japanese Treaty," *Radio Liberty Research Bulletin*, August 24, 1978, p. 1.

73. For more on pressure brought to bear by the U.S. side upon Tokyo to conclude the Sino-Japanese peace treaty, see Krasin, *op. cit.*, p. 8; Mazurov, *op. cit.*, p. 105.

74. Krasin, "Iaponiia-KNR," p. 9.

75. Mazurov, *op. cit.*, p. 147.

76. Ibid.

77. *Izvestiia*, January 30, 1979; Mikhail G. Nosov, "Vliianie normalizatsii amerikano-kitaiskikh otnoshenii na politiku Iaponii," in *Iaponiia 1980: Ezhegodnik* (Moscow: Nauka, 1982), p. 154; I.I. Ivkov, "SShA: 'Kitaiskaia karta' v Azii," *PDV*, No. 1 [29] (1979), p. 86; Mazurov, *op. cit.*, p. 147.

78. *Pravda*, August 25, 1978.

79. Brzezinski, *op. cit.*, p. 218.

80. *Pravda*, August 25, 1978.

81. Ibid.

82. *Izvestiia*, August 25, 1978. This was the authoritative Soviet interpretation. See also Kapitsa, "Bor'ba SSSR za mir i sotrudnichestvo v Azii," p. 44.

83. Petrov, *Iaponiia nashikh dnei* p. 50.

84. Petrov, "Politika Iaponii v Azii," p. 121.

85. Ibid.

86. Ibid.

87. Nosov, *op. cit.*, p. 154.

88. Ibid. For a different Soviet view, see Markov, *op. cit.*, p. 217.

89. Petrov, "Politika Iaponii v Azii," p. 121.

90. Petrov, *Iaponiia nashikh dnei*, p. 52.

91. Petrov, *Iaponiia v mirovoi politike*, pp. 263–269.

92. Petrov, *Iaponiia nashikh dnei*, p. 53; Markov, *op. cit.*, pp. 205–214. See also Mazurov, *SShA-Kitai-Iaponiia*, p. 192.

93. *Pravda*, August 13, 1978. A similar statement appeared in *Novoe vremia*, dated August 18, 1978. See also Krasin, "Iaponiia-KNP," p. 9. See also Petrov, *Iaponiia nashikh dnei*, p. 9.

94. *Izvestiia*, August 25, 1978. For exactly the same argument, see *Trud*, September 13, 1978.

95. *Izvestiia*, August 25, 1978.

96. *Pravda*, August 13, 1978.

97. "Moscow Attacks Deng's Visit, Urges Closer Japan-USSR Ties," *FBIS: Trends in Communist Media* (November 1, 1978), p. 4.

98. G.V. Melikhov, "Politika KNR v Azii," in Petrov, ed., *Mezhdunarodnye otnosheniia v aziatsko-tikhookeanskom regione*, p. 142.

99. TASS, August 16, 1978.

100. Ibid.

101. Quoted from *FBIS-SOV*, September 13, 1978, p. M5.

102. *Sovetskaia Rossiia*, October 31, 1978.

103. *Pravda* and *Izvestiia*, September 9, 1978.

104. *Krasnaia zvezda*, September 18, 1978.

105. *Izvestiia*, May 21, 1979.

106. *Pravda*, February 9, 1979.

107. Ibid.

108. *FBIS-SOV*, February 22, 1979, p. M1.
109. *FBIS-SOV*, April 11, 1979, p. C1.
110. Ibid.
111. *Iaponia 1980: Izhegodnik*, p. 163.
112. Ibid.
113. *FBIS-SOV*, March 6, 1979, p. M1.
114. *FBIS-SOV*, April 6, 1979, p. C1.
115. Ibid.
116. *Izvestiia*, April 8, 1979; *Pravda*, April 13, 1979.
117. Ibid.
118. *Asahi Shimbun*, August 14, 1978.
119. For example, see *Pravda* and *Izvestiia*, August 25, 1978; Stanislav Levchenko, "Iaponiia: Na krutom povorote," *Novoe vremia*, No. 35 (1978), p. 15.
120. *FBIS-SOV*, August 28, 1978, p. M1.
121. *FIBS-SOV*, October 31, 1978, p. C1.
122. *FBIS-SOV*, June 22, 1979, p. C1.
123. *FBIS-SOV*, June 17, 1977, p. M1.
124. Nagao Hyōdō, *Saikin no nisso-kankei to hoppōryōdo mondai* (Recent Japan-Soviet Relations and the Territorial Question) (Tokyo: Minshu-gaikō Kyōkai, 1979), p. 11.
125. *Asahi Shimbun* (evening edition), September 25, 1978.
126. *Asahi Shimbun* (evening edition), September 9, 1978.
127. *Asahi Shimbun*, October 14, 1978.
128. Hyōdō, *op. cit.*, p. 7.
129. *Nihon Keizai Shimbun*, February 28, 1979.
130. *Asahi Shimbun*, September 18, 1979; "Siberia: Russian Hopes, Japanese Doubts," *The Economist* (London), Vol. 272, No. 7099 (September 24, 1979), p. 86.
131. *Asahi Shimbun*, September 7, 1978.
132. Peter Berton, "The Japanese Communists' Rapprochement with the Soviet Union," *Asian Survey* Vol. 20, No. 12 (December 1979), pp. 1210–1222.
133. *Yomiuri Shimbun*, October 7, 1978.
134. *Asahi Shimbun*, May 15, 1979.
135. *Asahi Shimbun*, May 20, 1979.
136. Hyōdroō, *op. cit.*, p. 10.
137. Reuter, June 6, 1978; *Washington Post, International Herald Tribune, Guardian*, 8une 8, 1978.
138. For example, *Pravda*, September 28, 1979; *Izvestiia*, September 29, 1979.
139. Dmitriev, *op. cit.*, p. 95; *Izvestiia*, November 23, 1980.
140. For example, *Izvestiia*, February 9, 1979.
141. *Izvestiia*, November 4, 1979.
142. *Izvestiia*, February 9, 1979.
143. Dmitriev, *op. cit.*, p. 96.
144. *Izvestiia*, November 23, 1979.
145. *Izvestiia*, February 9, 1979.
146. Reuter, June 6, 1978; *Wall Street Journal*, June 8, 1978; *International Herald Tribune*, June 8, 1978 and January 31, 1979; *Washington Post*, June 8, 1978.
147. Robert E. Bedeski, *The Fragile Entente: The 1978 Japan-China Peace Treaty in a Global Context* (Boulder, CO: Westview, 1983), p. 142.
148. Ibid., p. 161.

149. Ibid.
150. *FBIS-SOV*, October 4, 1979, p. C1.
151. *Pravda*, September 28, 1979.

Chapter 8. The Soviets Propose Substitute Treaties

1. Jonathan Alford, ed., *The Future of Arms Control. Part III: Confidence-Building Measures* (Adelphi Papers No. 149) (London: International Institute for Strategic Studies, 1979), p. 1.
2. *Conference on Security and Cooperation in Europe: Final Act* (London: The Majesty's Stationery Office, 1975), pp. 9–11; Coit D. Blacker and Gloria Duffy, eds., *International Arms Control: Issues and Agreements* (second edition) (Stanford, CA: Stanford University Press, 1984), pp. 441–445.
3. Kalevi Ruhala, *Confidence-Building Measures—Options for the Future* (Hamburg: Institut für Fiedemsforsc/chung und Sicherheitspolitik an der Universität Hamburg—Forschungsberichte Heft, August 18, 1980), p. 47.
4. *Confidence-Building Measures: Report of the Secretary General* (A/34/416) (New York: United Nations, 1982, p. 3; *Comprehensive Study on Confidence-Building Measures—Report of the Secretary General* (A/36/474) (New York: United Nations, 1982), p. 2.
5. Ruhala, *op. cit.*, pp. 47–49; Alford, *op. cit.*, p. 1.
6. *Confidence-Building Measures*, p. 29.
7. The general position of the Soviet Union on this subject is as follows: "The experience on the European continent in implementing confidence-building measures could be used in regional considerations of the question of reaching agreement on such measures, taking into account, of course, the specific conditions and requirements of each region" *Confidence-Building Measures*, p. 55.
8. For a similar argument, see Adam Ulam, *Expansion and Coexistence* (New York: Praeger, 1968), pp. 189–189.
9. Mikhail S. Kapitsa, then head of the First Far Eastern Division of the Soviet Foreign Ministry and later deputy foreign minister under Iurii Andropov, stated publicly that the Soviet Union should follow the model of the European collective security system in its appeal for a collective security scheme in Asia: "The successful completion of the European Conference on Security and Cooperation and the experience of strengthening security in Europe underscore the possibility and necessity of additional measures in which all the states of the continent would join with the aim of strengthening peace and security in Asia and ensuring friendly international cooperation in that area. There is, certainly, no question of copying or automatically transferring the European collective security system to Asia. The situation in Asia is different from and more complex than that in Europe. At the same time, there is no doubt that the peoples of Asia, which is one of the cradles of human civilization, will be able to find correct answers to the vital problems facing them, problems crucial not only for the present but for the future" Kapitsa, "Bor'ba SSSR za mir i sotrudnichestvo v Azii," pp. 52–53; for an English translation, see "The USSR's Struggle for Peace and Cooperation in Asia," *Far Eastern Affairs*, No. 2 [1979], pp. 49–50).
10. For the Soviet draft of the treaty, see *Pravda*, February 24, 1978.

11. *Vo imia mira, bezopasnosti i sotrudnichestva* (Moscow: Politizdat, 1975), p. 8.

12. *Pravda*, August 7, 1975.

13. Quoted from Golam W. Choudhury, *Brezhnev's Collective Security Plan for Asia* (Washington, DC: Center for Strategic & International Studies, 1976), p. 1.

14. Berezin, *op. cit.*, p. 112.

15. N. Nikolaev, "Zigzagi politiki Tokio," p. 46.

16. *Gunshuku-mondai to Nippon* (Arms Control Question and Japan) (Tokyo: Information and Culture Bureau, Japanese Ministry of Foreign Affairs, 1982), p. 29.

17. Ibid.; Toshiaki Mutō, "Saikin-no nisso-kankei to tai oushū, taiyōshū gaikō (Recent Japanese-Soviet Relations and Japan's Policy Toward Europe and the Pacific," in *Saikin no kokusaijōsei* (Recent International Situations) (Tokyo: Information and Culture Bureau, Japanese Ministry of Foreign Affairs, 1981), p.49. For a similar remark by a high-ranking Japanese Foreign Ministry official, see Yoshio Ōkawara, the former Japanese ambassador to the U.N. Disarmament Committee at Geneva—see *Asahi Shimbun*, January 8, 1983.

18. *Confidence-Building Measures*, p. 55.

19. Richard Haass, "Confidence-Building Measures and Naval Arms Control," in Alford, *op. cit.*, p. 24.

20. Mutō, *op. cit.*, p. 49.

21. Haass, *op. cit.*, p. 24.

22. Text in *World Armament and Disarmament: SIPRI Yearbook 1973* (Stockholm: Almqvist & Wikseel, Humanities Press, Paul Elek, 1973), pp. 36–39.

23. Luigi Vittorio Ferraris, ed., *Report on a Negotiation: Helsinki–Geneva–Helsinki 1972–1975* (Geneva: Institut Universitaire de Hautes Etudes Internationales, 1979), p. 183.

24. Johan Jørgen Holsti and Karen Alette Melander, "European Security and Confidence-Building Measures," *Survival*, Vol. 79, No. 4, (July/August 1977), p. 149.

25. Holsti and Melander, "European Security and Confidence-Building Measures," pp. 152–154; Alford, *The Future of Arms Control*, pp. 1, 5; Ruhala, *op. cit*, pp. 52–73.

26. Alford, *op. cit.*, p. 5.

27. *XXVI s"ezd KPSS* (23 feuralia–3 marta 1981 goda), Vol. 1, p. 46.

28. Timofei B. Guzhenko, "Sovetsko-Iaponskie otnosheniia," *PDV*, No. 3 [43] (1982), p. 18; Kuznetsov, "Kuda tolkaiut Iaponiiu," p. 108.

29. Guzhenko, *op. cit.*, p. 18; Kuznetsov, *op. cit.*, p. 108.

30. *Defense of Japan: 1982* (Tokyo: Defense Agency, 1982), pp. 34–35.

31. G.D. Loescher, "Human Rights and the Helsinki-Belgrade Process," in *The Year Book of World Affairs 1981* (London: London Institute of World Affairs, 1981), p. 62.

32. M. L'vov, "Obshcheevropeiskoi soveshchanie: Opyt i znachenie," *MZ*, No. 3 (1976), p. 47.

33. William I. Bacchus, "Multilateral Foreign Policy Making: The Conference on Security and Cooperation in Europe," in David A. Caputo, ed., *The Politics of Policy Making in America: Five Case Studies* (San Francisco: W.H. Freeman, 1977), p. 136.

34. Mutō, *op. cit.*, p. 48.

35. Strictly speaking, the Helsinki Final Act was nothing but a confirmation by the West of what had been already recognized by the Federal Republic of Germany in its treaties with the USSR and Poland concerning normalization of borders. For more details, see Harold S. Russell, "The Helsinki Declaration: Brobdingnag or Lilliput?" *American Journal of International Law*, Vol. 70, No.

2 (April 1976), pp. 249–253.

36. Coit D. Blacker, and Gloria Duffy, eds., *International Arms Control: Issues and Agreements* (2d ed.) (Stanford, CA: Stanford University Press, 1984), p. 442.

37. *New York Times*, July 5–7, 1968, quoted by Stephan, in "The Kuril Islands: Japan versus Russia," pp. 327–328.

38. John J. Stephan, "Asia in the Soviet Conception," p. 42.

39. Swearingen, *op. cit.*, p. 287.

40. *Nihon Keizai Shimbun*, March 27, 1982. Mutō has made exactly the same kind of argument. See Mutō, *op. cit.*, p. 49. An editorial in *Mainichi Shimbun* on March 26, 1982 also expressed a strikingly similar view to that of Prime Minister Suzuki: "It is a fact that one must doubt that the Soviet proposal [calling for an agreement with Japan on CBMs] lacks concrete deeds underlining their seriousness. . . . The proposal to talk on CBMs cannot in itself be said to be meaningless. The point is, however, why is there not much confidence [between the Soviets and the Japanese]. . . . We have repeatedly written that the largest problem which has prevented us from building confident relations [between Japan and the USSR] is the Northern Territories issue. . . . The invasion of Afghanistan has strengthened distrust of the Soviet Union" (*Mainichi Shimbun*, March 26, 1982).

41. *Asian Security 1982* (Tokyo: Research Institute for Peace and Security, 1980), p. 172.

42. *The Economist*, November 6, 1982, p. 17.

43. For instance, Reinhard Drifte, "Disarmament and Arms Control in Japanese Politics," unpublished paper, September 1981, pp. 25–26, 29–30; *Asahi Shimbun*, January 8, 1983; Takeshi Igarashi, "Nisso-kankei o dakaisuru michi (The Way to Break the Deadlock in Japanese-Soviet Relations)," *Sekai*, No. 8 (August 1982), p. 100. A majority of the Japanese participants in the first session of the third Japanese-USSR roundtable, held in Tokyo on April 20–22, 1982, seemed to take a positive attitude toward CBMs, judging from the final summary of that subcommittee, which states: "The subcommittee recognized that there is a need to establish a security system in Asia, and the Soviet proposal on CBMs is worth discussing. . . ." *Jiyū*, No. 7 (July 1982), p. 49. However, the important point to be remembered is that the Soviets regarded only the *official* position of the Japanese government as relevant.

44. *Comprehensive Study on Confidence-Building Measures*, p. 4.

45. Ibid., p. 3; *Confidence-Building Measures*, p. 26.

46. *Confidence-Building Measures*, p. 12.

47. Ibid., p. 31; Ruhala, *op. cit.*, p. 49.

48. *Comprehensive Study on Confidence-Building Measures*, p. 4; *Confidence-Building Measures*, p. 20.

49. Ruhala, *op. cit*, p. 4.

50. Igarashi, *op. cit.*, p. 100.

51. V. Dal'nev, *Nisso-kankei dakai no michi—Soren wa dō Kangaeru ka* (The Way to Make a Breakthrough in Japanese-Soviet Relations: What Are the Thoughts of the Soviet Union?) (Tokyo: Asia-shobō 1981), p. 88.

52. *Yomiuri Shimbun*, January 3, 1983.

53. *Nihon Keizai Shimbun*, December 9, 1982.

54. Ibid.

55. Ibid.

56. *Report on Comprehensive National Security* (English Translation) (To-

kyo: The Comprehensive National Security Study Group, June 2, 1980), pp. 9, 42. This concept is believed to have been borrowed from Glenn H. Snyder's article, "Deterrence by Denial and Punishment," in Bobrow, ed., *op. cit.*, pp. 209–210, 209–237.

57. *Report on Comprehensive National Security*, p. 42; *Defense of Japan: 1982*, p. 81.

58. For a Soviet account of the shift in emphasis to intensive development of Western Siberia, see, for instance, B.P. Orlov, "Razvitie ekonomiki Sibiri na otdel'nykh etapakh sotsialisticheskogo stroitel'stva," *Izvestiia sibirskogo otdeleniia Akademii Nauk SSSR* (seriia Obshchestvennykh nauk), No. 11, vypusk 3, 1982, pp. 68–69.

59. Believing that "in a potential form a negotiating power is most effective," Professor Yōnosuke Nagai at the Tokyo University of Technology argued that Japan's bargaining power with the Soviet Union has such potentialities. See Yōnosuke Nagai, "Moratoriamu-kokka no boei-ron (The Defense Theory of the Moratorium State)," *Chūō Kōron*, (January 1981), pp. 104–105.

60. Charles Gati, "History, Social Science, and the Study of Soviet Foreign Policy," in Hoffmann and Fleron, eds., *op. cit.*, p. 8.

61. In most cases, when the Soviets spoke of a peace treaty with Japan, they had in mind a peace treaty that excluded the territorial issue, which, in their view, had been resolved. In general, however, even in Soviet understanding, a peace treaty also would have to deal with the territorial question, as admitted by Brezhnev in his interview given to Mr. Shōryū Hata, editor-in-chief of *Asahi Shimbun* on June 5, 1977, when he stated: "Any peace treaty naturally includes . . . questions dealing with broad matters, including border issues" (*Pravda*, June 7, 1977).

62. Dal'nev, *op. cit.*, p. 61.

63. Ibid.; Nikolaev, "Dobrososedstvo i sotrudnichestvo," p. 52; Modenov, "Tokio v farvatere politiki Vashingtona," p. 71; *Pravda*, April 14, 1982; Kuznetsov, *op. cit.*, p. 108.

64. Dal'nev, *op. cit.*, p. 52.

65. Nikolaev, *op. cit.*, p. 52.

66. Dal'nev, *Nisso-kankei dakai no michi*, p. 68.

67. *Sankei Shimbun*, January 3, 1981.

68. *Pravda*, June 8, 1969.

69. Victor Zorza, "Collective Security," *Survival*, Vol. 11, No. 8 (August 1969), p. 248; Peter Howard, "A System of Collective Security," *Mizan*, Vol. 11, No. 4 (July/August 1969), pp. 199–201, 203; Hemem Ray, "Soviet Diplomacy in Asia," *Problems of Communism*, Vol. 19 (March/April 1970), p. 46; Ian Clark, "Collective Security in Asia," *The Round Table*, No. 252 (October 1973), pp. 477–478; Alexander O. Ghebhardt, "The Soviet System of Collective Security in Asia," *Asian Survey*, Vol. 13, No. 12 (December 1973), p. 1076; Arnold L. Horelick, "The Soviet Union's Asian Collective Security Proposal: A Club in Search of Members," *Pacific Affairs*, Vol. 47, No. 3 (Fall 1974), p. 269; Howard M. Hensel, "Asian Collective Security: The Soviet View," *Orbis*, Vol. 19, No. 4 (Winter 1976), pp. 1564, 1579; Alfred Biegel, "Moscow's Concept for Collective Security in Asia," *Military Review*, Vol. 57, No. 2 (February 1977), pp. 3, 7, 11.

70. *Pravda*, March 21, 1972.

71. Ghebhardt, *op. cit.*, p. 1084.

72. For instance, Nobuhiko Ushiba, Japanese ambassador to the United States, was

quoted as saying that "the Soviet proposal aims at encircling China, and it will not be easily accepted by the United States." *Asahi Shimbun* (evening edition) and *Mainichi Shimbun* (evening edition), May 23, 1972.

73. Ghebhart, *op. cit.*, p. 1579; Horelick, *op. cit*, p. 282; Biegel, *op. cit.*, p. 10.

74. Horelick, *op. cit.*, p. 274; Horelick, "Soviet Policy Dilemma in Asia," *Asian Survey*, Vol. 17, No. 6 (June 1977), p. 511.

75. *Pravda*, September 19, 1977.

76. *Izvestiia*, February 23, 1978; *Pravda*, February 24, 1978.

77. *Izvestiia*, June 25, 1978.

78. Of course, verbally, the Soviets were also saying that "the Soviet Union is making an effort toward the development of *all-round* [*vsestoronnye*], mutually-beneficial relations with Japan" (emphasis added by H.K.). (Gromyko, "Programma mira v deistvii," p. 16).

79. Swearingen, *op. cit.*, p. 225; Stephan, *The Kuril Islands*, p. 247; Jōhō-bunka-kyoku, Gaimushō, *Warera-no Hoppōryōdo* (Our Northern Territories) (Tokyo: Gaimushō, March 1981), p. 46.

80. *Pravda*, October 10, 1973.

81. *Pravda* and *Izvestiia*, February 17, 1982.

82. Swearingen, *op. cit.*, p. 89.

83. Drifte, *op. cit.*, p. 25.

84. *Nihon Keizai Shimbun*, December 9, 1982.

85. For an argument that almost all disarmament proposals and negotiations have propagandistic elements as an integral feature, see Joseph L. Nogee, "Propaganda and Negotiation: The Case of the Ten-Nation Disarmament Committee," *Journal of Conflict Resolution*, Vol. 7, No. 3 (September 1963), pp. 510–511; John W. Spanier and Joseph L. Nogee, *The Politics of Disarmament: A Study in Soviet-American Gamesmanship* (New York: Praeger, 1962), pp. 32–36.

86. *XXVI s"ezd KPSS* (23 fevralia–3 marta 1981 goda), Vol 1, p. 46.

87. *Pravda* and *Izvestiia*, April 23, 1981.

88. *XXVI s"ezd KPSS* (23 fevralia–3 marta 1981 goda), Vol. 1, p. 46.

89. *Sovetskaia programma mira dlia 80–kh godov v deistvii: Materialy i dokumenty* (Moscow: Politizdat, 1982), p. 108.

90. *Pravda*, March 25, 1982.

91. V.V. Ovchinnikov, "Sonichi-kyōryoku wa kyokutō-niokeru heiwa-notameni" (Soviet-Japanese Cooperation for Peace in the Far East, *Jiyū*), No. 279 (July 1982), p. 59.

92. *Izvestiia*, March 1, 1982; *Pravda*, March 2, 1982; Kuznetsov, *op. cit.*, p. 108. See also N. Nikolaev and A. Pavlov, *op. cit.*, p. 33.

93. *Pravda*, November 23, 1982.

94. For the Soviet message conveyed by Polianskii to Itō, see *FBIS-SOV*, March 17, 1981, p. C1.

95. *Nihon Keizai Shimbun*, March 27, 1982.

96. John Garnett, "Disarmament and Arms Control Since 1945," in Laurence Martin, ed., *Strategic Thought in the Nuclear Age* (Baltimore, MD: John Hopkins University Press, 1979), p. 216.

97. Ibid.

98. *Pravda*, June 7, 1977.

Part Four. A Changing Global Environment

1. *XXVI s" ezd KNCC* (*23 fevralia–3 marta 1981 goda*), Vol. 1, p. 42.
2. Iurii Kuznetsov, op. cit., p. 106.
3. Nikolaev and Pavlov, op. cit., p. 33.
4. Ibid., pp. 32–33.
5. Ibid., p. 33.
6. Ibid., p. 34.
7. Ibid., p. 38.
8. Iurii Kuznetsov, op. cit., p. 106.
9. Donald C. Hellmann, "The Impact of Sino-Soviet Dispute on Noretheast Asia," in Herbert J. Ellison, ed., *The Sino-Soviet Conflict: A Global Perspective* (Seattle: University of Washington Press, 1982), p. 180.

Chapter 9. The Impact of the Soviet Invasion of Afghanistan (1979)

1. *Asahi Shimbun, Asahi Evening News,* and *Japan Times,* January 6, 1980.
2. Ibid.
3. Professor Kei Wakaizumi similarly, but from a slightly different viewpoint, discerned two trends of thinking in postwar Japan, namely, "the conservative" or "the realist," and "the reformist" or "the idealist." See Kei Wakaisumi, "Japan's Dilemma: To Act or Not to Act," *Foreign Policy,* No. 16 (1974), pp. 30–47.
4. *Asahi Shimbun,* January 5, 1980, and *Japan Times,* January 6, 1980.
5. *Japan Times; Sankei Shimbun* and *Asahi Shimbun,* January 6, 1980; and *Sankei Shimbun,* January 8, 1980.
6. *Asahi Shimbun* and *Japan Times,* January 6, 1980.
7. *Asahi Shimbun, Yomiuri Shimbun,* and *Nihon Keizai Shimbun,* January 8, 1980.
8. *Asahi Shimbun,* January 9, 1980.
9. Ibid.
10. *Asahi Shimbun* and *Nihon Keizai Shimbun,* January 12, 1980.
11. *Yomiuri Shimbun,* January 9, 1980.
12. *Asahi Shimbun,* January 12, 1980.
13. *Asahi Shimbun* (evening edition), January 16, 1980.
14. *Yomiuri Shimbun,* January 19, 1980.
15. Ōhira's visit to these Pacific Ocean countries was bitterly criticized by the Soviets. See, for example, *FBIS-SOV,* January 21, 1980, p. C1.
16. *Asahi Shimbun* (evening edition), January 23, 1980.
17. *Asahi Shimbun* (evening edition), January 25, 1980.
18. Ibid.
19. *Hokkaido Shimbun, Asahi Shimbun,* and *Japan Times,* February 1, 1980.
20. Ibid.
21. *Asahi Shimbun* (evening edition), February 5, 1980.
22. Ibid.
23. *Sankei Shimbun,* February 5, 1980.
24. Ibid.
25. *Asahi Shimbun* and *Sankei Shimbun,* February 2, 1980.
26. *Asahi Shimbun,* February 8, 1980.
27. *Nihon Keizai Shimbun,* February 8, 1980.
28. *Sankei Shimbun,* February 10, 1980.

29. *Asahi Shimbun* (evening edition), February 19, 1980, and *Yomiuri Shimbun*, February 20, 1980.

30. Members of *Seisaku-kōsō* (Policy-Design) Forum, like Yasusuke Murakami, professor of the University of Tokyo, Chikashi Moriguchi, professor of Kyoto University, and Saizaburo Satō, professor at the University of Tokyo, were advocates for this argument. *Asahi Shimbun*, January 26, 1980.

31. *Asahi Shimbun*, March 13, 1980.

32. *Asahi Evening News*, May 3, 1980.

33. *Asahi Shimbun*, March 7, 1980.

34. Naohiro Amaya, "Chōnin kokka Nippon: Tedai no kurigoto," *Bungei Shunjū*, March 1980, pp. 232–234; Amaya, "Nichibei-jidōsha-mondai to chōnin kokka," *Bungei Shunjū*, June 1980, pp. 94–112.

35. *Sankei Shimbun*, March 11, 1980.

36. *Mainichi Shimbun*, May 14, 1980.

37. *Nihon Keizai Shimbun*, May 23, 1980.

38. Ibid.

39. Masamori Sase, "'Chōnin kokka'ron o haisu," *Bungei Shunjū*, April 1980, pp. 222–235.

40. *Asahi Shimbun*, *Hokkaido Shimbun*, and *Sankei Shimbun*, July 19, 1980.

41. Ibid.

42. *Japan Times*, July 18, 1980; *Asahi Shimbun*, August 1, 1980 and August 8, 1980.

43. *Hokkaido Shimbun* (evening edition), July 21, 1980; *Asahi Shimbun*, *Nihon Keizai Shimbun*, and *Japan Times*, July 22, 1980.

44. Ibid.

45. Ibid.

46. *Sankei Shimbun*, August 2, 1980.

47. See, for example, Malcolm Mackintosh, "Soviet Interests and Policies in the Asian-Pacific Region," *Orbis*, Vol. 19, No. 3 (1975): pp. 763–765; Thomas W. Robinson, "Soviet Policy in Northeast Asia: Determinants, Options and Possible Changes," a paper read at the International Conference on Triangular Relations of Mainland China, the Soviet Union, and North Korea, held at the Asiatic Research Center, Korea University, Seoul, on June 23–25, 1977, pp. 1–4.

48. Petrov, *Iaponiia v mirovoi politike*, p. 42.

49. *Pravda*, January 20, 1980.

50. *FBIS-SOV*, January 30, 1980, p. C1.

51. *Izvestiia*, February 9, 1980.

52. *Izvestiia.*, May 27, 1980.

53. *FBIS-SOV*, May 5, 1980, p. C7.

54. *FBIS-SOV*, May 20, 1980, p. C1.

55. The Soviets were concerned about the Japanese idea of a "Pacific Ocean Community" for quite a long time. In his book *Iaponiia v mirovoi politike* (1973), Dmitrii V. Petrov, a Soviet expert on Japan, mentioned this phrase 17 times.

56. Iurii Bandura, "Tikhookeanskoe soobshchestvo—porozhdenie diplomatii imperializma," *MZ*, No. 5 (1980), pp. 62–64.

57. S.N. Nikonov regarded Ōhira as an initiator of this concept, and Iurii Bandura wrote that "in Japan this concept is connected with the name of Premier Ōhira." S.N. Nikonov "O planakh sozdaniia novoi regional'noi organizastii stran basseina Tikhogo okeana," *PDV*, No. 2 (1980), p. 170; Bandura, *op. cit.*, p. 64.

58. *Japan Times*, January 26, 1979.

59. *Kantaiheiyō rentai kōsō—chūkan hōkoku*—(Interim Report on the Pacific Basin Cooperation Concept) (unpublished), pp. 2, 4.

60. Ibid.

61. *Hokkaido Shimbun*, February 6, 1980.

62. *Nihon Keizai Shimbun*, January 22, 1980.

63. *Izvestiia*, January 17, 1980. Exactly the same comment was made by Bandura in his "Tikhookeanskoe soobshchestvo," p. 63.

64. Ibid.

65. Ibid., p. 70.

66. Osamu Miyoshi, professor of Kyoto Sangyō University noted that in the meeting held in April 1976 in Kyoto, the Soviet delegation mentioned the USSR as a *"Pacific"* power. Osamu Miyoshi, *Soren-teikokushugi no sekai-senryaku* (Kyoto: PHP Kenkyusho, 1980), pp. 267, 299. See also note 22 in Chapter 4. A book entitled *International Relations in the Asia-Pacific Region* was published in the Soviet Union in 1979. D.V. Petrov, ed., *Mezhdunarodnye otnosheniia v aziatsko-tikhookeanskom regione* (Moscow: Nauka, 1979), 280 pp.

67. *Hokkaido Shimbun*, February 6, 1980.

68. *FBIS-SOV*, January 8, 1980, p. C2.

69. Nikonov, *op. cit.*, p. 124.

70. *Izvestiia*, February 24, 1980.

71. *APN News*, February 28, 1980, p. 1.

72. Brezhnev, *Leninskim kursom*, Vol. 2, p. 413.

73. Ibid.

74. *Izvestiia*, January 17, 1980.

75. *Izvestiia*, February 9, 1980.

76. *Krasnaia zvezda*, March 25, 1980.

77. Ibid.; *Krasnaia zvezda*, June 22, 1980; *Izvestiia*, February 9, 1980.

78. According to what the Soviets were saying, the change in the leadership of the Japan Defense Agency from Enji Kubota to Kichizō Hosoda was carried out by Premier Ōhira under conditions of "intensifying pressure from Washington, which is trying to involve Japan more extensively in its strategy in the Far East and in Asia as a whole" (see *FBIS-SOV*, February 6, 1980, p. C2). *Izvestiia* claimed that the tour of Sunao Sonoda, Ōhira's special envoy, to the Middle East, Pakistan, and India in March 1980 also was dictated by the United States. *Izvestiia*, March 19, 1980.

79. *FBIS-SOV*, March 24, 1980, p. C1.

80. *Izvestiia*, May 31, 1980.

81. *FBIS-SOV*, June 9, 1980, p. C1.

82. *Izvestiia*, June 20, 1980.

83. *FBIS-SOV*, June 9, 1980, p. C1.

84. *Izvestiia*, February 16, 1980.

85. *Japan Times*, February 10, 1980.

86. *FBIS-SOV*, March 5, 1980, p. C2.

87. Ibid.

88. *FBIS-SOV*, March 11, 1980, p. C1.

Chapter 10. From Clouded to "Somewhat Crystal": Suzuki to Nakasone

"Somewhat Crystal" was the title of a novel that became a bestseller in Japan in 1980–1981.

1. "Address by Ambassador Mike Mansfield at the International Symposium on Security, Peace, and Survival, Tokyo, December 4, 1981," *Press Release* (Tokyo: Press Office, International Communication Agency, American Embassy, 8–24R), p. 5.

2. *Asahi Shimbun*, *Sankei Shimbun*, and *Hokkaido Shimbun*, July 19, 1980.

3. *Asahi Shimbun* (evening edition), May 2, 1981.

4. *Yomiuri Shimbun* (evening edition), May 9, 1981.

5. *Yomiuri Shimbun*, September 14, 1981.

6. Shūichi Katō, *Zasshu bunka* (Hybrid Culture: A Small Hope for Japan) (Tokyo: Kōdamsha, 1974), pp. 28–64.

7. Hichihei Yamamoto, *"Kūki" no Kenkyū* (The Study of 'Air') (Tokyo: Bungei Shunjū-sha, 1977), p. 16.

8. *Japan Times*, *Sankei Shimbun*, and *Asahi Shimbun*, January 6, 1980; *Sankei Shimbun*, January 8, 1980.

9. Kenneth B. Pyle, *The Japanese Question: Power and Purpose in a New Era* (2nd edition) (Washington, DC: American Enterprise Institute, 1996), p. 87.

10. Gary D. Allinson, *Japan's Postwar History* (Ithaca, NY: Cornell University Press, 1997), p. 156.

11. *Yomiuri Shimbun*, December 11, 1982.

12. *Yomiuri Shimbun*, December 10, 1982.

13. For the meaning of "alliance" according to Nakasone, see *Yomiuri Shimbun*, January 20, 1983.

14. For what Nakasone meant by "unmei kyōdōtai," see *Yomiuri Shimbun*, January 20, 1983; *Christian Science Monitor*, January 31, 1983; Yoshiaki Iizaka, "Nakasone-hushō no Narushisuto-shūjigaku" (Narcissistic rhetoric of Prime Minister Nakasone), *Chūō Kōron* (August 1983), p. 116.

15. For the text in English and in Japanese of the nuclear arms control statement issued on May 29, 1983 in the names of the leaders of seven countries (U.S., Britain, France, West Germany, Italy, Canada, and Japan) at the summit in Williamsburg, see *Washington Post*, May 30, 1983, and *Yomiuri Shimbun* (evening edition), May 30, 1983, respectively.

16. *Washington Post*, June 1, 1983.

17. In this paragraph, I am indebted to the succinct report by Clyde Haberman of the *New York Times* on June 22, 1983. For those who want to know more about the incident, see coverage in Japanese newspapers of the so-called "Levchenko incident," starting on December 1982, and the following books: John Barron, *KGB Today: The Hidden Hand* (New York: Reader's Digest Press, 1983), 489 pp; Shūkan-bunshun, ed., *Refuchenko wa Shōgen-suru* (Levchenko Testifies) (Tokyo: Bungeishujū-sha, 1983) 230 pp ; Masahiro Miyazaki, *Soren-supai no Tekuchi: Refuchenko Jiken no Yomikata* (The Tactics of a Soviet Spy: How to Interpret the Levchenko Incident) (Tokyo: Yamate Shobō, 1983), 254 pp.

18. Hearings Before the Permanent Select Committee on Intelligence, House of Representatives (97th Congress, Second Session) (July 13 and 14, 1982) (Washington, DC: U.S. Government Printing Office, 1982), p. 153. See also Hiroshi Shioya, "Nihon wa Supai-tengoku datta" (Japan was a Paradise for Spies: Interview with Levchenko), *Readers' Digest* (Japanese edition, June–July 1982), pp. 35–45.

19. Shūkan-bunshun, ed., *Refuchenko wa Shōgen-suru*, p. 209.

20. Ibid., p. 62.

21. Japanese Foreign Minister Shintarō Abe, for example, made it clear that the Japanese government would tighten the regulations on the transfer of Japanese advanced technology to the Soviet Union, saying that "one cannot completely deny that

Japan's export of advanced technology may serve to strengthen the Soviet military capability," in his speech made on July 27, 1983 (*Nihon Keizai Shimbun*, July 28, 1983).

22. *Kyodo News*, January 14, 1983.

23. For a discussion of a discrepancy in the views on the defense of sea-lanes of communication between Japan and the United States, see Hiroshi Kimura, "The Naval Buildup of the Soviet Union and the Defense of Sea Lanes of Communication," a paper read at the First Security Conference on Asia and the Pacific, held at Okinawa on May 11–13, 1982, pp. 15–29.

24. *Yomiuri Shimbun* and *Nihon Keizai Shimbun*, September 15, 1982; *Nippon no Bōei* (Defense of Japan) (Tokyo: Defense Agency, 1982), p. 79. Cf. *Defense of Japan 1982* (Tokyo: Japan Times, 1982), p. 69; *Asahi Shimbun*, May 15, 1983.

25. *Washington Post*, January 19, 1983.

26. *Yomiurii Shimbun*, January 20, 1983.

27. *Asahi Shimbun*, May 15, 1983; *Defense of Japan: 1983* (Tokyo: Japan Times, 1983), pp. 75–77.

28. *Washington Post*, January 19, 1983.

29. *Asahi Shimbun*, June 7, 1983.

30. For criticism of Nakasone's remarks, see Hiroshi Momose, "Finrando-gaikō no Imi" (The Meaning of the Finnish Diplomacy), *Sekai* (November 1983), pp. 70–84.

31. The term *Finlandation* means, according to the definition by Walter Laqueur, "that process or state of affairs in which, under the cloak of maintaining friendly relations with the Soviet Union, the sovereignty of a country becomes reduced" (Walter Laqueur, "Europe: The Specter of Finlandization)," *Commentary*, Vol. 64, No. 6 (December 1977), p. 37.

32. *Yomiuri Shimbun*, April 23, 1983.

33. *Yomiuri Shimbun* (evening edition), April 23, 1983.

34. *Nihon Keizai Shimbun* (evening edition), March 18, 1983.

35. For example, see *Yomiuri Shimbun*, January 13, 1983; June 10, 1983; July 2, 1983.

36. *Yomiuri Shimbun*, March 12, 1983.

37. *Asahi Shimbun* and *Hokkaido Shimbun*, February 7, 1983.

38. *Hokkaido Shimbun*, February 8, 1983.

39. *Nihon Keizai Shimbun*, December 7, 1982.

40. Ibid.

41. *Hokkaido Shimbun*, *Nihon Keizai Shimbun*, and *Yomiuri Shimbun*, February 17, 1982. The Japanese ambassador to Moscow, Masuo Takashima, expressed a similar view in an indirect way. See *Nihon Keizai Shimbun*, February 2, 1983.

42. *Yomiuri Shimbun*, February 18, 1983.

43. *Mainichi Shimbun*, February 1, 1983; *Hokkaido Shimbun*, February 14, 1983.

44. *Mainichi Shimbun* (evening edition), February 21, 1983; *Nihon Keizai Shimbun*, March 28, 1983; *Asahi Shimbun*, April 10, 1983.

45. *Hokkaido Shimbun*, June 24, 1983.

Chapter 11. Andropov's Policy: Any Change?

1. *Pravda*, November 23, 1982.

2. Ibid.

3. For two types of data used in all political and historical research, "words" and

"deeds," see Gati, *op. cit.*, pp. 12–15; Dallin, "The Domestic Sources of Soviet Foreign Policy," p. 359.

4. *FBIS-SOV*, November 22, 1982, p. C1.

5. Kobysh, *op. cit.*, p. 9.

6. *Izvestiia*, October 30, 1973. This exceptionally candid Soviet remark was noted by Western Soviet-watchers Professors Schwartz and Stephan. See Schwartz, *op. cit.*, p. 6, and Stephan, "Asia in the Soviet Conception," p. 29.

7. *Izvestiia*, October 30, 1973.

8. Ibid.

9. Kobysh, *op cit.*, p. 9.

10. *Pravda*, November 23, 1982.

11. Kuznetsov, *op. cit.*, p. 25.

12. Konstantin Andreev, Kirill Chereuko, "Vydumka i pravda o 'severnykh territoriiakh,'" *MZ*, No. 3 (1983), pp. 114–115, 117–118.

13. *XXV s˝ezd KPSS (23 fevralia–5 marta 1981 goda)*, Vol. 1, p. 45.

14. *New York Times*, November 7, 1982; *Yomiuri Shimbun*, June 30, 1983. *Asian Security: 1983* (Tokyo: Research Institute for Peace and Security, 1983), p. 92.

15. *Sankei Shimbun*, November 1, 1982; *Asian Security: 1983* (Tokyo: Research Institute for Peace and Security, 1983), p. 91.

16. *New York Times*, November 7, 1982.

17. Referring to the arrival of MiG-23 fighters on Etorofu island, Masaharu Gotōda, Nakasone's Chief Cabinet Secretary, said in a press conference on August 30, 1983: "It is part of the consequent Soviet military buildup on our inherent territory. It is deeply regretful" (*Hokkaido Shimbun, Sankei Shimbun*, and *Japan Times*, August 31, 1983).

18. *Sankei Shimbun*, September 29, 1983, and *Japan Times*, September 30, 1983.

19. *Asahi Shimbun, Yomiuri Shimbun, Sankei Shimbun*, and *Japan Times*, October 16, 1983.

20. *Yomiuri Shimbun* and *Sankei Shimbun*, October 16, 1983.

21. *Yomiuri Shimbun* and *Japan Times*, October 16, 1983.

22. *Japan Times, Yomiuri Shimbun*, and *Sankei Shimbun*, November 16, 1983.

23. *Die Welt*, January 17, 1983; *Mainichi Shimbun* and *Yomiuri Shimbun* (evening edition), January 18, 1983; *Washington Post*, January 18 and 19, 1983; *Times* (London), January 19, 1983; *Christian Science Monitor*, January 21, 1983.

24. *Die Welt*, January 19, 1983; *Mainichi Shimbun* and *Yomiuri Shimbun*, January 19, 1983.

25. *Der Spiegel*, January 24, 1983, p. 84.

26. *Asahi Shimbun*, February 24, 1983.

27. *Asahi Shimbun*, March 13, 1983.

28. *Pravda*, April 3, 1983; *Asahi Shimbun, Yomiuri Shimbun*, and *Hokkaido Shimbun*, April 3, 1983.

29. *Asahi Shimbun*, April 12, 1983.

30. Ibid.

31. *Asahi Shimbun*, March 13, 1983.

32. *Pravda*, August 27, 1983; *Japan Times, Mainichi Daily News*, August 28, 1983; *Asahi Shimbun* (evening edition), *Yomiuri Shimbun* (evening edition), *Sankei Shimbun* (evening edition), *Kyoto Shimbun* (evening edition), and August 27, 1983.

33. *Japan Times*, August 28, 1983.

34. Ibid.

35. Ibid; *Mainichi Daily News*, August 28, 1983.

36. *Sankei Shimbun* and *Japan Times*, October 5, 1983. During a press conference at the Soviet Embassy in Tokyo held on November 18, 1983, Georgii A. Arbatov, head of the Soviet Institute of the USA and Canada, confirmed reports that there were 108– SS 20s in the Soviet Far East (*Japan Times*, November 19, 1983).

37. *Yomiuri Shimbun* (evening edition), October 15, 1983.

38. Ibid. According to confidential information provided by the United States in late November 1983, the Soviet Union had already deployed 117 SS-20s and was preparing to deploy 27 more, bringing the total number of SS-20s deployed in the Far East to 144. *Yomiuri Shimbun* (evening edition), November 26, 1983.

39. *New York Times*, May 8, 1983; *Asahi Shimbun*, May 9 and May 10, 1983.

40. *Sankei Shimbun*, August 30, 1983.

41. Ibid.

42. *Arms Control and Disarmament Agreements: Texts and Histories of Negotiations* (1980 edition) (Washington, DC: United States Arms Control and Disarmament Agency, 1980), pp. 86–87.

43. *Yomiuri Shimbun* and *Japan Times*, April 13, 1983.

44. *Asahi Shimbun*, February 3, 1983.

45. *Kakushin*, No. 152 (April 1983), p. 83.

46. *Mainichi Shimbun*, May 18, 1981.

47. Ibid.

48. For a discussion on this subject, see, for example, *Asian Security: 1981* (Tokyo: Research Institute for Peace and Security, 1981), p. 15.

49. Many books and articles have been written on this incident, including, for example, the following books in English: Alexander Dallin, *Black Box: KAL 007 and the Superpowers* (Berkeley: University of California Press, 1985); Oliver Clubb, *KAL Flight 007: The Hidden Story* (Sag Harbor, NY: Permanent Press, 1985); Michel Brun, translated by Robert Boronno, *Incident at Sakhalin: The True Mission of KAL Flight 007* (New York: Four Walls Eight Windows, 1985); Seymour M. Hersh, *"The Target is Destroyed": What Really Happened to Flight 007 and What America Knew About It* (New York: Random House, 1986); R.W. Johnson, *Shoot-Down: Flight 007 and the American Connection* (New York: Viking Penguin, 1986); David Pearson, *KAL 007: The Cover-Up* (New York: Summit Books, 1987).

50. *Pravda*, September 10, 1983.

51. *Vedomost' Verkhovnogo Soveta SSSR*, No. 48 [2174], 1982, pp. 887–888.

52. *Newsweek*, September 19, 1983, p. 12.

53. Cited in Dallin, *Black Box*, p. 87.

54. *Mainichi Shimbun*, January, 1983.

55. *Asahi Shimbun*, August 15, 1983.

56. *Asahi Shimbun*, *Yomiuri Shimbun*, *Sankei Shimbun*, and *Hokkai Times*, August 22, 1983.

57. For an unofficial English translation of the whole text of the speech, see *Japan Times*, September 11, 1983.

58. For the entire resolution, see, for example, *Yomiuri Shimbun* (evening edition), September 9, 1983.

59. Pearson, *op. cit.*, p. 189; Johnson, *op. cit.*, pp. 127–128.

60. *Yomiuri Shimbun* and *Japan Times*, September 29, 1983.

61. *Asahi Shimbun* (evening edition), *Yomiuri Shimbun* (evening edition), and *Hokkaido Shimbun* (evening edition), October 5, 1983; *Japan Times*, October 6, 1983.

62. *Asahi Shimbun*, August 14, 1983.
63. *Japan Times*, September 10, 1983.
64. *New York Times*, September 4, 1983.
65. *Japan Times*, September 10, 1983; *Asahi Shimbun*, September 27, 1983.
66. *Yomiuri Shimbun*, September 21, 1983.
67. *New York Times*, September 8, 1983; *Time*, September 19, 1983, p. 6.
68. *Pravda*, September 7 and 10, 1983.
69. *Japan Times*, September 22, 1983.

Conclusions

1. Sunao Sonoda revealed more than he intended to at a meeting of the Foreign Relations Committee of the Liberal Democratic Party on January 26, 1978: "Japan's close cooperation with the U.S. is the basic pivot of Japanese foreign policy. In this context, the Japan-China Peace Treaty is not to be regarded as a simple bilateral agreement but rather as a more advanced form of cooperation with the U.S. That is, we consider the Treaty as one facet of the U.S. world strategy." *Asahi Shimbun*, January 26, 1978; *FBIS-SOV*, September 28, 1979, p. C1.

2. Oleg N. Bykov, "Vneshnepoliticheskaia strategiia SShA v aziatsko-titkhookeanskom regione," in D.V. Petrov, ed., *Mehdunarodnye otnosheniia v aziatsko-tikhoukeanskom regione* (Moscow: Nauka, 1979), p. 53.

3. Andrei G. Bochkarev, and Don L. Mansfield, eds., *The United States and the USSR in a Changing World: Soviet and American Perspectives* (Boulder, CO: Westview, 1992), p. 42.

4. Derek da Cunha, *Soviet Naval Power in the Pacific* (Boulder, CO: Lynne Rienner, 1990), p. 18.

5. Geoffrey Jukes, *Russia's Military and the Northern Territories Issue* (Working Paper No. 277) (Canberra: Australian National University, Strategic and Defense Studies Centre, 1993), p. 7.

6. da Cunha, *op. cit.*, p. 18.

7. Jukes, *op. cit.*, p. 7.

8. Ibid.

9. *Asahi Shimbun*, *Sankei Shimbun*, and *Hokkaido Shimbun*, July 19, 1980.

10. Ibid.

Selected Bibliography

I. Newspapers and Periodicals

Asahi Shimbun (Tokyo)
Asia Pacific Community (Tokyo)
Asian Security (Tokyo)
Asian Survey (Berkeley)
Aziia i Afrika segodnia (Moscow)
Christian Science Monitor (Boston)
Chūō Kōron (Tokyo)
Current Digest of the Soviet Press (Ohio)—abbreviated as CDSP
Defense of Japan (Tokyo)
Economist (London)
Far Eastern Economic Review (Hong Kong)
Foreign Affairs (New York)
Foreign Broadcast Information Service: Soviet Union (Washington, DC)—abbreviated as *FBIS-SOV*
Foreign Policy (New York)
Hokkai Times (Sapporo)
Hokkaido Shimbun (Sapporo)
Iaponiia: Ezhegodnik (Moscow)
International Herald Tribune (Paris)
International Security
Izvestiia (Moscow)
Japan Quarterly (Tokyo)
Japan Times (Tokyo)
Journal of Northeast Asian Studies (Washington, DC)
Kommunist (Moscow)
Komsomol'skaia pravda (Moscow)
Krasnaia zvezda (Moscow)
Literaturnaia gazeta (Moscow)
Mainichi Shimbun (Tokyo)
Mezhdunarodnaia zhizn' (Moscow)—abbreviated as *MZ*
Mirovaia ekonomika i mezhdunarodnye otnosheniia (Moscow)—abbreviated as *MEiMO*

Military Balance (London)
Narody Azii i Afriki (Moscow)
Newsweek (New York)
New York Times (New York)
Nihon Keizai Shimbun (Tokyo)
Novoe vremia (Moscow)
Pacific Community (London)
Pravda (Moscow)
Problemy dal' nego vostoka (Moscow)—abbreviated as *PDV*
Problems of Communism (Washington, DC)
Radio Liberty Research Bulletin (Munich)
Sankei Shimbun (Tokyo)
Sekai (Tokyo)
Sovetskaia Rossiia (Moscow)
Time (New York)
Tsūsan Hakusho (Tokyo)
Vneshniaia torgovlia SSSR (Moscow)
Wall Street Journal (New York)
Washington Post (Washington)
Yomiuri Shimbun (Tokyo)

II. Books and Monographs: English Sources

Aganbegian, A.G., ed. *Regional Studies for Planning and Projecting: The Siberian Experience* (Hague: Mouton, 1981).

Arbatov, A. Georgii, and William Oltmans. *The Soviet Viewpoint* (New York: Dodd, Mead, 1983).

Bedeski, Robert E. *The Fragile Entente: The 1978 Japan-China Peace Treaty in a Global Context* (Boulder, CO: Westview, 1983).

Beloff, Nora. "Escape from Freedom: A Defector's Story," *Atlantic Monthly*, (November 1980).

Berton, Peter. "The Japanese Communists' Rapprochement with the Soviet Union," *Asian Survey*, Vol. 20, No.12 (December 1979).

Bialer, Seweryn, ed. *The Domestic Context of Soviet Foreign Policy* (Boulder, CO: Westview, 1981).

Black, Cyril E. et al. *The Modernization of Japan and Russia* (New York: Free Press, 1975).

Blaker, Michael. *Japanese International Negotiating Style* (New York: Columbia University Press, 1977).

Byrnes, Robert F., ed. *After Brezhnev: Sources of Soviet Conduct in the 1980s* (Bloomington: Indiana University Press, 1983).

Christopher, Robert C. *The Japanese Mind: The Goliath Explained* (New York: Linden Press, 1983).

Clemens, Walter C., Jr. *The U.S.S.R. and Global Interdependence: Alternative Futures* (Washington, DC: American Enterprise Institute for Public Policy Research, 1978).

Comprehensive National Security Group. *Report on Comprehensive National Security* (English Translation) (Tokyo: Prime Minister's Cabinet Office, 1980).

Dmytryshyn, Basil. "Current Trends in Soviet Foreign Policy," unpublished paper read at the Japan-U.S. Society in Sapporo, February 1979.

Drifte, Leinhard. "Disarmament and Arms Control in Japanese Politics" (unpublished paper).

Dzirkals, Lilita. *Soviet Perceptions of Security in East Asia: A Survey of Soviet Media Comments* (Santa Monica, CA: RAND Corporation, 1978).

Edmonds, Richard L. *Siberian Resource Development and the Japanese Economy: The Japanese Perspective* (Washington, DC: Association of American Geographers, 1979).

Emmerson, John K. *Arms, Yen & Power: The Japanese Dilemma* (New York: Dunellen, 1971).

Eran, Oded. *Mezhdunarodniki: An Assessment of Professional Expertise in the Making of Soviet Foreign Policy* (Ramat Gan, Israel: Turtledove Publishing, 1979).

Falkenheim, Peggy L. "Some Determining Factors in Soviet-Japanese Relations," *Pacific Affairs*, Vol. 50, No. 4 (Winter 1977/1978).

———. "The Impact of the Peace and Friendship Treaty on Soviet-Japanese Relations," *Asian Survey*, Vol. 19, No. 12 (December 1979).

Given, D.W. "The Sea of Okhotsk: U.S.S.R.'s Great Lake?," *United States Naval Institute Proceedings*, Vol. 96, Nos. 9/811 (September 1970).

Glaubitz, Joachim. "Anti-Hegemony Formulas in Chinese Foreign Policy," *Asian Survey*, Vol.16, No. 3 (March 1976).

———. "Some Aspects of Recent Soviet Policy toward East and Southeast Asia," in Lawrence L. Whetten, ed., *The Political Implications of Soviet Military Power* (New York: Crane, Russak, 1977).

Goldman, Stuart D. *Soviet-Japanese Relations and the Strategic Balance in Northeast Asia* (unpublished paper at the Congressional Research Service, Library of Congress).

Gorshkov, Sergei G. *The Sea Power of the State* (Oxford: Pergamon, 1979).

Gottemoeller, Rose E., and Paul F. Langer. *Foreign Area Studies in the USSR: Training and Employment of Specialists* (Santa Monica, CA: RAND Corporation, 1983).

Gupta, Bhabani Sen. *Soviet-Asian Relations in the 1970's and Beyond: An Interperceptional Study* (New York: Praeger, 1976).

———. "Japanese Perceptions of the Soviet Union," *Pacific Community*, Vol. 7, No. 3 (April 1976).

Ha, Joseph M. "Moscow's Policy Toward Japan," *Problems of Communism*, Vol. 26, No. 5 (September/October 1977).

Haselkorn, Avigdor. "Impact of Sino-Japanese Treaty on the Soviet Security Strategy," *Asian Survey*, Vol. 19, No. 6 (June 1979).

Hellmann, Donald C. *Japanese Foreign Policy and Domestic Politics* (Berkeley: University of California Press, 1969).

———. "The Impact of the Sino-Soviet Dispute on Northeast Asia," in Herbert J. Ellison, ed., *The Sino-Soviet Conflict: A Global Perspective* (Seattle: University of Washington Press, 1982). 172–184.

Hinton, Harold C. *Three and a Half Powers: The New Balance in Asia* (Bloomington: Indiana University Press, 1975).

Hoffmann, Erik P., and Frederic J. Fleron, Jr., eds. *The Conduct of Soviet Foreign Policy* (expanded 2nd edition) (New York: Aldine, 1980).

Jain, R.K. *The USSR and Japan: 1945–1980* (New Delhi: Harvester, 1981).

Jervis, Robert. *Perception and Misperception in International Politics* (Princeton, NJ: Princeton University Press, 1976).

Jönsson, Christer. *Soviet Bargaining Behavior: The Nuclear Test Ban Case* (New York: Columbia University Press, 1979).

Jukes, Geoffrey. *Russia's Military and the Northern Territories Issue* (Working Paper No. 277) (Camberra: Australian National University, Strategic & Defense Studies Centre, 1993).

Kennan, George F. *Memoirs: 1925–1950* (Boston: Atlantic, Little, Brown, 1967).

Kim, Hong N. "The Fukuda Government and the Politics of the Sino-Japanese Peace Treaty," *Asian Survey*, Vol. 19, No. 3 (1979).

Kim, Young C. *Japanese-Soviet Relations: Interactions of Politics, Economics and National Security* (Beverly Hills, CA: Sage, 1974).

Kimura, Hiroshi. "The Soviet Union and Japan," *Asian Security: 1981* (Tokyo: Research Institute for Peace and Security, 1981).

———. "Failure of Soviet Policies toward Japan," *Asia Pacific Community*, Vol. No.16 (Spring 1982).

———. "Soviet Policy toward Japan," in Dan Coldwell, ed., *Soviet International Behavior and U.S. Policy Options* (Lexington, MA: Lexington, 1985).

———. "The Soviet Proposal on Confidence-Building Measures and the Japanese Responses," in Joshua D. Katz and Tilly C. Friedman-Lichtschein, eds., *Japan's New World Role* (Boulder, CO: Westview, 1985).

———. "Japan and the Soviet Union—Why 'Distant Neighbors'?" *Trialogue* (New York: Trilateral Commission), No. 37 (1985).

———. "The Soviet Military Buildup: Its Impact on Japan and Its Aims," in Richard H. Solomon and Masataka Kōsaka, eds., *The Soviet Far East Military Buildup: Nuclear Dilemmas and Asian Security* (Dover, MA: Auburn House, 1986).

Kirsch, Marian P. "Soviet Security Objectives in Asia," *International Organization*, Vol. 25, No. 3 (Summer 1970).

Kuno, Yoshi S. *Japanese Expansion on the Asiatic Continent* (Berkeley: University of California Press, 1940), Vol. 2.

Langdon, Frank. "Japanese-Soviet 200-mile Zone Confrontation," *Pacific Community*, Vol. 9, No. 1 (October 1977).

Lebra, Takie Sugiyama. *Japanese Patterns of Behavior* (Honolulu: University Press of Hawaii, 1976).

Lee, Edmund [pseudonym]. "Beijing's Balancing Act," *Foreign Policy*, No. 51 (Summer 1983).

Lensen, George A. *The Strange Neutrality: Soviet-Japanese Relations during the Second World War: 1941–1945* (Tallahassee, FL: Diplomatic, 1972).

Mackintosh, Malcolm. "Soviet Interests and Policies in the Asian-Pacific Region," *Orbis*, Vol. 19, No. 3 (Fall 1975).

Mathieson, Raymond S. *Japan's Role in Soviet Economic Growth: Transfer of Technology Since 1965* (New York: Praeger, 1979).

Miyauchi, Kuniko. "No Slowdown in Soviet Security Buildup: Why USSR Switched From Introvert, Economic National Policy to Extrovert Military One," *Japan Times*, May 13, 1979.

Mochizuki, Mike M. "Japan's Search for Strategy: The Security Policy Debate in the 1980s" (Occasional Paper, 82–01, Program on U.S.-Japan Relations, Center for International Affairs, Harvard University, 1982).

Morgenthau, H.J. *Politics Among Nations: The Struggle for Power and Peace* (third edition) (New York: Alfred A. Knopf, 1961).

Nakane, Chie. *Japanese Society* (Berkeley, CA: University of California Press, 1972).

Nakasone, Yasuhiro. *My Life in Politics* (private edition, 1982).

Ogarkov, N.V. "Always in Readiness to Defend the Homeland," *Soviet Press* (September/October 1982; November/December 1982; January/February 1983).

Rees, David. *Soviet Border Problems: China and Japan* (Institute for the Study of Conflict, 1982).

Reischauer, Edwin O. *The Japanese* (Cambridge, MA: Belknap, 1977).

Rejai, Mostafa, ed., *Decline of Ideology* (Chicago: Aldine-Atherton, 1971).

Robinson, Thomas W. "Sino-Soviet Relations During the 1980s as a Factor in Northeast Asian Security" (unpublished paper).

Rosecrance, Richard, *The Rise of the Trading State: Commerce and Conquest in the Modern World* (New York: Basic Books, 1986).

Saeki, Kiichi. "Toward Japanese Cooperation in Siberian Development," *Problems of Communism*, Vol. 21, No. 3 (May/June 1972).

Samelson, L.J. *Soviet and Chinese Negotiating Behavior: The Western View* (Beverly Hills, CA: Sage, 1976).

Scalapino, Robert A., ed. *The Foreign Policy of Modern Japan* (Berkeley: University of California Press, 1977).

Shabad, Theodore, and Victor L. Mote. *Gateway to Siberian Resources: The BAM* (Washington, DC: Scripta, 1977).

Sinha, Mira. "The Sino-Japanese Peace Treaty: Moscow Loses Round One to Peking," *China Report*, Vol. 14, No. 4. (July–August 1978).

Solomon, Richard H., ed. *Asian Security in the 1980s: Problems and Policies for a Time of Transition* (Cambridge, MA: Oelgeschlager, Gunn & Hain, 1979).

Stephan, John J. *The Kuril Islands: Russo-Japanese Frontier in the Pacific* (Oxford: Clarendon Press, 1974).

———. "The Kuril Islands: Japan versus Russia," *Pacific Community* (Tokyo), Vol. 7, No. 3 (April 1976).

———. "Japan and the Soviet Union: The Distant Neighbors," *Asian Affairs*, 8, Part III (October 1977).

———. "Japan in the Soviet Mirror: The Search for Rapprochement," *Bulletin of Peace Proposals*, Vol. 13, No. 1 (1982).

———. "Japan and the Soviet Union in the 1980's: Persistence of Historical Patterns or a New Departure?" (Fukuoka: Fukuoka UNESCO Association, 1982).

———. "Soviet Approaches to Japan: Images Behind the Policies," *Asian Perspective* (Seoul: Institute for Far Eastern Studies, Kyungnam University), Vol. 6, No. 2 (Fall/Winter, 1982).

Sternheimer, Stephen. *East-West Technology Transfer: Japan and the Communist Bloc* (Beverly Hills, CA: Sage, 1980).

Stuart, Douglas T., and William T. Tow. *China, the Soviet Union, and the West: Strategic and Political Dimensions in the 1980s* (Boulder, CO: Westview, 1982).

Sutter, Robert G. *Future Sino-Soviet Relations and Their Implications for the United States* (Congressional Research Service Paper No. 83–10F) (Washington, DC: Library of Congress, 1982).

Swearingen, Rodger. *The Soviet Union and Postwar Japan: Escalating Challenge and Response* (Stanford, CA: Hoover Institution Press, 1978).

Tretiak, Daniel. "The Sino-Japanese Treaty of 1978: The Senkaku Incident Prelude," *Asian Survey*, No. 12 (1978).

Weinstein, Martin E. "Trends in Japan's Foreign and Defense Policies," in William J. Barnds, ed., *Japan and the United States: Challenges & Opportunities* (New York: New York University Press, 1979).

Whiting, Allen S. *Siberian Development and East Asia: Threat or Promise?* (Stanford, CA: Stanford University Press, 1981).

Wolfers, Arnold. *Discord and Collaboration: Essays on International Politics* (Baltimore, MD: Johns Hopkins University Press, 1962).

Yoshida, Shigeru. *The Yoshida Memoirs: The Story of Japan in Crisis*, translated by Kenichi Yoshida (Boston: Houghton Mifflin Company, 1962).

Zagoria, Donald S. "Gauging the Sino-Soviet Thaw," *The New Leader*, Vol. 65, No. 22 (November 29, 1982).

————. "The Moscow-Beijing Détente," *Foreign Affairs*, Vol.61, No.4 (Spring 1983).

————, ed. *Soviet Policy in East Asia* (New Haven, CT: Yale University Press, 1982).

III. Books and Monographs: Russian Sources

Aleksandrov, V.A. "Mesto Sibiri i dal'nego vostoka v ekonomicheskikh sviaziakh SSSR i Iaponii," *PDV*, No. 1 [41] (1982).

Andreev, K., and K.E. Cherevko. "Vydumka i pravda o 'severnykh territoriiakh,' " *MZ*, No. 3 (1983).

Bandura, Iurii N. " 'Tikhookeanskoe soobshchestvo'porozhdenie diplomatii imperializma," *MZ*, No. 5 (1980).

Berezin, V.N. *Kurs na dobrososedstvo i sotrudnichestvo v ego protivniki: Iz istorii normalizatsii otnoshenii SSSR s poslevoennoi Iaponiei* (Moscow: Mezhdunarodnye otnosheniia, 1977).

Bogdanov, O.V. *Peregovory—osnova mirnogo uregulirovaniia mezhdunarodnykh problem* (Moscow: Znanie, 1958).

Brezhnev, L.I. *Leninskim kursom*, Vols. 1–8 (Moscow: Gospolitizdat, 1970–1981).

Cherevko, K.E. "Vneshniaia politika SSSR v krivom zerkale iaponskoi sovetologii," *PDV*, No. 2 [46] (1983).

Chikunov, I. "SSSR-Iaponiia: Strannye tolkovaniia," *Novoe vremia*, No. 8 [1706] (February 17, 1978).

Dal'nev, V. "Chto meshaet razvitiiu sovetsko-iaponskikh otnoshenii," *MZ*, No. 1 (January 1981).

Deborin, G.A. "Novyi istoricheskii etap v razvitii sovetskoi vneshnei politiki i diplomatii," in V.Z. Lebedev, ed., *O sovremennoi sovetskoi diplomatii* (Moscow: Institut mezhdunarodnykh otnoshenii, 1963).

Dmitriev, I.D. "Antisovetizm—orudie reaktsii," in *Iaponiia 1981: Ezhegodnik* (Moscow: Nauka, 1982).

Dolgorukov, P.D. "Torgovo-ekonomicheskie otnosheniia SSSR s Iaponiei," a paper read at the Japan-Soviet Symposium jointly held by the Soviet Academy of Sciences and *Sankei Shimbun* at Osaka in November 1979.

XXV s" ezd Kommunisticheskoi partii Sovetskogo Soiuza (24 fevralia—5 marta 1976 goda): Stenograficheskii otchet (Moscow: Politizdat, 1976).

XXVI s" ezd Kommunisticheskoi partii Sovetskogo Soiuza (23 fevralia—3 marta 1981 goda): stenograficheskii otchet (Moscow: Politizdat, 1981).

Dvina: Voiskovye manevry provedennye na territorii belorussii v marte 1970 goda (Moscow: Ministerstvo oborony SSSR, 1970).

Eidus, Kh. T. *SSSR i Iaponiia: Vneshnepoliticheskie otnosheniia posle vtoroi mirovoi voiny* (Moscow: Nauka, 1964).

Epishev, A. "Istoricheskaia missiia armii sotsialisticheskogo gosudarstva," *Kommunist*, No. 7 [1035] (May 1972).

Feinberg, E. Ia. *Russko-iaponskie otnosheniia v 1697–1875 gg.* (Moscow: Izdatel'stvo vostochnoi literatury, 1960).

Filosofskoe nasledie V.I. Lenina i problemy sovremennoi voiny (Moscow: Ministerstvo oborony SSSR, 1972).

Gantman, V.I. "Politika, preobrazuiushchaia mir: O roli vneshnei politiki SSSR v sovremennykh mezhdunarodnykh otnosheniiakh," *Kommunist*, No. 7 [1053] (May 1973).

Golovnin, V. "Tikhookeanskie mirazhi tokiiskikh politikov," *Aziia i Afrika segodnia*, No. 7 [277] (July 1980).

Gorshkov, S. *Morskaia moshch' gosudarstva* (Moscow: Voennoe izdatel'stvo Ministerstva oborony SSSR, 1976 and 1979).

——. "Voennomorskie floty v voinakh i v mirnoe vremia," *Morskoi sbornik*, No. 2 (1972), 20–29; No. 3 (1972), 20–32; No. 4 (1972), 9–23; No. 5 (1972), 12–24; No. 6 (1972), 11–21; No. 8 (1972), 14–24; No. 9 (1972), 14–24; No. 10 (1972), 13–21; No. 11 (1972), 24–34; No. 12 (1972), 14–22; No. 2 (1973), 13–25.

Grechko, A.A. *Na strazhe mira i stroitel'stva kommunizma* (Moscow: Voenizdat, 1971).

——. "Rukovodiashchaia rol' KPSS v stroitel'stve armii razvitogo sotsialisticheskogo obshchestva," *Voprosy istorii KPSS*, No. 5 (1974).

Gromyko, A. "Programma mira v deistvii," *Kommunist*, No. 14 [1096] (September 1975).

——. *Vo imia torzhestva leninskoi vneshnei politiki: izbrannye rechi i stat'i* (Moscow: Politizdat, 1978).

Guzhenko, T. "Sovetsko-iaponskie otnosheniia," *PDV*, No. 3 [43] (1982).

Iosilevich, A. "Pekin i bezopasnost' v Azii," *Aziia i Afrika segodnia*, No. 7 [229] (July 1976).

Ivanov, M.I. *Rost militarizma v Iaponii* (Moscow: Voennoe Izdatel'stvo Ministerstva oborony SSSR, 1982).

Ivkov, I.I. "Iaponskii militarizm podnimaet golovu," *PDV*, No. 3 [27] (1978).

——. " SShA: 'kitaiskaia karta' v Azii," *PDV*, No. 1 [29] (1979).

Kapitsa, M.S. *Na razhykh paralleriakh: zapiski diplomata* (Moscow: Kniga I biznes, 1996).

——. "Bor'ba SSSR za mir i sotrudnichestvo v Azii," *PDV*, No. 1 [29] (1979).

—— et al. *Istoriia mezhdunarodnykh otnoshenii na dal'nem vostoke: 1945–1977* (Khabarovsk: Khabarovskoe knizhnoe izdatel'stvo, 1978).

Kassis, V. *Kamikadze beret shturval* (Moscow: Sovetskaia Rossiia, 1980).

Kobysh, V. "Est' vykhod iz tupika: Tak schitaiut uchastniki traditsionnoi Sovetsko-iaponskoi vstrechi," *Literaturnaia gazeta*, No. 51 [4909] (December 22, 1982).

Kovalenko, I.I. *Sovetskii Soiuz v bor'be za mir i kollektivnuiu bezopasnost' v Azii* (Moscow: Nauka, 1976).

Krasin, G. "Iaponiia-KNR: V farvatere 'gegemonizm,'" *Novoe vremia*, No. 34 [1732] (August 18, 1978).

——. "Sovetsko-iaponskie otnosheniia," *MZ*, No. 4 (1976).

——. "SSSR-Iaponiia: Uglubliaia doverie," *Novoe vremia*, No. 4 [1702] (January 20, 1978).

Krupianko, M.I. *Sovetsko-iaponskie ekonomicheskie otnosheniia* (Moscow: Nauka, 1982).

Krutskikh, A.V. *Amerikanskaia politika 'partnerstva' v vostochno-aziatskom regione* (Moscow: Mezhdunarodnye otnosheniia, 1980).

Kulish, V.M., ed. *Voennaia sila i mezhdunarodnye otnosheniia: Voennye aspekty vneshne-politicheskikh kontseptsii* (Moscow: Mezhdunarodnye otnosheniia, 1972).

Kutakov, L.N. *Vneshnaia politika i diplomatiia Iaponiia* (Moscow; Mezhdunarodnye otnosheniia, 1964).

Kuznetsov, Iu. "Kuda tolkaiut Iaponiiu," *Kommunist*, No. 4 [1230] (March 1983).

Lebedev, V.Z., ed. *O sovremennoi sovetskoi diplomatii* (Moscow: Institut mezhdunarodn ykh otnoshenii, 1963).

Lenin, V.I. *Polnoe sobranie sochineniia* (5th edition) (Moscow: Gospolitizdat, 1965–70).

Leonov, P.A. "Zhemchuzhina Sovetskogo Dal'nego Vostoka," *PDV*, No. 4 [24] (1977).

Levchenko, Stanislav. "Iaponiia: Na krutom povorote," *Novoe vremia*, No. 35 [1733] (August 25, 1978).

Lukin, V.P. et al., eds. *SShA i problemy Tikhogo okeana: Mezhdunarodno-politicheskie acpekty* (Moscow: Mezhdunarodnye otnosheniia, 1979).

Markov, A.P. *Poslevoennaia politika Iaponii v Azii i Kitai: 1945–1977* (Moscow: Nauka, 1979).

Mazurov, V.M. *SshA–Kita—Iaponiia: Perestroika mezhgosudarstvennykh otnoshenii: 1969–1979* (Moscow: Nauka, 1980).

Mirov, A. "Aziia: Ne konfrontatsiia, a sotrudnichestvo," *Aziia i Afrika segodnia*, No. 8 [242] (August 1977).

Modenov, Stanislav S. "Pod militaristskimi shtandartami" *MZ*, No. 1 (1980).

———. "Tokio v farvatere politiki Vashingtona," *MZ*, No. 4 (1981).

Nikolaev, N.N. "Rasshirenie sovetsko-iaponskikh sviazei," *MZ*, No. 7 (1973).

———. "K 50–letiiu ustanovleniia diplomaticheskikh otnoshenii SSSR s Iaponiei," *PDV*, No. 2 [14] (1975).

———. "Dobrososedstvo i sotrudnichestvo—v interesakh SSSR i Iaponii," *MZ*, No. 1 (1978).

———. "Zigzagi politiki Tokio," *MZ*, No. 10 (1981).

———. "Vozrozhdenie iaponskogo ekspansionizma" in S.N. Morozov, ed., *Gegemonizm: S epokhoi v konflikte* (Moscow: Progress, 1982).

———, ed. *Mezhdunarodnye otnosheniia v aziatsko-tikhookeanskom regione* (Moscow: Nauka, 1979).

Nikolaev, N.N., and Aleksandrov, A.N. "Iapono-amerikanskie otnosheniia: Starye problemy, novye tendentsii," *PDV*, No. 4 [44] (1982).

Nikolaev, N.N., and Andreev, B.V. "Kitaisko-iaponskie peregovory o zakliuchenii dogovora o mire i druzhbe," *PDV*, No. 3 [15] (1975).

Nikolaev, N.N., and A. Pavlov. "SSSR-Iaponiia: kurs na dobrososedstvo i ego protivniki," *MZ*, No. 7 (1982).

Nikonov, S.N. "O planakh sozdaniia novoi, regional'noi organizatii stran basseina Tikhogo okeana," *PDV*, No. 2 [34] (1980).

Nosov, M.G. "Vliiania normalizatsii amerikano-kitaiskikh otnoshenii na politiku Iaponii," *Iaponiia 1980: Ezhegodnik* (Moscow: Nauka, 1981), pp. 153–65.

Orlov, B.P. "Razvitie ekonomiki sibiri na otdel'nykh etapakh sotsialisticheskogo stroitel'stva," Izvestia sibirskogo otdeleniia akademii Nauk SSSR (seriia obshchestvennykh nauk), No. 1, vypusk 3, 1982.

Pavlovskii, V. "Kollektivnaia bezopasnost'—put' k miru v Azii," *MZ*, No. 6 (1972).

————. "Aziia-kollektivnuiu bezopasnost',"

Petrov, D.V. *Iaponiia nashikh dnei* (Moscow: Znanie, 1979).

————. *Iaponiia v mirovoi politike* (Moscow: Mezhdunarodyne otnosheniia, 1973).

————. "Militarizatsiia Iaponii—Ugroza miru v Azii," *PDV*, No. 1 [39] (1981).

————. "Vneshnaia politika Iaponii na rubezhe 70-80-kh godov," *Iaponiia 1980:Ezhegodnik* (Moscow: Nauka, 1981).

————. "Vozrozhdenie iaposkovo ekspansionizma" in S.N. Morozov, ed., *Gegemonizm: S epokhoi v knoflikte* (Moscow: Progress, 1982) pp. 186–204.

————. ed. *Mezhdunarodnye otnosheniia v aziatsko-tikookeanskom regione* (Moscow: Nauka, 1979).

Pinaev, L.P. *Evoliutsiia voennoi politiki Iaponii: 1959–1980 gg.* (Moscow: Nauka, 1982).

Polevoi, B.P. *Pervootkryvateli kuril'skikh ostrovov* (Iuzhno-Sakhalinsk, Sakhalin: Dal'nevostochnoe knizhnoe izdatel'stvo, 1982).

Sergiev, A.V. "Marksizm-Leninizm o sootnoshenii vnutrennei i vneshnei politiki," in *Vzaimosviaz' i vzaimovliianie vnutrennei i vneshnei politiki* (Moscow: Nauka, 1982).

————. "Leninizm o sootnoshenii sil kak faktore mezhdunarodnykh otnoshenii," *MZ*, No. 4 (1975).

Shakhnazarov, G. "K probleme sootnosheniia sil v mire," *Kommunist*, No. 3 [1067] (February 1974).

Smolin, N.A. "Vazhneishie sobytiia vnutripoliticheskoi zhizni Iaponii v 1980 g.," in *Iaponiia 1981: Ezhegodnik* (Moscow: Nauka, 1981).

Solov'ev, A. *Kuril'skie ostrova* (Moscow: Izdatel'stvo Glavnomorskogo upravlenie severnogo puti, 1945 and 1947).

Spandar'ian, V.B. "Sovetsko-iaponskie torgovo-ekonomicheskie otnosheniia," *PDV*, No. 3 [35], 1980.

Stalin, I.V. *Sochineniia*, 3 volumes, edited by Robert H. McNeal (Stanford, CA: Hoover Institution on War, Revolution, and Peace, 1967).

Stepanov, A.I. "V.I. Lenin o kompromissakh vo vneshnei politike i sovremennost'," in Lebedev, ed. *O sovremennoi sovetskoi diplomatii.*

Sushkov, V.N. "O torgovo-ekonomicheskom sotrudnichestve s kapitalisticheskimi stranami v stroitel'stve v SSSR krupnykh promyshlennykh ob"ektov," *Vneshniaia torgovlia*, No. 2, 1976.

Tikhvinskii, S.L. et al., eds. *Istoriia mezhdunarodnykh otnoshenii na dal'nem vostoke: 1945–1977* (Khabarovsk: Khabarovskoe knizhnoe izdatel'stvo, 1978).

Tolkunov, L. "Iaponiia segodnia," *Novoe vremia*, No. 31 [1833] (August 1, 1980).

Ustinov, D.F. *Izbrannye rechi i stat'i* (Moscow: Politizdat, 1979).

Vasil'ev, O.V. "Nekotorye problemy vneshnei politiki Iaponii v 1980 g.," *Iaponiia 1981: Ezhegodnik* (Moscow: Nauka, 1982).

Vedomosti Verkhovnogo Soveta SSSR, No. 48 [2174] (1982).

Verbitskii, S.I. "'Tikhookeanskaia doktrina' Vashingtona," *Aziia i Afrika segodnia*, No. 8 [230] (August 1976).

Verbitskii, S.I., and I.I. Kovalenko, eds. *SSSR-Iaponiia: K 50-letiiu ustanovleniia sovetsko-iaponskikh diplomaticheskikh otnoshenii (1925–1975)* (Moscow: Nauka, 1978).

Vorontsov, V.B. *Kitai i SShA: 60–70-e gody* (Moscow: Nauka, 1979).

Zanegin, B. "Aziatskaia bezopasnost': Dva podkhoda," *Aziia i Afrika segodnia*, No. 3 [249] (March 1978).

Zorin, V.A. *Osnovy diplomaticheskoi sluzhby* (izdanie vtoroe, ispravlennoe i dopolnennoe) (Moscow: Mezhdunarodnye otnosheniia, 1977).

IV. Books and Monographs: Japanese Sources

Akizuki, Toshiyuki. "Nichiro-kankei to Ryōdo-ishiki" (Japanese-Russian Relations and Views on Territory)," *Kyosanshugi to Kokusaimondai* (Communism and International Affairs) (Tokyo: Japanese Institute of International Affairs), Vol. 4, No. 1 (July/September 1979).

Bandura, Iurii. "Soren wa nihon ni nanio nozomuka?" (What Does the Soviet Union Want from Japan?)," *Jiyū* (January 1982).

Dal'nev, V. *Nisso-kankei dakai no michi: Soren wa dō Kangae'ru ka* (The Way to Make a Breakthrough in Japanese-Soviet Relations: How Does the Soviet Union Think?) (Tokyo: Asia-shobo, 1981).

Gondō, Mitsuru. *Nihyaku-kairi Gyōgyō-suiiki* (The 200-mile Fishing Zone) (Tokyo: Kyōikusha, 1978).

Hyōdo, Nagao. *Saikin no Nissokankei to Hoppōryōdo Mondai* (Recent Japanese-Soviet Relations and the Territorial Question) (Tokyo: Minshu-gaiko Kyokai, 1979).

Kim, Yan C. *Kuremurin no Tainichi Senryaku* (The Kremlin's Strategy Toward Japan) (Tokyo: TBS Buritanika, 1983).

Kimura, Hiroshi, ed. *Hoppōryōdo o kangaeru* (How to Think on the Northern Territories Issue?) (Hokkaido: Hokkaido Shimbun-sha, 1981).

Kōsaka, Masataka. *Saishō Yoshida Shigeru* (Tokyo: Chūō Kōron-sha, 1967).

Mainichi Shimbun-sha. *200-kairi Sakana Senso* (The 200-mile Fish War) (Tokyo: Mainichi Shimbun-sha, 1977).

Nakajima, Mineo. *Chūso-domei no shōgeki: Nihon no anzen to keizai wa dōnaru ka* (Shock of Sino-Soviet Alliance: What Will Be the Security and Economy of Japan?) (Tokyo: Kōbun-sha, 1982).

Nakasone, Yasuhiro. *Nippon no Shuchō* (Japan Speaks) (Tokyo: Keizai Ōrai-sha, 1954).

Ovchinnikov, V.V. "Sonichi-kyōryoku wa Kyokutō ni okeru Heiwa no Tameni" (The Soviet-Japanese Cooperation for Peace in the Far East), *Jiyū*, No. 279 (July 1982).

Shimizu, Takehisa. *Hoppōryōdo-mondai kaiketsu no yon-hōshiki* (Four Formulas for Resolving the Northern Territories Issue) (Tokyo: Kasumigaseki-shuppankai, 1977).

Suzuki, Keisuke. "Shiberia-kaihatsu to Nisso-keizai kankei: wagakuni no taiso-seisaku o megutte" (Siberian Development and Japanese-Soviet Economic Relations: How Does Japan Have to Act?), in Kiichi Mochizuki, ed. *Shiberiya-kaihatsu to Hokuyōgyogyō* (Sapporo: Hokkaido Shimbun-sha, 1982).

Takada, Kiyoshi. *200-kairj Sensō* (The 200-mile War) (Tokyo: K.K. World Photo Press, 1977).

Takano, Akira, "Soren ni okeru Hoppōryōdo Kenkyū ni tsuite" (Studies in the Soviet Union on the Northern Territories), *Shikan* (Historic View) (Tokyo: Waseda University), No. 95 (March 1977).

Tanaka Sōri wa kataru: Nisso-shuno kaidan nitsuite (Prime Minister Tanaka Speaks on the Summit Meeting) (Tokyo: Hoppōryōdo mondai taisaku kyokai, 1974).

Teratani, Hiromi. "Nisso doji-chosa: Daigakusai no ishiki no chigai" (The Soviet-Japanese Simultaneous Survey: Difference in College Students Consciousness), *Seiron* (February 1978).

Warera-no Hoppōryōdo (Our Northern Territories) (Tokyo: Ministry of Foreign Affairs).

Yamagata, Taizō. *Chishima wa uttaeru: ninjū no nijūkyūnen* (The Kurils Sue: 29 Years of Submission) (Tokyo: Nippon Kyōbun-sha, 1973).

Yamamoto, Hichihei. "*Kūki no Kenkyū*" (The Study of 'Air') (Tokyo: Bungei Shunjū-sha, 1977).

Yoshida, Shien. *Hoppōryōdo* (Northern Territories) (revised edition) (Tokyo: Jiji-Tsusin-sha, 1973).

Name Index

A

Abe, Shintarō, 239, 257–258, 259–260
Afanas'ev, Viktor, 173
Afornin, Iurii, 120, 169, 242
Aichi Kiichi, 65
Akagi Munenori, 4
Akizuki Toshiyuki, 62
Aleksandrov, A., 47
Alekseyev, 33
Amaya Naohiro, 212–213
Anatolyev, 170
Andreev, Konstantin, 244
Andropov, Iurii, 24, 26, 47, 71, 103, 111, 181, 184, 197, 201, 240, 241–262, 265, 267
Arai Hirokazu, 252
Arbatov, Georgii A., 24–25, 57, 186, 249, 250–251
Arita Keisuke, 147
Asukata Kazuo, 173

B

Bandura, Iurii N., 11, 67, 96, 120, 160, 168, 174, 175, 216, 218, 221, 281n.39
Bendasan, Isaiah (pseud.), 27
Berezin, V.N. (pseud.), 6, 179
Bialer, Seweryn, 9
Blaker, Michael, 136–137
Bogdanov, O.V., 134

Bohlen, Charles, 137
Bovin, Aleksander, 56, 93, 243
Brezhnev, Leonid I., 14, 28, 45, 56, 65, 71, 79, 81, 95, 102, 103, 105, 111, 134, 146, 152–154, 155, 178–179, 180–181, 184, 191–192, 195–196, 197, 201, 220, 234, 241, 245, 248, 253, 255, 265, 267
Brown, Harold, 285n.2
Brzezinski, Zbigniew, 141, 142, 162–163, 264
Bull, Hedley, 42
Bykov, Oleg N., 264–265

C

Carter, Jimmy, 120, 141, 142, 212, 216, 224, 234, 264
Cherevko, Kirill E., 244
Chernenko, Konstantin U., 195, 245, 247
Clausewitz, Carl von, 26

D

Dallin, Alexander, 9, 108, 109
Dal'nev, V., 4, 186, 190
Demchenko, Mikhail, 165, 166, 222
Deng Xiaoping, 103–104, 143, 144, 167, 170, 266
Dmitriev, Iurii D., 174–175
Doi Takeo, 119
Dolgorukov, Pavel D., 33, 86–87, 155

Subject Index

Hiroshi Kimura is a Professor at the International Research Center for Japanese Studies in Kyoto and serves as first vice president of the International Council for Central and East European Studies (ICCEES). After graduating from Kyoto University with a B.A. in law he continued his graduate studies at Columbia University and received his Ph.D. in political science. He was a Fulbright-Hays Visiting Professor at the Institute for Sino-Soviet Studies, George Washington University, and at Stanford University. He was also a special research fellow at the Japanese Embassy in Vienna and Moscow. Before assuming his present post, Professor Kimura was Director of the Slavic Research Center at Hokkaido University. His recent research has focused on Russian foreign policy toward Japan. His major publications in English include *Prospects for East-West Relations* (New York, 1986); *Gorbachev's Reform: U.S. and Japanese Assessments* (New York, 1988); *Beyond Cold War to Trilateral Cooperation in the Asia-Pacific Region: Scenarios for New Relationships Between Japan, Russia, and the United States* (Cambridge, 1992); and *International Negotiation: Actors, Structure/Process, Values* (New York, 1999).